Managing Your Money

A practical guide to personal finance

Tony Boczko

BLOOMSBURY ACADEMIC
LONDON • NEW YORK • OXFORD • NEW DELHI • SYDNEY

BLOOMSBURY ACADEMIC
Bloomsbury Publishing Plc
50 Bedford Square, London, WC1B 3DP, UK
1385 Broadway, New York, NY 10018, USA
29 Earlsfort Terrace, Dublin 2, Ireland

BLOOMSBURY, BLOOMSBURY ACADEMIC and the Diana logo are trademarks of Bloomsbury Publishing Plc

First published by Palgrave Macmillan 2016
Reprinted by Bloomsbury Academic, 2024

A catalogue record for this book is available from the British Library.

A catalogue record for this book is available from the Library of Congress.

ISBN 978–1–137–47187–1 paperback

For
Reece David, India Mai, Zoe Marie, and Laura Alice

Contents

List of figures and tables

Figures

Tables

Preface

With personal debt (including student debt) now at record levels, and people both young and old struggling to meet personal financial commitments, this book provides a practical guide to personal financial planning. It also explores a range of personal finance topics, including savings and investments, borrowing, personal taxation, pensions, insurance, and debt.

The primary aims of this book are:

- to enhance personal financial management skills
- to promote a clearer understanding of the sometimes complex language of personal finance
- to increase awareness of the importance of personal financial planning.

Acknowledgements

My thanks to:

- Kirsty Reade at Palgrave for her patience and professionalism
- Pat Mould for providing the initial idea for the book
- the various anonymous reviewers for their constructive and helpful comments.

Part 1
Budgeting and borrowing

Overview

Chapter 1 provides an introduction to the social and economic framework within which individuals make financial decisions during their lifetime, from student life through their working life to eventual retirement.

Chapter 2 explores the need for budgeting and controlling what we spend, when we spend and how much we spend, on the products and services we consume. It also considers how simple personal financial management techniques can be used not only to identify possible cash-flow problems and to highlight areas that may require corrective action, but also to identify possible short-term strategies.

Chapter 3 explores the alternative types of secured and unsecured borrowing that are available; the alternative types of lending institutions a borrower may use; the risks associated with each type of borrowing and each institution; the role of credit-rating agencies; and the usefulness of credit scoring.

1

Introduction to *Managing Your Money*

Learning outcomes

By the end of this chapter, you should be able to:

- explain the key features of financial literacy
- identify the main objectives and key issues associated with personal financial management.

1.1 Introduction

Money changes lives. It can make a person's life better or it can make a person's life worse – its impact and influence depend entirely on how the money is managed and how it is used. As suggested by Ayn Rand, 'Money is only a tool. It will take you wherever you wish, but it will not replace you as the driver' (Rand 1957: 387).

In today's ever more complex and ever more chaotic financial environment, being able to manage money – being financially literate and a skilled and competent driver, to use Rand's analogy – is a crucial life skill: and it is a skill that can no longer be relegated to the sidelines of our daily activities.

1.2 Being financially aware: the need for financial literacy

'Financial literacy' refers to the set of competencies and capabilities that allows you to make informed and effective decisions about your available financial resources. It is, in essence, about empowerment – about taking control, and understanding how money works. In particular, financial literacy considers:

- how to manage earnings
- how to meet financial commitments
- how and where to borrow money (if necessary)
- how and where to invest any surplus funds.

In a survey in 2013, the Money Advice Service found that whilst 86% of people surveyed were financially aware and did keep track of their income and expenditure (what they earned and what they spent), nearly 48% of people surveyed were concerned about the state of their finances and their levels of debt (Money Advice Service 2013: 9). Over 51% of people surveyed said they were struggling to keep up with bills and credit commitments (ibid.: 10). More importantly, only 63% of people surveyed were making sure they had 'some' money saved for a 'rainy day' (ibid.: 11).

So what factors affect a person's financial literacy, and what are the key benefits of being financially literate?

1.3 Managing your money: key factors

A range of factors can have an impact on your financial literacy, the most important being: understanding, knowledge, and confidence.

Life events – from the large one-off events (such as moving home, getting married, having a baby, or retiring), to the unforeseen day-to-day events that arise out of the uncertainty and unpredictability of modern life (such as the arrival of unexpected bills or invoices, or accidents and emergencies) – can have a dramatic effect on personal finances. The ability to navigate successfully through the financial turmoil created by such life events requires:

- an understanding of the personal implications and financial consequences of such life events
- a knowledge of the potential sources of information and advice that can be used in managing such life events
- the confidence to use a wide range of emotional, intellectual and behavioural skills, including financial mathematics, budgeting and planning, self-control, decision-making, and problem-solving.

1.4 Managing your money: key benefits

The key benefits of effective money management are:

- controlling spending and managing personal cash flow
- avoiding (excessive) debt
- maintaining a healthy credit score
- fulfilling personal goals
- reducing stress and improving your health and well-being.

Controlling spending and managing personal cash flow

Managing what you spend and controlling how much you spend are key features of responsible, proactive money management. In particular:

- Avoid penalties and interest charges by properly scheduling payment of debts (for example, personal loans, car loans, mortgage payments, utility bills, and credit-card bills).
- Invest surplus funds in interest-bearing savings accounts (preferably tax-exempt savings accounts), however small the surplus may be.
- Avoid excessive unnecessary spending by shopping around, asking for discounts, and buying what you need rather than what advertisers tell you you want.

Avoiding (excessive) debt

Being in debt – being unable to pay outstanding bills or accounts or to make repayments of outstanding loans and personal borrowing – can be very difficult to deal with. Yet, surprisingly, many people often fail to deal with their personal debts, and especially long-term chronic debt. Unfortunately, the more you ignore debt, the larger it becomes, and the worse the situation tends to get. Debt will not go away on its own, and nor will the people to whom you owe the money.

Good personal financial management, including understanding how to manage your money better and how to budget and manage spending, can help you get out of debt or prevent you from being in debt in the first place.

Maintaining a healthy credit score

A credit score is a numerical representation of a person's creditworthiness. Whilst its precise calculation varies between different lending institutions and credit agencies, these differences are matters of degree: accruing a poor credit history by failing to pay outstanding bills or accounts or by defaulting on payment agreements could have a serious, long-lasting and detrimental impact on your credit score and your future financial health, including your ability to borrow and to obtain credit.

Fulfilling personal goals

Whilst money cannot buy happiness, it can certainly help!

For many people, long-term financial goals are inextricably linked to personal dreams and aspirations. Whether you dream of owning your own home, working for yourself and owning your own business, travelling the world, or merely retiring early, only money can make your dream become reality. Effective money management, good financial planning and regular saving can help to fulfil those financial goals and make those personal dreams come true.

Reducing stress and improving personal well-being

Effective money management can not only reduce levels of debt and prevent excessive debt, but can also reduce personal stress. The stress, worry and anxiety associated with poor money management may not only have a dramatic effect on an individual's physical health and mental well-being, it may also have a significant impact on their relationships with other people, and especially partners and other family members.

> **Activity 1**
>
> Based on their importance to you personally, prioritise the key benefits of effective money management mentioned above.

1.5 Managing your money: personal financial management

This guide to personal financial management explores the following key issues and areas:
- budgeting and cash management
- borrowing, loans, and credit
- taxation (including personal Income Tax, business tax for unincorporated and small incorporated businesses, Capital Gains Tax, and Inheritance Tax)
- savings and investments
- pensions

- insurance and assurance
- fraud
- regulation, legislation, and codes of practice
- debt, Individual Voluntary Arrangements (IVAs), and bankruptcy.

Budgeting and cash management

To manage and control what you spend money on, when you spend your money, and how much you spend on the products and service you consume, it is important to be able to distinguish between the different types of personal spending, to recognise how to manage spending and make money work harder, and to know how to use the growing variety of (increasingly online) payment technologies now available. You need to be able to create, manage, and use a personal cash budget, and to understand how you can use simple personal financial management techniques to recognise possible cash-flow problems, to highlight areas that may require corrective action, and to identify possible short-term strategies.

Borrowing, loans, and credit

Credit cards, charge cards, unsecured personal loans, high-cost subprime lending and mortgage borrowing have all become important features of today's increasingly challenging financial environment. Essential features of any money management survival toolkit are your understanding of:

- the alternative types of secured and unsecured borrowing that are available to borrowers
- the alternative types of lending institutions that are available to borrowers (for example, banks, building societies, credit unions and loan companies)
- the risks and costs that are associated with each type of borrowing and each type of lending institution.

Taxation

The current framework of taxation in the UK is regulated and administered by HM Revenue and Customs (HMRC), which is responsible for the assessment and collection of taxes, both direct taxes and indirect taxes.

Direct taxes are taxes that are paid directly by an individual or organisation, with the individual or organisation upon which the taxes are levied being responsible for the fulfilment of the tax payment. These are taxes levied on the individual's or organisation's income or profits.

Indirect taxes are taxes that are related to consumption, expenditure, privilege, or right, and are taxes levied on goods and services.

In terms of taxes payable, it is important to understand:

- what personal tax allowances and tax exemptions are available
- what Income Tax is payable on earned income, on employee-related benefits in kind ('perks' in addition to wages or a salary), and on investment income
- what taxes are payable by both unincorporated businesses (for example, a sole trader or a partnership) and small incorporated businesses (for example, a small private limited company)
- what Capital Gains Tax is payable on profits or gains made on the sale of property and investment assets
- what Inheritance Tax is payable on property and money acquired by gift or by inheritance.

Savings and investments

There is an enormous variety of savings and investments products available, including:

- low-risk savings and investments, such as cash-related savings and investments (including ISAs), cash bonds, Premium Bonds, Savings Certificates, Children's Bonds, Pensioner Bonds, Investment Bonds, Gilts, and pensions
- medium-risk investments, such as endowments and friendly society tax-exempt savings plans, company bonds, shares, property, offshore savings accounts, and pooled investment funds
- higher-risk investments, such as commodities, structured products, Venture Capital Trusts, spread betting, Contracts for Difference, land banking, and other unregulated collective investment schemes.

Before investing, it is important to understand:

- the risks and uncertainty associated with any savings account or other financial investment
- the underlying nature of the investment (is it cash-based, asset-based, or debt-based?)
- the nature (and timing) of any investment return (is it based on investment growth or income, or a combination of both?)
- the level of certainty of any possible investment returns.

Pensions

Although pensions are merely a type of tax-efficient long-term savings plan, they are undergoing a revolution. Economic necessity, industry pressure and government legislation continue to change the very nature and scope of many pension schemes – especially many public sector pension schemes. For those concerned about their future financial security and their retirement well-being, it has become an absolute necessity to understand changes in the State Pension scheme (from April 2016), changes in access to private sector pension schemes (from April 2015), the advantages of workplace occupation-related pension schemes, and the alternative types of individual contract-based pension schemes available.

Insurance and assurance

Held hostage to a future that is both uncertain and unpredictable, we are constantly bombarded with a confusing array of often very costly insurance and assurance products and schemes: from life-related policies to asset-protection policies, from health-related policies to activity-related policies, from travel-related policies to income-protection policies and investment-related policies. But which of these types of insurance and assurance policies do we actually need? More importantly, what actual purpose do such insurance and assurance policies actually serve?

Fraud

Fraud is the use of false representation or criminal deception, or both, to gain an unjust personal advantage or to avoid a legal or moral obligation. In today's increasingly web-based, cyber-connected, online society, it is crucially important to understand and appreciate:

- how person-related fraud (for example, financial fraud, credit-card fraud, identity theft and fraud, false-billing fraud and advance-fee fraud) are perpetrated

- what impact such person-related frauds can have on the lives of those targeted
- how you can protect yourself – your identity, your assets and your money – from identity impostors, cyber fraudsters and online scammers.

Regulation, legislation, and codes of practice

There is a staggering array of financial products and services now available in an ever-expanding and ever more complex and interconnected financial marketplace. Of necessity, a similar array of organisations and guidelines have been developed to supervise financial interactions, including the Financial Conduct Authority, the Prudential Regulatory Authority, the Competition and Markets Authority, the Lending Standards Board code of practice, and the Financial Conduct Authority's Consumer Credit sourcebook. Those who provide financial products and services (including independent financial advisers) are regulated by various legislative requirements (for example, the *Data Protection Act 1998*, the *Limitations Act 1980*, and s.40 *Administration of Justice Act 1970*; and the Financial Ombudsman Service is available to assist in resolving disputes between product and service providers and their customers or clients. These arrangements have been devised:

- to protect those purchasing the financial products and services
- to enhance the stability of the financial marketplace
- to maintain confidence in the products and services sold.

Debt, voluntary arrangements, and bankruptcy

Debt is a complex issue that can be very difficult to deal with. The stress, the worry and the anxiety associated with excessive personal debt can have a substantial effect on a person's physical and mental health. Understanding what debt is, being able to distinguish between different types of debt (secured debt and unsecured debt), and appreciating the consequences of not dealing with personal debt – County Court Judgments, bailiffs, the seizure of personal goods or possessions, and ultimately bankruptcy – are vitally important.

It is also important to understand how a personal debt issue can be managed: whether by using a (free) debt advice service or a (paid for) debt management company; by applying for an Individual Voluntary Arrangement (IVA), or if applicable, a Debt Relief Order; or even by making a formal application for bankruptcy.

1.6 *Data Protection Act 1998*

The *Data Protection Act 1998* is designed to protect personal information held about individuals, and regulates the processing of data relating to individuals – or in the terminology used – 'data subjects'.

The *Data Protection Act 1998* applies to all personal data. It gives rights to the individual data subjects (those to whom the data relates). It also imposes responsibilities:

- on the individual data subjects
- on the companies and organisations that hold the data
- on the employees of those organisations who use the information.

The *Data Protection Act 1998* implemented part of the European Convention on Human Rights. It applies only to information about individuals (such as names, addresses, personal reference numbers, income, or entitlement to benefits). It does not apply to non-personal data, such as that relating to other businesses or limited companies.

Note: The *Data Protection Act 1998* only protects personal data about people who are alive.

All companies are required to be registered with the Information Commissioner and to comply with:

- the provisions of the *Data Protection Act 1998*
- the guidelines and interpretations issued by the Information Commissioner.

Failure to do so can result in the imposition of substantial fines, and, if deemed appropriate by the Information Commissioner, closure of the company.

Data Protection Act 1998: definitions

The *Data Protection Act 1998* provides the following definitions:

- *Data subject:* An individual who is the subject of the personal information (data). For the provisions of the Act to apply, the data subject must be living.
- *Data controller:* A person who determines the purposes for which, and the manner in which, personal data are processed or will be processed. Processing may be by an individual or by an organisation, and may be carried out jointly or in common with other persons or organisations.
- *Data processor:* A person who processes data on behalf of a data controller. Responsibility for correct processing under the *Data Protection Act 1998* remains, however, with the data controller.

Data Protection Act 1998: principles

The *Data Protection Act 1998* also contains eight data protection principles, which are designed to ensure that data are properly handled. These principles are as follows:

- 1st principle: 'personal data shall be processed fairly and lawfully'.
- 2nd principle: 'personal data shall be obtained only for one or more specified and lawful purposes, and shall not be further processed in any manner incompatible with that purpose or those purposes'.
- 3rd principle: 'personal data shall be adequate, relevant and not excessive in relation to the purpose or purposes for which they are processed'.
- 4th principle: 'personal data shall be accurate and, where necessary, kept up to date'.
- 5th principle: 'personal data processed for any purpose or purposes shall not be kept for longer than is necessary for that purpose or those purposes'.
- 6th principle: 'personal data shall be processed in accordance with the rights of data subjects under this Act'.
- 7th principle: 'appropriate technical and organisational measures shall be taken against unauthorised or unlawful processing of personal data and against accidental loss or destruction of, or damage to, personal data'.
- 8th principle: 'personal data shall not be transferred to a country or territory outside the European Economic Area, unless that country or territory ensures an adequate level of protection of the rights and freedoms of data subjects in relation to the processing of personal data'.

Activity 2

Miss Wainwright, a Manchester-based dentist, discloses her patients' details, including their home addresses, telephone numbers and email addresses, to her son, who manages a mail-order company, so that he can use them to market his own products. Does this disclosure contravene the *Data Protection Act 1998*?

Activity 3

A business consulting company routinely transfers staff-related personal data between its UK-based offices using unencrypted storage devices. Does this action contravene the *Data Protection Act 1998*?

Data Protection Act 1998: rights

The *Data Protection Act 1998* also gives rights to individuals in respect of personal data held about them by others. The rights are:

- the right to access by the data subject (*Data Protection Act 1998*, s.7, s.8 and s.9)
- the right to prevent processing likely to cause damage or distress (ibid., s.10)
- the right to prevent processing for the purposes of direct marketing (ibid., s.11)
- rights in relation to automated decision-making (ibid., s.12)
- the right to take action for compensation if the individual suffers damage by any contravention of the Act by the data controller (ibid., s.13)
- the right to take action to rectify, block, erase or destroy inaccurate data (ibid., s.12(a), s.14, and s.62).

Activity 4

Distinguish between a *data subject*, a *data controller*, and a *data processor*.

Note: It should be noted that the approach to data protection in Europe differs from that in the USA, where a more fragmented sectorial approach is used which relies primarily on a combination of legislation, regulation and self-regulation, rather than on governmental regulation alone. The USA has no single data protection law comparable to the EU's *Data Protection Directive*.

Sensitive personal data

Special rules exist regarding the processing of sensitive personal data. 'Sensitive personal data' is defined as personal data consisting of information relating to:

- a data subject's racial or ethnic origin
- a data subject's political opinions
- a data subject's religious beliefs or other beliefs of a similar nature
- a data subject's membership of a trade union

- a data subject's physical or mental health condition
- a data subject's sexual life or sexual orientation
- any criminal offences committed (or allegedly committed) by a data subject.

Activity 5

You have been informed that LME Ltd, a UK-based personal loan company with which you have an account, is investigating the possibility of opening offices in France, Germany, South Africa, and Malaysia. Because of the company's operations, all customer personal data will be transferred between all of these locations. Which of the data processing principles (contained in the *Data Protection Act 1998*) would apply to transferring personal data outside the EU?

1.7 Case study: the Carter family

The following case study relates to the Carter family: Stuart and Mary Carter, and their three children, Jonathan, Michelle, and Anthony.

Note: Discussion questions related to this case study scenario feature at the end of each chapter.

The Carter Family

It is 31 May 2016.

On 1 January 1982, three years after they were married, Stuart and Mary Carter decided to start their own business, CLB Ltd, a specialist hand-crafted furniture manufacturer and retailer. The business started its operations from a single-storey building in York. Originally, Stuart Carter and Mary Carter were the only full-time employees of the company. Stuart Carter was responsible for the design and construction of the business's products, and Mary Carter was responsible for the marketing and retail of the business's products as well as the day-to-day management of the company and its business finances.

During the late 1990s and early 2000s, the company quickly expanded and since then has grown substantially. By the end of 2015 the company operated a total of twelve retail outlets and two production workshops, located around the UK. On 31 December 2015, after 34 years of trading, the financial statements of the company showed a turnover of £16m, and a pre-tax profit of £3.5m.

Stuart and Mary Carter together own 100% of the 20,000 ordinary shares in issue. A recent valuation of CLB Ltd suggested that the shares were worth approximately £46 each.

Jonathan Carter is a 31-year-old chartered accountant who is now employed as a senior executive manager within the company and who has been involved in the business since leaving university nine years ago. He is at present in charge of the Finance and Administration office, which is still located in the company's original location in York. Jonathan is married and has three children: twin girls India-May and Zoe Marie, aged 5, and a boy Reece David, aged 3.

Jonathan's younger sister, Michelle, is 24. His younger brother, Anthony, is 21. Both are in full-time education.

Michelle has completed an MSc in International Politics at the London School of Economics and has decided not to join the business but to pursue a career in academia. In March 2016, she was awarded a three-year EU scholarship grant of £9,500 per year, which will allow her not only to complete her PhD at the London School of Economics but also to take an 18-month teaching sabbatical at the University of Lausanne, Switzerland, commencing in January 2017.

Unlike his sister, Anthony left sixth-form college with no clear career ambitions. In early 2013, following completion of his A-levels, Anthony suddenly decided that he would like to 'experience the world' and, contrary to his parents' wishes, took a gap year (which actually lasted 22 months), and travelled around Europe, Australasia, South East Asia and South America. Anthony returned to the UK in early 2015. He spent six months working in Harrogate as a commis chef for a well-known chain of international hotels, but is now reading for a degree in Facilities Management at the University of Lincoln.

Stuart and Mary Carter

Whilst Mary Carter, who is now 58, has not worked in the family business since suffering a minor stoke six months ago, Stuart Carter, who has now celebrated his 60th birthday, has continued to work a 50-hour week at the company, as he has done for the last 34 years.

Although he himself is in good health, he grew concerned about his wife and spent more and more time over the last few months considering both the work he does (his role) and the responsibilities he carries (his position) in the company, his worth to the company, and whether he really wanted to continue as Managing Director at the helm of CLB Ltd.

On 7 May 2016, after a long discussion with his wife, Stuart Carter finally decided that he would retire from the family business and devote more time and energy to his wife and her recuperation, to their lifetime passion for sailing, and to the restoration of their summer home in Aubagne, near Marseilles in the South of France.

Stuart and Mary Carter have since made the following decisions:

- They will formally retire on 30 November 2016. Their son Jonathan will be appointed Managing Director of CLB Ltd, and will take over responsibility for the management of the company as of 1 December 2016.
- They have resolved to launch a Share Incentive Plan on 30 November 2016 for the benefit of all the company's employees.
- Each of their children, Jonathan, Michelle and Anthony, will receive an equal share of ownership of the family company. Stuart and Mary Carter have decided to transfer 22% of the share capital to each of their children and to retain ownership of the remaining 34% of the share capital for themselves (17% for Stuart Carter and 17% for Mary Carter).
- They will sell their apartment in Bath, and the city apartments in Siena and Barcelona (see below), and move to their house in the South of France, where they expect to live for at least ten months of each year. The proceeds of the sales will be placed in trust for the benefit of their grandchildren. They will retain ownership of their house in York.
- They will sell all of their investments in UK Gilts and Commercial Bonds and invest the total amount in a diversified portfolio of UK-based FTSE 100 equities.
- They will amend their wills to provide that on the death of the first spouse the estate will pass to the remaining spouse absolutely. At the death of the second spouse, the assets will be divided equally between the three children.

The values (in pounds) of Stuart and Mary Carter's assets are estimated to be as shown.

	Mr Stuart Carter £	Mrs Mary Carter £	Total £
UK Assets			
House, York (main residence)			750,000
City apartment, Bath			450,000
Overseas Assets			
House, Aubagne, France			450,000
City apartment, Siena, Italy			250,000
City apartment, Barcelona, Spain			350,000
Quoted Investments			
Shares	140,000	25,000	165,000
UK Gilts	56,000	43,000	99,000
Commercial Bonds	67,000	54,000	121,000
Non-Quoted Investments			
Shares in CLB Ltd	460,000	460,000	920,000
Bank deposits	15,500	12,700	28,200

Note: The UK and overseas properties are held jointly and are owned without mortgage. The yacht is owned by Mr Stuart Carter and has a permanent all-year mooring in Marseilles. The quoted and non-quoted investments are held individually.

In addition to the assets above, Stuart Carter has a whole-of-life assurance policy, which on his death would pay out £100,000 to his wife. Mary Carter has a similar policy for £80,000, which will go to her husband on her death.

The earnings of Stuart and Mary Carter over the last two years have been as follows:

	Mr Stuart Carter £	Mrs Mary Carter £
Year ended 31 March 2015:		
Salary	90,000	75,000
Bonus (1% of profits)	40,000	40,000
Dividends	70,000	70,000
Year ended 31 March 2016:		
Salary	96,000	52,000
Bonus (1% of profits)	60,000	30,000
Dividends	80,000	80,000

Note: Bonuses and dividends are normally paid in July, approximately 4 weeks after the company's AGM.

For a number of years, Stuart and Mary have each paid a percentage of their salaries, matched by an equal contribution from the company, into a small self-administered pension fund run for the company. Stuart is estimated to be due a lump sum of £95,000 on retirement and a (reduced) pension of £15,000 per annum. Mary will be due a lump sum of £60,000 and a (reduced) pension of £7,000 per annum.

Jonathan Carter

Jonathan, his wife Claire (whom he married six years ago), and their young family live in an old Victorian four-bedroom detached house in a small village seven miles north of Beverley, near York. They purchased the house three years ago. Although the house is in need of urgent repair and refurbishment – the roof needs replacing, the house needs rewiring, the kitchen needs some cosmetic refurbishment, and the house needs double-glazing – it has a market value of £270,000. There is, however, an outstanding mortgage on the property of approximately £180,000. The mortgage is a Lloyds Bank standard variable-rate repayment mortgage in the name of Jonathan Carter only.

Claire, who is a graduate of the University of Hull Business School, owns and manages a fashion boutique called 'Image 20', which trades in a retail park four miles outside York. The business is not a limited company but an unincorporated business, and commenced trading on 1 April 2012. The financial results for 'Image 20' for the year ending 31 March 2016 are detailed below:

Income Statement for the year ended 31 March 2016

	£	£
Sales		185,605
Cost of Sales	90,855	
Gross Profit	94,750	
Less:		
Wages and Salaries	25,962	
Rent	10,773	
Rates	6,355	
Heating	8,004	
Lighting	5,120	
Advertising	5,926	
General Expenses	8,525	
Depreciation	2,450	
		73,115
Net Profit		21,635
Less:		
Drawings		18,986
Profits retained for the year		2,649

(Continued)

Notes:

1. Sales include £1,650 of fashion accessories (valued at the retail price) which Claire took for her personal use.
2. Wages and salaries include Claire's annual salary of £15,000, which she withdraws in cash from the business on a monthly basis. She is not registered for PAYE.
3. Capital allowances for 2015/16 are £1,200.
4. The business employs two part-time staff who are paid in cash (from till receipts) at the end of each working day.
5. As at 31 March 2016, the business had an overdraft of £2,530.
6. Image 20 is not registered for VAT purposes.

Note: Claire has not paid any National Insurance contributions since she started to trade as 'Image 20' in April 2012.

For the year ending 31 March 2016, Jonathan earned a salary of £65,000 from CLB Ltd (including a performance-related bonus). His wife Claire earned a salary of £15,000, plus personal drawings from Image 20 of £18,986.

Despite their joint income, their large house, their new cars, and the fact that they take expensive overseas holidays, Jonathan and Claire are in serious financial trouble. They have no savings, their joint account is always overdrawn, and for the last 18 months their monthly financial commitments have exceeded their monthly income.

In terms of monthly outgoings, the couple have the following costs:

- nursery fees: £490 per month
- private medical insurance: £256 per month
- food costs: £460 per month
- other costs (for mortgage repayments, utility bills, private medical insurance, motor expenses and overdraft interest): £1,340 per month
- monthly personal loan repayments: £856 per month (including £67 per month for payment protection insurance)
- credit-card and store-card payments: £435 per month.

Note: Each month Jonathan and Claire pay only the minimum repayments on their credit cards and store cards (approximately 2.5% of the outstanding balance).

As at 31 May 2016, Jonathan has personal credit-card debts of £4,010, and an outstanding personal loan of £8,500. Claire has personal credit-card debts of £9,650, an outstanding personal loan of £17,000 (used four months ago to purchase a car), and various store cards with an outstanding balance of £3,655.

Claire is rather blasé about the ever-increasing levels of personal debt, despite receiving three final demand letters and a notice of court action in the last two months. Indeed, two weeks ago she booked a two-week summer Mediterranean cruise for the family, at a cost of £4,790. Jonathan, however, has become increasingly concerned, not only about the state of their finances and the levels of debt they have, but also about how they will pay for the urgent refurbishment to the house which estimates suggest will cost between £50,000 and £60,000.

Jonathan, who recently celebrated his 35th birthday, has only just become a member of the CLB Ltd's pension scheme. He has made no other provision for his future or his family's future. He has no life insurance (he cancelled the life insurance policy that had been attached to the mortgage) and no savings. Claire does not contribute to a pension scheme. She has no life insurance. Neither Jonathan nor Claire has made a will.

Note: Six days ago Jonathan Carter received an invoice for £1,862.76 from Pandel plc, a Norwich-based glazing company, for work undertaken over seven years ago on a property Jonathan owned before he married Claire. The company is now demanding payment and threatening legal action if payment is not made in full within 14 days.

Michelle Carter

Michelle has lived away from the family home in York for over four years: three years as an undergraduate student at the University of Bath, where she graduated with a first-class degree in Political and Social Sciences, and then a Masters year as a postgraduate student at the London School of Economics, where she graduated with distinction. She has now been offered a PhD place at LSE. She has a life independent of the family and the family business. As far as CLB Ltd is concerned, Michelle does not want any involvement at all, and is happy that her older brother Jonathan is so committed to the company and its future.

Michelle lives alone in a small two-room basement flat, which she rents from a Mr and Mrs Williams, long-time friends of her father. Because she occasionally babysits their two small children, Michelle rents the basement flat at a heavily discounted monthly cost. Michelle owns a three-year-old Citroen DS3. She passed her driving test only 15 months ago and bought the car a few weeks later, while she was at home in York. To minimise the expense, Michelle only has third-party vehicle insurance (bought online through the AA). To reduce the insurance premiums even further, Michelle also informed the insurers that her home address was in York (her parents' address), not in London.

Michelle's monthly expenses are as follows:

- rent: £250 per month
- rates: £28 per month
- water, gas and electricity: £19 per month
- food: £120 per month
- clothes: £32 per month
- vehicle insurance: £65 per month
- travel expenses: £65 per month.

Other than her student loan of £12,600, Michelle has no other debts. She receives a personal allowance of £350 per month from her parents. Her parents have told her that this will continue until she completes her PhD.

Whilst her PhD will cost £5,650 per year for the next three years, and the cost of the 18-month teaching sabbatical at the University of Lausanne, Switzerland, will be approximately £9,400, these costs will be more than covered by the three-year EU scholarship grant of £9,500 per year.

Michelle's bank account has a balance of £1,605, and she has an ISA account with a balance of £9,650.

Last year, whilst completing her MSc, Michelle also undertook some part-time teaching, for which she received an honorarium of £65 per month. Michelle also works part-time as a bar assistant in the student bar at the London School of Economics. Her net take-home pay is approximately £250 per month. It is expected that these employments will continue for the first year of her PhD.

Although Michelle is not a shy person, unlike her brothers she has only a small circle of friends, and whilst she does frequently socialise with her student friends, she is far happier on her own and in the company of her books. Michelle has never been a gambler. She has never visited a bookmaker's, has never played bingo, and has never bought a lottery ticket. Three weeks ago, however, whilst shopping on Oxford Street with two of her friends, she decided to buy a silver National Lottery scratch card. Michelle did not check the scratch card until she got home, when to her absolute amazement she found she had won £250,000!

Michelle's first reaction was that it was a mistake: a huge error. It couldn't possibly be correct. After contacting Lottery HQ, however, and checking and rechecking the details, she realised it was correct. Five days after she had confirmed her bank account details and a few other personal details, the money was paid into her account by CHAPS transfer. Michelle has yet to tell her family of her astonishing win.

Anthony Carter

Like his sister, Anthony does not want any involvement in the family business. Once he completes his degree, in June 2019, Anthony would like to open a boutique restaurant, somewhere in the Yorkshire region, specialising in South American cuisine.

As part of his degree, for his penultimate academic year (commencing in September 2017), Anthony has the opportunity to study overseas. Whilst there are no additional study fees to pay, Anthony has to fund his accommodation costs, his living costs and his travel costs himself. He estimates that in total the cost of the year-long academic placement will be approximately £7,500. Anthony is planning to go back to Argentina, to study at the Universidad de Buenos Aires. He spent the final five months of his gap-year travels working in a small restaurant on the Plaza Dorrego in the San Telmo neighbourhood of Buenos Aires, and would like to visit some of the friends he left behind when he returned to the UK.

Anthony is hopeless with money, however, and still seems unable to get to the end of a semester without getting into debt. He has an overdraft of £2,479, a credit-card debt of £2,593, a personal loan with an outstanding balance of £6,097 (which he used to purchase a car), and a student loan of £8,500.

Anthony lives in a small three-bedroom terrace student house near St Catherine's, approximately two miles away from the University of Lincoln city campus. He shares the rent, rates and utilities costs equally with two other students. Anthony's monthly expenses are as follows:

- rent: £84 per month
- rates: £28 per month
- water, gas and electricity: £32 per month
- food: £176 per month
- clothes: £32 per month
- going out: £120 per month
- other costs: £218 per month.

Note: 'Other costs' relate to the running costs of his car, a minimum credit-card repayment, payment of overdraft interest, and a personal loan repayment.

Anthony works part-time (approximately 50 hours a month) as a warehouse assistant at the local Tesco superstore. His net take-home pay is approximately £300 per month. He also receives an allowance from his parents of £350 per month. He has no idea how he will pay off his personal loans, his credit card or his overdraft, or save the money he needs for his year overseas to Argentina in 16 months' time.

Note: Seven weeks ago, Anthony's student accommodation was broken into. His phone, tablet, laptop, debit card and credit card were stolen. He reported the loss of his debit card and credit card to his bank, which immediately cancelled the cards. Two weeks later, however, Anthony noticed that an overseas purchase totalling £2,065 had been charged to his credit-card account. He complained to his bank, which agreed that the credit-card charge was a fraudulent 'identify theft'-related transaction. Nevertheless, as yet, and despite repeated requests, the money has not been returned to his account.

1.8 Concluding comments

Financial literacy is about personal empowerment and financial responsibility: it is about taking control of, and being responsible for, your own financial well-being. Whilst the ability to manage your money efficiently and effectively involves the understanding of a wide range of techniques and the use of an array of complex skills and competencies, it is nonetheless a crucial component of your everyday survival toolkit.

Key points

- 'Financial literacy' refers to the set of competences that allows a person to make decisions about her or his financial resources.
- The key components of financial literacy are: skills and confidence, understanding and knowledge, attitude, motivation, and opportunity.
- Good personal financial management can help to reduce personal stress, to avoid excessive debt, and to fulfil personal goals.

Self-review questions

1. What is meant by 'financial literacy'?
2. Briefly describe the factors that can affect a person's financial literacy.
3. Distinguish, with examples, between direct taxes and indirect taxes.
4. What are the main objectives of good personal financial management?
5. Briefly explain the eight principles contained within the *Data Protection Act 1998.*

Case study discussion questions

1. Given Stuart and Mary Carter's plans for the future, to what direct taxes do you think they would be liable?
2. Jonathan and Claire Carter are clearly experiencing financial problems. What factors do you think are affecting their ability to manage their finances?

Suggested answers to chapter activities

Activity 1

Although the prioritisation of benefits can vary considerably between individuals, a common ranking would be:

- avoiding (excessive) debt
- reducing stress

- controlling spending and managing personal cash flow
- maintaining a healthy credit score
- fulfilling personal goals.

Activity 2

This would contravene the 2nd principle – the disclosure of such information is incompatible with the purposes for which the information was initially obtained.

Activity 3

This would contravene the 7th principle, which provides that appropriate technical and organisational measures should be undertaken to prevent unauthorised or unlawful processing of personal data or the accidental loss or destruction of, or damage to, personal data.

Activity 4

A *data subject* is a living person who is the subject of the personal information (the data). A *data controller* is a person who determines the purposes for which, and the manner in which, personal data are, or will be, processed. A *data processor* is a person who processes data on behalf of a data controller, although the responsibility for correct processing remains with the data controller.

Activity 5

The relevant data protection principles would be: the 6th principle (that personal data shall be processed in accordance with the rights of data subjects under this Act); the 7th principle (that appropriate technical and organisational measures shall be taken against accidental loss or destruction of, or damage to, personal data); and the 8th principle (that personal data shall not be transferred to a country or territory outside the European Economic Area, unless that country or territory ensures an adequate level of protection of the rights and freedoms of data subjects in relation to the processing of personal data.

2

Budgeting and cash management

Learning outcomes

By the end of this chapter, you should be able to:

- describe the growing variety of payment technologies now in use
- distinguish between the different types of personal spending
- recognise how to manage spending and make money work harder
- describe and explain the key stages in creating a personal budget
- explain the difference between an annual percentage rate (APR) of interest and an annual equivalent rate (AER).

2.1 Introduction

In a society driven by mass media marketing and advertising targeted at individuals, financial survival in today's web-based online society requires a knowledge and understanding of how to plan the use of personal finances, how to manage personal spending, and how to make money work harder and go further.

This chapter considers a range of topics related to payment technologies, personal spending, and most importantly of all, budgeting and cash management.

2.2 Paying for products and services

There can be little doubt that the technologies we use to pay for the products we buy and the services we use have changed in recent years, and the change has been both dramatic and substantial.

The more notable developments over the last 50 years include these:

- 1968: BACS (Bankers' Automated Clearing Services), the company responsible for the clearing and settlement of direct debit and direct credit[1] payments, was established.
- 1974: The UK *Consumer Credit Act* was introduced.
- 1976: SWIFT (Society for Worldwide Interbank Financial Telecommunication) payments were launched, paving the way for international payments.
- 1984: The CHAPS (Clearing House Automated Payments System) system was introduced for high-value electronic payments.
- 1986: The LINK network[2] was created.
- 1987: The first UK debit card was issued, by Barclays Bank.

- 1990: The UK cashback scheme (see below) was introduced.
- 1997: Online banking was introduced by Nationwide Building Society (followed a few months later by the Royal Bank of Scotland).
- 2003: The 'chip and PIN' system was introduced.
- 2008: The Faster Payment[3] system was introduced.
- 2008: Contactless UK payment cards were issued.
- 2011: Mobile phones were first used as debit cards.
- 2012: A mobile payment app (pingit) was launched by Barclays.
- 2014: A mobile payment system (Paym[4]) was introduced.

Today there are many alternative ways of paying for the products we buy and the services we use, including: cash, cheques, debit cards, credit cards, charge cards, prepaid cards, direct debits, standing orders, CHAPS, prepayment plans, and mobile payments. Whilst some of these can only be used to pay for in-store purchases, of course, many can be used to pay for both in-store and online purchases.

Cash

Cash – the use of legal tender currency – is still a widely accepted method of payment. It is an immediate method of payment without additional cost (although some cash machines (ATMs) may charge a fee for withdrawing cash). No bank account is required – although carrying large amounts of cash can of course present a security issue: if you lose your purse or wallet, any cash lost can only be recovered if you have an appropriate insurance policy.

Will cash continue to be used as a method of payment? Yes, it will – mainly because there will always be a need for, and a demand for, a method of payment that protects the anonymity of both the payer and the payee.

Cheques

Although cheques can still be used to pay for a wide variety of transactions, many retailers (including Tesco, Asda, Sainsbury, and Marks & Spencer) and many service providers (including many utility providers) have stopped accepting cheques as a method of payment. Consequently, their use is declining rapidly. Providing a bank account has a credit balance (equal to or greater than the value of any cheques), then cheques are usually free to use. An exception is cashing a cheque with a 'cheque chaser', an organisation or a company that charges a fee (usually a fairly large fee) for doing so (for example, see The Money Shop[5]).

Cheques can take up to three days to clear – that is, for the money to be received by the payee – and, if not cashed, remain legally valid for up to six years.

Debit cards

Debit cards are now widely used. Many businesses now accept debit-card payments as the 'default' method of payment for products and services. Debit cards can be used to withdraw cash from ATMs, both in the UK and overseas, and can also be used to make payments online (although this is *not* recommended – see 'Credit cards', below).

To use a debit card, a bank account is required. Provided that the bank account is in credit, debit cards are free to use, although some retailers impose a 'minimum spend' level (commonly £10 or £15) below which a small transaction cost is incurred. Payments are processed on the day of the transaction.

Note: If an account holder or cardholder is the innocent victim of fraud, then normally all funds will be returned and the account holder or cardholder will not be held liable.

Sometimes things go wrong – a purchased product may not arrive or may arrive but prove faulty; a service may not be provided or may be provided incorrectly; a charge may be made multiple times or be charged incorrectly; or the retailer or service provider may have ceased trading. In such circumstances, the customer or cardholder can request a 'chargeback' and claim back any money paid. Visa, MasterCard and American Express all offer chargeback schemes, and these are applicable to all debit cards, prepaid cards, and credit cards. There is no limit (although MasterCard impose a minimum amount of £10), but claims must be made within 120 days of the purchase or expected service provision.

Note: Some debit cards have now been upgraded to include contactless technology, which enable small payments (up to £30 in value) to be made by simply holding the card up to a special card reader, without the need to enter a PIN number or provide a signature.

Credit cards

Currently accepted by over a million retailers and service providers in the UK, credit cards based on Visa or MasterCard[6] are now widely used and accepted in over 150 countries, with some credit cards also facilitating contactless payment technologies (see above).

Many credit cards offer a range of payment rewards and loyalty-related schemes, cash-back offers, and 0% interest transfers.

Some retailers may impose a minimum spend level (commonly £10 or £15) below which a small transaction cost is incurred. In general, transactions are usually processed on the same day, though payment is not required until the end of the accounting period, usually every 6 weeks. If payment is made in full, no interest charge is accrued – if not, interest will be charged on any outstanding balance carried forward. A minimum payment is normally required.

Note: Interest charges (and interest rates) can vary between banks and card issuers. For example, in June 2015[7] a MBNA Low Rate Credit Card charged 6.6%, NatWest Cashback Plus Credit Card charged 17.4%, a Lloyds Bank Avios Reward Credit Card charged 23.7%, and a Virgin Atlantic Black Credit Card charged 52% (Money 2015).

Although no bank account is required to be able to use a credit card, credit-card companies will normally undertake a credit check (see Chapter 3) on any applicant before issuing a credit card.

When shopping, and especially when shopping online, you should always use a credit card, primarily because of s.75 of the *Consumer Credit Act 1974*,[8] which provides that 'if the debtor under a debtor-creditor-supplier agreement falling within section 12(b) or (c) has, in relation to a transaction financed by the agreement, any claim against the supplier in respect of a misrepresentation or breach of contract, he shall have a like claim against the creditor, who, with the supplier, shall accordingly be jointly and severally liable to the debtor.' If you use a credit card to pay for products or services costing between £100 and £60,260,[9] therefore, the credit-card provider is equally liable if something goes wrong. S.75 also applies to store cards, store instalment credit and some car finance agreements (although not to hire purchase). It does not, however, apply to the following:

- products or services costing less than £100 or more than £60,260
- purchases for which a debit card or charge card is used
- products or services paid for by a secondary cardholder

- products or services bought through an intermediary
- purchases for which a credit card is used indirectly
- for hire purchase agreements.

Where s.75 does *not* apply, a chargeback facility (see above) could be used. This is especially useful for purchases costing less than £100.

Charge cards

Charge cards are very different from credit cards. They do not offer a credit facility, and generally do not impose a spending limit or charge interest. Cardholders can spend without restriction, but *must* pay the outstanding amount *in full* at the end of the accounting period. If this is not done, significant penalty costs are imposed.

An annual membership fee is normally payable for a charge card, and such cards are generally available only to those earning above a minimum income requirement. Many charge cards offer a range of loyalty rewards, including a concierge service, access to special airport lounges, and insurances.

Note: Charge cards are not covered by s.75 of the *Consumer Credit Act 1974*, although charge-card companies (such as American Express) all have chargeback schemes which enable customers to claim for a refund within 120 days of discovering a problem.

Prepaid cards

Prepaid cards are essentially top-up payment cards. All retailers who accept Visa and MasterCard will also accept payments using a prepaid card. These cards can be used to purchase products and services in-store or online. They can also be used to withdraw funds from ATMs.

Prepaid cards are usually free, although some issuers may charge a fee either to purchase a card or to top it up, and a bank account is not required. As with debit cards and credit cards, payments are processed on the day of the transaction.

Activity 1

Explain the main advantages of using a credit card to pay for products or services.

Direct debits

Direct debits are mainly used for making regular payments – for example, utilities, Council Tax, loan repayments, and subscriptions. The bank account holder (the payer) must authorise the creation of a direct debit – in writing, over the telephone, or online. Thereafter, the payee may amend the amount paid and other details, but must notify the account holder (in writing or by email), normally 10 working days in advance of the change. Over 20,000 companies in the UK accept direct-debit payments.[10]

Direct-debit payments are free to use (providing the bank account is in credit) and are processed using BACS (Bankers' Automated Clearing Services). A bank account is required, and payments are processed immediately on the due date, or if necessary on the next weekday. All direct-debit payments are covered by the direct-debit guarantee scheme which provides a refund should any direct-debit payments be incorrectly made or processed.

For further information on direct debits, see: www.directdebit.co.uk.

Standing orders

Standing orders are also used for making regular payments, and again the bank account holder (the payer) must authorise the creation of a standing order – in writing, over the telephone, or online. Unlike a direct debit however, the payee cannot amend the amount paid. A bank account is required, and payments are processed immediately on the due date, or if necessary on the next weekday. Standing-order payments are free to use, providing the bank account is in credit; and like direct debits are processed using BACS.

If a standing-order payment is made fraudulently, the bank account holder will normally receive a refund, provided that the account holder is an innocent victim of the fraud.

Note: Whereas a direct debit gives permission to a company to take money from an account holder's account, a standing order is an instruction by an account holder to a bank or building society to make payments. With a standing order, only the account holder can change the date or the payment amount, whereas with a direct debit these details can be changed by the person or organisation being paid.

CHAPS

CHAPS (Clearing House Automated Payments System) is mainly used for very high-value payments, as for example when buying a house. CHAPS payments can cost between £25 and £30 per transaction and payments are processed immediately (on the same day). A bank account is required, and the CHAPS payment must be authorised in advance.

Note: For most payments, it would be cheaper the use the Faster Payment Service.[11] This is a UK banking service that enables payments between different banks' customer accounts to occur swiftly, typically within two hours.

Any fraudulent payment will normally be refunded, provided that the account holder is an innocent victim of the fraud.

Prepayment plan

Prepayment plans are payment facilities offered by some retailers and service providers that allow a customer to pay for products or services in advance of their receipt or use. Examples are mobile phone prepayment plans, funeral services prepayment plans, and wine club membership prepayment plans.

Mobile payment (Paym)

Paym allows an account holder to make secure payments to account holders of other participating banks or building societies using their mobile number.[12] By September 2015, seventeen banks and building societies are able to use the Paym system.[13]

Promoted by the Payments Council as a fast, safe, secure, convenient and simple-to-use payment system, Paym payments are generally made immediately (as are payments using the Faster Payments or LINK payment mechanisms), although some payment periods may vary depending on the type of bank account used.

To send and receive payments, both the sender and the recipient must register with their respective banks in order to link their mobile phone number to their bank account. This registration process can be undertaken online.

Future alternative payment methods

The way we pay for the products we buy and the services we use is of course changing: as technology changes, so does the availability of alternative (and hopefully improved) methods of payments. Whilst many alternative payment technologies will undoubtedly be developed, many of them will be short-lived. Those payment technologies that do survive to gain widespread social acceptance will of course need to be secure, reliable and accessible. More importantly, they will need to exemplify two key notions: simplicity and naturalness. Future payment technologies will need to adapt to people. They will need to become more person-orientated – more flexible, more mobile, and, perhaps most importantly, less visible.

An example of this new payment technology is Apple Pay, launched in 2015, a mobile payment and digital wallet service provided by Apple Inc. that allows users to make payments using the iPhone 6, Apple Watch, the iPad Air or iPad Mini, using the Visa, MasterCard and American Express payment facilities.

So what does the future hold?

In the shorter term, it is likely that mobile payment technologies and contactless (or 'near-field communication') payment technologies will continue to develop and gain wider social acceptance. The demise of card-based payment technologies that require authentication in two distinct ways[14] will accelerate with the development of more secure, universal, interchangeable and convenient electronic cash systems – surpassing existing 'open source' electronic cash systems, such as the controversial bitcoin.[15]

In the longer term, it is likely that the development of biometrically-based payment technologies will grow, using for example enhanced fingerprint recognition, iris imaging, and skin-based scanning systems, in which a persons' unique individuality will become the foundation of future payment technologies.

> **Activity 2**
>
> Distinguish between the following alternative ways of paying for products and services: *direct debit, standing order*, and *CHAPS.*

2.3 Spending patterns

General spending (or consumption) patterns can be categorised into three groups:
- rational spending
- symbolic spending
- conspicuous spending.

Rational spending

Rational spending is personal spending that focuses on essential products and services: that is, spending on products and services that are deemed necessary for sustaining social and economic well-being. Although it is often associated with low-price, non-branded products and services, this is not necessarily the case since rational spending would also include spending on utility services such as water, gas and electricity, for example.

Symbolic spending

Symbolic spending is personal spending that focuses on the meanings and symbols attached to products and services, rather than on their underlying purposes or functional usefulness. In this context, products and services are seen as social tools, serving to communicate membership of a socially constructed group, and individuals are often prepared to pay a premium to claim membership in this way.

Conspicuous spending

Conspicuous spending is a conscious public display of discretionary economic power. It comprises personal spending that focuses on using luxury products and services whose purchase displays accumulated wealth and attaining or maintaining a particular social status. Conspicuous spending is normally associated with high-value branded products and services purchased by, or used by, high-earning individuals with substantial levels of disposable income.

Note: 'Invidious consumption' is the deliberate conspicuous consumption of products and services in order to display wealth and superior social status and to provoke the envy of others.

Buying products and services

The 2014 survey of UK household spending (Office of National Statistics 2014),[16] which used COICOP[17] classifications, suggested that total average UK household spending during 2013 was £517.20 per week (ibid., p.1),[18] divided as shown in Table 2.1.

Table 2.1 UK household spending

Classification of expenditure	Actual spending (£)	Proportion of total spending (%)
Transport	70.40	14
Recreation and culture	63.90	12
Housing and utilities	74.40	15
Restaurants and hotels	40.40	8
Food and non-alcoholic drinks	58.80	11
Miscellaneous products and services	39.10	8
Clothing and footwear	22.60	4
Household products and services	33.10	6
Alcohol and tobacco	12.00	2
Communication	14.50	3
Health	6.20	1
Education	8.80	2
Other	73.00	14
Totals	517.20	100

Source: Data from Office of National Statistics (2014).

Note: 'Housing and utilities' excludes mortgage costs and Council Tax.

There are of course significant variations between different geographical regions of the UK, especially between London, the South East, Wales, the East Midlands, the North East, and Scotland (ibid., p.8); and between different income groups in the UK, for example the lowest-earning 10% of UK households spent an average of £189.80 per week, whereas the highest-earning 10% of UK households spent an average of £1,119.50 per week (ibid., p.10). Such variations are influenced by two key groups of factors: firstly social and cultural heritage, and secondly economic status.

Whilst the interaction of a variety of social and cultural factors, such as demographic characteristics (ethnicity, age and gender), cultural background and social history, and family and marital status (married or single, and with or without children), clearly conditions an individual's patterns of spending , such as the products they buy and the types of services they use, it is an individual's economic status – such as her or his employment status (employed, unemployed, pensioner, student, etc.), level of after-tax income, accumulated wealth and personal assets, and access to unearned funds and borrowing – that clearly influences levels of expenditure: that is, how much people actually spend.

2.4 Budgeting and cash management

A budget is simply a financial plan – a financial plan that covers a specific future timescale. The most common type of budget is an annual budget, which is usually divided into 12 monthly budgets to show expected inflows and outflows of resources – that is, the income to be received and the expenditure (or expenses) to be incurred.

Advantages of creating a personal budget and financial plan

As a plan for the future, a personal cash budget can be used:

- to control spending and identify possible cash-flow problems
- to manage borrowing and outstanding debts (overdrafts, credit cards, bank loans, and the like)
- to highlight areas that may require corrective action
- to identify any possible savings.

More importantly, a personal cash budget can be used to identify strategies to manage unexpected occurrences (such as loss of employment or large, unanticipated expenses) and to assist in the planning for expected but expensive future events (such as marriage, having children, or buying a house).

Disadvantages of creating a personal budget and financial plan

Unless properly managed, a personal cash budget can become prescriptive. It can lead to inflexibility and become very de-motivating – especially if unrealistic/unachievable targets are set. More importantly, because they need to be regularly updated to reflect current circumstances a personal cash budget can, unless properly managed, become very time-consuming.

Sources of income

Before creating a personal cash budget, it is important to identify:

- the various sources from which income may be received
- the alternative types of expenditure that may be incurred, based on the products and services used.

Wages and salaries

Wages and salaries are earned income, associated with full- or part-time employment – monetary remuneration (including benefits in kind[19]) paid by an employer to an employee in exchange for work done.

With a *wage*, remuneration is generally calculated as a fixed amount per task (or unit) completed, or per hour or per day worked. With a *salary*, remuneration is generally a fixed amount (usually specified in an employment contract) paid on a regular basis (every four weeks or every calendar month), regardless of tasks completed, units produced, or hours worked. Such remuneration may also include commission payments, performance bonuses, and performance-related pay.

Where an employment contract exists, all payments of wages and salaries must be made net of Income Tax and National Insurance using HM Revenue and Custom's PAYE (Pay As You Earn) system.

Note: PAYE deductions are normally applied to all wages and salaries, including sick pay, maternity pay, directors' fees and pensions, but not to payments of the State Pension (see Chapter 5).

Grants

Grants (or more specifically personal grants) are non-repayable disbursements made for example by a government department, a company, or a foundation or trust, to a recipient individual once a specified qualifying criterion has been satisfied.

Such personal grants can be for example:

- disaster-related (made to victims of natural disasters)
- business-related (made to individuals seeking to start a business or to invest in a business project)
- education-related (made to individuals to cover education fees or tuition costs).

Benefits

Benefits are payments made to individuals by the government via the Department for Work and Pensions (DWP) or in some instances HM Revenue and Customs. There are various benefits, designed to meet different kinds of need. Here are some examples:

- The State Pension is payable to people who have reached State Pension age.
- Child Benefit and Child Tax Credit are payable to people who have children.
- Statutory Sick Pay is payable to employees who are absent from work due to illness.
- Income Support is payable to people on a low income.
- Income-based Jobseeker's Allowance (JSA) is payable to people who are out of work and seeking employment.
- Employment and Support Allowance (ESA)[20] is payable to people who are unable to work due to illness or disability and who are not receiving Statutory Sick Pay.

- Working Tax Credit is payable to people who work but have a low income, and can be claimed by working individuals, childless couples, and working families with dependent children (up to a maximum of two children[21]).
- Housing Benefit is payable to help people on a low income pay their rent.
- Council Tax Benefit is payable to help those on low income pay their Council Tax.
- Personal Independence Payments (PIP; formerly Disability Living Allowance or DLA) is payable to people with disabilities who have ongoing care needs.
- Attendance Allowance is payable to people whose ability to keep safe and to care for themselves is affected by a physical or mental illness or disability.
- Carer's Allowance is payable (subject to qualifying criteria) to people who provide care for someone else.

Note: By 2017, Universal Credit, a new non-taxable, means-tested benefit for working-age individuals will have replaced the following benefits and tax credits: Income Support, income-based Jobseeker's Allowance, income-related Employment and Support Allowance, Child Tax Credit, Working Tax Credit, and Housing Benefit. Universal Credit will be payable monthly.

Note: To help people assess their eligibility for benefits, independent online benefit calculators are available (see: www.gov.uk/benefits-calculators).

Pensions

Pensions are income received from the State Pension scheme (for those over the State retirement age), from an occupational (or workplace) pension scheme, or from a contract-based pension scheme (see Chapter 10).

With the exception of income received from the State Pension scheme, all pension-based income is subject to Income Tax, which is payable through HM Revenue and Custom's PAYE system or using the Income Tax self-assessment service.

Savings and investment income

Investment income is income such as interest receipts from savings and cash investments, and dividend income from equity investments. Interest receipts (income from savings), and dividends (income from equity investments) are usually paid 'net of tax' – that is, after the tax has been deducted at source.

Other income

'Other income' comprises all other personal income, including for example:
- rental income from property assets
- profits or capital gains on the sale of investment securities or other assets
- winnings from betting and gambling.

Types of expenditure

Housing

These are costs and expenses related to the repayment of mortgages, together with related insurance costs and other property maintenance and repair costs.

For rental property, expenditure on housing would comprise only rental fees and charges.

Utilities and services

These are costs and expenses related to the supply of water services and other utility-related services, including for example energy charges such as electricity, gas and other fuel costs. Utilities and services can be paid either quarterly (every three months) or monthly. The cost of such utilities and services is usually based on a tariff selected by the utility or service user.

Activity 3

Mark pays his electricity bill every quarter. His estimated usage for the next 6 months is as follows:
- 3 months ending 31 March: 9,500kWh
- 3 months ending 30 June: 8,250kWh.

Mark's current tariff charges 22.7p for the first 1,000 kWh and then 7.8p for each additional kWh. Mark is considering changing to an alternative tariff, which charges a fixed fee of £100 per quarter and 9.4p per kWh.

Based on his estimated usage, should Mark change to the alternative tariff?

Furniture and fittings

These are costs and expenses related to furnishings and household equipment, and would include, for example, textiles and appliances, tableware and utensils, house and garden equipment and tools, and goods and services related to routine household maintenance.

Food and clothing

These are costs and expenses related to the purchase of food (including takeaways), beverages (both alcoholic and non-alcoholic), and clothing and footwear.

Transport and communication

These are costs and expenses related to the use of public transport, car ownership or usage (for example, petrol costs, insurance costs, road tax, and repair and maintenance costs), and communication (including landline telephone charges, internet service provision, mobile phone charges, and postal services).

Recreation and entertainment

These are costs and expenses related to:
- the purchase of audiovisual products and services
- subscription to recreational and entertainment services
- the purchase of holidays
- the use of hotels, restaurants and other catering services.

Health and education

These are costs and expenses related to the purchase of private healthcare, and the provision of private education (from pre-primary or primary education, to secondary education, post-secondary non-tertiary education, and higher or tertiary education).

Other expenses

These are costs and expenses related to miscellaneous goods and services, including the cost of personal insurance and financial services. It also includes costs and expenses related to the repayment of loans and associated interest charges.

Savings and investments, and loans and borrowing

Savings and investments

Where over a period of weeks or months a surplus of income exists – that is, where income exceeds expenditure – it may be useful to save or invest any such surplus. Remember: money can earn money!

In general, savings (and investments) can be categorised as:

- low-risk savings and investments, such as cash-related savings and investments, (including ISAs), cash bonds, Premium Bonds, Savings Certificates, Children's Bonds, Pensioner Bonds, Investment Bonds, Gilts, and pensions
- medium-risk investments, such as endowments and Friendly Society tax-exempt savings plans, company bonds, shares, property, offshore savings accounts, and pooled investment funds
- higher-risk investments, such as commodities, structured products, Venture Capital Trusts, spread betting, Contracts for Difference, land banking, and other unregulated collective investment schemes.

We will consider these in more detail in Chapter 9.

Loans and borrowing

Where surplus expenditure exists – that is, where expenditure exceeds income – it may be necessary to borrow funds or to use a credit facility. Both of these usually require repayment of the amount borrowed or credit used, together with any agreed interest.

There are many different sources of borrowing and credit: from high street retail banks, to building societies, consumer finance companies, credit unions, and subprime lenders (payday loan companies, logbook lenders, and doorstep lenders). Similarly, there are many different types of borrowing and credit: from short-term loans or overdrafts, to medium-term personal loans, product finance, credit facilities, and longer-term secured homeowner loans.

We will consider these in more detail in Chapter 3.

Preparing and using a personal cash budget

Before we look at the four key stages in preparing and using a personal cash budget, here are a few important general guidelines:

- Keep your personal cash budget simple and do not over-complicate issues.
- There is no single perfect record-keeping method – use a method that suits you.
- Set a time period that is long enough for you to be able to see the results of your personal cash budgeting efforts.
- Try to build an emergency fund into your personal cash budget.
- Be flexible – make adjustments to your personal cash budget as circumstances change.
- Set an achievable goal so that it will motivate you.

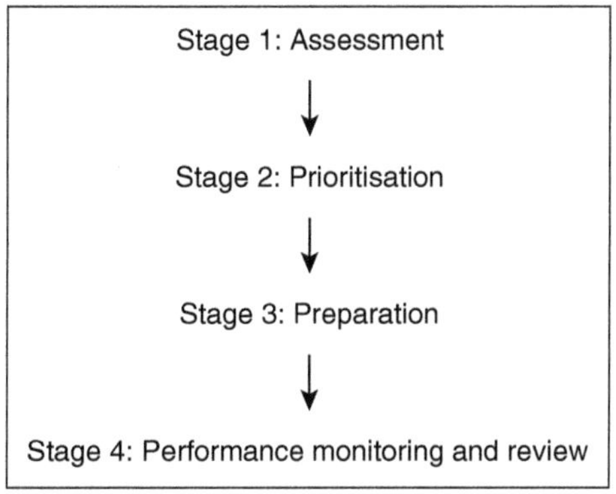

Figure 2.1 Key stages in preparing and using a personal cash budget

If your budget affects other people, such as your spouse or partner, it is important to be open with her or him and to explain what you are doing and why you are doing it: this can help to create a support system.

There are four key stages to preparing and using a personal cash budget (see Figure 2.1).

Stage 1: assessment

The assessment stage is concerned with:

- identifying how much you have – for example, balances on current accounts, savings accounts, investment accounts and any other financial investments
- ascertaining how much you earn – for example, weekly wages, monthly salaries, and any overtime payments
- determining how much you owe – for example, monthly payments such as car loans, mortgages, credit cards, personal loans, utility or energy bills, and all other recurring debts
- establishing a personal financial goal or objective.

Your choice of a personal financial goal will depend on a range of factors, including your age, health, marital status, dependent status, current financial status, current level and sources of income, and future income prospects.

Stage 2: prioritisation

The prioritisation stage is concerned with putting your commitments and expenses in order of urgency and identifying any constraints. It involves separating the 'needs' from the 'wants'! At this stage, it is important to be honest, realistic and consistent, and to ensure that your budget includes not only those occasional 'one-off' expenses, but also both fixed and variable expenses.

Stage 3: preparation

The preparation stage is concerned with creating a budget or financial plan. There are a variety of tools that can be used to create and manage a personal cash budget, from pen and paper, to a simple spreadsheet (using Microsoft Excel, for example) or more sophisticated money management software, to an online money management modeller or budget builder (such as those provided by The Money Advice Service and The Money Saving Expert[22]).

Stage 4: Performance monitoring and review

The performance monitoring and review stage is concerned with reviewing your budgeting work and comparing your actual income and expenses with your budgeted, or planned income and expenses. This will allow you to adjust your future expectations as necessary.

To help you record daily, weekly or monthly payments and expenses, you could use a mobile app such as The Money Charity 'spendometer',[23] which can be used to record and monitor your 'spending speed' (how often you incur expenses) and to set budget limits to prevent overspending.

> **Activity 4**
>
> Describe the key stages of preparing a personal cash budget.

2.5 Personal cash budget

Below is a (fictitious) personal cash budget for Amanda Gates for 2016, as at 31 January 2016.

Note: In Table 2.2, the January 2016 budgeted figures have been replaced with actual income and actual spending during the month. The closing balance for January 2016, which is also the opening balance for February 2016, therefore represents the balance on Ms Gates' current account. As shown in Table 2.2, at the end of January 2016 Amanda Gates was overdrawn by £456.03.

2.6 Personal statement of financial position

A personal statement of financial position is essentially a statement of everything you own (your total assets[24]) and everything you owe (your liabilities[25]), and is therefore a statement of your net worth. It is essentially a snapshot of your financial condition or situation at a given moment in time.

Table 2.3 shows a personal statement of financial position for Amanda Gates, as at 1 January 2016. As you can see, at 1 January 2016 Ms Gates' net worth was £51,251.35.

Personal statements of financial position are often used when someone applies for extended credit (such as a personal secured loan or a mortgage) to allow the lender to assess the person's financial situation and to make an informed decision as to whether the proposed borrowing should be approved.

> **Activity 5**
>
> Distinguish between a *personal cash budget* and a *statement of financial position.*

2.7 Managing spending and making money work harder

There are many commonsense ways in which money can be made to work harder: here are a few simple examples.

Table 2.2 A personal cash budget

Cash Budget 2016														
Summary	**January**	**February**	**March**	**April**	**May**	**June**	**July**	**August**	**September**	**October**	**November**	**December**	**Total**	**Average**
Opening Balance	*-£236.53*	*-£456.03*	*-£1,338.03*	*-£1,075.03*	*£992.97*	*-£659.53*	*-£446.53*	*-£328.53*	*-£283.53*	*-£33.53*	*-£108.53*	*-£193.53*		
Income	£2,754.50	£2,754.50	£2,829.50	£5,354.50	£2,754.50	£2,829.50	£2,954.50	£2,754.50	£2,829.50	£2,754.50	£2,754.50	£3,029.50	£36,354.00	£3,029.50
Expenses	£2,974.00	£3,636.50	£2,566.50	£3,286.50	£4,407.00	£2,616.50	£2,836.50	£2,709.50	£2,579.50	£2,829.50	£2,839.50	£2,599.50	£35,881.00	£2,990.08
Closing Balance	*-£456.03*	*-£1,338.03*	*-£1,075.03*	*£992.97*	*-£659.53*	*-£446.53*	*-£328.53*	*-£283.53*	*-£33.53*	*-£108.53*	*-£193.53*	*£236.47*		
Income	**January**	**February**	**March**	**April**	**May**	**June**	**July**	**August**	**September**	**October**	**November**	**December**	**Total**	**Average**
Salary	£2,754.50	£2,754.50	£2,754.50	£2,754.50	£2,754.50	£2,754.50	£2,754.50	£2,754.50	£2,754.50	£2,754.50	£2,754.50	£2,754.50	£33,054.00	£2,754.50
Annual Bonus				£2,600.00									£2,600.00	£216.67
Dividend Income							£200.00					£200.00	£400.00	£33.33
Investment Income			£75.00			£75.00			£75.00			£75.00	£300.00	£25.00
Expenses	**January**	**February**	**March**	**April**	**May**	**June**	**July**	**August**	**September**	**October**	**November**	**December**	**Total**	**Average**
Mortgage	£850.00	£850.00	£850.00	£850.00	£850.00	£850.00	£850.00	£850.00	£850.00	£850.00	£850.00	£850.00	£10,200.00	£850.00
Food	£325.63	£350.00	£350.00	£350.00	£350.00	£350.00	£350.00	£350.00	£350.00	£350.00	£350.00	£350.00	£4,175.63	£347.97
Car Loan	£345.00	£345.00	£345.00	£345.00	£345.00	£345.00	£345.00	£345.00	£345.00	£345.00	£345.00	£345.00	£4,140.00	£345.00
Personal Loan	£285.00	£285.00	£285.00	£285.00	£285.00	£285.00	£285.00	£285.00	£285.00	£285.00	£285.00	£285.00	£3,420.00	£285.00
Credit card (Visa)	£263.86	£200.00	£250.00	£250.00	£250.00	£250.00	£250.00	£250.00	£250.00	£250.00	£250.00	£250.00	£2,963.86	£246.99
Property Insurances		£800.00											£800.00	£66.67
Life Insurance	£29.75	£30.00	£30.00	£30.00	£30.00	£30.00	£30.00	£30.00	£30.00	£30.00	£30.00	£30.00	£359.75	£29.98
Telephone/Internet	£45.37	£50.00	£50.00	£50.00	£50.00	£50.00	£50.00	£50.00	£50.00	£50.00	£50.00	£50.00	£595.37	£49.61
Mobile Phone	£71.02	£70.00	£80.00	£70.00	£75.00	£80.00	£90.00	£73.00	£73.00	£73.00	£73.00	£73.00	£901.02	£75.09
Sky TV	£56.00	£56.00	£56.00	£56.00	£56.00	£56.00	£56.00	£56.00	£56.00	£56.00	£56.00	£56.00	£672.00	£56.00
Clothing	£87.86	£75.00	£75.00	£75.00	£75.00	£75.00	£75.00	£75.00	£75.00	£75.00	£75.00	£75.00	£912.86	£76.07
Electricity	£263.35			£200.00			£200.00			£200.00			£863.35	£71.95
Water				£450.00									£450.00	£37.50
Gas		£300.00			£200.00			£100.00			£200.00		£800.00	£66.67
Entertainment	£85.48	£90.00	£60.00	£140.00	£60.00	£110.00	£120.00	£110.00	£80.00	£130.00	£140.00	£100.00	£1,225.48	£102.12
Council Tax					£1,645.50								£1,645.50	£137.13
Bupa Healthcare	£85.50	£85.50	£85.50	£85.50	£85.50	£85.50	£85.50	£85.50	£85.50	£85.50	£85.50	£85.50	£1,026.00	£85.50
TV Licence	£145.50												£145.50	£12.13
Other	£34.68	£50.00	£50.00	£50.00	£50.00	£50.00	£50.00	£50.00	£50.00	£50.00	£50.00	£50.00	£584.68	£48.72

Table 2.3 A statement of financial position

	£	£
Assets		
Property	282,000.00	
Car	6,250.00	
Personal property	3,562.00	
Current a/c	230.24	
ISAs	16,525.00	
Shares (market value)	10,256.35	
Other investments	563.87	
		319,387.46
Liabilities		
Mortgage	262,236.00	
Personal loans	5,636.25	
Credit cards	263.86	
		268,136.11
Total net worth		51,251.35

Paying by direct debit

Where possible, pay bills by direct debit; not only is this more convenient, but paying by direct debit often attracts a discount or a reduced standing (or fixed) charge, especially from utility providers.

Note: Regularly check your account balance, especially with utility providers. If your account has a substantial credit balance, ask for the money back.

Paying when you have to

You should always pay outstanding bills, invoices and accounts by their due date, but remember to take advantage of any notice period. If you have 14 days to pay, you should take 14 days to pay. If an invoice is due to be paid on the 21st of a month – pay on the 21st. Never ever pay an outstanding bill, invoice or account when you receive it, but only when it is due.

Asking for a cash discount

Always shop around for goods and services. If you are purchasing an expensive item, always ask the retailer for a discount if you pay cash – the worst that can happen is that she or he says no!

0% credit cards

Credit cards are a popular and convenient form of payment. Whilst they can be used to pay for a wide variety of products and services, they can be very expensive. High interest charges normally accrue on any outstanding unpaid balance following a short interest-free period (usually about 56 days).

Where possible, transfer any outstanding credit-card balance to a credit card with a lower interest rate or, if available, one with a 0% interest rate. Although 0% interest rate offers are usually only available for a limited period, and only apply to any balance transferred, they can reduce monthly payments considerably.

Note: At the time of writing, there is no limit to how many times a credit-card balance can be transferred.

Paying as you go

Pioneered by magazines and newspapers, the subscription model,[26] whereby an individual pays for access to the product or service, is now used by many businesses, including satellite television, mobile phone networks, internet providers, software providers, and various clubs and societies. Always read the conditions that apply to a subscription service, and do not subscribe to, or commit to subscribe to, any product or service that you will not use fully.

Buying generic products and services

Where possible, buy generic products and services rather than equivalent branded products and services. Whilst the branded versions may appear more appealing, they are usually more expensive and are often of no better quality than their non-branded equivalents.

Minimising mobile phone costs

Mobile phones have become an essential component of who we are: they are part of our daily lives. Unfortunately, mobile phone providers can be very clever at marketing and selling expensive bundles of services, some of which subscribers never use. Take care not to subscribe to tariffs or service bundles that include services or facilities you never use.

Earning as you shop

Where possible, use shops or online sites that provide cashback offers on purchases or large discounts on shopping. Although amounts can vary, savings of between 3% and 10% of the total amount spent are fairly common.[27]

Checking the bill!

Before you pay any invoice or outstanding account, always check the details of amounts owed and make sure that these are correct.

Decluttering and making money

Whenever you have finished using something, whether old clothes that you no longer wear, technology such as laptops, mobiles or tablets that you have replaced, or embarrassing old CDs that you bought on a whim and will never listen to again, sell it! Somebody somewhere will buy it. You can advertise it locally or sell it online.

Learning to cook

From Chinese food to Indian food, from Thai food to Italian food, from fish and chips to pizzas, kebabs, and burgers, the demand for fast-food takeaways and supermarket ready-made meals is enormous – even though many have low nutritional value and high calorific content. In 2014, nearly £30bn was spent on takeaways in the UK, with the typical person spending £109 per month on convenience meals (Huffington Post 2015).

Learn to cook – it's healthier, so not only will it save you money but you will probably live longer!

2.8 Interest rates

Interest is a charge made for using money. When *borrowing* money – for example using a current account overdraft, a personal loan, or an outstanding balance on a credit card – the interest is the cost of borrowing. This cost is usually expressed as an annual percentage of the total sum borrowed.

When *investing* money – for example in a savings account, a bond, or a cash ISA – the interest is the return received for investing that money. This return is usually expressed as an annual percentage of the total sum invested.

There are two ways of calculating interest: simple interest and compound interest.

Simple interest

Simple interest is calculated by multiplying the loan amount (or principal) by the interest rate, and then by the number of payment periods over the life of the loan.

For example, assume a loan amount of £5,000, an interest rate of 3% per annum, and a repayment period of 36 months. What would the interest charge be?

The *simple* interest charge could be calculated as follows:

(£5,000.00 ∗ 3% p.a.) ∗ 3 years (as opposed to 36 months) would be £450.00.

Compound interest

Compound interest is calculated by multiplying the loan amount *plus* the interest outstanding by the interest rate, and repeating this for each of the payment periods over the life of the loan.

For example, assume (as above) a loan amount of £5,000, an interest rate of 3% per annum, and a repayment period of 36 months. What would the interest charge be?

The *compound* interest charge could be calculated as follows:

Year 1: £5,000.00 ∗ 3% p.a. = £150.00
Year 2: £5,150.00 ∗ 3% p.a. = £154.50
Year 3: £5,304.50 ∗ 3% p.a. = £159.14

The total interest charge for the period would therefore be:

(£150.00 + £154.50 + £159.14) = £463.64[28]

Note: In this example interest has been compounded annually. Interest may also be compounded monthly, weekly or even daily. As this can obviously increase the overall interest charge, be sure to check the terms whenever you borrow or invest money.

Activity 6

Helen has £2,000 to invest for 3 years. She can choose between two different savings accounts. Account A will pay 2.18% p.a. simple interest, paid out at the end of each year. Account B will pay 2.15% p.a. compound interest paid at the end of each year. Which account would give Helen the greatest amount of interest over the 3-year period?

Annual percentage rates (APRs)

As different lenders offer differing rates and have differing additional charges, it can be hard to compare the true costs to find the best deal. The *annual percentage rate* (APR) makes such comparisons easier. Expressed as a single percentage, the APR is the total amount that a loan or credit facility will cost over a period of one year. It includes interest charges and all other fees (for example, arrangement fees or administration fees) and indicates the true overall cost of the loan or credit facility. Even so, the APR on a loan or credit facility may be fixed or variable, and the rate charged will vary with the lender or credit provider and with the duration of the loan or credit facility.

Note: It is a legal requirement that all lenders and credit providers must supply information about the APR for each loan product or credit facility they offer.

Representative APR

Following the *Consumer Credit (EU Directive) Regulations 2010*, which came into force on 1 February 2011, the term 'representative APR' was introduced. Put simply, the *representative APR* must reflect what at least *51%* of successful applicants will be charged. Offers to other applicants may differ widely, depending on the lender's or credit provider's assessment of the risk.

Note: If a lender or credit provider advertises a loan or credit facility, the advertisement must contain certain standard information. This must include a representative APR, which must be prominent, clear, and concise.

Annual equivalent rates (AERs)

The *annual equivalent rate* (AER) is quoted on savings accounts and current accounts (provided that they have a credit balance). The AER reflects how much interest will be earned or accrued over a period of one year. This takes into account how often the interest is paid, what effect compounding will have, and the impact of any applicable withdrawal charges or fees.

Note: AERs are quoted gross (not net): they do not take into consideration any Income Tax that may have to be paid on savings interest.

Activity 7

Alan Blake recently arranged a personal loan with his local bank. The loan amount is £12,000, the interest rate is 5% p.a., and the repayment period is 4 years. Using compound interest, calculate the total amount of interest payable.

2.9 Concluding comments

A personal cash budget is an invaluable personal finance tool. Not only can a personal cash budget help to prioritise spending and identify wasteful expenditure, it can also help prepare for future financial emergencies and (perhaps more importantly) assist in achieving future financial goals, no matter how large or small those may be.

2.10 Suggested further reading

For further reading on the following topics, see the references given.
Alternative methods of payment in the UK:
- www.ukpayments.org.uk/

Benefits:
- www.moneyadviceservice.org.uk/en/categories/benefits

Budgeting and money management:
- www.moneyadviceservice.org.uk/en/categories/budgeting-and-managing-money

Key points

- Alternative ways of paying for products and services include: cash, cheques, debit cards, credit cards, charge cards, prepaid cards, direct debits, standing orders, CHAPS, pre-payment plans, and mobile payments.
- What we buy and how much we spend are influenced by two key groups of factors: social or cultural heritage, and economic status.
- A budget is a financial plan that covers a specific future timescale.
- A personal statement of financial position is a statement of total assets and liabilities.
- Simple interest is calculated by multiplying the loan amount (or principal) by the interest rate, and then by the number of payment periods over the life of the loan.
- Compound interest is calculated by multiplying the loan amount *plus* the interest outstanding by the interest rate, and repeating this for each of the payment periods over the life of the loan.
- 'APR' is an abbreviation for 'annual percentage rate'.
- A 'representative APR' must be available to at least 51% of customers.
- 'AER' is an abbreviation for 'annual equivalent rate' and is quoted on savings accounts and current accounts.

Self-review questions

1. Briefly explain the key stages in preparing a personal cash budget.
2. Describe five commonsense ways in which our money can be made to work harder.
3. Briefly explain why, if possible, regular occurring payments should always be made by direct debit.
4. Distinguish between the following methods of payment:
   - a debit card
   - a prepaid (or top-up) card
   - a credit card
   - a charge card.
5. Identify and describe five alternative sources of personal (or household) income, and five alternative types of personal (or household) expenditure.

Case study discussion questions

1. Based on her expected income and expenditure, advise Michelle Carter on how to manage her money.
2. Advise Anthony on how a personal budget could help him to reduce his level of debt.

Suggested answers to chapter activities

Activity 1

The main advantages of using a credit card to pay for products and services are that they provide a quick and easy way to borrow, interest-free credit (for up to 56 days), and consumer protection (primarily because of s.75 of the *Consumer Credit Act 1974*).

Activity 2

A *direct debit* is an instruction from an account holder to her or his bank or building society which authorises a company or an organization to collect varying amounts from that account. A *standing order* is an instruction to a bank or building society to make regular fixed payments to a particular person, company or organisation. *CHAPS* is a same-day automated payment system for processing payments made within the UK: it is primarily used for very high-value payments.

Activity 3

Existing tariff

3 months ending 31 March:

$$(1000\text{kWh} * 22.7\text{p}) + (8{,}500\text{kWh} * 7.8\text{p}) = (£227 + £663) = £890$$

3 months ending 30 June:

$$(1{,}000\text{kWh} * 22.7\text{p}) + (7{,}250\text{kWh} * 7.8\text{p}) = (£227 + £565.50) = £792.50$$

Total cost based on the existing tariff: £890 + £792.50 = £1,682.50

New tariff

3 months ending 31 March:

$$£100 + (9{,}500\text{kWh} * 9.4\text{p}) = (£100 + £893) = £993$$

3 months ending 30 June:

$$£100 + (8{,}250\text{kWh} * 9.4\text{p}) = (£100 + £775.50) = 875.50$$

Total cost based on the alternative tariff: £993 + £875.50 = £1,868.50

As the alternative tariff would be more expensive, Mark should not change tariff.

Activity 4

The key stages of preparing a personal cash budget are:

1. The assessment stage, concerned with identifying cash resources and debts.
2. The prioritisation stage, concerned with prioritising commitments and expenses, and identifying any constraints.
3. The preparation stage, concerned with creating a budget or financial plan.
4. The performance monitoring and review stage, concerned with reviewing the plan and comparing the actual income and expenses with the budgeted or planned income and expenses.

Activity 5

A personal cash budget is simply a financial plan that covers a specific future timescale. A personal statement of financial position is essentially a statement of total assets (everything you own) and total liabilities (everything you owe), and is thus a statement of net worth.

Activity 6

Account A would pay:

$$(£2{,}000 * 2.18\%) * 3 = £130.80$$

Account B would pay:

$$\text{Year 1: } £2{,}000.00 * 2.15\% \text{ pa} = £43.00$$
$$\text{Year 2: } £2{,}043.00 * 2.15\% \text{ pa} = £43.92$$
$$\text{Year 3: } £2{,}086.92 * 2.15\% \text{ pa} = £44.87$$

$$\text{Total interest: } (£43.00 + £43.92 + £44.87) = £131.79$$

(This could also be calculated as follows: the total interest receivable would be £2,000 * $(1.0215)^3$ = £2,131.79. The total interest receivable would therefore be £2.131.79 – £2,000 = £131.79.)

Helen should therefore choose Account B.

Activity 7

The compound interest charge could be calculated as follows:

$$\text{Year 1: } £12{,}000.00 * 5\% \text{ pa} = £600.00$$
$$\text{Year 2: } £12{,}600.00 * 5\% \text{ pa} = £630.00$$
$$\text{Year 3: } £13{,}230.00 * 5\% \text{ pa} = £661.50$$
$$\text{Year 4: } £13{,}891.50 * 5\% \text{ pa} = £694.58$$

The total interest charge for the period would therefore be:

$$(£600.00 + £630.00 + £661.50 + £694.58) = £2{,}586.08$$

(This could also be calculated as follows: the total repayable (principal and interest) would be £12,000 * $(1.05)^4$ = £14,586.08. The total interest repayable would therefore be £14,586.08 – £12,000 = £2,586.08.)

Notes

1. Direct credit is a secure transfer service which enables organisations to make payments directly into bank or building society accounts. Direct credits are mainly used for paying wages and salaries, although they are also used for a wide variety of other applications such as payments of pensions, payments of employees' expenses, insurance settlements, payments of dividends and interest, and payment refunds.
2. See: www.link.co.uk/.
3. See: www.fasterpayments.org.uk/.
4. See: www.paymentscouncil.org.uk/mobile_payments/what_is_Paym/.
5. The Money Shop: see www.moneyshop.com.
6. Visa and MasterCard are worldwide payment-processing companies, both providing rules and standards for the way in which card transactions are accepted, authorised, and processed. Visa and MasterCard do not issue credit cards themselves. Instead they negotiate the setting up of payment systems with different banks and building societies around the world.
7. See: www.money.co.uk/credit-cards.htm.
8. S.75 of the *Consumer Credit Act 1974* provides that 'if the debtor under a debtor-creditor-supplier agreement falling within section 12(b) or (c) has, in relation to a transaction financed by the agreement,

any claim against the supplier in respect of a misrepresentation or breach of contract, the debtor shall have a like claim against the creditor, who, with the supplier, shall accordingly be jointly and severally liable to the debtor'.

9. S.75 of the *Consumer Credit Act 1974* protects purchases between £100 and £30,000 against a retailer ceasing to trade, and against products proving to be faulty or damaged when delivered. This protection was extended to purchases up to £60,260 by the *2011 Consumer Credit Directive* (effective from 1 January 2013).
10. See: www.payourway.org.uk/.
11. Faster Payments Service, see: www.fasterpayments.org.uk.
12. The underlying network technology is provided by VocaLink (www.vocalink.com/), a member of the wider SEPA (Single Euro Payments Area) network.
13. Banks able to use Paym are: Bank of Scotland, Barclays, Clydesdale Bank, Cumberland Building Society, Danske Bank, First Direct, Halifax, HSBC, Isle of Man Bank, Lloyds Bank, Nationwide, NatWest, RBS, Santander, TSB, Ulster Bank and Yorkshire Bank.
14. So-called 'two-factor authentication' requires users to identify themselves using a combination of two different components – something that the user knows (such as a PIN or password), something that the user possesses (such as a physical swipe card), or something that is inseparable from the user (typically biometric data such as a fingerprint). To use an ATM, for example, a user must present a valid card (something they possess) and key in a valid matching PIN (something they know).
15. For bitcoin, see: www.bitcoin.org/en. (Concerns have been expressed about bitcoin because it is not accepted in all countries, its price and value can be volatile, and there have been allegations of its use by organised crime.)
16. For further details and analysis of each expenditure item in Table 2.1, see: www.ons.gov.uk/ons/dcp171766_385729.pdf.
17. COICOP (Classification Of Individual Consumption by Purpose) is an internationally recognised functional classification designed to classify groups of transactions. See: http://stats.oecd.org/glossary/detail.asp?ID=352.
18. Note that the summary Table 1.1 on p. 2 is incorrect – the total expenditure is £517.20, not £517.30.
19. A 'benefit in kind' is a benefit which an employee (or a director) receives from their employment but which is not included in their wage or salary. They are sometimes referred to as 'perks' or 'fringe benefits'.
20. There are two types of Employment and Support Allowance. Contributory Employment and Support Allowance, and Income-Related Employment and Support Allowance. For further information, see: www.gov.uk/employment-support-allowance/overview.
21. There are some exceptions – for example multiple births (for example triplets) will be excluded.
22. For the Money Advice Service online budget planner, see: www.moneyadviceservice.org.uk/en/tools/budget-planner. For the Money Saving Expert online budget planner, see: www.moneysavingexpert.com/banking/Budget-planning#bplanner.
23. Available on iTunes at: https://itunes.apple.com/gb/app/spendometer/id305360397?mt=8.
24. An asset can be defined as the right to receive a future economic benefit as a consequence of a past transaction or event – for example, a contract of exchange.
25. A liability represents a legally enforceable economic claim against an individual, and can be defined as an obligation to transfer economic benefits as a result of a past transaction or event.
26. A variation of the subscription model is the 'freemium' model whereby some services and access to some content is provided free, while access to premium features is available only to paying subscribers.
27. For a list of top cashback sites, see: www.moneysavingexpert.com/shopping/cashback-websites.
28. For those who are more mathematically orientated, this could be calculated as follows:

$$\text{Total repayable (principal and interest): } £5{,}000 * (1.03)^3 = £5{,}463.64.$$

$$\text{Total interest repayable: } £5{,}463.64 - £5{,}000 = £463.64.$$

3

Borrowing, loans, and credit

Learning outcomes

By the end of this chapter, you should be able to:

- distinguish between different types of lenders
- distinguish between different types of secured and unsecured borrowing
- identify the key characteristics of different types of borrowing
- appreciate the risks and costs associated with different types of borrowing
- explain the role of credit reference agencies in the borrowing process.

3.1 Introduction

We live in a world dominated by material consumption – by the irrationalities of a marketplace where tomorrow is too late and only today will do. Credit cards, charge cards, unsecured personal loans, high-cost subprime lending and mortgage borrowing now fuel the engine of a demand-led, possession-crazy consumer society in which we borrow from the future to buy today: where an ever-spiralling level of personal debt has become a key feature of our increasingly challenging daily lives.

This chapter explores the most popular types of borrowing, and considers the costs and risks associated with each type of borrowing.

3.2 Types of lenders

For consumers, there are many different sources of borrowing. The most widely known and widely used alternative lenders and credit providers in the UK are as follows:

- high street commercial (retail) banks
- building societies
- consumer finance companies
- credit unions
- subprime lenders (for example, payday loan companies, logbook lenders, and doorstep lenders).

Banks

Banks[1] are licensed financial institutions, regulated by the Prudential Regulatory Authority and the Financial Conduct Authority, that deal in money (and its various substitutes and derivatives), and provide a range of money-related financial services. They accept deposits and use these deposits for lending and investment activities. In essence, banks are financial intermediaries which link those customers who have surplus funds with those customers who require additional funds.

Broadly speaking, there are two main types of banks:

- corporate (investment) banks
- commercial (retail) banks.

Corporate (investment) banks

Corporate (investment) banks focus primarily on providing services to large businesses, corporate entities and institutional clients, and other related activities on the financial markets – for example, foreign exchange trading, commodity or equity trading, futures and options trading, and money-market trading.

Commercial (retail) banks

Commercial (retail) banks are mainly concerned with managing the savings and deposits, loans and mortgages, and insurance and credit facilities of individual customers, although these banks may sometimes provide business banking services to small- or medium-sized non-corporate businesses, and private banking or wealth management services to individuals and families with high net worth. These banks are often referred to as the 'high street' banks.

In this book, our focus is primarily on commercial (retail) banking, whose ancestry can be traced back to the ancient civilisations of Babylonia and Mesopotamia, although the origins of modern retail banking clearly have their roots in early Renaissance Italy and the bench or counter[2] lenders of Florence, Lucca, Siena, Venice and Genoa.

Today, commercial banks provide a range of different deposit, savings, investment and payment services[3] for customers; and with banks now offering a wide variety of different service and product access channels – for example, ATMs, mobile banking, online banking, telephone banking, call centres, video banking, and traditional mail based services – a bank account is now considered an indispensable component in the day-to-day management of personal finance.

Within the UK, high street commercial banking is dominated by HSBC, Barclays, the Lloyds Banking, the Royal Bank of Scotland, and the Spanish-owned bank Santander. There are also a number of smaller commercial banking businesses owned by retail groups, including Sainsbury's Bank (owned by Sainsbury's), Tesco Bank (owned by Tesco), M&S Bank (owned by Marks & Spencer and operated through HSBC), Virgin Money (owned by the Virgin Group), the Co-operative Bank (owned by the Co-operative Group), and Harrods Bank (owned by Harrods). In addition, there are a small number of independent specialist banks, including Aldermore, C. Hoare & Co., N. M. Rothschild's & Sons, and Weatherby's.[4]

All banks are covered by the Financial Services Compensation Scheme (FSCS), which protects savings in banks up to £75,000.

Note: Whilst most banks are profit-making, privately owned corporate institutions, some are Government-owned – for example, National Savings and Investments is a Government-run savings bank wholly owned by the UK Government, whereas Lloyds Banking is (in 2015) partly owned by the UK Government.

Building societies

Building societies[5] are financial institutions that are owned by their members. Created for the purpose of making secured loans on residential property,[6] they are mutual organisations that today offer a range of banking and related financial services, including mortgage lending. Emerging out of the rapid economic and physical expansion in Birmingham in the late 18th century (Ashworth 1980: 4), the first permanent building societies were created in the late 1830s.

Building societies were originally regulated by the *Building Society Act 1874* (as amended). The late 19th and especially the early 20th centuries saw a rapid expansion in the number of societies within the UK. During the 1960s and 1970s, nearly every main city in the UK had its own locally named building society. Since then, however, changes such as these:

- the demutualisation[7] of many established societies, following the *Building Society Act 1986*
- successive waves of acquisitions by many high street banks of their mortgage- lending neighbours
- the merger of many once-competing high street building societies.

have substantially reduced the number of societies in the UK. As of 31 August 2015, there are now only 46[8] building societies in the UK, and although these remaining building societies actively compete with banks in offering a wide range of financial products and consumer banking services, including mortgage lending and savings accounts, their dominance and influence in the market has declined substantially over the last few decades.

All building societies in the UK are registered with and members of the Building Societies Association,[9] and (as of 31 August 2015) the largest five building societies in the UK were: the Nationwide Building Society, the Yorkshire Building Society, the Coventry Building Society, the Skipton Building Society, and the Leeds Building Society.

Note: As with commercial (retail) banks, all deposits in building societies (up to £75,000) are covered by the Financial Services Compensation Scheme.

Finance companies

Finance companies, or more accurately non-banking financial companies (NBFCs), are specialist financial institutions that supply credit for the purchase of consumer goods and services, either:

- by purchasing the sales contracts directly from suppliers or manufacturers
- by providing small loans directly to consumers or through a services or retail company.

Finance companies may also extend credit for consumer purchases, for example by providing financing for instalment-plan sales or credit sales agreements – one of the most common of these being motor car financing.

In essence, finance companies act as a lending institution by extending credit. The main difference between a bank and a finance company is that, unlike a bank, a finance company does not, and cannot, accept deposits from the public. To acquire funds, finance companies generally borrow from banks or issue debt instruments via the money market. However, many finance companies are closely affiliated with existing high street banks, as for example Blackhorse Finance,[10] a motor car finance company affiliated to Lloyds Bank.

All finance companies are regulated by the Prudential Regulatory Authority and by the Financial Conduct Authority.

Credit unions

Credit unions are member-owned financial co-operatives or financial membership organisations, controlled by their members and operated for the purpose of providing financial services to their members. First established in the UK in the 1960s,[11] credit unions offer many of the same financial services as a high street bank, and are generally 'not-for-profit[12] community-oriented institutions that provide services intended to support local community development.

Whilst UK-based credit unions vary in size, in membership, and in the range of products and services they offer, broadly speaking they offer three main types of financial product: current accounts, savings accounts, and loans. In addition, some now offer ISAs and insurance-related products.

Regulated by the *Credit Unions Act 1979*, as amended by the Legislative Reform (Industrial and Provident Societies and Credit Unions) Order 2011 which came into force on 8 January 2012 to allow credit unions greater flexibility in the services they provide, the members to whom they can provide them and the charges they can make for the services they provide,[13] all credit unions in the UK are also regulated by the Prudential Regulation Authority for prudential purposes and the Financial Conduct Authority for conduct purposes. More importantly, since October 2008 all UK credit unions have been covered by the Financial Services Compensation Scheme, which protects savings in banks and similar institutions up to £75,000.

With a varied history, dating back to the work of Franz Hermann Schulze-Delitzsch in Germany in the mid-19th century (Moody and Fite 1984: 4), credit unions have now become a substantial international movement: there are over 40,250 credit unions in around 80 countries, enabling 118 million members to access affordable financial services.[14]

As at December 2014, there were 392 credit unions in England, Scotland and Wales, employing more than 1,500 staff. With an annual turnover of £26 million (year to 30 September 2014), total assets of £1.26 billion, total loans of £718 million and total deposits of £1.07 billion, credit unions now provide current accounts for more than 35,000 people.[15]

Examples of credit unions are 6 Towns Credit Union and the Angus Credit Union.[16] A list is available showing UK credit unions registered with, and subscribing to, the Association of British Credit Unions Limited's code of governance.[17]

Subprime lenders

Subprime lenders (also called near-prime lenders or non-prime lenders) are lenders that specialise in lending money to customers with a poor, a limited, a volatile, or an incomplete credit history: often those who have a low income or are unemployed, or who have a County Court Judgment (CCJ) or recent credit default.[18]

Although subprime lenders use a risk-based pricing system to calculate the terms of any loans they offer to customers, their loan terms are often criticised as being unfair and discriminatory. Subprime lenders are sometimes referred to as 'predatory lenders'. Examples of subprime lenders include:

- Payday loan companies that provide small, high-interest, short-term loans intended to cover short-term expenses – see, for example, Wonga short-term loans, at: www.wonga.com.

- Logbook loan companies that provide asset-based loans secured on the borrower's car; the company will hold the car's V5 registration documents until the loan has been repaid in full – see, for example, Auto Advance logbook loans, at: www.autoadvance.co.uk.
- Doorstep loan (or door-to-door loan) providers that offer personal loans in cash, delivered to the borrower's home by locally employed agents; loan repayments are also collected from the borrower's home – see, for example, Provident Personal Credit, at: www.providentpersonalcredit.com/home-credit/doorstep-loans.
- Text loan providers offer small loans for very short periods (usually days) – see, for example, Bongaloans, at: www.bongaloans.com.
- Guarantor loan companies provide 'bad credit' loans that require a guarantor, someone with a good credit history who will guarantee the borrower's application and make repayments if the borrower is unable to do so – see, for example, Amigo loans, at: www.amigoloans.co.uk.
- Pawnbroker loan companies offer personal cash-based loans secured on the borrower's personal assets – see, for example, H and T pawnbrokers, at: https://www.handt.co.uk/.

3.3 Types of borrowing

There are essentially two alternative types of borrowing: *unsecured* borrowing and loans and *secured* borrowing and loans (see Figure 3.1):

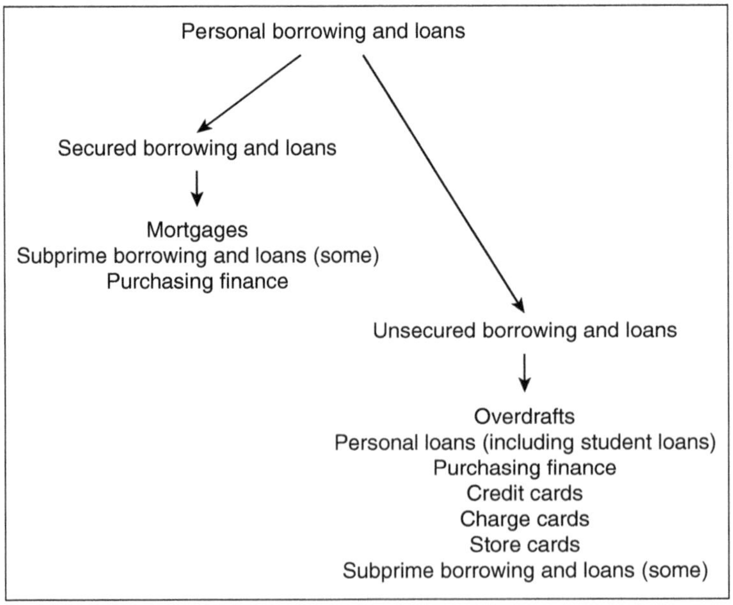

Figure 3.1 Types of personal borrowing

Unsecured borrowing and loans

Unsecured borrowing and loans are supported only by a borrower's credit history and creditworthiness, and are obtained without the use of property or assets as collateral for the borrowing or loan. In the absence of any underlying collateral, interest rates on unsecured borrowing and loans tend to be higher than those for secured loans. As indicated in Figure 3.1, the most popular types of unsecured borrowing and loans include overdrafts, personal loans (including student loans), purchasing finance, credit cards and charge cards, store cards, and some subprime loans or borrowing.

Secured borrowing and loans

Secured borrowing and loans rely on using property or an asset as collateral for the borrowing or loan: that is, in the event of non-repayment or loan default, the provider of the borrowing or loan (often a bank) can take possession of the property or asset and use it to repay the loan. Because of this underlying collateral, interest rates for secured loans tend to be lower than those for unsecured loans. As indicated in Figure 3.1, the most popular type of secured borrowing is of course a mortgage, often called a homeowner loan; but others exist, for example some subprime borrowing, and some forms of purchasing finance, can be secured on property or assets.

3.4 Overdrafts

An overdraft is an automatic (or arranged) borrowing facility linked to a bank current account. It is designed to help manage short-term borrowing needs, and is repayable on demand. That is, a bank could demand repayment of an overdraft in full at any time – although in practice it is unlikely to do so unless there has been a significant deterioration in the customer's credit status or a significant breach of the bank's regulations.

Note: If a bank does cancel an overdraft without warning and without good cause, and if as a result the account holder incurs substantial additional charges, the account holder may have grounds for complaint – first to the bank, and then if necessary to the Financial Ombudsman Service.

Authorised overdrafts

An authorised overdraft (or planned overdraft) is a pre-agreed overdraft whereby the account holder is allowed to borrow up to a preset overdraft limit. Whilst some banks offer a limited interest-free authorised overdraft (usually up to £100), in general overdraft charges are made up of a daily, weekly or monthly fee, together with an overdraft interest charge. The overdraft fee and interest charge will of course vary between banks and between accounts. It will also depend on the size of the overdraft.

For example, overdraft charges on a Lloyds Bank current account in January 2015 (Lloyds Bank 2015) were:

- a fixed monthly fee of £6, and
- a monthly interest charge of between 1.34% and 1.53% (an equivalent annual rate of between 17.28% p.a. and 19.94% p.a.).

Unauthorised overdrafts

An unauthorised (or unplanned) overdraft occurs when an account holder exceeds her or his authorised overdraft limit, or allows the account to be overdrawn when no agreed overdraft limit is in place. Such an overdraft should be avoided in all circumstances – fees can be very high. Again, fees vary between banks and between accounts, but the fees would normally include:

- a daily fee: from £10 a day to £35 a day, usually up to a maximum set limit (say 6 to 8 days) per accounting period or per month *and*
- a transaction fee: from £10 per item to £25 per item, for any ATM withdrawal, direct debt, standing order, or debit-card payment (irrespective of whether the transaction has been approved or declined by the bank).

3.5 Personal loans

A personal loan is a loan provided by a bank or other loan provider that is not secured against any personal asset. Such loans are, for obvious reasons, also known as unsecured loans. A minimum age, a standard credit check and minimum earnings requirements often apply. Interest charges vary between loan providers, and will be dependent on the amount borrowed and the period over which the amount is borrowed. In general, personal loans can be between £1,000 and £25,000 and for periods between 2 years and 5 years. Although interest rates vary considerably, interest rates on 'prime' personal loans in January 2015 varied between 4.1% and 13.6% APR (Santander 2015).

For example, a personal loan of £13,000 for 36 months at an APR of 4.3% would give a monthly repayment of £385.07. The total repayable would be £13,862.52.

Advantages of a personal loan

The main advantages of a personal loan are that:

- large amounts are usually available
- interest rates are fixed
- monthly loan repayments are fixed
- variable loan periods are often available
- this kind of loan can be used to consolidate several debts into a single personal loan.

Disadvantages of a personal loan

The main disadvantages of a personal loan are that:

- personal loans can be costly, especially for smaller amounts
- some personal loans have variable interest rates
- early repayment charges may apply (especially to pre-2011 loans).

Note: With a personal loan you have a 14-day cooling-off period, from the date of the loan agreement or from when you receive a copy of the agreement, whichever is later. If the agreement is cancelled, you must return (repay) the capital and any accrued interest within 30 days.

Student loans

A student loan[19] is a specific type of personal loan, aimed at a particular demographic group. It is designed to assist students in paying for university-related or college-related costs: tuition fees, books, and living expenses. Interest rates are very low – substantially lower than for many other personal loans – and loan repayments are usually deferred while the student remains in higher education.

The student loan or student finance package includes four components:

- a tuition fee loan
- a maintenance loan
- a maintenance grant
- a special support grant (where applicable).

The maintenance loan, maintenance grant and special support grant are only available to full-time students.

Note: Different student loan or student finance rules apply if the student's course of study began before September 2012.

Tuition fee loans

All UK and EU full-time or part-time students can apply for a tuition fee loan. Although this loan is repayable by the student, it is paid directly to the student's university or college.

As of 31 August 2015, tuition fee loans are limited, as follows:

- full-time student: maximum tuition fee loan up to £9,000[20]
- full-time student at a private university or college:[21] maximum tuition fee loan up to £6,000
- part-time student: maximum tuition fee loan up to £6,750
- part-time student at a private university or college: maximum tuition fee loan up to £4,500.

Maintenance loans

Maintenance loans are only available to full-time UK students. They are not available to part-time students, EU students, or students aged 60 and over.

Table 3.1 Maintenance loans

Full-time student	Loans for courses commencing September 2015	Loans for courses commencing August 2016
Living at home	Up to £4,565	Up to £4,675
Living away from home (outside London)	Up to £5,740	Up to £5,878
Living away from home (in London)	Up to £8,009	Up to £8,202
Year overseas (part of a UK course)	Up to £6,820	Up to £6,984

Source: Data from https://www.gov.uk/student-finance/loans-and-grants.

Maintenance grants

Maintenance grants are only available to full-time UK students and are based on household income.[22] They are not available to part-time students or EU students.

Note: Maintenance grants are not repayable, but can be used by the recipient to reduce any maintenance loan received.

Table 3.2 **Maintenance grants**

Household income	Grants for courses commencing September 2015	Grants for courses commencing September 2016
£25,000 or less	£3,387	£3,387
£30,000	£2,441	£2,441
£35,000	£1,494	£1,494
£40,000	£547	£547
£42,620	£50	£50
Over £42,620	No grant	No grant

Source: Data from https://www.gov.uk/student-finance/loans-and-grants.

Special support grants

Special support grants are only available to full-time UK students. They are not available to part-time students or EU students.

A special support grant is available *instead* of a maintenance grant if the full-time UK student qualifies for:
- Income Support
- income-related Employment and Support Allowance
- Housing Benefit *or*
- the housing element of Universal Credit.

Qualifying for a student loan and student finance

Eligibility for a student loan or student finance depends on:
- the university or college course[23] the student is attending or due to attend
- the student's previous higher education studies, if any[24]
- the age of the student[25]
- the nationality or residency status of the student.[26]

Repaying a student loan

Loan repayments (tuition fee loan and maintenance loan) are earnings-related – that is, a minimum level of earnings is required before repayments begin.

The amount of the repayment changes each year. For example, former students whose course of study began before 1 September 2012 will start repaying their student loan when they earn over £17,335 p.a. (From April 2016, the repayment threshold will rise to £17,495 p.a.) Interest on such loans is accrued at 1.5% p.a. Loan repayments are 9% of the former student's income in excess of £17,335 (Student Loans Company 2015a).

Former students whose course of study began on or after 1 September 2012 will start repaying their student loan when they earn over £21,000 p.a. Interest on such loans is accrued at inflation plus 3% p.a. Loan repayments are 9% of the former student's income in excess of £21,000 (Student Loans Company 2015b).

Note: Interest is added to the loan from the date when the loan (or the first instalment of the loan) is received.

Loan repayments are made through HM Revenue and Customs:
- as a PAYE deduction, if employed *or*
- through self-assessment, if self-employed *or*
- directly to the Student Loans Company, if living and working outside the UK.

Note: For further details on student loans, minimum earnings requirements, and interest rates, see the Student Loans Company's website (www.slc.co.uk).

Activity 1

Jane Mason expects to earn £30,000 p.a. when she graduates from the University of Leeds with a BSc (Hons) in Social Anthropology. She commenced her undergraduate degree in September 2013 and expects to graduate in June 2016. Using this information, estimate Jane Mason's student loan repayments. (*Note:* Ignore interest.)

3.6 Conditional sales, hire purchase, and credit sales

Conditional sale agreement

A conditional sale is a type of borrowing, although it differs from other types of borrowing inasmuch as the purchaser does not *own* the goods – the purchaser does not have legal title to the goods – until she or he has paid for the goods in full. A conditional sale is a legally binding agreement in which a purchaser agrees to pay for goods over a number of agreed payment periods (weeks or months). Once a sum equal to the purchase price of the goods and any accrued interest has been paid, usually in equal instalments, title to the goods is transferred to the purchaser. This is called 'getting good title'.

The *Consumer Credit Act 1974* provides strict requirements in relation to the form and contents of conditional sale agreements.

Credit sale agreement

A credit sale agreement is very similar to a conditional sale agreement, and is a legally binding agreement in which a purchaser agrees to pay for goods over a number of agreed payment periods (weeks or months). The key difference is that with a credit sale agreement the purchaser obtains legal title to the goods immediately – that is, the property (legal title) is transferred at the commencement of the agreement and the purchaser pays the total purchase price by instalments.

Hire purchase agreement

A hire purchase agreement is very similar to a conditional sale agreement, and is also a legally binding agreement in which a purchaser agrees to pay for goods over a number of agreed payment periods (weeks or months). The key difference is that with a hire purchase agreement, the purchaser *may* then exercise an option to buy the goods, on payment of an additional nominal sum, and if not must return the goods to the owner. Under a hire purchase agreement, the purchaser is under no obligation to take title of the goods, whereas with a conditional sale agreement the transfer of the title occurs automatically on completion of the agreement.

Hire purchase agreements are commonly used by high street 'rent-to-own' retailers, such as Brighthouse (see: www.brighthouse.co.uk) and PerfectHome (see: www.perfecthome.co.uk), who often impose very high interest rates (up to 70%) and normally require purchasers to pay for in-house product insurance cover. This can often mean that the total amount payable as per the hire purchase agreement is many times the original recommended retail price of the product being purchased.

Note: During the agreement or contact period, for both a conditional sale agreement and a hire purchase agreement, the purchaser may not sell or dispose of the goods without the seller's permission.

Ending an agreement

A purchaser can end a conditional sale agreement or a hire purchase agreement at any time during the agreement period. Notice must be given in writing; the goods to which the agreement relates must be returned to the seller; and the purchaser will have to pay all payment instalments due – up to the date the agreement was ended.

Note: If the total payments made by the purchaser are less than half of the total price of the goods, the purchaser may still have to pay the balance – under a conditional sale agreement or hire purchase agreement the seller is normally entitled to this amount. If the purchaser has paid more than half of the total price of the goods when the agreement is ended, no refund will be paid.[27]

The seller can end a conditional sale agreement or a hire purchase agreement if the purchaser defaults on instalment repayments during the agreement period, and may then repossess the goods to which the agreement relates. A court order will normally be required; but if the purchaser has paid less than one-third of the total amount due, a court order may not be required.

3.7 Personal leasing

Personal leasing, or personal contract hire, is a common form of leasing widely used by the motor car industry. Personal leasing agreements generally last for a fixed period – between 24 and 60 months – during which time the lessee (the customer) pays a monthly fee. At the end of the lease, the lessee returns the motor car to the leasing company and, if she or he wishes, takes out another leasing agreement on a new motor car. Strict conditions usually apply to, for example, mileage and maintenance requirements.

Advantages of personal leasing

The main advantages of personal leasing are that:

- it is a cost-effective way of acquiring the use of a motor car
- monthly payments are fixed
- optional maintenance packages are usually available
- it gives the customer access to a wide range of 'upmarket' motor cars.

Disadvantages of personal leasing

The main disadvantages of personal leasing are that:

- comprehensive car insurance is necessary on any leased motor car
- the customer will never own the motor car
- a 'wear and tear' policy will apply, as well as a mileage limit
- there is no option to buy the motor car.

An alternative to a personal contract hire agreement is a personal contract purchase agreement, where the customer has the option to purchase the motor car at the end of the contract.

Activity 2

Compare and contrast a *conditional sale agreement*, a *hire purchase agreement*, and a *credit sale agreement*.

Note: The Finance and Leasing Association (FLA) is the UK's leading trade body for asset finance, consumer finance and motor finance providers. Members include banks, building societies, the major retailers and manufacturers, and a range of independent firms. All members must adhere to the FLA's code of practice.

3.8 Credit cards

Because most companies, including both 'dotcom' and 'dotbam' companies, now accept credit-card payments, over the last 25 years credit cards became one of the most popular, convenient and widely used forms of payment for consumer goods and services in the UK. (A 'dotcom company' is a company that has only an online presence; a 'dotbam company' has both an online presence and a high street presence – such companies are often referred to as 'clicks and bricks' companies.) Nevertheless, it is important to remember that a credit card is merely a loan vehicle – or, more specifically, a revolving credit instrument. When using a credit card, the cardholder is essentially borrowing money. Following an interest-free period (usually about 56 days), interest charges will usually accrue on any outstanding unpaid balance. Although some credit cards offer 0% interest charges for a limited period (usually on balance transfers – that is, the transfer of a balance from another credit card), in general credit cards are expensive and tend to have interest rates that are normally higher than most 'prime' personal loans. They should therefore be used with caution, and primarily for short-term financing purposes.

Minimum-age and standard credit-check requirements apply, with the credit-card limit – the maximum a cardholder can spend using the card – determined by the issuer (for example, a bank, a building society or even a retailer[28]), being based on the cardholder's income and credit history. This limit will often change as the cardholder establishes a credit profile and a payment history with the card issuer. Normally, if a cardholder pays the full outstanding balance on the credit card each month, the card issuer will seek to increase the credit limit, as an incentive to the cardholder to spend more and leave an outstanding balance on the credit card at the end of the accounting period so that interest can be charged. Remember: a card issuer's favourite customer is one who has a consistently high outstanding balance at the end of each accounting period and who pays off only the minimum amount of the outstanding balance each month.

Advantages of a credit card

The main advantages of a credit card are that:
- it is easy to use and widely accepted
- it is safer to carry than cash
- you can buy now and pay later, with interest-free credit for up to 56 days

- using s.75 of the *Consumer Credit Act 1974* you are protected for any purchases over £100 and below £60,260 (see Chapter 2)
- you can accumulate reward points and take advantage of cashback offers, *and*
- you are protected against credit-card theft and fraudulent misuse.

Disadvantages of a credit card

The main disadvantages of a credit card are that:

- interest charges can be very high if the outstanding balance is not paid in full at the end of the accounting period
- there are excessive charges for missing payments
- there are additional high fees for cash withdrawals at ATMs
- deposits and pre-authorisations can reduce the available credit limit on the card, *and*
- it can be very expensive to use overseas.

3.9 Charge cards

A charge card is a card that charges no interest but requires the user to pay the balance in full at the end of each accounting period, usually monthly – that is, no balance can be carried forward from one month to the next (without excessive penalty charges). Charge cards generally have a much higher spending limit than a credit card, and are often unlimited; they often impose a high minimum earnings requirement for members; and they normally charge a set annual membership fee. Some also provide additional (point-based) membership benefits.

Examples of such cards are: American Express (see: www.americanexpress.com/uk) and Diner's Club (see: www.dinersclub.co.uk).

3.10 Store cards

A store card is a company- or retailer-specific credit card that can *only* be used with the issuing high street retail store (or a group to which it belongs). Store cards are often promoted using unusually high discount offers – for example, 10% off purchases for the next 6 months. Minimum age and standard credit-check requirements apply.

Store cards can be used to purchase items on credit and to defer payment until the end of the accounting period – usually a month. However, interest charges can accrue on any unpaid balance, and store cards often impose very high interest charges – much higher than an average credit card.

Although store cards can be useful in obtaining discounts and other retail-related membership benefits – especially from a high street retail shop that is used regularly – they are very expensive and frequently mis-sold. *Never let a balance accrue on a store card account. Always pay the balance off in full at the end of the accounting period.*

Note: Store cards should not be confused with the branded credit cards issued by high street retailers, which can be used anywhere; or with retail-based reward cards or loyalty cards, which allow you to collect points that can be redeemed at a later date for discounted products or services.

3.11 Subprime borrowing and loans

Subprime borrowing and subprime loans are often described as 'bad credit' finance. These are borrowing and loans for those who cannot obtain finance elsewhere: for example, people on benefits or Jobseeker's Allowance, people with a bad credit history or no credit history, people with a low income, or people who have CCJs or existing loan arrears or who have received default notices for late or unpaid loan repayments.

The underlying characteristics of subprime borrowing and loans are:

- Borrowing or loan periods and repayment schedules are usually very short, often less than a month.
- Interest-rate charges are often a very high multiple of existing high street bank-based borrowing (in some instances, an APR in excess of 4,000% p.a.[29]).
- Default charges for non-payment or late payment arrears are usually excessively high.
- Additional high-cost charges and fees are often imposed for account administration services, payment collection services, and the early repayment of loans or the early settlement of borrowing.

There are many types of subprime borrowing and loans, the most popular being payday loans, logbook loans, doorstep loans, text loans, guarantor loans, and pawnbroker loans.

Payday loans

Payday loans are small, high-interest, very short-term loans that are intended to be repaid on or by the borrower's next payday. They are typically available for amounts between £100 and £1,500, and are substantially more expensive than an unsecured loan or a personal loan, although they can (in some instances) be a lot cheaper than an unauthorised overdraft. On average, the interest payback on a payday loan over the agreed loan period (usually less than a month) is between £20 and £50 for each £100 borrowed.

Note: All payday lenders *must* disclose their representative annual percentage rate (APR), which represents the interest that would be payable on the loan if the borrower maintained the payday loan, at the agreed rate, for a whole year.

Loan applications can be made online, over the phone, or at one of the many payday-loan company high street outlets. Following a minimal credit check (some payday loan companies offer 'no credit check' loans), confirmation of identity, employment and employer details, and bank account details, the loan funds for any accepted applications are normally paid out within a couple of days of the application, and some payday lenders offer instant or 24-hour loans.[30]

The loan money is available for the length of the agreed term and at the agreed cost (interest charge), unless early repayment is made. At the agreed date – usually the borrower's next payday – the full amount of the loan, together with any interest, should be repaid, usually by deduction from the borrower's debit card. If required, however, the borrower can, with the agreement of the payday lender, 'roll over' the loan repayment to the borrower's *next* payday – that is, extend the loan period for a further month – although doing so will incur substantial additional fees and interest charges.

Advantages of payday loans

The main advantages of a payday loan are that:

- it gives quick access to cash advances for salaried employees with a poor credit history
- the application process is simple
- the eligibility criteria are minimal
- it is an 'equal opportunity' loan (that is, it does not discriminate between good or bad credit histories)
- it can help to rebuild the borrower's credit history.

Disadvantages of payday loans

The main disadvantages of a payday loan are that:

- the interest rates can be very high
- extra charges are often applied or incurred
- failing to meet agreed payments can damage or completely destroy a borrower's credit profile, and worsen a borrower's debt problem.

Payday loans can be very expensive and should be used only with caution.

Logbook loans (V5 loans)

Logbook loans (also known as V5 loans, or bill-of-sale lending) are asset-based loans secured on a borrower's vehicle – usually a car, but it could be a van or a motorcycle. The logbook loan company holds the vehicle's V5 registration document (historically referred to as the vehicle's logbook) until the loan is paid back in full.

Loans are available online and from loan company high street outlets, and the amount borrowed can vary between £500 and £50,000, depending on how much the vehicle is worth – although some logbook loans companies limit the loan to 50% of the vehicle's current value. In a 2014 study, the Citizens Advice Bureau found that the average (median) loan was only £1,286 (Citizens Advice Bureau 2014: 3).

To be approved for a logbook loan, an applicant must have proof of a steady source of income. Loans are normally paid within a few days of a successful application, although some logbook loan companies will, on payment of an additional administration fee, pay immediately on approval.

So how do logbook loans work? When a borrower applies for a logbook loan, she or he will be asked to surrender the vehicle's registration document. This proves she or he is the registered keeper of the vehicle. The borrower will also be asked to sign a credit agreement and a 'bill of sale'. The 'bill of sale' effectively means that the lender now owns the vehicle – on a temporary basis (until the loan is fully repaid), with the borrower still able to use the vehicle as long as she or he maintains repayments on the loan. These documents are legally recognised[31] in England, Wales and Northern Ireland, but not in Scotland.[32]

Interest charges on logbook loans vary between lenders, but rates between 300% p.a. and 600% p.a. are not unusual. Most logbook loans last between 6 to 18 months, although borrowers are able to repay loans early if they wish.

Note: If a borrower cannot meet the payment schedule of a logbook loan, the logbook loan company has the right to employ enforcement officers (bailiffs) to seize and to repossess the borrower's vehicle without a court order. If the company then sells the vehicle for an amount that is less than the amount outstanding on the loan, the logbook loan company can take the borrower to court to recover the balance.

Advantages of logbook loans

The main advantages of a logbook loan are that:

- it provides a quick and easy access to borrowing, even for those with a bad credit history
- the application process is simple
- the interest rate is often fixed.

Disadvantages of logbook loans

The main disadvantages of a logbook loan are that:

- the borrower's vehicle could be repossessed if the borrower fails to make the repayments to the logbook loan company
- interest rates are very high
- this kind of loan is much more expensive than conventional unsecured loans
- early repayment charges may apply
- borrowing is limited by the value of the vehicle.

Logbook loans are very expensive and very risky, imposing high interest rates and potentially unfair terms and conditions. Also, logbook loan companies are sometimes accused of employing harsh and aggressive collection tactics.

In general, logbook loans are only used by people who have a very poor rating, often people with other multiple outstanding loans[33] and debts and who may need cash quickly.

Note: Many logbook loan providers are members of the Consumer Credit Trade Association (CCTA). For the CCTA code of practice on bill of sale lending, see: www.ccta.co.uk/admindocs/codes_of_practice/bills_of_sale_code.pdf.

Doorstep loans

Doorstep loans (also known as door-to-door loans or home credit) are small-amount personal loans – usually between £50 and £500. Loans are granted subject to status and are available to UK residents only. They are generally only used by borrowers with a very poor credit history. The cash is delivered to the borrower's home by the loan company's locally employed agents. Loan repayments are also collected from the borrower's home – usually on a weekly basis, although borrowers may make loan repayments by direct debit. Doorstep lenders may also offer trading cheques and vouchers which can be exchanged for goods, usually clothing and soft furnishings at specific shops.

As with other forms of subprime borrowing, the costs can be very high – in some cases the interest rates can exceed 1,500% APR – making doorstep loans much more expensive than a bank loan or the average credit card. In addition, doorstep lenders may also impose additional interest charges and administrative fees if the borrower defaults on loan repayments.

The cost of alternative home-credit loan lenders can be compared on an independent comparison website, at: www.lenderscompared.org.uk.

All doorstep lenders (but not necessarily their individual agents or employees) *must* be authorised and licensed[34] by the Financial Conduct Authority. Offering a doorstep lending facility without appropriate authorisation is a criminal offence. In addition, it is also a criminal offence for a lender to make 'cold calls' on prospective borrowers and to offer to lend them money – any home visit *must* be made in response to a request by the borrower.

Advantages of doorstep loans

The main advantages of a doorstep loan are that:
- it gives quick access to small cash advances
- the home-based application process is simple
- the eligibility criteria are minimal.

Disadvantages of doorstep loans

The main disadvantages of a doorstep loan are that:
- the interest rates may be very high
- extra charges can often be applied or incurred.

Text loans

Text loans (also known as SMS borrowing) are borrowing or loan arrangements made using text messaging to complete the loan application. Loans are typically up to £1,500. Once accepted, the agreement is signed and verified (using text messaging) and the funds deposited into the borrower's bank account, usually the same day. No paper and no documents to sign –the application is completely online, using mobile messaging.

So how do text loans work? Once a borrower has completed an online application, the lender will complete a series of credit checks and affordability checks to assess the borrower's eligibility for a loan, and will then make an instant decision. If provisionally accepted, the borrower will be required to verify the loan. The lender will then send an email link to an online loan agreement page, which will display the terms and conditions of the loan. Once he or she has confirmed acceptance of the terms and conditions, the borrower will e-sign the loan agreement, usually using a SMS code sent by the lender. Some text loan lenders may then contact the borrower to confirm their employment status (some lenders impose a minimum earnings criteria), or may request copies of pay-slips or bank statements. Once all details have been confirmed, the money will be transferred to the borrower's bank account.

There are two main types of text loans. Text-based *payday* loans generally last between 14 and 30 days and are for up to £1,000 – the borrower receives the funds in full and repays the loan, and the interest on the loan, on her or his next pay date. Text-based *instalment* loans are repaid over periods between 2 months and 12 months, or even a few years.

Note: Many text loan lenders use a collection process known as a Continuous Payment Authority (CPA),[35] which allows the text loan lender to set up recurring payments from a borrower's account.

For UK-based text loan providers, borrowers must be resident and employed in the UK to be eligible. Loans are paid in pounds sterling. Text loans are only available to those with an active bank account.

Advantages of text loans

The main advantages of a text loan are that:
- there is no paperwork involved in the application
- the application process is simple and quick.

Disadvantages of text loans

The main disadvantages of a text loan are that:
- some text loan lenders charge an application fee

- the interest rates can be very high
- additional fees and interest charges will be incurred if a repayment default occurs
- failing to meet agreed payments can damage or completely destroy a borrower's credit profile, and worsen a borrower's debt problem.

Text loans can be very expensive and should be used with caution.

> **Activity 3**
>
> What are the main advantages and disadvantages of payday loans, doorstep loans and text loans?

Guarantor loans

Marketed as 'the all new good old fashioned loan',[36] guarantor loans are 'bad credit' loans that require a guarantor – that is, a third party is required to guarantee a borrower's application, promising to make repayments if the borrower is unable to do so or defaults on agreed payments. Guarantor loans are generally offered for amounts between £1,000 and £7,500 and over periods up to 5 years, and are aimed at borrowers with poor credit history, recent payment defaults or County Court Judgments, who are unable to obtain finance or to borrow money through more traditional channels. Interest rates of up to 60% are not unusual, although they do vary between guarantor loan providers; but even these high rates are still much lower than many other types of subprime borrowing.

Applicants must be over 18 years old, must have a UK bank account from which loan repayments will be collected, and must demonstrate 'affordability' and 'capability' – that is, that they can afford the loan repayments and are capable of making them in a timely fashion. The person acting as guarantor may not be financially linked to the borrower (for example, she or he may not be a dependent spouse), but could be a family member, a friend, or even a work colleague. The loan company will undertake appropriate credit and identity checks both for the borrower and for the guarantor. To be accepted, the guarantor will usually need to be over 21, to be a UK resident and a UK homeowner, and to have a good credit history. The guarantor will also need to demonstrate affordability and capability.

Note: Guarantor loans are not payday loans: interest charges are much lower, and generally there are no administration or arrangement fees.

Advantages of guarantor loans

The main advantages of a guarantor loan are that:

- it is a flexible form of lending and ideal for someone with a poor credit history
- usually no credit check is required for the borrower
- it is cheaper than many other types of subprime borrowing
- it is a simple, old-fashioned, trust-based way of borrowing.

Disadvantages of guarantor loans

The main disadvantages of a guarantor loan are that:

- although interest rates are lower than those associated with other types of subprime borrowing, they are still fairly high

– finding a guarantor who will agree to co-sign a borrowing agreement may be difficult because of the impact on the guarantor's own credit score and credit file should the borrower default on the loan agreement.

Pawnbroker loans

Pawnbrokers generally offer two services:
– a purchasing facility: a customer may sell a personal asset to a pawnbroker for cash
– a borrowing facility: a customer may offer a personal asset as security for a loan.

We will focus on the latter.

A pawnbroker loan is a secured loan, which can be secured against a range of personal assets, such as jewellery, watches, diamonds, electrical goods, cameras, life and endowment policies, collectables, shares, computer hardware, cars, vehicles, motorbikes – essentially, any item of value. As at 31 August 2015, there were 2,000 pawnbrokers in the UK, operating in a market valued at £930 million.[37]

So how do pawnbroker loans work? When a prospective borrower offers a personal asset as possible security for a loan, the pawnbroker will examine and value the personal asset and then make an offer of the maximum amount he or she is prepared to lend. Before any transaction occurs, the pawnbroker will also provide the prospective borrower with pre-contract information providing details of the pawnbroker's credit terms.

If the offer is acceptable, the borrower will be required to sign a credit agreement with the pawnbroker and will be offered a period of time after which the loan must be repaid. The maximum loan period is 6 months, but it can be much less. As with all credit agreements, there is a 14-day cooling-off period during which the borrower has the right to withdraw from the agreement.

During the loan period, the personal asset remains the property of the borrower but is in the possession of the pawnbroker, as security for the loan. The personal asset can be redeemed at any time during the loan period by repaying the capital borrowed, together with the interest accrued up to the point of redemption. Interest rate charges vary not only between pawnbrokers but also depending on the amount being borrowed. Pawnbrokers typically charge an annualised interest rate; this can vary between 80% and 130%, which equates to approximately 6% to 9% a month.[38]

If the loan remains unpaid or is not renewed at the end of the loan period, subject to legal requirements[39] the pawnbroker can sell the personal asset to retrieve the outstanding loan and the accrued interest owing. Any surplus, after expenses have been taken, will normally be returned to the borrower. Any loss – if the personal asset can only be sold for an amount less than the outstanding loan and the accrued interest – will still be (legally) recoverable from the borrower.

Advantages of pawnbroker loans

The main advantages of a pawnbroker loan are that:
– there is no credit check, so borrowers with a poor credit history or credit rating can still borrow funds
– it is simple and very quick to arrange a loan – normally the money is available immediately on signing the agreement
– pawned goods can (usually) be redeemed at any time
– interest is only charged for the period for which the funds are borrowed.

Disadvantages of pawnbroker loans

The main disadvantages of a pawnbroker loan are that:

- it can be a relatively expensive way to borrow
- the amount of the loan is limited to a percentage of the value of the asset being pawned
- if the loan is not repaid on time, the pawnbroker can sell the borrower's asset (after giving the borrower appropriate notice), and if the sale value is less than the value of the outstanding loan, the borrower will still be legally liable for the remaining debt.

For further details on UK-based pawnbrokers, see the National Pawnbrokers' Association's website, at: http: www.thenpa.com.

Loans: Financial Conduct Authority ruling

Following a Financial Conduct Authority investigation, from 2 January 2015 the following conditions apply to all high-cost short-term credit (HSCTC), including payday loans, logbook loans, doorstep loans and guarantor loans:

- There is an initial cost cap of 0.8% per day: that is, for all high-cost short-term credit loans, interest and fees must not exceed 0.8% per day of the amount borrowed.
- All fixed default fees will be capped at £15: that is, if borrowers do not repay their loans on time, default charges may not exceed £15, and interest on unpaid balances and default charges must not exceed the initial rate.
- There will be a total cost cap of 100% to protect borrowers from escalating debts: that is, borrowers will never have to pay back more in fees and interest than the amount borrowed.

The Financial Conduct Authority has indicated that a review of the above cap will take place in the first six months of 2017. For further information on the price cap, see: www.fca.org.uk/news/fca-confirms-price-cap-rules-for-payday-lenders.

3.12 Mortgages

A mortgage is a loan in which a borrower, the mortgagee, offers property or land as security to a lender, the mortgagor, until the loan (both capital and interest) has been repaid. Mortgages can be obtained directly from a bank or building society, or negotiated through a mortgage broker.[40]

Perhaps one of the largest financial commitments a borrower will ever make, a mortgage is a form of secured borrowing: if the borrower does not maintain agreed mortgage repayments, the lender can seize (and sell) the property on which the mortgage is secured, and recover the outstanding balance of the mortgage (both capital and interest). This process is often referred to as a 'mortgage repossession', and during 2013 in the UK 28,900 properties were repossessed due to mortgage arrears, compared with 33,900 in 2012.[41] The Money Charity estimated that for the first three months of 2014 a house was repossessed in the UK every 20 minutes and 15 seconds (Money Charity 2014b: 2).

Mortgage repayments are usually made on a monthly basis over a long period of time – typically 25 years, but it can be up to 40 years. The amount that can be borrowed, and the cost at which it can be borrowed (the interest rate), are usually determined by a number of factors, including the credit score or credit history of the borrower (or borrowers, if it is a joint mortgage application), the current employment status of the borrower (or borrowers), the earnings capacity of the borrower (or borrowers), and the value of the house or property on which the mortgage will be secured.

Provided that the borrower has a good current credit score and a good credit history and is in full-time employment, the possible mortgage will be determined by a salary multiple of her or his earnings, but limited (if necessary) to a percentage value of the house or property being purchased.

Activity 4

Andrew Bishop's annual earnings are £55,000 p.a. He wants to buy a local small semi-detached property which is currently on the market for £180,000. His bank has advised him that it offers mortgages of up to three times the applicant's salary, but limits mortgages to a maximum of 85% of the value of the property. How much can Andrew borrow?

Repaying a mortgage

There are basically just two ways of repaying a mortgage, giving rise to two kinds of mortgage: the 'interest-only mortgage' and the 'repayment mortgage'.

With an interest-only mortgage, the monthly payments made by the borrower do not reduce the actual sum borrowed (the capital), but simply cover the cost of borrowing the money (the interest). At the end of the mortgage period, the full capital sum will still be outstanding and will need to be repaid. To be able to do this, the borrower also arranges an investment that will build up sufficient funds to pay off the capital sum at the end of the mortgage term. With this type of mortgage repayment, however, there is always a risk that the value of the investment may not be sufficient to repay the full capital sum borrowed. The most common form of investment used is an endowment plan.[42]

With a repayment mortgage, in contrast, the borrower's repayment each month consists of part interest and part capital, so that by the end of the mortgage period the borrower will have paid the interest and repaid the capital and will owe nothing.

Some lenders may also offer a part-interest-only and a part-repayment mortgage, which would be a combination of both of the above.

Note: Changes to mortgage rules from 26 April 2014 mean that lenders and mortgage providers must now make sure that any prospective borrower will be able to afford the initial mortgage repayments and other associated household costs.

Further information on what a lender or mortgage provider is required to check is available on the Financial Conduct Authority's website, at: www.fca.org.uk.

Types of mortgage

There are many different types of mortgages, the most popular of which are variable-rate mortgages, fixed-rate mortgages, discount-rate mortgages, cash-back mortgages, tracker mortgages, current account mortgages, capped mortgages, and endowment mortgages; but there are also other types of mortgage, including subprime mortgages.

Variable-rate mortgages (standard variable-rate mortgages)

A standard variable-rate mortgage (also known as an SVR or reversion-rate mortgage) is a mortgage for which the lender can increase or decrease its standard variable rate (the interest rate on the mortgage) at any time. Although the standard variable rates will be influenced by the Bank of England's base rate, a lender can also change its standard variable rate while the base rate remains unchanged. Standard variable-rate mortgages typically range between 2% and 6% above the Bank of England base rate. (As at 31 August 2015, the Bank of England base rate was 0.5%.) Remember that if the interest rate changes, so will the monthly repayments.

Fixed-rate mortgages

Unlike a variable-rate mortgage, a fixed-rate mortgage is one for which the mortgage interest rate is fixed for a period of years (usually for up to 10 years), with a guarantee that there will be no change in monthly mortgage repayments over the period – that is, no matter what happens to interest rates, monthly mortgage repayments will stay the same for the period of the agreement. Once the fixed-rate period has ended, the mortgage will normally revert to a standard variable-rate mortgage.

Discount-rate mortgages (discounted variable-rate mortgages)

A discounted variable-rate mortgage is one that uses a reduced interest rate – most commonly the lender's standard variable rate.

The discount could be for a period 2, 3 or 5 years, or it could even be for the entire term of the mortgage (a 'lifetime discounted rate'). In addition, the discount could be a fixed discount rate for the period (for example, a 1% discount for 5 years) or a tapered discount rate (for example, 1% discount for years 1 and 2; a 0.75% discount for years 3 and 4; and a 0.5% discount for year 5).

Once the discount interest rate period has ended, the mortgage will normally revert to a standard variable-rate mortgage.

Cash-back mortgages (money-back mortgages)

A cash-back mortgage is a mortgage – usually a standard variable-rate mortgage or a tracker mortgage – for which a cash lump sum is paid to the borrower once the mortgage agreement has been completed. The size of this cash lump sum depends on the size of the mortgage and the type of mortgage: some lenders restrict cash-back offers to a very limited range of mortgages. Remember: nothing is free, and the cash lump sum will be funded by a higher mortgage interest rate, paid by the borrower. Cash-back mortgages are popular with first-time buyers.

Tracker mortgages

Unlike the standard variable-rate mortgages, a tracker mortgage mirrors the Bank of England's base rate. If the Bank of England's base rate increases by 1%, the tracker mortgage interest rate will also increase by 1%. Similarly, if the Bank of England's base rate decreases by 1%, the tracker mortgage interest rate will decrease by 1%.

Some tracker mortgages have a floor – that is, a minimum level below which the tracker mortgage interest rate will not drop. In addition, as with fixed-rate mortgages, tracker mortgages are available over different terms: most commonly 2 or 5 years, although it is possible to arrange a lifetime or full-term tracker mortgage.

Current account mortgages (offset mortgages)

This type of mortgage combines a borrower's mortgage account and a borrower's current account to give a single net balance. Some lenders also link savings accounts, credit cards and personal loans into a single combined account, and refer to such mortgages as offset mortgages.

With this type of mortgage, the borrower is charged interest (usually using a standard variable rate) only on the total *net* amount owed to the lender – that is, the amount of the total outstanding mortgage *less* any savings or current account balances.

Capped-rate mortgages (capped mortgages)

A capped-rate mortgage is a type of standard variable-rate mortgage that has an interest-rate ceiling, or cap, beyond which the mortgage interest rate cannot rise. Capped-rate mortgages are normally offered only for an introductory period of between 2 years and 5 years, after which the capped-rate mortgage will normally be converted to a standard variable-rate mortgage. With a capped-rate mortgage, the mortgage repayments are guaranteed not to increase beyond a certain level, but because they are a kind of variable-rate mortgage the repayments can also benefit from a decrease in interest rates.

Capped-rate mortgages are the rarest of all types of mortgages, and tend to be offered at a higher variable rate than the best tracker-rate mortgages and discounted-rate mortgages, because of the security that the interest cap provides.

Endowment mortgages

As discussed above, an endowment mortgage is a mortgage arranged on an interest-only basis with the intention that the capital be repaid on the maturity of a low-cost endowment policy. In essence, the borrower is required to have two separate agreements: an agreement with the lender for the mortgage and an agreement with the insurer for the endowment policy. Such mortgages, whilst popular in the 1980s and early 1990s, are now very rare.

Why endowment mortgages became unpopular Endowment mortgages were very popular in the 1980s because they benefited from tax relief on premiums paid into the endowment plan and tax relief on mortgage interest payments. Premium relief was abolished in 1984, however, while mortgage interest relief was abolished in 2000, which made endowment mortgages much more expensive.

More importantly, stock market uncertainty and volatility during the 1990s resulted in many endowment plans failing to achieve their targeted returns. This resulted in many investors who held mortgage-related endowment plans being unable to pay off their mortgage loans in full when those became due. This, together with widespread claims of mis-selling by insurance companies, resulted in a dramatic decline in the popularity of, and demand for, endowment mortgages.

Other types of mortgages

Equity-release mortgages Equity-release mortgages enable a property owner to release cash from the equity accumulated in their property. These mortgages are targeted at older homeowners: the minimum age is typically 55 on lifetime mortgages and 60 on home-reversion plans.

Lifetime mortgages are the most common type of scheme. These enable a property owner to borrow money secured on their property, either as a lump sum or as regular income, or as a combination of the two. The mortgagee continues to own the property.

Monthly repayments are not usually made; instead, the amount borrowed, together with all accrued interest, is repaid when the property owner dies or moves into long-term care. An alternative type of lifetime mortgage is a drawdown version, designed for property owners who do not need a large cash lump sum but merely a pot of money that they can use as and when required. Interest is only charged on the cash drawn (or released).

With a home-reversion plan mortgage, the property owner sells a percentage of their home to a financial institution, either for a lump sum or for regular income. The owner retains the right to live at the property. When the property is eventually sold (for example, on the death of the property occupier and part-owner), the financial institution receives their percentage of the sale receipts.

Subprime mortgages A subprime mortgage (also known as a 'bad credit' mortgage or an impaired credit mortgage) is a mortgage granted to a borrower with a poor credit history who would not qualify for a conventional mortgage.

Prior to 2007, many lenders offered special mortgages to people classed as 'subprime' borrowers, usually at interest rates that were considerably higher than those generally charged on the more widely available high street mortgages. Such borrowers included discharged bankrupts, those who had fallen into arrears on a previous mortgage, and those who had suffered other debt problems in the past or had outstanding County Court Judgments.

Since the 2007/2008 credit crunch, the subprime mortgage market in the UK has almost disappeared. Although a small number of specialist lenders still cater for the so-called 'near-prime' mortgage borrower – those who may have a very slight credit impairment – there are very few institutions (banks or building societies) currently offering subprime mortgages.[43]

Islamic mortgages 'Islamic mortgage' is a term used to describe a sharia-compliant method of purchasing a house or property.[44] In an Islamic mortgage, the bank or building society enters into an agreement of shared ownership, so that the bank and the purchaser own their respective percentages of the property, based on their relative contributions to the cost of the purchase. During the term of the agreement, the borrower pays the bank rent, the amount of the rent being partly based on the proportion of the property that the bank owns. Over time, the rent contributes to paying back the sum borrowed and to the bank's profit (which has been deferred over the term of the agreement).

Additional factors to consider

Apart from factors such as affordability and availability, additional factors to consider when selecting a mortgage include these, for example:

- How flexible is the mortgage? Can payments be deferred or missed without penalty?
- How portable is the mortgage? Can it be moved to another property?
- Are there charges or penalties for early repayment of the mortgage?

Note: Failure to meet repayment obligations can result in:

- debt consolidation, whereby any outstanding amount is (with the agreement of the mortgage provider) added to the capital amount of the mortgage; or, if this is not possible
- legal action to recover the amounts outstanding, and thus possible loss of the property on which the mortgage is secured.

3.13 Credit reference agencies

Before agreeing to offer a loan or to give credit, banks, building societies, finance companies, loan companies and retailers want to be confident that you can repay the money they lend. Most companies now use credit reference agencies, which can provide a range of information about a potential borrower – information that lenders and retailers can use to make their lending or credit-provision decisions.

The *Consumer Credit Act 1974*[45] defines a credit reference agency as: '... a person carrying on a business comprising the furnishing of persons with information relevant to the financial standing of individuals, being information collected by the agency for that purpose' (1974: s.145(8)). As such, credit reference agencies can collect and record information (either public information or credit account information) on a person's credit-worthiness, which can then be supplied to lenders, retails and credit providers.

There are three main credit reference agencies in the UK:
- Experian, at: www.experian.co.uk
- Equifax, at: www.equifax.co.uk
- Callcredit, at: www.callcredit.co.uk.

Note: The lender must obtain the borrower's permission to check the information on his or her credit reference file. If a lender refuses to offer a loan or provide a credit facility after checking the borrower's credit reference file, the lender must:
- inform the borrower why a loan application or credit application has been refused
- provide details of the credit reference agency used.

Remember also that credit reference agencies do not *advise* lenders or retailers – they do not make decisions on behalf of lenders or retailers: they simply provide information. The decision is for the lender or retailer to make.

Different banks, building societies, finance companies, loan companies and retailers use different credit reference agencies, and some may use more than one credit reference agency. For details, see: www.moneysavingexpert.com/credit-cards/credit-reference.

Note: All credit reference agencies are regulated by the Financial Conduct Authority.

Information kept by credit reference agencies

Credit reference agencies keep information about personal borrowing and financial behaviour. They collect information from a variety of sources, more specifically:
- The Electoral Roll, which shows the address of a person who has registered to vote, and the date on which the person was registered there.
- Public records,[46] including court judgments, bankruptcies, Individual Voluntary Arrangements, Debt Relief Orders, and Administration Orders.
- A range of financial institutions which provide account information on how a person has managed their existing bank accounts, how they have managed their financial commitments, whether they make payments on time, and details of people to whom they are financially connected (for example, joint bank accounts).
- The Council of Mortgage Lenders (CML), regarding home repossessions or homes voluntarily surrendered. (*Note:* This information is only available to other CML registered members).

- The Gone Away Information Network (GAIN), which is a network of organisations whose members submit and share details of people who have moved home and left behind an outstanding credit account or a loan account that is at least 30 days in arrears, without having notified the lender of a forwarding address. Equifax holds records on behalf of the GAIN organisation. (*Note:* This information is only available to companies who are members of GAIN.)

Credit reference agencies also record details of previous searches made on a person's credit file – that is, details of companies and organisations that have looked at the information on a person's credit file in the last 12 months (although not if they made 'soft searches'[47]), as well as details of any illegal activity (fraud or identity theft) of which the person may have been a victim. If a lender believes that it may have detected a fraud or attempted fraud on a person's account (for example, a possible identity theft), or if a person believes that her or his identity may be at risk (for example, they may have recently lost confidential personal documents), a CIFAS[48] marker may be placed on the person's credit reference file. Such protective registration does not affect a person credit score, and is intended to warn lenders and to protect innocent consumers.

Information not kept by credit reference agencies

Credit reference agencies do not keep details of the following:

- student loans (except pre-1998 'mortgage style' student loans)
- local Council Tax arrears
- parking or driving fines
- information about family or relatives (unless there is a financial association)
- declined loan or credit applications (lenders can only see whether a loan or credit application has been made)
- payment defaults that are more than 6 years old
- Payment Protection Insurance (PPI), bank charges, and other claims
- race, religion, or ethnicity
- wages or salary
- any savings accounts
- medical history
- criminal convictions
- child support payments.

How long is information kept by credit reference agencies?

With a few exceptions, credit reference agencies normally keep information they collect for 6 years. There are exceptions:

- information from the Electoral Roll is kept indefinitely
- information on credit searches is kept for 1 year (2 years for debt collection searches) by Experian and Equifax, and for 2 years by Callcredit
- association information is kept until the financial link ends, or until a disassociation request (or notice of disassociation) is received by the credit reference agencies
- information concerning linked addresses is kept as long as the information is relevant
- any CIFAS flag is kept for as long as there is evidence of fraud or potential fraud
- information regarding bankruptcy may be held for longer than 6 years if a County Court or High Court has imposed a Bankruptcy Restrictions Order for a period greater than 6 years.

> **Activity 5**
>
> Describe the main types of information that a credit reference agency would keep, and for how long the information would be retained.

Checking your credit reference file

Using s.7 of the *Data Protection Act 1998*, a person can request a copy of their credit reference file from any of the credit reference agencies. This is known as a Statutory Credit Report, for which a small fee (£2) is payable. The credit reference agency *must* provide the report within seven working days of receiving the request. Requests can be made by letter or online.

Changing information on a credit reference file

If a person believes that information held by a credit reference agency on their credit file is incorrect, she or he can formally request (in writing) that the credit reference agency changes or removes the incorrect information.

Note: A person cannot ask for information to be removed or changed simply because she or he does not want prospective lenders to see it.

The credit reference agency must reply within 28 days of the request and report whether it has removed the entry from the credit file, amended the entry in the credit file, or taken no action. If the entry has been amended, the credit reference agency must provide a copy of the amended entry, and must also send those details to any lender that has searched the credit reference file in the last 6 months. If the credit reference agency does not amend the entry on the credit file, amends it but incorrectly, or does not reply to the request within 28 days, the person can refer the issue to the Information Commissioner.

In addition, a person can if necessary request a credit reference agency to add a 'notice of correction' to an entry on the credit file. This notice is a personally written statement (to a maximum of 200 words) that seeks to clarify an entry on a credit file. If the credit reference agency believes that the notice of correction is incorrect and unsuitable for publication, however, the agency must pass the notice to the Information Commissioner, and the Commissioner will then make an order to say what notice, if any, should be added to the credit reference file.

3.14 Credit scoring

A credit score is a statistically derived numerical expression, and is based on an analysis of a person's credit file or files. It is used as a representation of a person's creditworthiness – that is, the score indicates a person's likely future behaviour based on their past history, although for the lender or credit provider this has less to do with assessing risk and more to do with assessing profitability.

Individual lenders, credit providers and credit reference agencies employ their own unique methodologies, varying, for example, in what information is taken into account, how that information is quantified, what weighting is used, and how the credit score is calculated. In general, however, the higher the number of the credit score, the more creditworthy the person is deemed to be. Most lenders and credit providers impose a minimum threshold level – if a person's credit score is below the minimum threshold, this could significantly reduce the likelihood of any finance or credit facilities being provided. In determining whether to approve a loan or credit application, lenders and credit providers will use details provided in the loan or credit application,[49] any past history the applicant may have with that lender or credit provider, *together* with the applicant's credit score.

Note: Because different providers of finance and credit facilities use different calculation methodologies and impose different threshold levels, it is possible that a prospective borrower refused by one lender or credit provider might not be refused by others.

Improving a low credit score

There are many ways in which a low credit score can be improved. Some of the most popular are these:

- regularly check your credit file (and especially after making a loan or credit application that has been rejected)
- appeal against unfair payments notices or defaults (if necessary, use the Financial Ombudsman Service or the Information Commissioner)
- register to vote and ensure that you appear on the Electoral Roll
- ensure that payments are made on time
- cancel unused credit cards, charge cards, and store cards
- build a predictable credit history
- time any loan or credit applications correctly.

Also, never withdraw cash on a credit card, as this may indicate bad personal financial management; and never use payday loans, as these can have a detrimental impact of your credit score and on any future mortgage application.

3.15 Concluding comments

In today's world of 'buy now and pay later', there is an ever-increasing variety of lending institutions, finance companies and credit providers willing to offer an almost endless assortment of borrowing opportunities to help consumers buy tomorrow's dream today. From unsecured personal borrowing and credit sale options, to hire purchase 'rent-to-own' and conditional sale agreements, from secured loans and mortgages to short-term borrowing, from credit cards, charge cards and store cards to subprime loans, loans are available (subject to status) at a price – and some at a very high price.

Be careful of offers that appear too good to be true, and be honest with yourself about what you can truly afford. And always, *always* read the small print on any loan agreement, credit agreement or sales agreement.

3.16 Suggested further reading

For further reading on the following topics, see the references given.

Loans and credit cards:

- www.moneysavingexpert.com/credit-cards

Mortgages (beginner's guide):
- www.moneyadviceservice.org.uk/en/articles/mortgages-a-beginners-guide

Key points

- The most widely used lenders and credit providers in the UK are: high street commercial (retail) banks, building societies, consumer finance companies, credit unions, and subprime lenders.
- All banks, building societies and finance companies are regulated by the Prudential Regulatory Authority and by the Financial Conduct Authority.
- Credit unions are member-owned financial co-operatives controlled by their members and operated for the purpose of providing financial services to their members.
- Subprime lenders (also called near-prime lenders or non-prime lenders) specialise in lending money to customers with a poor, a limited, a volatile or an incomplete credit history.
- Unsecured borrowing and loans are supported only by a borrower's credit history and creditworthiness.
- Secured borrowing and loans rely on property or an asset as collateral for the borrowing or loan.
- An overdraft is a borrowing facility linked to a bank current account. It may be authorised (planned) or unauthorised (unplanned).
- A personal loan is a loan provided by a bank or other loan provider that is not secured against any personal asset.
- A credit card is simply a loan vehicle.
- A charge card is a card that requires the user to pay the balance in full at the end of each accounting period.
- Subprime borrowing or subprime loans are 'bad credit' finance, the most popular being payday loans, logbook loans, doorstep loans, text loans, guarantor loans, and pawnbroker loans.
- A mortgage is a secured loan in which a borrower offers property or land as security to a lender until the loan (both capital and interest) has been repaid.
- The most common types of mortgages are: variable-rate mortgages, fixed-rate mortgages, discount-rate mortgages, cash-back mortgages, tracker mortgages, current account mortgages, capped mortgages, endowment mortgages, and subprime mortgages.
- Credit reference agencies collect and record information (either public information or credit account information) on a person's creditworthiness.
- A credit score is a statistically derived numerical representation of a person's creditworthiness.

Self-review questions

1. What are the key differences between a high street bank and a building society?
2. What are the main advantages and disadvantages of using a credit card?
3. What are the main types of subprime lending, and should subprime lending be avoided at all costs?
4. What are the main types of mortgages currently available?
5. What information do credit reference agencies keep, and for how long may they keep the information?

Case study discussion questions

1. Advise Anthony Carter on how he may be able to raise the money he needs for his trip overseas to Argentina in 16 months' time.
2. Advise Jonathan Carter on how he could finance the refurbishment of his house, and the possible strategies he could adopt to minimise his own and his wife's levels of debt.

Suggested answers to chapter activities

Activity 1

Because her course of study began after September 2012, Jane Mason's loan repayments would commence once her earnings exceed £21,000 p.a.

$$£30{,}000 - £21{,}000 = £9{,}000$$

$$£9{,}000 * 9\% = £810 \text{ p.a.}$$

Her monthly repayment would therefore be: £810/12 = £67.50.

Activity 2

A *conditional sale agreement* is a type of borrowing that differs from other types of borrowing inasmuch as the purchaser does not *own* the goods (does not have legal title to the goods) until she or he has paid for the goods in full.

A *hire purchase agreement* is a legally binding agreement in which a purchaser agrees to pay for goods over a number of agreed payment periods (weeks or months), after which the purchaser *may* then exercise an option to buy the goods, on payment of an additional nominal sum, or if not must return the goods to the owner.

A *credit sale agreement* is a legally binding agreement in which a purchaser agrees to pay for goods over a number of agreed payment periods (weeks or months). With a credit sale agreement, the purchaser obtains legal title to the goods immediately – that is the property (legal title) is transferred at the commencement of the agreement and the purchaser pays the total purchase price by instalments.

Activity 3

The main advantages of payday loans, doorstep loans, and text loans are:
- they give quick access to cash advances
- the application process is often quick and simple
- they generally have a very low eligibility criteria.

The main disadvantages are:
- interest rates can be very high
- extra charges often apply
- failing to meet agreed payments can damage or completely destroy a borrower's credit profile, and worsen a borrower's debt problem.

Activity 4

The bank would in principle lend up to a maximum of £165,000 (£55,000 * 3). However, for this house it would limit the mortgage to £153,000 (£180,000 * 85%). Andrew could therefore borrow £153,000. To buy this house, Andrew would therefore need to be able to make a deposit of £27,000 (£180,000 – £153,000).

Activity 5

Credit reference agencies keep information about personal borrowing and financial behaviour. With a few exceptions, credit reference agencies normally keep information they collect for 6 years.

Notes

1. This statement excludes the Bank of England. The Bank of England, the central bank of the United Kingdom, was established in 1694 and nationalised in 1946. In 1998 it became an independent public organisation, wholly owned by the Government, but accountable to Parliament. The entire capital of the Bank of England is held by the Treasury solicitor on behalf of HM Treasury. The Bank of England is one of eight banks authorised to issue banknotes in the United Kingdom; it has a monopoly on the issue of banknotes in England and Wales, and regulates the issue of banknotes by commercial banks in Scotland and Northern Ireland.
2. The word 'bank' is borrowed, or more accurately derived, from the old-Italian word *banca*, meaning 'bench' or 'counter'. During the Renaissance, benches were used by Florentine lenders as desks or exchange counters for the undertaking of financial transactions.
3. Such services include, for example, the domestic direct debits (DD) and standing orders (SO), as well as Faster Payments Systems (FPS) using CHAPS (Clearing House Automated Payments System), and BACS (Bankers' Automated Clearing Service).
4. For Aldermore, see www.aldermore.co.uk; for C. Hoare & Co., see www.hoaresbank.co.uk; for N. M. Rothschilds & Sons, see www.rothschild.com; and for Weatherbys, see www.weatherbys.co.uk.
5. Building societies are not unique to the UK but exist internationally: in Australia, Jamaica, the Republic of Ireland, New Zealand, and Zimbabwe. In other countries, mutual institutions similar to building societies exist, for example the Co-operative Banks in Austria, and the Savings and Loans Institutions in the United States.
6. As defined by the *Building Society Act 1986*, a building society is a society whose 'purpose or principal purpose is that of making loans which are secured on residential property and are funded substantially by its members' (s.5(1)(a)).
7. 'Demutualisation' allowed building societies to become public limited companies.
8. See: http://www.bankofengland.co.uk/pra/Documents/authorisations/buildingsocietieslist1508.pdf.
9. See: www.bsa.org.uk/.
10. See: www.blackhorse.co.uk.
11. The first recorded credit union in the UK was formed in Derry, Northern Ireland, in October 1960. See: www.derrycu.com/content.asp?section=1.
12. Credit unions are 'not for profit' because their purpose is to serve their members rather than to maximise profits.
13. The Reform Order also allowed them to offer interest on savings, instead of paying a dividend.
14. See: www.abcul.org/credit-unions/history-world-facts.
15. See: www.abcul.org/media-and-research/facts-statistics. *Note:* The Association of British Credit Unions Limited (ACBUL) is the largest credit union trade association in the UK. See: http://www.abcul.org/home.
16. For 6 Towns Credit Unions, see www.sixtowns.co.uk; for the Angus Credit Union, see www.anguscreditunion.co.uk.
17. Association of British Credit Unions Limited: for the code of governance, see: www.abcul.org/about/abcul-credit-unions.
18. Such borrowers are often referred to as 'NINJA' borrowers – that is, borrowers with 'No Income, No Job or Assets'.
19. For further details, see: www.gov.uk/student-finance.
20. In the July 2015 budget, the Chancellor of the Exchequer announced the Government's intention to allow tuition fees to rise with inflation, above £9,000, for those institutions offering high-quality teaching in 2017–18.
21. Private universities and colleges are institutions not operated by the Government. As of September 2015, there are four fully-fledged private universities in the UK: the University of Buckingham, BPP University, Regent's University London, and the University of Law.

22. In the July 2015 Budget, the Chancellor of the Exchequer announced that as from September 2016 (academic year 2016–17), the student maintenance grant would be abolished and replaced with a student loan facility.
23. The course must be a qualifying course. It must be in the UK, and must be one of the following:
    - a first degree (for example a BA, a BSc or a BEd)
    - a Foundation Degree
    - a Certificate of Higher Education
    - a Diploma of Higher Education (DipHE)
    - a Higher National Certificate (HNC)
    - a Higher National Diploma (HND)
    - a Postgraduate Certificate of Education (PGCE)
    - an Initial Teacher Training course.
24. Generally, student finance is only available for a student's *first* higher education qualification, although limited additional funding may be available if, for example:
    - the student has changed the higher education course of study
    - the student terminated a higher education course of study but later decided to start again
    - the student is 'topping up' a higher education qualification.
25. Although there is no upper age limit for a tuition fee loan, a maintenance loan is only available to those who are under the age of 60 at the start of the course.
26. To be eligible for student finance, a student must:
    - be a UK national or have 'settled status'
    - be living in England
    - have lived in the UK, the Channel Islands or the Isle of Man for three years before the start of the course.
27. Some companies may suggest that if a conditional sale agreement or a hire purchase agreement is ended during the agreement period, the purchaser must pay the total price of the goods to which the agreement relates. This is wrong.
28. Companies such as Visa, Mastercard and Barclaycard are merely payment-services companies – they just process card-based transactions and payments on behalf of the card issuer.
29. For example, see THL Direct at www.thldirect.co.uk.
30. In October 2014, after a review of its policies and procedures and discussions with the Financial Conduct Authority, payday lender Wonga announced that following new affordability checks it was writing off £220m of payday loans debts in relation to 330,000 borrowers. It also announced that it was suspending interest charges for a further 45,000 borrowers. See: 'Wonga to write off £220m of customer debts', at: www.bbc.co.uk/news/business-29457044.
31. The law only recognises a bill of sale if the lender registers the bill with the High Court. If the bill is not registered, the lender must get Court approval to repossess a borrower's vehicle.
32. In England, legislation allows a bill of sale to act as security; whereas in Scotland, a bill of sale cannot be used as security and is not legally binding. In Scotland, the lender is required to demonstrate that she or he properly purchased and took physical possession of the borrower's vehicle for a reasonable time before hiring it back to the borrower under a hire purchase agreement.
33. See: www.citizensadvice.org.uk/index/campaigns/current_campaigns/logbook-loans.htm.
34. A list of licensed doorstep lenders is available from the FCA register, at: www.fca.org.uk/register.
35. Continuous Payment Authority (CPA) is a form of regular payment, whereby an account holder provides a business or retailer with her or his debit-card details and authorises the business or retailer to deduct a set or variable amount from that account on an ongoing basis – until the agreement ends, or until the CPA is cancelled. CPAs are different from standing orders and direct debits in that they do not provide the account holder with the same level of protection, and they allow the business or retailer more flexibility in taking payments.
36. See: http://guarantorloansuk.net/amigo-loans/.
37. See: www.thenpa.com/press-and-media/keyfacts.asp.
38. See: www.thenpa.com/press-and-media/keyfacts.asp.
39. The requirements are these:
    - If the amount borrowed is greater than £75 and the loan (with interest) is not repaid, the pawnbroker can sell the goods.
    - If (after 6 months) goods are not reclaimed and the amount borrowed was less than £75, the pawnbroker can sell the goods.

- If (after 6 months) goods are not reclaimed and the amount borrowed was greater than £75, the pawnbroker can sell the goods following an agreed period (without notice).
- If the value is greater than £100, the pawnbroker can sell the goods following an agreed period but must give notice to the lender.

40. From 26 April 2014, a broker must tell a prospective borrower if there are limits on the range of mortgages that the broker can recommend – for example, mortgages from particular lenders rather than from the whole mortgage market.
41. See: www.cml.org.uk/cml/media/press/3817.
42. An endowment plan is a savings plan designed to pay a lump sum after a specific period – that is, on its 'maturity'.
43. Magellan Homeloans (a trading name of Mars Capital Finance Limited) was the first subprime mortgage lender to enter the market following the 2007/2008 credit crisis, and targeted borrowers with adverse credit histories who had suffered a financially damaging 'one-off' event. See: www.magellan-homeloans.co.uk.
44. An underlying principle of sharia finance is that money cannot be generated from money.
45. The *Consumer Credit Act 1974* is available at: www.legislation.gov.uk/ukpga/1974/39/contents.
46. In Scotland, such records also include decrees, sequestration orders, Debt Arrangement Schemes, Debt Payment Programmes, and Trust Deeds.
47. A 'soft search' (also known as a 'quotation credit search') is not a full credit search. Because a soft search does not leave a note on a person's credit reference file, a soft search has no impact on a person's credit score or future creditworthiness.
48. CIFAS is a UK-based fraud prevention service, providing the UK's most comprehensive database of confirmed fraud data in the UK, together with an extensive range of fraud prevention services. For further information, see: www.cifas.org.uk.
49. Many lenders and credit providers use National Hunter (see: www.nhunter.co.uk), a data-sharing facility primarily concerned with the prevention of application fraud within the banking, finance and insurance industry. *Note:* Data is shared only between member organisations.

Part 2
Taxation

Overview

Chapter 4 explores the current framework within which taxes are assessed and collected in the UK; the current administrative system used for the collection of taxation in the UK; and the various types of income, profits and gains on which taxes are levied.

Chapter 5 explores the basic structure of UK Income Tax, and considers the alternative types of incomes and benefits in kind that are currently taxable. It also discusses the range of personal allowances now available.

Chapter 6 explores how tax is levied on small businesses, both unincorporated and incorporated.

Chapter 7 explores the scope of Capital Gains Tax and considers basic elementary calculations for individuals.

Chapter 8 explores the scope and the nature of Inheritance Tax as a wealth tax, the requirements and exemptions of current inheritance tax legislation, and how Inheritance Tax can be minimised through careful planning.

These chapters aim to provide a useful introduction to these taxes, but for full details of each tax you should consult the HMRC website.

Note: Unless otherwise stated, the rates and allowances used in this part of the book are those applicable to income and gains earned in, and/or related to, the tax year 2015/2016.

4

UK tax and the UK tax system

Learning outcomes

By the end of this chapter, you should be able to:

- describe the key characteristics of a tax system
- explain how the UK tax system is administered
- distinguish between the different types of direct and indirect taxes
- distinguish between tax evasion and tax avoidance.

4.1 Introduction

Often seen as a necessary evil, taxation is the process by which the Crown raises income to contribute to the necessary expense of government. A widely accepted and commonly used method of apportioning the cost of government among those who are assumed to enjoy its benefits, taxation is merely the price paid for civilisation.

This chapter explores:

- the current framework within which taxes are assessed and collected in the UK
- the current administrative system used for the collection of taxation in the UK
- the various types of income, profits and gains on which taxes are levied.

4.2 A brief history of taxation in the UK

The history of taxation in the UK is an archaic mosaic of confrontational monarchs, hostile feudal lords, and belligerent governments: a complex tale, littered with warring nobles, treacherous politicians, economic chaos and social upheaval.

In the UK (and especially in England) taxation was essentially designed to raise money to fund Royal expenses and the ever-growing cost of government. The main forms of taxation were land taxes (originally known as Danegeld[1]), property taxes, and to a smaller extent custom duties and food rent (a tax in kind levied on essential foodstuffs). Norman England saw the introduction of variable taxes on movable property and income and taxes on trade, together with a new revised land tax (originally known as Carucage[2]); late medieval England saw the introduction of a short-lived poll tax,[3] an export tax on wool, and a tax on wine; and Elizabethan England saw the development of a local Poor Law tax (which later became a national tax), in 1667, with Charles II introducing a coal tax in 1667 and 1670 (repealed in 1889), a revised land tax in 1692, and a window tax in 1696.

Whilst the United Kingdom of Great Britain came into being on 1 May 1707, the first *permanent* UK income tax was not introduced until 1842. Although income tax was first introduced in the UK in 1798, by William Pitt the Younger, it was abolished by Henry Addlington in 1801 but then reintroduced in 1803, allowing for taxation at the source and for the creation and introduction of five schedules[4] of taxable income. Income tax was again repealed by Chancellor of Exchequer Nicholas Vansittart in 1816; but made a surprise (and ultimately permanent) return in 1842, when it was reintroduced by Sir Robert Peel.

Whilst 19th century politicians Benjamin Disraeli and William Gladstone tried repeatedly (albeit unsuccessfully) to revise and repeal the imposition of income tax, it was the 20th and 21st centuries that saw a number of significant changes not only to UK Income Tax but to taxation generally. These included:

- the introduction of Corporation Tax in 1965, and the removal of companies from Income Tax liability
- the introduction of Capital Gains Tax in 1965,[5] to minimise the increasing avoidance of Income Tax
- the progressive deletion of the Income Tax schedules (introduced in the early 19th century) under which Income Tax was levied[6]
- the introduction of Capital Transfer Tax[7] in 1975, which was eventually replaced by Inheritance Tax in 1986
- the amendment of tax liability rules and the growing use of differential rates of Income Tax.

Note: During the 1940s the lowest rate of Income Tax was 50%. with a highest rate of Income Tax of 98%.[8] During the 1950s and 1960s the rate was progressively reduced. In 1971 the highest rate of Income Tax was reduced to 75%, and it fell to 40% in 1988. In 1997 the lowest rate of Income Tax was reduced to 23%, and to 20% in 2007. In 2010 a new higher rate of Income Tax of 50% was introduced, which was subsequently reduced to 45% from 2013.

4.3 The function and purpose of taxation

In their simplest form, taxes are merely mandatory financial payments that are determined by the Government on behalf of the Crown, these payments being justified by their benefit to society and sanctioned by law. The main functions of such taxes include:

- raising revenue for the Government
- repricing goods and services
- redistributing wealth
- reorganising the economy
- controlling and co-ordinating social behaviour.

Taxes are used by governments:

- to achieve (their) specific social and political goals
- to encourage economic growth and stability
- to discourage the use of certain products and services
- to protect and strengthen socially and economically important sectors.

4.4 The characteristics of a good tax system

A good tax system should have a number of key characteristics. For example:

- it should be equitable
- it should be balanced
- it should be universal
- it should be transparent
- it should be flexible
- it should be cost-effective.

Equitability

An equitable tax system is a tax system in which everybody pays a fair and appropriate share of taxes.

There are two important concepts of equity: horizontal equity and vertical equity. *Horizontal equity* means that taxpayers in a similar financial condition should pay a similar amount of taxes. *Vertical equity* means that wealthier taxpayers should pay at least the same proportion of income in taxes as those who are less well off.

Balance

A balanced tax system is a tax system that has not only a balanced arrangement of progressive, regressive or proportional taxes, but more importantly a combination of both direct and indirect taxes.

Universality

In a good tax system, taxes are universally applicable in the sense that persons with the same ability to pay are treated in the same way with no discrimination whatsoever.

Transparency

A tax system is transparent if information is provided about who is subject to tax, how much tax they should pay, and what benefits, exemptions, deductions and credits are available.

Flexibility

A tax system should be flexible and able to accommodate:

- the changing demands of an economy
- the changing needs of a modern government.

Cost-effectiveness

A tax system should be cost-effective and administratively efficient – the cost of collecting taxes should not exceed the revenue received from those taxes.

4.5 The UK tax system

HM Treasury

HM Treasury[9] (Her Majesty's Treasury) is a UK Government ministry responsible for:

- controlling public spending

- co-ordinating the UK's financial services policy
- ensuring sustainable economic growth
- providing strategic supervision of the UK's tax system, including the imposition and collection of taxation.

The management of the Treasury is the responsibility of the Chancellor of the Exchequer.

HM Revenue and Customs

HM Revenue and Customs[10] (also referred to as HMRC) is the UK's tax authority. It is responsible for ensuring that funds are available to finance the UK's public services and to assist couples, families and individuals with targeted financial support (for example, Tax Credits).

Replacing the Inland Revenue and Customs and Excise, HM Revenue and Customs was established by the *Commissioners for Revenue and Customs Act 2005* (CRCA 2005). Its main responsibilities include:

- the administration and collection of both direct and indirect taxes
- the administration and collection of National Insurance contributions
- the distribution of Child Benefit and some other forms of State support
- the payments of Tax Credits
- the enforcement of the national minimum wage
- the recovery of Student Loan repayments
- the administration of statutory payments (for example Statutory Sick Pay and Statutory Maternity Pay)
- the administration of anti-money laundering registrations
- the administration of the Government Banking Service.

HM Revenue and Customs consists of:

- the Commissioners for HM Revenue and Customs
- the Officers of HM Revenue and Customs.

It is HM Revenue and Customs that is responsible for:

- the assessment of tax liabilities
- the collection of taxes
- the supervision of the self-assessment system.

Note: Rules on the administration of the UK tax system are contained in the *Taxes Management Act 1970* (*TMA* 1970).

Revenue Scotland

The *Scotland Act 2012* provided the Scottish Parliament with powers to introduce devolved taxes. Revenue Scotland[11] was established as a non-ministerial government department on 1 January 2015. From 1 April 2015 Revenue Scotland became responsible for the administration and collection of devolved taxes in Scotland.

4.6 Classification of taxes

Taxes can be classified either by their nature or by their type (see Figure 4.1).

By nature

By nature, taxes can be categorised as proportional, progressive or regressive.

Proportional taxes

Proportional taxes (or level or flat taxes) are taxes that are applied at a constant rate against a taxpayer's income – the *rate* is the same, irrespective of the taxpayer's income or earnings. The UK has no proportional taxes.

Progressive taxes

Progressive taxes are taxes that are applied at a rate dependent on a taxpayer's income, with each rate being applied to a particular income band – from band to band, the larger an individual's income, the larger the percentage of tax the individual will pay. An example of a progressive tax would be Income Tax.

Regressive taxes

Regressive taxes are taxes that are applied, in effect, at a decreasing rate – the larger an individual's income, the smaller the percentage of tax the individual will pay. An example of a regressive tax would be VAT, because in practice the kinds of goods that are subject to VAT will represent a higher proportion of the spending of people who are less well off.

By type

By type, taxes can be categorised as either direct or indirect.

Direct taxes

Direct taxes are taxes that are paid directly by an individual or an organisation – the individual or organisation upon which the taxes are levied is responsible for the fulfilment of the tax payment. These are taxes levied on income or profits. Examples of direct taxes to which an individual may be subject include: Income Tax (including tax collected under Pay As You Earn, or PAYE, and under self-assessment), National Insurance, Capital Gains Tax, Inheritance Tax, and Stamp Duty Tax.

Note: If an individual owns an incorporated business, she or he would also be responsible for ensuring that any Corporation Tax due on profit made by the company is fully paid.

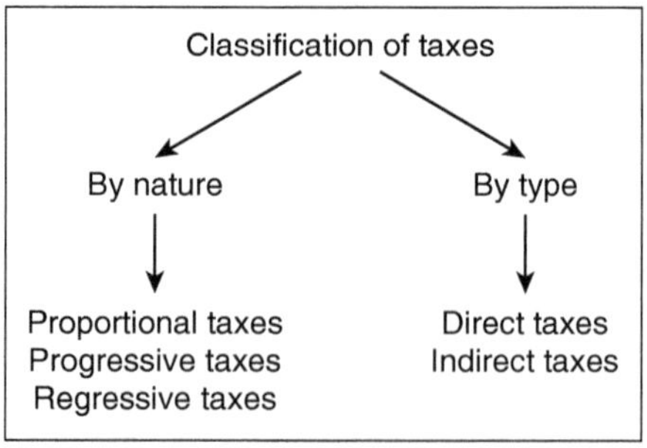

Figure 4.1 Classification of taxes

Indirect taxes

Indirect taxes are taxes that are related to consumption, expenditure, privilege or right. These are taxes levied on goods and services. Examples of indirect taxes to which an individual may be subject include: Value Added Tax (VAT), Air Passenger Duty (APD), Insurance Premium Tax, Customs Duty, Excise Duty, Tobacco and Alcohol Duty, Fuel Duty, and Vehicle Excise Duty (also known as Road Tax or Vehicle Tax).

In addition, at a local level an individual may also be subject to, or responsible for paying, Council Tax and business rates.

4.7 Different types of taxes

Income Tax

Income Tax is a tax paid on any earnings, pensions, benefits, savings or investment income, rents and fringe benefits received from an employer that exceeds an initial tax-free allowance.

> **Activity 1**
>
> During the year ending 31 March 2016, Alan was paid £27,550 a year. If his Personal Allowance for the year was £10,600 and his income was taxed at 20%, how much Income Tax would Alan pay?

Income Tax may also be payable on assets that have been gifted away but continue to be used: this is known as a Pre-Owned Asset Tax (POAT).

Note: We will consider Income Tax in more detail in Chapters 5 and 6.

National Insurance

National Insurance is paid on earnings and business profits, and payment of National Insurance entitles the payee to qualify for a range of State benefits. Class 1 National Insurance contributions are paid by employees; Class 2 and Class 4 National Insurance contributions are paid by the self-employed.

A person is required to pay National Insurance if he or she is:

- 16 years of age or older *and*
- an employee earning more than £156 a week *or*
- self-employed and making a profit of over £8,060 a year (unless exempted).

Note: We will consider National Insurance in more detail in Chapter 5.

Corporation Tax

Corporation Tax is a tax paid by companies on their taxable profits for an accounting period. It also applies to many unincorporated associations (for example, clubs, associations and co-operatives) and to foreign companies that have a UK branch or office.

Note: We will consider Corporation Tax (in relation to small businesses) in more detail in Chapter 6.

Capital Gains Tax

Capital Gains Tax is a tax paid on the profit made at the disposal of any possession or investment; or, if the assets have been gifted, on the increase in value from the date the asset was acquired (providing that the asset is not exempt).

For standard-rate taxpayers, capital gains are taxed at a standard rate of 18%. For higher-rate taxpayers – those paying Income Tax at 40% – capital gains are taxed at a higher rate of 28%.

Note: We will consider Capital Gains Tax in more detail in Chapter 7.

Inheritance Tax

Inheritance Tax is a tax paid on an estate of a particular value – more than £325,000 during 2015/2016, or up to £650,000 for a married couple or a civil partnership. Inheritance Tax may also be due on lifetime transfers, depending on the overall value of the estate.

Note: In the July 2015 Budget, the Chancellor of the Exchequer announced Government proposals to add a tapered[12] family home allowance of £175,000 per person to the existing £325,000 tax-free allowance (from April 2017). We will consider Inheritance Tax in more detail in Chapter 8.

Stamp Duty Tax

There are three types of Stamp Duty Tax: Stamp Duty, Stamp Duty Reserve Tax, and Stamp Duty Land Tax. Stamp Duty applies to paper-based transfers of shares and securities; whereas Stamp Duty Reserve Tax (SDRT) applies to electronic paperless transfers of shares and securities, which are usually actioned using an electronic system called CREST.[13] Both Stamp Duty and Stamp Duty Reserve Tax are payable by the purchaser (unless the transfer is exempt), and charged at 0.5% of the consideration value.

Stamp Duty Land Tax applies to land transactions.[14] The tax is payable by the purchaser, with the percentage charge dependent on the nature of the land (whether it is residential, non-residential, or mixed-use[15]), and the value of the land.

As at 31 August 2015, charges were as shown in Tables 4.1 and 4.2.

Table 4.1 Stamp Duty Land Tax: residential property

Rate (%)	Residential property
0	Up to £125,000
2	£125,001–£250,000
5	£250,001–£925,000
10	£925,001–£1,500,000
12	Over £1,500,001

Source: Data from https://www.gov.uk/stamp-duty-land-tax/residential-property-rates.

Table 4.2 **Stamp Duty Land Tax: non-residential property (and mixed use)**

Rate (%)	Non-residential property
0	Up to £150,000 (*if annual rent is less than £1,000*)
1	Up to £150,000 (*if annual rent is more than £1,000*)
3	£150,001–£250,000
4	£250,001–£500,000
5	Over £500,001

Source: Data from https://www.gov.uk/stamp-duty-land-tax/nonresidential-and-mixed-use-rates.

Note: Once the relevant Stamp Duty Land Tax band has been determined, the rate applies to the *whole* of the value, not just to the value within the band limit.

Value Added Tax (VAT)

Regulated by the *Value Added Tax Act 1994*, and administered by HM Revenue and Customs, VAT is a tax paid on the taxable supplies of goods[16] and services[17] made in the UK by a taxable person.[18]

Current rates of VAT

As at 31 August 2015, taxable supplies[19] were taxable at:
- a standard rate of VAT (20%) *or*
- a reduced rate of VAT (5%) *or*
- a zero rate of VAT.[20]

Note: There are some goods and services that are not subject to VAT. These include:
- insurance, finance and credit
- education and training
- fund-raising events by charities
- subscriptions to membership organisations
- the selling, leasing and letting of commercial land and buildings.

VAT registration

VAT charged on goods and services sold is known as *output tax*; VAT paid on goods and services purchased is known as *input tax*. Where the value of taxable supplies or taxable turnover (that is, goods and services sold) exceeds £81,000 in a 12-month period (or is likely to exceed £81,000 in the next 30 days), then a person *must* register for VAT with HM Revenue and Customs. A person can also register voluntarily, even though their taxable turnover is less than the registration limit. The benefit of registration is that it can allow for the recovery of any input tax paid on goods and services purchased.

Note: If a person provides only zero-rated goods, she or he may apply for exemption from VAT registration. In addition, a registered person may be eligible for voluntary deregistration if HM Revenue and Customs is satisfied that the person's taxable supplies in the following year will not exceed £79,000.

VAT returns

Although some small businesses may submit an *annual* VAT return, the vast majority of registered persons provide a VAT return every 3 months (with the VAT periods determined by HM Revenue and Customs). VAT returns are submitted online, and must be submitted within 1 month and 7 days after the end of the VAT period.

> **Activity 2**
>
> Which goods and services are not subject to VAT?

Air Passenger Duty

Air Passenger Duty[21] is a tax paid on flights from the UK, which is usually included as part of the cost of the flight. How much is paid depends on the distance travelled and the class of travel. There are currently three rates of Air Passenger Duty: reduced-rate, standard-rate, and higher-rate.

Reduced-rate Air Passenger Duty

Reduced-rate Air Passenger Duty is normally charged on the lowest class of travel.[22]

Table 4.3 Reduced-rate Air Passenger Duty

Band	Distance from London	Cost (from April 2015)	Cost (from April 2016)
A	Up to 2,000 miles	£13	£13
B	Over 2,000 miles	£71	£73

Source: Data from https://www.gov.uk/tax-on-shopping/air-passenger-duty.

Standard-rate Air Passenger Duty

Standard-rate Air Passenger Duty is charged on any other class of travel in most aircraft.

Table 4.4 Standard-rate Air Passenger Duty

Band	Distance from London	Cost (from April 2015)	Cost (from April 2016)
A	Up to 2,000 miles	£26	£26
B	Over 2,000 miles	£142	£146

Source: Data from https://www.gov.uk/tax-on-shopping/air-passenger-duty.

Higher-rate Air Passenger Duty

Higher-rate Air Passenger Duty is charged on travel in aircraft of 20 tonnes or more that are equipped to carry fewer than 19 passengers.

Table 4.5 Higher-rate Air Passenger Duty

Band	Distance from London	Cost (from April 2015)	Cost (from April 2016)
A	Up to 2,000 miles	£78	£78
B	Over 2,000 miles	£426	£438

Source: Data from https://www.gov.uk/tax-on-shopping/air-passenger-duty.

Insurance Premium Tax

Insurance Premium Tax is a tax paid on (most) insurance policy premiums, with the rate of Insurance Premium Tax depending on the type of insurance. (It is usually included as part of the cost of the insurance.)

A standard Insurance Premium Tax rate of 6% (increased to 9.5% from November 2015) is applied to most types of insurance, including car insurance, pet insurance, and home (buildings and contents) insurance. A higher Insurance Premium Tax rate of 20% is applied to travel insurance, and to insurance arranged by the supplier on vehicles (including hire vehicles), electronic goods, and other household products (including gas central heating).

Note: There is no Insurance Premium Tax on life insurance or income-protection insurance.

Tobacco and Alcohol Duty

Both Tobacco Duty and Alcohol Duty are included in the price paid for the product. However, Tobacco Duty varies depending on the type of tobacco products, and Alcohol Duty varies depending on the nature of the alcoholic beverage.

Note: VAT at 20% is charged on all tobacco and alcoholic products.

Tobacco Duty

The level of Tobacco Duty depends on whether the tobacco product is cigarettes, cigars, or another tobacco product.

Table 4.6 Tobacco Duty

Tobacco product	Rate of Tobacco Duty
Cigarettes	16.5% of the retail price + £3.79 per packet of 20
Cigars	£2.36 on a 10g cigar
Hand-rolling tobacco	£4.64 on a 25g packet
Other smoking (pipe) tobacco	£2.60 on a 25g packet
Chewing tobacco	£2.60 on a 25g packet

Source: Data from https://www.gov.uk/tax-on-shopping/alcohol-tobacco.

Beer Duty

The level of Beer Duty depends on the strength of the beer or its 'alcohol by volume' (ABV).

Table 4.7 Beer Duty

Beer strength (ABV)	Beer Duty per litre for each % of alcohol
More than 1.2% but less than 2.8%	8.10p
More than 2.8% but less than 7.5%	18.37p
More than 7.5%	23.85p

Source: Data from https://www.gov.uk/tax-on-shopping/alcohol-tobacco.

Cider Duty

The level of Cider Duty depends on the nature of the cider and the strength of the cider.

Table 4.8 Cider Duty

Type of cider	Strength (ABV)	Cider Duty per litre
Still	More than 1.2% but less than 7.5%	38.87p
Still	More than 7.5% but less than 8.5%	58.75p
Sparkling	More than 1.2% but less than 5.5%	38.87p
Sparkling	More than 5.5% but less than 8.5%	264.61p

Source: Data from https://www.gov.uk/tax-on-shopping/alcohol-tobacco.

Wine Duty

As with Cider Duty (above), Wine Duty depends on the nature of the wine and the strength of the wine.

Table 4.9 Wine Duty

Type of wine	Strength (ABV)	Wine Duty per litre
Still	More than 1.2% but less than 4%	84.21p
Still	More than 4% but less than 5.5%	115.80p
Still	More than 5.5% but less than 15%	273.31p
Still	More than 15% but less than 22%	364.37p
Sparkling	More than 5.5% but less than 8.5%	264.61p
Sparkling	More than 8.5% but less than 15%	350.07p

Source: Data from https://www.gov.uk/tax-on-shopping/alcohol-tobacco.

Note: Duty for wine with an ABV greater than 22% is the same as for spirits.

Spirit Duty

Spirit Duty is £27.66 per litre of pure (100%) alcohol. The duty is included in the price paid for the spirit (https://www.gov.uk/tax-on-shopping/alcohol-tobacco).

Fuel Duty

Fuel Duty is a tax paid on petrol, diesel and other fuels used in vehicles or for heating. The duty is included in the price paid for the fuel.

Note: VAT at 20% is *also* charged on petrol, diesel and other fuels. VAT at 5% is charged on domestic heating fuel.

The rate of Fuel Duty depends on the type of fuel, as follows:

Table 4.10 Fuel Duty

Type of fuel	Rate of Fuel Duty
Petrol, diesel, biodiesel and bioethanol	57.95p
Liquefied petroleum gas (LPG)	31.61p
Natural gas used as fuel in vehicles	24.70p
Fuel oil used for heating (or burned in a furnace)	10.70p

Source: Data from https://www.gov.uk/tax-on-shopping/fuel-duty.

Customs Duty

Customs Duty is a tax paid on goods that are transported across international borders (but not within the EU). It is charged on gifts and other goods sent from outside the EU, as follows:

Table 4.11 Customs Duty

Type and value of goods	Customs Duty
Anything under £135	No charge
Gifts worth £135 to £630	2.5% (but reduced for some goods)
Gifts above £630 and other goods above £135	Rate depends on the type of goods and their country of origin

Source: Data from https://www.gov.uk/goods-sent-from-abroad/tax-and-duty.

For Custom Duty, the value includes the price paid for the goods, and any postage, packaging and insurance costs.

Note: VAT is also payable on goods sent from non-European Union countries and European Union special territories (for example, the Canary Islands) if they are:
- gifts worth more than £36
- other goods worth more than £15
- alcohol, tobacco products and fragrances of any value.

Excise Duty

If alcohol or tobacco products are received from outside the European Union, Excise Duty is charged at current rates (as above).

Vehicle Excise Duty

Vehicle Excise Duty is an excise duty which must be paid for most types of vehicles used (or parked) on UK public roads. It is collected and enforced by the Driver and Vehicle Licensing Agency (DVLA).[23]

For cars registered before 1 March 2001, the Vehicle Excise Duty is based on engine size For vehicles registered on or after 1 March 2001, the Vehicle Excise Duty is based on theoretical carbon dioxide (CO_2) emission rates per kilometre. (See: https://www.gov.uk/vehicle-tax-rate-tables/rates-for-cars-and-light-goods-vehicles-registered-before-1-march-2001 and https://www.gov.uk/vehicle-tax-rate-tables/rates-for-cars-registered-on-or-after-1-march-2001.)

From 1 April 2017, however, new Vehicle Excise Duty (VED) bands will be introduced:

- a zero rate (for vehicles emitting zero CO_2)
- a standard rate (£140 p.a.)
- a premium rate (for vehicles costing more than £40,000).

Note: The new rates will not apply in the first year after registration. There will be special first-year rates linked to the vehicle's CO_2 emissions.

Council Tax

Council Tax is a property-based tax which contributes to financing local services such as policing, fire services, support services for the elderly, parks and recreation services (including libraries), refuse disposal, street cleaning and street lighting. Council Tax was introduced in 1993, replacing the socially (and politically) controversial Community Charge (or 'Poll Tax' as it was more commonly called). Council Tax is payable for individual properties and dwellings and is the responsibility of owner-occupiers or (for rented accommodation) tenants.

How much Council Tax is payable

The amount of Council Tax payable depends on how much money the local authority needs to raise, and the Council Tax band in which the property or dwelling appears.

As at 31 August 2015, Council Tax bands were:

Table 4.12 Council Tax bands

Council Tax valuation band	Ranges of value
A	Up to £40,000
B	More than £40,000 and up to £52,000
C	More than £52,000 and up to £68,000
D	More than £68,000 and up to £88,000
E	More than £88,000 and up to £120,000
F	More than £120,000 and up to £160,000
G	More than £160,000 and up to £320,000
H	More than £320,000

Source: Data from http://manuals.voa.gov.uk/corporate/publications/Manuals/CouncilTaxManual/council_tax_man_s1/b-ct-man-sect1-pt1.html.

Properties exempt from Council Tax

Properties currently exempt from Council Tax include:

- properties that are occupied entirely by full-time students

- properties that are occupied by people under the age of 18 only
- Armed Forces accommodation
- properties that are unoccupied and undergoing major repair work[24]
- properties that are unoccupied and part of the estate of someone who has died[25]
- unoccupied and repossessed property.

Business rates

Business rates are charged on most non-domestic properties. Such properties include shops, offices, public houses, warehouses, factories, and holiday rental homes and guest houses. They may also be payable if part of a building is used for non-domestic purposes.

Business rates payable are calculated by multiplying the rateable value of your property (which is determined by the Valuation Office Agency[26]), and the business rates multiplier (which is determined by central government).

Exemptions from business rates

The following properties are exempt from business rates:
- farm buildings and land[27]
- fish farms
- places of public religious worship
- buildings used for the training or welfare of disabled people.

4.8 Tax allowances and tax-free income

Tax allowances are allowances that reduce the amount of tax a person has to pay. There are two types of allowances:
- allowances that give full relief
- allowances that give restricted (partial) relief.

Table 4.13 shows a summary of tax allowances for 2015/2016.

Table 4.13 Tax allowances

Type of allowance	Allowance (2015/2016)
Personal Allowance[28] (*born after 6 April 1948*)	£10,600
Income limit for Personal Allowance (*born after 6 April 1948*)	£100,000
Age-related Personal Allowance (*born before between 6 April 1938 and 6 April 1948*)	£10,600
Age-related Personal Allowance (*born before 6 April 1938*)	£10,660
Income limit above which you start to lose age-related allowance (*born before 6 April 1948*)	£27,700

(Continued)

Table 4.13 (Continued)

Married Couple's Allowance (*born after 6 April 1935*)	£8,355
Married Couple's Allowance (*born before 6 April 1935 only*)	£3,220
Blind Person's Allowance	£2,290
Transferrable Tax Allowance (*for married couples and civil partners*)	£1,060
Capital Gains Tax (annual) threshold	£11,100
Inheritance Tax threshold	£325,000

Source: Data from www.gov.uk/government/publications/tax-and-tax-credit-rates-and-thresholds-for-2015-16/tax-and-tax-credit-rates-and-thresholds-for-2015-16.

Note: In the March 2015 Budget, the Chancellor of the Exchequer announced Government proposals to introduce a new Personal Savings Allowance of £1,000 (or £500 for higher-rate taxpayers) from April 2016.

4.9 Tax rates

Table 4.14 shows a summary of tax rates and Income Tax bands for 2015/2016.

Table 4.14 Tax rates and Income Tax bands

Type	Tax rate for (2015/2016)
Basic-rate Income Tax	20%
Higher-rate Income Tax	40%
Additional-rate Income Tax	45%
Dividend: ordinary rate	10%
Dividend: upper rate	32.5%
Dividend: additional rate	37.5%
Trust rate	45%
Basic-rate band	£0 to £31,785 (after allowances)
Higher-rate band[29]	Over £31,785
Additional-rate band	Over £150,000
Starting rate limit (*for savings income*)	£5,000
Capital Gains Tax (*for gains over a threshold of £11,100*)	18% or 28%
Inheritance Tax (*for transfers over a threshold £325,000*)	40%

Source: Data from www.gov.uk/government/publications/tax-and-tax-credit-rates-and-thresholds-for-2015-16/tax-and-tax-credit-rates-and-thresholds-for-2015-16.

Income Tax

Classification of income

The amount of Income Tax payable on income depends on the *type* of income. For Income Tax purposes, there is a range of different types of taxable income, including:
- income from employment
- income from pensions
- profits from trades, professions and vocations
- profits from properties
- income from a trust
- income from (some) social or welfare benefits
- income from savings and investments (which includes interest and dividends)
- other miscellaneous income.

Note: In Chapters 5 and 6 we will consider the Income Tax treatment of these alternative types of income in more detail.

National Insurance

The amount of National Insurance contributions payable depends on three factors:
- the class of National Insurance payable
- the level of income (if employed) or profit (if self-employed)
- the nature of the employment (employed or self-employed).

Table 4.15 National Insurance classes and rates

Type	Cost
Class 1 (Employed contracted in)	
Employer	
£0.01 to £156.00 earnings per week	0%
£156.01 to £815.00 earnings per week	13.8%
Over £815.00 earnings per week	13.8%
Employee	
£0.01 to £156.00 earnings per week	0%
£156.01 to £815.00 earnings per week	12%
Over £815.00 earnings per week	2%
Classes 1A and 1B (Employers only)	13.8%
Class 2 (Self-employed)	£2.80 per week
Small earnings exemption	£5,965
Class 3 (Voluntary)	£14.10 per week
Class 4 (Self-employed)	
Profits up to £8,060 p.a.	0%
Profits from £8,060 to £42,385 p.a.	9%
Profits above £42,385 p.a.	2%

Source: Data from www.gov.uk/government/publications/tax-and-tax-credit-rates-and-thresholds-for-2015-16/tax-and-tax-credit-rates-and-thresholds-for-2015-16.

Note: The life of Class 2 National Insurance may be limited – in the March 2015 Budget, the Chancellor of the Exchequer announced Government proposals to abolish Class 2 National Insurance during the next Parliament[30] (that is, the one that began in May 2015).

Corporation Tax

For 2015/2016, the rate of Corporation Tax is 20% for all companies. (See: https://www.gov.uk/corporation-tax-rates/rates.)

Note: In the July 2015 Budget the Chancellor of the Exchequer announced that for 2017/2018 the rate of Corporation Tax would be 19% for all companies, and that by 2020 the rate of Corporation Tax would be reduced to 18% for all companies.

Capital Gains Tax

For 2015/2016, Capital Gains Tax is only payable on gains above the annual exemption threshold of £11,100. For trusts, the annual exemption threshold is £5,550. (See: https://www.gov.uk/capital-gains-tax/allowances.)

The current rate of Capital Gains Tax is either 18% or 28% (depending on the chargeable person's taxable income).

Inheritance Tax

Inheritance Tax only applies to non-exempt transfers that total more than £325,000. The rate of Inheritance Tax is 40% on any transfers above the threshold of £325,000, although the rate of Inheritance Tax may be reduced to 36% if 10% or more of an estate is left to a charity. (See: https://www.gov.uk/inheritance-tax.)

Additional exemptions include:

- annual gifts: £3,000
- small gifts: £250
- gifts on marriage by a parent: £5,000
- gifts on marriage by a grandparent or other relative: £2,500
- gifts on marriage by any other: £1,000.

Note: Some lifetime gifts are taxed at 20%.

4.10 Collection of taxes

Taxes are collected on behalf of the government by HM Revenue and Customs. Income Tax and National Insurance contributions are commonly collected at source, using the PAYE (Pay As You Earn) scheme. An alternative, for taxes not collected using the PAYE scheme, is payment after self-assessment.

Pay As You Earn (PAYE)

If a person works for an employer (full-time or part-time), receives an employment-based pension, or receives a personal pension, any Income Tax and any National Insurance contributions payable are normally collected using the PAYE scheme.

How PAYE works

The PAYE scheme is a method of deducting Income Tax and National Insurance contributions from wages or salaries,[31] or from occupational or personal pension payments before they are paid to the employee or pension recipient. That is, the employee or pension recipient receives the payment net of Income Tax and National Insurance contributions. Deductions are made from each weekly or monthly payment. The amount of deductions depends on the employee's or pension recipient's tax code.

Note: The employer or pension provider is responsible for ensuring that any Income Tax or National Insurance deductions are paid to HM Revenue and Customs.

Details of any Income Tax or National Insurance deductions will be provided on the employee's or pension recipient's payslip (if she or he receives one). At the end of the tax year, all employees and pension recipients receive a P60, a statement that details the total amounts of pay or pension received, and the Income Tax or National Insurance deductions made during the previous (recently ended) tax year.

Note: A tax year is from 6 April to 5 April in the following year, so the tax year for 2015/2016, for example, is from 6 April 2015 to 5 April 2016.

The PAYE scheme can also be used to collect:

- Income Tax payable on other taxable income (for example, investment interest or rental income)
- Income Tax due on State retirement pension payments (for those in receipt of an occupational pension)
- money owed to HM Revenue and Customs (for example, overpaid tax credits, tax debts from previous tax years, and unpaid or underpaid National Insurance contributions).

PAYE and personal tax codes

Personal tax codes are determined by HM Revenue and Customs, and are used by employers and pension providers to calculate how much Income Tax should be deducted from any payment of wages, salaries or pensions.

Personal tax code information is available on:

- any payslips received from the employer or pension provider
- the P45 received from an employer at the end of an employment contract
- the P60 received from an employer at the end of the tax year
- a PAYE coding notice received from HM Revenue and Customs.

A personal tax code has two components:

- a number, which refers to how much income can be earned before Income Tax is payable
- a letter (or sometimes two letters), which refers to how much Income Tax should be deducted from any payment of wages, salary or pension.

Personal tax codes usually change each tax year: this is because of changes to the annual Personal Allowance, and also changes to income and benefits received.

The number in a tax code

The number in a tax code informs an employer or a pension provider how much tax-free income a person can receive in a given tax year, and is calculated as follows. First, any income or benefits received (for example, untaxed interest, or company car benefit) are added up. This value of income and benefits received is then deducted from the tax-free Personal Allowance. The remaining amount is the amount of income that is tax-free in that the tax year.

This amount, divided by 10, becomes the numerical component of a person's tax code.

Activity 3

During 2014/2015, Bryan Myers received untaxed income of £3,890 and company benefits amounting to £1,860. The tax-free Personal Allowance for 2015/2016 is £10,600. What would the numerical component of his personal tax code be for 2015/2016?

The letter in a tax code

The letter or letters in a tax code help an employer or a pension provider to calculate how much Income Tax should be deducted from any wages, salaries or pension. The letters are as shown in Table 4.16.

Table 4.16 Tax code letters

Tax code letter	Meaning
L	You are entitled to the basic tax-free Personal Allowance.
P	You were born between 6 April 1938 and 5 April 1948 and are entitled to a larger full tax-free Personal Allowance.
Y	You were born before 6 April 1938 and are entitled to a larger full tax-free Personal Allowance.
T	Your tax code includes other calculations.
0T	Your Personal Allowance has been used up.[32]
BR	All your income from this employment or pension is taxed at the 20% basic rate.
D0	All your income is taxed at the 40% higher rate.
D1	All your income is taxed at the 45% additional rate.
NT	You are not paying any tax on this income.
K	You have untaxed income or benefits that exceed your Personal Allowance.

Source: Data from https://www.gov.uk/tax-codes/letters-in-your-tax-code-what-they-mean.

Note: A personal tax code with a suffix 'W1' (meaning 'Week 1') or 'M1' (meaning 'Month 1') is an emergency code (sometimes referred to as a non-cumulative code), and means that any Income Tax deduction is based on what has been paid in the current pay period rather than the whole year.

Self-assessment

Self-assessment entails providing the necessary information about yourself to permit the calculation of taxable income and gains (after any allowances or reliefs) and Income Tax and Capital Gains Tax (after allowing for tax deducted at source and tax credits on dividends). If you make your return online, the calculation is done for you. If you make the return on paper before 30 September, the calculation is also done for you; but after that date you must calculate the outstanding tax yourself.

A taxpayer is required to complete a self-assessment tax return if in the previous tax year she or he:

- was self-employed, a business partner, a director[33] or a trustee
- received income over £100,000
- had work expenses of £2,500 or more
- received more than £2,000 in untaxed income
- received income over £50,000 and also received Child Benefit (or has a partner who did)
- received more than £10,000 in savings or investment income (before tax)
- has taxable foreign income *and/or*
- made gains on the disposal of chargeable assets and needs to pay Capital Gains Tax.

(See: www.gov.uk/self-assessment-tax-returns/who-must-send-a-tax-return.)

Activity 4

Which taxpayers are required to complete a self-assessment tax return?

Keeping records

All self-assessment taxpayers must retain records to enable them to provide and submit an accurate and correct tax return.[34] However there are no specific rules or requirements about how such records should be maintained.

Note: HM Revenue and Customs can impose a penalty if records are not usable, are inaccurate, or are incomplete.

Records must be maintained as follows:

- for tax returns submitted before the deadline: records must be kept for at least 22 months after the end of the tax year to which the tax return relates
- for tax returns submitted after the deadline: records must be kept for at least 15 months after the tax return was submitted.

So what records or documents should be maintained?

Income from employment For income from employment, documents should include:

- form P45 (if employment was terminated during the tax year)
- form P60 (showing income and tax for the tax year)
- form P11D (for expenses and benefits)
- information about any redundancy or termination payment.

In addition, documents should be kept that record:

- any tips received, any employment benefits (for example, meal vouchers), and any lump-sum payments not included on your P60 or P45 (for example, incentive payments or 'golden hellos')

- any legitimate (tax-deductible) expenses (for example, tools of trade, work-related travel costs, and costs of specialist clothing for work)
- any benefits claimed and received (for example, Social Security Benefits, Statutory Sick Pay, Statutory Maternity, Paternity or Adoption Pay, and Jobseeker's Allowance).

Income from employee share schemes or share-related benefits The following documents or records should be retained:
- share-option certificates and exercise notices
- details of any changes to share options and share-related benefits
- details related to any payments made for the shares
- details of any benefits received as an employee shareholder.

Savings, investments, and pensions The following documents or records should be retained:
- bank or building society statements and passbooks
- statements of interest or income from savings and investments
- tax deduction certificates
- dividend vouchers (from UK companies)
- unit trust tax vouchers
- profits made from life insurance policies
- details of any trust income
- details of any 'unusual' income received (for example, an inheritance).

Pension information The following documents or records should be retained:
- form P160 (which details when the pension commenced)
- form P60 (annual pension)
- details of any tax deduction.

Rental income The following documents or records should be retained:
- details of the dates when the property was let
- details of all rent received
- details of any income from other services provided for tenants (for example, repairs and maintenance)
- rent books, receipts, invoices and bank statements
- details of (tax-deductible) expenses related to the property (for example, paid-for services such as cleaning or gardening).

Overseas income The following documents or records should be retained:
- evidence of earned overseas income (for example, payslips, bank statements, and payment confirmations
- receipts for any relevant (tax-deductible) overseas expenses
- dividend certificates from overseas companies
- details (proof) of the taxes already paid.

Activity 5

For self-assessment taxpayers, how long must records be kept?

Submitting a self-assessment tax return

Once a person has registered, she or he may submit a self-assessment tax return using HM Revenue and Customs' self-assessment online service, or may still use a traditional paper submission.

Self-assessment deadlines The deadlines for submitting a self-assessment tax return to HM Revenue and Customs and paying any money owed are as shown in Table 4.17.

Table 4.17 Self-assessment deadlines (for 2015/2016)

Self-assessment	Date
Registration	5 October 2016
Submission of paper tax return	31 October 2016
Submission of online tax return	31 January 2017
Payment of Income Tax owed:	
– 1st payment on account	31 January 2016
– 2nd payment on account	31 July 2016
– Final payment	31 January 2017

Source: Data from https://www.gov.uk/self-assessment-tax-returns/deadlines.

If the amount of tax due is less than £3,000, HM Revenue and Customs can (if the taxpayer is eligible) collect the tax through the PAYE scheme; however the online return must be submitted by 30 December following the end of the tax year.

Note: Capital Gains Tax is usually due on 31 January following the end of the tax year – for example, for 2015/2016 it would be due on 31 January 2017.

Penalties for non-submission

For 2015/2016, for example, the penalties stipulated are as follows:

- if a tax return is not filed by its due date, a late filing penalty of £100 is charged
- if a tax return is not filed 3 months after its due date, daily penalties are charged at £10 per day, up to a maximum of 90 days[35]
- if a tax return is not filed 6 months after its due date, a late filing penalty is charged: the penalty is the greater of £300 or 5% of the amount of the tax due
- if a tax return is not filed 12 months after its due date, a late filing penalty is charged: the penalty is the greater of £300 or 5% of the amount of the tax due.

(See: https://online.hmrc.gov.uk/information/help?helpcategory=selfAssessment&helpid=penaltiesHelp.)

Penalties for non-payment

For 2015/2016, for example, the penalties stipulated are as follows (ibid.):

- a first late-payment penalty is imposed where a liability is outstanding for more than 30 days: this penalty is 5% of the amount that was outstanding 30 days after it was due

- a second late-payment penalty is imposed where a liability is outstanding more than 30 days plus 5 months after its due date: this penalty is 5% of the amount that was outstanding 30 days plus 5 months after it was due
- a third-late payment penalty is imposed where a liability is outstanding more than 30 days plus 11 months after its due date: this penalty is 5% of the amount that was outstanding 30 days plus 11 months after it was due.

Amending a self-assessment tax return

Corrections can be made to a self-assessment tax return for up to 12 months after the original submission date. Once the corrections have been submitted (and approved), HM Revenue and Customs will update the taxpayer's account, and:

- issue a refund for any overpaid taxes, with interest[36] (refunds can be paid electronically into a bank account; paid by cheque; or deducted from the taxpayer's next self-assessment tax bill, if it is a small amount) *or*
- issue a revised account for any additional tax, including interest, that is now due (detailing how the outstanding tax can be paid, and the deadline for the payment).

Note: In the March 2015 Budget, the Chancellor of the Exchequer announced Government proposals to abolish the self-assessment annual return – a welcome proposal that would, if delivered, ease the self-assessment burden on many millions of individuals and small businesses.

4.11 Tax avoidance and tax evasion

What is tax avoidance?

Tax avoidance is the conscious organisation of one's personal financial affairs to minimise a possible tax liability. Whilst HM Revenue and Customs has described tax avoidance as bending the rules of the tax system to gain a tax advantage that the government never intended,[37] this is in essence a lawful practice. It is simply the use of legal means to pay the least amount of tax possible, and is a practice that can perhaps be traced as far back as the late 17th century, when house owners bricked up windows to minimise the levy of the Window Tax.[38]

Note: Tax avoidance involving the use of 'legitimate' but nonetheless manufactured artificial transactions – transactions designed for no other purpose other than to obtain a tax advantage and to reduce a tax liability – is often referred to as 'aggressive tax avoidance' and has been the subject of some high-profile media stories[39] and HM Revenue and Customs decisions.

Signs of tax avoidance

Whilst there are some tax avoidance schemes that are openly sponsored by the Government – for example, the use of ISAs to eliminate Income Tax liability on savings interest – any scheme that relies on 'concealment, pretence, non-disclosure or misrepresentation of the facts' (HM Revenue and Customs 2014: 2) to reduce or to eliminate a tax liability could constitute aggressive tax avoidance. If proven (following investigation and if necessary tribunal hearing), such a scheme could result in serious sanctions ranging from possible financial penalties to prosecution or imprisonment, or both.

In March 2014 HM Revenue and Customs published guidelines,[40] identifying the following as possible signs of tax avoidance:
- the scheme promises to eliminate a tax liability at little or no cost
- the scheme tax benefits are out of proportion to any 'real' economic activity, expense or investment risk
- the scheme involves overly complex, artificial or contrived business or financial arrangements
- the scheme involves money going around in a circle, back to where it originated
- the scheme involves the use of offshore companies or trusts for little or no sound commercial reason
- the scheme involves the use of a tax haven or banking secrecy
- the scheme contains exit arrangements designed to circumvent tax consequences
- the scheme agreement contains secrecy or confidentiality clauses
- the scheme requires the payment of upfront fees
- the scheme is a 'no win, no fee' arrangement.

What is tax evasion?

Tax evasion is the illegal non-payment or under-payment of tax, including the dishonest claiming of tax allowances. It includes, for example:
- the fraudulent evasion of Income Tax
- the fraudulent evasion of VAT
- the falsification of information
- the evasion of Excise Duty
- cheating the Public Revenue.

Tax evasion (or tax-based fraud) is investigated by HM Customs and Revenue or by the Economic Crime Command (ECC) of the UK National Crime Agency (NCA), or both.

Fraudulent evasion of Income Tax

Following the *Taxes Management Act 1970*, it is a criminal offence knowingly, dishonestly and fraudulently to evade a declaration or payment of Income Tax to HM Revenue and Customs.

On conviction in a Crown Court, the maximum penalty for the fraudulent evasion of Income Tax is 7 years' imprisonment or an unlimited fine, or both. On summary conviction in a Magistrates' Court, the maximum penalty is 6 months' imprisonment or a financial penalty not exceeding £5,000, or both.

Fraudulent evasion of VAT

Value Added Tax (VAT) is charged on:
- the supply of most goods and services
- the acquisition of goods from countries in the European Union (EU)
- the importation of goods from countries outside the EU.

Businesses (individuals, partnerships, and companies) who supply goods and services are required to be registered with the HMRC for VAT purposes if their annual turnover exceeds the prescribed limit.[41] Criminal liability arises if a person:
- knowingly commits fraudulent evasion (for example, by deliberately failing to submit a tax return) *or*

- purposefully takes steps to evade liability (for example, by failing to register for VAT) *or*
- knowingly acquires possession of goods or accepts the supply of services on which VAT has been or will be evaded *or*
- purposefully provides false or inaccurate information with intent to deceive (for example, reducing sales income or increasing purchase costs).

On conviction in a Crown Court, the maximum penalty for the VAT evasion is 7 years' imprisonment or an unlimited fine, or both. On summary conviction in a Magistrates' Court, the maximum penalty is 6 months' imprisonment or a financial penalty not exceeding three times the amount of VAT owed.[42]

Falsification of information

Following the *Customs and Excise Management Act 1979*, it is a criminal offence knowingly and recklessly to make a false declaration to HM Revenue and Customs (including the counterfeiting of documents).

On conviction in a Crown Court, the maximum penalty is 2 years' imprisonment or an unlimited fine, or both. On summary conviction in a Magistrates' Court, the maximum penalty is 6 months' imprisonment or a financial penalty, or both.

Evasion of Excise Duty

The evasion of duty involves the deliberate avoidance of Excise Duty, and/or being knowingly concerned in the deliberate non-payment of Customs Duty on the importation of goods (see *Customs and Excise Management Act 1979*, s.170)

The maximum penalty – on conviction in the Crown Court is an unlimited fine or a term of imprisonment not exceeding seven years or both. On summary conviction in a Magistrates' Court, the maximum penalty is a fine which can range from £2,500 to over £500,000, depending on the nature of the offence.[43]

Cheating the Public Revenue

Cheating the Public Revenue is illegal (contrary to common law). Examples include:

- VAT carousel fraud
- missing trader intra-community fraud (MTIC fraud), within the EU
- Income Tax fraud (for example, failing to deduct Income Tax from payments made to employees).

The offence of 'cheating the Public Revenue' can only be tried in a Crown Court, and whilst there are no minimum or maximum sentencing requirements, factors that can aggravate the offence and increase the sentence include the level of fnancial consideration involved, the profits generated, the period of offending, and the impact of the offending on other ('third') parties.

Activity 6

What are the main types of tax evasion?

Consequences of tax evasion

Civil investigation of fraud Wherever appropriate, HM Revenue and Customs use civil fraud investigation procedures under Code of Practice 9 (COP9)[44] to investigate tax evasion.[45]

Criminal investigations are generally reserved for cases where the conduct of those involved is such that only a criminal sanction is appropriate, although HM Revenue and Customs can if necessary:

- conduct a criminal investigation in any case
- carry out these investigations across a range of offences.

A Code of Practice 9 challenge is normally issued with a Contractual Disclosure Facility (CDF), whereby the taxpayer is invited to make a full disclosure of all irregularities in return for a civil settlement including a financial penalty and a guarantee of no prosecution for the irregularities disclosed.

Once a challenge has been received, a taxpayer has 60 days either to admit or deny the fraud.

Criminal prosecutions for tax offences Following investigations by HM Revenue and Customs, the Crown Prosecution Service (CPS) is responsible for prosecuting tax evasion or tax-based fraud, with criminal prosecutions generally reserved for only the most serious cases. Examples of such cases would be ones where:

- organised crime is suspected to be involved
- the individual or organisation suspected of tax fraud is held in a position of trust
- individuals or organisations have provided materially false statements during a civil investigation
- there has been deliberate concealment of material facts
- deception, conspiracy or corruption is suspected
- there have been repeated offences or instances of unlawful conduct, or both.

Tax appeals

Where there is a dispute between a taxpayer and HM Revenue and Customs, the dispute or disagreement can be resolved by either an internal review or by a tribunal hearing (see Figure 4.2).

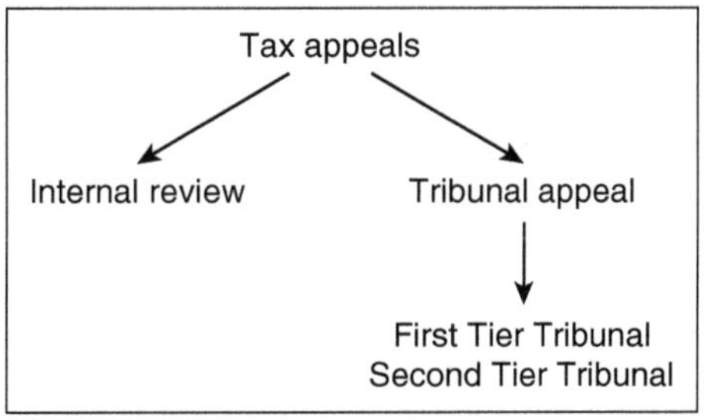

Figure 4.2 Tax appeals

Internal reviews

An internal review is a review undertaken by an officer from HM Revenue and Customs who is unconnected with the case or assessment under dispute. This is an informal and cost-effective method of resolving assessment disputes.

A taxpayer must either accept the conclusions and recommendations of the internal review or appeal to a tribunal. Any appeal can be made only once any internal review has been completed, and must be made within 30 days of the review being completed.

Tribunal hearings

Without an internal review, or if the taxpayer disagrees with the findings of an internal review, the taxpayer can appeal to a tax tribunal. Such appeals are heard either by a First Tier Tribunal or by a Second Tier Tribunal.

First Tier Tribunal

A person can appeal to a First Tier Tribunal if she or he wants to challenge a decision made by HM Revenue and Customs. A First Tier Tribunal would normally hear:
- cases that are simple: for example, cases involving fixed filing penalties
- cases that are straightforward: for example, cases that involve a limited exchange of documentary evidence
- cases that require only minimal case management: for example, cases that can be dealt with in writing and without a hearing.

A decision of a First Tier Tribunal can be appealed to the Second Tier Tribunal.

Second Tier Tribunal

The Second Tier Tribunal would generally only consider cases that:
- require lengthy formal hearings
- involve the presentation of complex evidence
- require the consideration of important principles of law *and/or*
- involve substantial amounts of money.

A decision of the Second Tier Tribunal is binding on tribunals and other affected authorities and can only be appealed to the Court of Appeal.

4.12 Concluding comments

With its ever-changing compendium of benefits, allowances, reliefs and exemptions, the UK tax system is a complex collection of rules and regulations that has evolved over many centuries. A constantly shifting landscape of both direct and indirect taxes, it remains universally feared and loathed in equal measure.

4.13 Suggested further reading

For a brief history of taxation in the UK, see:
- http://webarchive.nationalarchives.gov.uk/
- http://www.hmrc.gov.uk/education-zone/secondary-history.htm
- http://www.parliament.uk/about/living-heritage/transformingsociety/private-lives/taxation/

Key points

- HM Revenue and Customs (also referred to as HMRC) is the UK's tax authority. It is responsible for ensuring that funds are available to finance the UK's public services.
- Taxes can be classified by either their nature or by their type. By nature, taxes can be categorised as proportional, progressive or regressive. By type, taxes can be categorised as direct or indirect.
- Direct taxes include: Income Tax (including tax collected under Pay As You Earn or self-assessment), National Insurance, Capital Gains Tax, Inheritance Tax, and Stamp Duty Tax.
- Indirect taxes include: Value Added Tax, Air Passenger Duty, Insurance Premium Tax, Customs Duty, Excise Duty, Tobacco and Alcohol Duty, and Fuel Duty.
- Taxes are commonly collected using either the PAYE (Pay As You Earn) scheme or by self-assessment.
- Tax avoidance is the conscious organisation of one's personal financial affairs to minimise a possible tax liability.
- Tax evasion is the illegal non-payment or under-payment of tax, including the dishonest claiming of tax allowances.

Self-review questions

1. Distinguish between *direct taxes* and *indirect taxes*, providing examples of each.
2. What are the main responsibilities of HM Revenue and Customs?
3. Briefly describe the characteristics of a good tax system.
4. Distinguish between *tax evasion* and *tax avoidance.*
5. Who would normally be required to complete a self-assessment Income Tax return?

Case study discussion questions

1. Briefly explain to Claire Carter the possible implications of not using the PAYE scheme for the payment of wages and salaries.
2. Advise Claire Carter of the current requirements for VAT registration, and the consequences of not registering 'Image 20' for VAT purposes.

Suggested answers to chapter activities

Activity 1

Alan would pay the following Income Tax for the year ending 31 March 2016:

$$(£27{,}550 - £10{,}600) * 20\% = £3{,}390.$$

Activity 2

Goods and services that are not subject to VAT include goods and services-related insurance, finance and credit, education and training, fund-raising events by charities, subscriptions to membership organisations, and selling, leasing and letting of commercial land and buildings.

Activity 3

Bryan Myers' tax-free entitlement would be:

$$£10{,}600 - (£3{,}890 + £1{,}860) = £4{,}850.$$

His tax code (number) would therefore be:

$$4{,}850/10 = 485.$$

Activity 4

A taxpayer is required to complete a self-assessment tax return if in the previous tax year she or he:

- was self-employed, a business partner, a director[46] or a trustee
- received income over £100,000
- had work expenses of £2,500 or more
- received more than £2,000 in untaxed income
- received income over £50,000 and also received Child Benefit (or has a partner who did)
- received more than £10,000 in savings or investment income (before tax)
- has taxable foreign income *and/or*
- made gains on the disposal of chargeable assets and needs to pay Capital Gains Tax.

Activity 5

For HM Revenue and Customs purposes, records must be maintained as follows:

- for tax returns submitted before the deadline: records must be kept for at least 22 months after the end of the tax year to which the tax return relates
- for tax returns submitted after the deadline: records must be kept for at least 15 months after the tax return was submitted.

Activity 6

The main types of tax evasion are:

- the fraudulent evasion of Income Tax
- the fraudulent evasion of VAT
- the falsification of information
- the evasion of Excise Duty
- cheating the Public Revenue.

Notes

1. Danegeld was originally a tax levied as a tribute to buy off the Danes (the Viking raiders), but eventually became a permanent land tax.
2. Carucage was an English land tax introduced by King Richard I in 1194, based on the size of the estate owned by the taxpayer.
3. A flat-rate poll tax was introduced in 1377, and a graduated poll tax was introduced in 1379. The inequity and unpopularity of these poll taxes contributed to the Peasants' Revolt in 1381.
4. See: https://en.wikipedia.org/wiki/History_of_taxation_in_the_United_Kingdom.
   These schedules were: schedule A (tax on income from UK land), schedule B (tax on commercial occupation of land), schedule C (tax on income from public securities), schedule D (tax on trading income, income from professions and vocations, interest, overseas income and casual income), and schedule E (tax on employment income). A further schedule, schedule F (tax on UK dividend income), was added later.
5. Capital Gains Tax was introduced by the Labour Chancellor of the Exchequer, James Callaghan, to prevent people avoiding Income Tax by switching their earnings from income into capital.

6. Schedule B was abolished in 1988, schedule C was abolished in 1996, and schedule E was abolished in 2003. For Income Tax purposes, the remaining schedules (schedule A, schedule D, and schedule F) were superseded by the *Income Tax (Trading and Other Income) Act 2005*.
7. The origins of Capital Transfer Tax can be traced back to the tax on estates in 1796 (originally called Legacy, Succession and Estate Duty), and the introduction of Death Duty in 1894.
8. See: http://webarchive.nationalarchives.gov.uk/+/http://www.hmrc.gov.uk/history/taxhis6.htm.
9. For further information, see: www.gov.uk/government/organisations/hm-treasury.
10. For further information, see: www.gov.uk/government/organisations/hm-revenue-customs/about.
11. For further information, see: www.revenue.scot/who-we-are.
12. The additional allowance is to be gradually withdrawn for estates worth more than £2m.
13. CREST is an electronic settlement and registration system administered by Euroclear. See: www.euroclear.com/en.html.
14. A land transaction is a transaction in which there is transfer of land, including a legal interest in or legal right over such land.
15. Non-residential and mixed-use property includes:
    - commercial property such as shops or offices
    - agricultural land
    - forests
    - any other land or property that is not used as a dwelling
    - six or more properties bought in a single transaction.
16. Goods are deemed to have been supplied if there is a transfer of ownership.
17. A supply of services is any supply (undertaken for consideration) that is not a supply of goods.
18. A 'taxable person' includes a sole trader, a partnership, a company, a club, an association, and a charity.
19. In addition, goods imported into the UK, and services received from overseas, may also be subject to VAT.
20. See: www.gov.uk/vat-rates and www.gov.uk/rates-of-vat-on-different-goods-and-services.
21. See: www.gov.uk/tax-on-shopping/air-passenger-duty.
22. If there is a gap of more than 40 inches between two rows of seats, the standard rate is charged. See: www.gov.uk/tax-on-shopping/air-passenger-duty.
23. Before 1 October 2014, it was necessary to display a vehicle licence tax disc on a vehicle, but since that date this is no longer a requirement.
24. Exemption ends after 12 months.
25. For up to 6 months after the grant of probate.
26. See: www.gov.uk/government/organisations/valuation-office-agency.
27. Excluding buildings used as offices or for other business activities.
28. The Personal Allowance will increase to £10,800 from 6 April 2016 and increase to £11,000 from 6 April 2017.
29. The basic rate limit for 2016/2017 will be increased to £31,900 and to £32,300 for 2017/2018. Together with changes to Personal Allowances, this will mean that the higher-rate threshold above which individuals pay Income Tax at 40% will be £42,700 for 2016/2017 and £43,300 for 2017/2018.
30. See: www.ft.com/cms/s/0/ecf1dd40-cd81-11e4-a15a-00144feab7de.html#axzz3WhrFN6sH.
31. 'Wages' includes Sick Pay, Maternity Pay, Paternity Pay and Adoption Pay.
32. Or you have started a new job and do not have a form P45; or you did not provide your new employer the details she or he needs in order to give you a tax code.
33. Unless it was a directorship of a non-profit organisation and no remuneration (including benefits) was received.
34. For further details, see: www.gov.uk/keeping-your-pay-tax-records/overview.
35. If a tax return is filed during the 90 days, the daily penalty is charged up to and including the day the tax return is filed.
36. Once approved, refunds can take between 4 weeks and 6 weeks.
37. See: www.bbc.co.uk/news/business-27372841.
38. First imposed in England in 1696, the Window Tax was finally repealed in 1851 after campaigners successfully argued that it was not only a tax on light and air, but more importantly an unequal tax because the greatest burden fell on the lower and middle classes.

39. Such media stories include those regarding tax-avoidance schemes used by Gary Barlow (of Take That), comedian Jimmy Carr, radio DJ Chris Moyles, and others. See: www.mirror.co.uk/3am/celebrity-news/gary-barlow-tax-evasion-celebrity-3531247.
40. Available at: www.gov.uk/government/publications/tempted-by-tax-avoidance.
41. See: www.gov.uk/vat-registration.
42. See *Value Added Tax Act 1994*, s.72(1).
43. See: www.cps.gov.uk/legal/s_to_u/sentencing_manual/evasion_of_excise_duty_with_intent_to_defraud_her_majesty/.
44. See: www.gov.uk/government/uploads/system/uploads/attachment_data/file/366583/cop9_1_.pdf.
45. HM Revenue and Customs' Civil Investigation of Fraud (CIF) teams investigate frauds for amounts up to £500,000. Amounts greater than £500,000 are generally investigated by HM Revenue and Customs' Special Civil Investigations (SCI) team.
46. Unless it was a directorship of a non-profit organisation and no remuneration (including benefits) was received.

5

Income Tax and National Insurance

Learning outcomes

By the end of this chapter, you should be able to:

- distinguish between the different types of taxable and non-taxable income
- describe the treatment (for Income Tax purposes) of alternative types of taxable income
- distinguish between taxable and non-taxable benefits
- describe the different classes of National Insurance contributions.

5.1 Introduction

Income Tax and National Insurance are now the principal forms of direct personal taxation in the UK. Charged on a wide variety of income and benefits in kind (after allowing for an ever-growing complexity of deductions, reliefs and personal allowances), they are assessable and payable using either the PAYE scheme or the increasingly popular self-assessment scheme.

This chapter explores:

- the basic structure of UK Income Tax and National Insurance
- the alternative types of incomes and benefits in kind that are currently taxable
- the range of personal allowances now available.

5.2 Non-taxable income

There are three types of non-taxable income:

- income from (some) social and welfare benefits
- income from (some) savings and investments
- other miscellaneous income.

Income from social and welfare benefits

The most common non-taxable social and welfare benefits include:

- age-related Christmas bonuses
- Child Benefit

- Child Tax Credit
- Disability Living Allowance
- free TV licence (for those over 75)
- some healthcare costs (including eye tests and prescriptions)
- Housing Benefit
- income-based Employment and Support Allowance
- Income Support
- industrial injuries benefits[1]
- lump-sum bereavement payments
- Maternity Allowance
- Pension Credit
- Personal Independence Payments
- Social Fund payments[2]
- Universal Credit
- War Widow's or Widower's Pension
- winter fuel payments
- Working Tax Credit.

Note: By 2017, income-based Employment and Support Allowance, Income Support, Housing Benefit, Child Tax Credit and Working Tax Credit will all be replaced by Universal Credit.

Income from savings and investments

Non-taxable income from savings and investments includes:
- income from National Savings and Investment (NS&I) certificates
- income from Individual Savings Accounts (ISAs)
- prizes from Premium Bonds
- lump-sum pension payments[3]
- annual withdrawals from Investment Bonds of up to 5% of the original investment.

Other miscellaneous income

The most common non-taxable miscellaneous income includes:
- National Lottery winnings
- educational grants and student loans
- compensation or damages awarded for personal injuries
- bonuses and profits on some life assurance policies
- lump-sum pension payments (maximum 25% of the capital value)
- insurance benefits (for example, benefits paid under mortgage protection insurance, permanent health insurance, and payment-protection insurance)
- strike pay and unemployment pay from trade unions
- Premium Bond prizes
- winnings from gambling (for example, horse racing)
- payments of compensation for loss of employment (the first £30,000)
- rental income from a 'live in' lodger (the first £4,250).

There are many others.

5.3 Taxable income

There is a range of different types of taxable income,[4] including:
- income from employment
- income from pensions
- profits from trades, professions and vocations
- profits from properties
- income from a trust
- income from (some) social and welfare benefits
- income from savings and investments[5]
- other miscellaneous income.

5.4 Income from employment

Income from employment[6] includes:
- any earnings arising from an employment contract
- any income paid to an office holder (for example, a director).

Such earnings or income include a salary, a wage, a fee, a commission, a gratuity, a profit, or an incidental benefit (one that has monetary value), as well as a redundancy payment, a payment made on the termination of employment, and any share-related income.

Note: If a company offers employees shares in the company, possible tax advantages may arise. However, such tax advantages only apply if the shares are offered through a Share Incentive Plan (SIP), a Save As You Earn (SAYE) scheme, a Company Share Option Plan (CSOP), or an Enterprise Management Incentive (EMI). Some tax advantages are also available to employee shareholders. (We will discuss such tax-advantaged share schemes in Chapter 7.)

For Income Tax purposes:
- earnings are deemed to be received either when the payment is made or (if earlier) when the employee becomes entitled to the payment of earnings
- taxable benefits are deemed to be received when the benefit is provided to the employee.

Employment or self-employment?

The distinction between employment and self-employment is:
- *employment* involves a contract *of* services, whereas
- *self-employment* involves a contract *for* services.

For Income Tax purposes, an individual is deemed to be employed if:
- there is external control or influence over the work and activities the individual undertakes *and*
- the individual must accept additional work if offered *and/or*
- the individual is entitled to receive employment benefits.

An individual is deemed to be self-employed if:
- the individual provides his or her own equipment and resources
- the individual can appoint assistants or helpers

- the individual can choose when and where to work
- the individual can select what activities to undertake
- the individual is responsible for his or her own management *and/or*
- the individual is liable for any financial loss resulting from his or her activities.

5.5 Benefits in kind

Covered by the *Income Tax (Earning and Pensions) Act 2003,* 'benefits in kind' are taxable benefits that an employee or director (but not an 'excluded employee' – see below) receives from her or his employment, but that do not form part of her or his financial remuneration: the wage or salary.

An excluded employee is:

- an employee in lower-paid employment who is not a director of a company *or*
- a director with 'no material interest'[7] in the company.

'Lower-paid employment' is employment for which earnings[8] in a tax year are below £8,500.

Note: Employees (including directors) who are not excluded employees are sometimes referred to as P11D[9] employees.

Some benefits in kind are tax-free; some are only taxed if the employee in receipt of the benefit is not in lower-paid employment; and some are taxable irrespective of the employee's level of earnings.

Non-taxable (tax-free) benefits in kind

The following are non-taxable benefits,[10] or tax-free benefits in kind:

- Contributions paid by an employer into an approved occupational or personal pension scheme for an employee.
- Meal vouchers, providing they are:
  - non-transferable
  - available to all employees and
  - can be used for meals only.
- Supplies and services provided on an employer's business premises so that an employee can perform her or his employment duties or activities.
- Accommodation, providing it is:
  - necessary for the proper performance of an employee's duties or activities
  - provided for the better performance of an employee's duties or activities
  - customary to provide accommodation as part of such employment *and/or*
  - necessary for the employee's security.
- Supplies and services provided by an employer but not on the employer's business premises, so that an employee can perform or undertake her or his employment duties or tasks (providing any private non-employment related use is insignificant).
- Free or subsidised canteen meals, providing they are available to all employees.
- Medical treatment overseas (where an employee becomes ill whilst working overseas).
- Health screening, medical examinations and check-ups.
- Nurseries and play schemes.

- Payments towards 'reasonable' additional household costs where an employee is required to work wholly or partly at home (up to £18 per month can be paid without the need for supporting evidence).
- Incidental overnight expenses (up to a maximum of £5 per night in the UK and £10 per night outside the UK[11]).
- Some travelling expenses.
- Up to £15,480 p.a. paid to an employee who is on a full-time course lasting a year (with an average full-time attendance of no less than 20 weeks).
- Certain retraining costs.
- Employer-funded or employer-reimbursed training.
- Long-service awards, providing no similar award has been made in the previous 10 years and the value of the award is no more than £50 per year of service.
- Goodwill entertainment (for example, a Christmas party or other annual party, limited to a value of no more than £150 per employee).
- Motor car, motorcycle and bicycle parking (near the employee's place of work).
- In-house sports facilities.[12]
- Health and safety clothing necessary for an employee to perform or undertake her or his employment duties or tasks.
- Welfare counselling, providing the service is available to all employees.
- Counselling services to redundant employees.
- Works buses or subsidies for public bus services, providing these relate to the transport of employees to and from work.
- Bicycle and cycling safety equipment provided for employees to travel to and from work.
- Reasonable relocation or removal expenses (up to a maximum of £8,000 for each move).
- Personal gifts provided for reasons unconnected with an employee's duties (for example, retirement gifts, other than cash, and wedding gifts).
- Employment-related personal gifts (other than cash) received from a third party (for example, tickets for sporting or cultural events), providing the total value is not worth more than £250 in a tax year.
- Some interest-free or low-interest loans provided by an employer.
- Equipment and facilities provided for disabled employees to enable them to perform their employment activities.

Taxable benefits in kind

Where a benefit in kind is taxable, the taxable value of the benefit is the cash-equivalent value of the benefit. In general this is the cost (paid by the employer) of providing the benefit, although there are some exceptions (see below).

Accommodation

The taxable benefit of accommodation provided for an employee (including an excluded employee) is:

- the value of the rent that would have been payable if the accommodation had been let at an amount equal to its annual value (normally its rateable value[13]), if the accommodation is owned by the employer *or*
- the higher of the rent actually paid for the accommodation and the annual value of the accommodation, if the accommodation is not owned by the employer.

(See: https://www.gov.uk/expenses-and-benefits-accommodation/work-out-the-value.)

There is an additional charge payable if the cost of providing the accommodation is more than £75,000 – this cost includes the cost of purchase and the cost of additional improvements made before the beginning of the tax year. The additional charge is calculated as follows:

(cost of providing the accommodation − £75,000) ∗ (HM Revenue and Customs official rate of interest[14] at the beginning of the tax year).

Note: Any contribution paid by the employee is deductible from the annual value of the accommodation.

Activity 1

The cost of providing accommodation for an employee is £106,400. The accommodation has an annual value of £4,870. The employee contributes £340 to the cost of providing the accommodation. The official rate of interest for 2015/2016 is 3%. What would the taxable benefit be for 2015/2016?

Exceptions Accommodation is a non-taxable benefit where (as indicated earlier) it is:

- necessary for the proper performance of an employee's duties or activities
- provided for the better performance of an employee's duties or activities
- customary to provide accommodation (as part of such employment) *and/or*
- necessary for the employee's security.

Expenses associated with living accommodation

Expenses for ancillary services associated with living accommodation provided for an employee (other than an excluded employee) that are paid by an employer are also a taxable benefit. Such ancillary services include, for example:

- utility services (for example, gas, electricity and water)
- cleaning services
- repair and maintenance services (including decorating services)
- the provision of furniture and fittings.[15]

The full cost of the above ancillary services is taxable as a benefit in kind. However, where accommodation is employment-related (and therefore non-taxable), then taxable ancillary services are limited to a maximum of 10% of the employee's net earnings.

(See: https://www.gov.uk/expenses-and-benefits-accommodation/what-to-report-and-pay.)

Cars

A taxable benefit arises where an employee (or a member of his or her family or household) is provided with the use of a car by reason of his or her employment, whether the car is provided by the employer or a third party.

Note: Pooled cars are exempt.[16]

The value of the benefit is based on a percentage of the list price of the car, with this percentage depending on the car's carbon dioxide (CO_2) emissions. The list price includes:
- the list price of the car for a single retail sale at the time of first registration
- the price (including fitting) of any additional optional accessories[17] fitted when the car was first provided to the employee
- the price (including fitting) of any additional optional accessories fitted later and costing at least £100.

Where an employee makes a capital contribution – that is, pays part of the purchase price of the car (with respect to its list price) or of any additional optional accessories – that capital contribution is a deductible contribution. In any tax year, the maximum deductible contribution is £5,000.

Note: Special rules exist for classic cars.[18]

Car benefit For 2015/2016, the car benefit depends on the amount of CO_2 emitted, measured in grams per kilometre:
- For ultra-low carbon cars (cars that emit up to 50 g/km), the taxable benefit is 5% of the list price.
- For cars that emit between 51 g/km and 75 g/km, the taxable benefit is 9% of the list price.
- For cars that emit between 76 g/km and 94 g/km, the taxable benefit is 13% of the list price.
- For cars that emit over 95 g/km, the percentage increases by 1% for every additional 5 g/km, up to a maximum of 37% for cars that emit over 210 g/km.

In addition, the benefit is reduced:
- on a time basis where the car is unavailable (for a period exceeding 30 days) during the tax year *and/or*
- by any payment the employee *must* make for private use (but car insurance does not count).

With the exception of the cost of providing a driver, any other associated benefits (for example, insurance costs, repair costs and parking costs) are not taxable.

Note: Lower-paid employees are not liable for any car-related benefit they receive, even if the car is used for private purposes.[19]

Fuel for cars

Any fuel provided by an employer is a taxable benefit, unless:
- the fuel provided is made available for business-related travel only *or*
- the employee pays (in full) the cost of any fuel provided for private use.

Note: A reimbursement by the employee of only part of the cost of the fuel does not reduce the taxable benefit.

The taxable benefit is a percentage of a base figure. The base figure for 2015/2016 is £22,100, with the percentage being the same as that used for the car benefit (the percentage based on CO_2 emissions).

As with car benefit, fuel benefit is reduced on a time basis where the car is unavailable (for a period exceeding 30 days) during the tax year.

(See: www.gov.uk/government/publications/tax-and-tax-credit-rates-and-thresholds-for-2015-16/tax-and-tax-credit-rates-and-thresholds-for-2015-16.)

Vans and heavier commercial vehicles

Where an employee has private use of a van (up to a maximum laden weight of 3,500 kg), there is an annual scale charge up to £3,150 p.a.[20] Where the employer also provides fuel for unrestricted private use, there is an additional annual charge of £594 p.a.[21] There is, however, no taxable benefit where an employee uses a van for home-to-work travel, but not for any other private use.

Statutory approved mileage allowance

Where an employee uses her or his own vehicle for employment purposes, no tax is payable on any allowance paid by an employer at or below certain statutory approved mileage allowances (see Table 5.1).

Table 5.1 Approved mileage allowances

Type of vehicle	Statutory approved mileage allowance per business mile (2015/2016)
Car	*For Income Tax purposes:* – 45p for the first 10,000 miles in a tax year, then 25p per mile *For National Insurance purposes:* – 45p for all business miles
Motorcycle	*For Income Tax and National Insurance purposes:* – 24p for all business miles
Cycle	*For Income Tax and National Insurance purposes:* – 20p for all business miles

Source: Data from https://www.gov.uk/guidance/rates-and-thresholds-for-employers-2015-to-2016.

Where an employer pays an amount *greater* than the statutory approved mileage allowance per business miles, the *additional* amount is a taxable benefit in kind. An employer can also pay up to an additional 5p per business mile (non-taxable) for any additional employee or passenger who makes the same business journey. Again, where an employer pays a *greater* amount, the *additional* amount is also a taxable benefit in kind.

Note: An employee can only claim tax relief up to the statutory approved mileage allowance. If an employer pays an amount per mile that is *lower* than the statutory mileage allowance, the employee can only claim tax relief on the lower amount received.

Other assets or goods made available for private use

Where other assets are made available to an employee (or to the employee's family or household) for private use, the taxable benefit is the higher of 20% of the market value of the asset when it was first made available or the rent (or charge) paid by the employee.

Note: The 20% charge is time-apportioned when the asset is not available for the whole tax year, with the adjusted 20% charge also reduced by any contribution made by the employee.

Where an asset made available to an employee (or to the employee's family or household) is subsequently acquired by the employee, the taxable benefit on the acquisition would be the greater of

- the current market value of the asset, less the amount paid by the employee *or*
- the market value of the asset when it was first made available to an employee (or to her or his family or household), less any amounts already taxed (ignoring contributions from the employee), less the price paid by the employee.

Beneficial loans

A taxable benefit arises where employment-related interest-free or low-interest loans are provided for employees or their relatives, or both (but not to excluded employees). The benefit is equal to any loan amounts written off (unless the employee has died) *plus* the difference between the HM Revenue and Customs official interest rate and the interest rate paid by the employee.[22]

Note: Where a loan is provided to an employee on normal commercial terms, it is not regarded as a low-interest loan; but a taxable benefit on amounts written off can still arise.

(See: https://www.gov.uk/expenses-and-benefits-loans-provided-to-employees.)

Qualifying loans and arrangements

Tax relief is available for interest on certain loans used for certain specific purposes.[23] These include:

- to buy ordinary shares in, or to lend money to, a close company[24]
- to acquire ordinary shares in an employee-controlled company
- to acquire a share or shares in, or to lend money to, a co-operative
- to acquire an interest in a trading or professional partnership other than an investment limited liability partnership (LLP)
- to provide a partnership (including an LLP) with funds to contribute to or to advance its business
- to buy equipment or machinery for use by a partnership.

Note: Tax relief cannot be claimed for interest on overdrafts or credit cards.

The limit on tax reliefs restricts the total amount of qualifying loan-interest relief and certain other reliefs in each year to the greater of £50,000 and 25% of 'adjusted total income'.[25]

Mobile phones

A taxable benefit arises if an employer provides a mobile phone to an employee,[26] but no taxable benefit arises if both of the following apply:

- the employer only provides an employee with one mobile phone (or SIM card) *and*
- the phone contract is between the employer and the supplier or mobile operator.

For further information, see: www.gov.uk/expenses-and-benefits-mobile-phones.

Hotels and temporary accommodation

The cost of hotel accommodation or other temporary accommodation provided while travelling for employment-related purposes is a non-taxable benefit. If, however, an employee is provided with a cash allowance to cover such costs, that cash allowance is a taxable benefit in kind – although any amounts spent on employment-related hotel accommodation or temporary accommodation can be deducted (as a tax relief) from taxable income.

Vouchers

Where an employee (including an excluded employee) receives a cash voucher, or uses a credit facility (for example, a credit card) to obtain cash, goods or services, or receives a non-cash voucher (or exchangeable voucher) to obtain goods or services, the employee is taxed on the cost (to the employer) of providing the cash voucher, the credit facility or the non-cash voucher, less any contribution or payment made by the employee.

Note: Where a voucher is provided as a non-taxable benefit, the provision of the voucher is also exempt from Income Tax.

Scholarships

A tax benefit arises where an employer provides a scholarship[27] (or bursary, or educational endowment) for a family member of an employee (but not excluded employees). The scholarship is not a taxable benefit if the scholarship is fortuitous – that is, if there is no direct connection between the employee and the awarding of the scholarship.

A scholarship is fortuitous if *all* of the following apply:

- the person with the scholarship is in full-time education *and*
- the scholarship would still have been granted to the person even if her or his family member was not an employee *and*
- the scholarship is managed by a trust fund or under a scheme *and*
- 25% or fewer of the payments made by the fund or scheme are for employment-linked scholarships.

Childcare

If an employer provides childcare[28] in the form of a workplace nursery or a play scheme at an employee's place of work, this is an exempt benefit.

If an employer contracts out with an approved childcare provider, or provides childcare vouchers[29] to pay for an approved (and registered) childcare provider, then only part of the childcare cost is free from tax. The childcare provision must, however, be usually available to all employees.

How much is tax-free depends on the rate of Income Tax paid by the employee. The limits are:

- £55 per week for a basic-rate taxpayer
- £28 per week for a higher-rate taxpayer
- £25 per week for an additional-rate taxpayer.

Note: If an employee accepts childcare vouchers, this can affect how much Tax Credit the employee can claim. The Working Tax Credit system provides support for childcare costs, but where costs are covered by employer-provided childcare vouchers, these cannot be included as part of a Working Tax Credit claim.

Other employment-related benefits

Other employment benefits include, for example:
- discounted goods and services
- holidays
- medical insurance
- travel expenses.

Note: Such benefits do not include accommodation, cars, fuel, vans and heavy vehicles, loans, or mobile phones, which are subject to special rules (see above).

Discounted goods and services Other employment-related benefits provided to an employee (other than an excluded employee) from within the employer's business are taxable in full. Cash allowances given in lieu of employment-related benefits are taxable for all employees.

Holidays An employee who receives a free holiday would have to pay tax on the full value of the holiday. For an excluded (or lower-paid) employee, such a holiday would be a tax-free benefit, provided that the holiday has no resale value and is not convertible to cash, for example.

Medical insurance Except for excluded employees, private medical insurance provided by an employer to an employee (or her or his family) is a taxable benefit.

Travelling expenses If an employer reimburses an employee for the costs of travelling from home to work, or pays such costs directly (for example, by purchasing a season ticket for an employee), the full value of the benefit is normally taxable.

5.6 Allowable deductions

Some expenses are specifically allowable (or deductible) from net taxable earnings. To be deductible, an expense must be for qualifying travel, or wholly, exclusively and necessarily incurred. Such expenses include:
- subscriptions to recognised professional bodies, providing the professional body is relevant to an employee's employment
- contributions (within prescribed limits) to registered pension schemes
- payments to charities made using the payroll-deduction scheme
- payments for liability insurance relating to the employee's employment duties or activities
- payments of liabilities arising from the employee's employment duties or activities
- mileage expenses (at or below the statutory approved mileage allowance – see the discussion above on taxable benefits in kind)
- expenses (paid by an employee) and incurred wholly, exclusively and necessarily for the performance of their employment duties or activities.

Activity 2

Reece Charlton is marketing director of DH Ltd. In 2015/2016 he earned a salary of £80,000 p.a. and received a performance bonus of £22,000. Because of the nature of his work, he also received £6,500 p.a. to cover general travelling and entertainments expenses.

He has a 5-year interest-free company loan of £15,600 (repayable in September 2017), and has use of a company car valued at £36,000 (with CO_2 emissions of 82 g/km). During 2015/2016 the company also provided personal medical health insurance costing £1,200.

Explain to Reece Charlton the Income Tax implications of each of these elements of income and benefits in kind.

5.7 Income from pensions

Tax is payable on any pension received. The amount of tax payable by an individual depends on the total income received, her or his tax-free personal allowance, and the applicable tax rate.

Note: Total income includes the State Pension, any private pensions income (whether from workplace, personal or stakeholder pensions), earnings from employment or self-employment, any taxable benefits received, and any other income received (for example, from investments, property and savings).

Receiving a State Pension and a private pension

When income (a pension) is received from a pension provider (or from an insurance company managing an individual's pension annuity or retirement income), the provider will deduct Income Tax at source – that is, before making the pension payment. The provider will also deduct any Income Tax due on the individual's State Pension.

If an individual receives a pension from more than one provider (for example, a private personal pension and an occupational pension), HM Revenue and Customs will ask *one* of the providers to deduct the Income Tax due on an individual's State Pension.

Note: A pension provider (or each pension provider, if there is more than one of them) will provide a P60 at the end of the tax year detailing how much tax has been deducted and paid.

Receiving a State Pension only

If an individual has no other income other than the basic State Pension, she or he will not pay Income Tax, providing that the State Pension is less than the current Personal Allowance. If any *additional* State Pension (S2P) is received (see Chapter 10), then Income Tax *may* become payable, depending on the total overall pension income received.

Receiving a State Pension only and continuing to work

If an individual continues to work in employment and also to receive a State Pension, his or her employer will deduct any Income Tax due on earnings *and* that due on the State Pension, using the PAYE scheme.

If an individual continues to work in self-employment and also to receive a State Pension, she or he must complete a self-assessment return at the end of the tax year and must declare her or his total overall income.

Receiving a State Pension and other income

If an individual receives other income – for property, investments or savings – in addition to a State Pension, she or he must complete a self-assessment return at the end of the tax year and must declare her or his total overall income.

Unauthorised payments

There are some payments made by pension providers on which recipients must pay up to 55% tax. These payments are referred to as 'unauthorised payments', and include:
- most lump sums over 25% of a pension pot (taxed at 55%)
- any payments before an individual is 55 (unless the pension scheme provides the individual with the right to receive such payments)
- regular payments after an individual has died.

5.8 Profits from trades, professions and vocations

The taxation of profits from trades, professions and vocations – or, more specifically, profits from unincorporated businesses – will be discussed in Chapter 6.

5.9 Profits from property

Income from land and buildings in the UK (including houseboats and caravans that are not moved) is taxable as non-savings income. All rental income and expenses for all properties are pooled together with profits and losses, which are calculated using an accruals basis rather than a cash basis. That is:
- all rental income is taxed in the tax year it is *due* to be received, even if the income has not yet been received *and*
- all allowable expenses are deductible in the tax year they are *due* to be paid, even if the expenses have not yet been paid.

Rental income

Rental income includes not only the rent received but also the income received from tenants for the use of furniture and fittings and for other services or facilities normally provided by a landlord.

If services or facilities are provided that would *not* normally be provided by a landlord – for example, a laundry service or a meal service – such income is usually treated as trading income, rather than rental income, and taxed separately.

Note: If a property is used as a hotel, a guesthouse, or a bed-and-breakfast facility, all the income is treated as trading income irrespective of the services and facilities provided.

Allowable expenses

To be allowable, expenses must have been incurred wholly and exclusively as a result of renting out a property or properties. The most common types of allowable expenses are:
- utility payments, for water, gas and electricity

- Council Tax payments
- property maintenance and repairs to the property (but not improvements to the property)
- contents insurance
- mortgage interest on a mortgage used to purchase the property[30]
- costs of services, including the wages of gardeners and cleaners (such services must be part of the rental agreement)
- rental or letting agency fees
- legal fees[31]
- accountants' fees
- rents, ground rents, and service charges
- other direct costs.[32]

Note: 10% of the net rent received (that is, the rent received less any costs paid that would usually be paid by a tenant) can be claimed as a wear-and-tear allowance for the furniture and equipment provided with a furnished residential letting. However, from April 2016 this automatic allowance will be abolished, and landlords will only be able to deduct *actual* costs incurred.

Losses

Any losses from UK rental properties (that is, where allowable expenses are greater than the rental income actually received) can be carried forward to set against future profits from UK properties. Although there is no time limit, such losses should be used as soon as possible.

Treatment of profits from property businesses

There is some variation to the treatment of profit from property businesses, for example where:
- one or more rooms are let in an individual's own home
- a property is let as a holiday home
- the property or properties are located overseas.

Rooms let in one's own home

Where an individual lets one or more furnished rooms in her or his main residence as living accommodation, the first £4,250 gross income received each year is tax-free (or £2,125, if the property is being let jointly). This is known as Rent-A-Room Relief.

Note: From April 2016, Rent-A-Room Relief will be increased to £7,500 (or £3,250 per person, if the property is being let jointly).

The relief does not apply to any room let as an office or for other business purposes. Also, if income from a property is being let jointly, each individual is entitled to half of the tax-free allowance (even if there are more than two people sharing the income).

Note: Any additional charges (for example, for meals, cleaning and laundry) must be added to the rent received to calculate the 'gross rent'. Expenses cannot be deducted.

Gross income less than the Rent-A-Room limit If the gross rent received is less than £4,250 (or £2,125 per person, if the property is being let jointly), such rents are exempt from Income Tax under the Rent-A-Room scheme. An individual can, however, elect to opt out of the Rent-A-Room scheme and be taxed in the normal way. For example, an individual who made a loss on Rent-A-Room accommodation might wish to set that loss against other letting income (not within the Rent-A-Room scheme).

Gross income greater than the Rent-A-Room limit If the gross rent received is greater than £4,250 (or £2,125 per person, if the property is being let jointly), an individual can choose either:
- to pay tax on the profits in the normal way for a rental property (by paying tax on the actual profit after deducting allowable expenses) *or*
- to pay tax on the gross income less the £4,250 (or £2,125) limit, with no allowance for expenses.

Note: The former method applies by default.

Activity 3

Suzanne charges her lodger Jane £500 a month rent to share her house. The annual rental income is therefore £6,000, and Suzanne's tax-allowable expenses are £2,900. How should Suzanne treat her rental income? (*Note*: Assume that Suzanne pays 20% Income Tax.)

Properties let as holiday homes (furnished holiday lets)

Income from a furnished holiday let is regarded as trading income, and as such capital allowances are available on furniture and fittings (instead of the 10% wear-and-tear allowances), as well as some Capital Gains Tax reliefs.[33]

The above can be claimed only if *all* of the following apply:
- the property is offered to let for at least 210 days a year *and*
- the property is actually let for more than 105 days a year *and*
- no single let is more than 31 days *and*
- the charge is the going rate for similar properties in the local area.

Any furnished holiday let must be situated in the UK or another state within the European Union.

Foreign properties

If an individual lives and pays tax in the UK, he or she must also declare rental income from overseas property lettings. How much Income Tax is payable depends on whether the individual is 'resident', 'ordinarily resident' or 'domiciled' in the UK.

An individual is *resident* in the UK if she or he:
- was in the UK for 183 days or more in a tax year *or*
- lives in the UK permanently *or*
- was in the UK for an average of 91 days or more in a tax year (over a maximum of 4 consecutive tax years).

An individual is *ordinarily resident* in the UK if she or he:
- was, or is, resident in the UK year after year *or*
- made clear to the UK Border Agency on the date of her or his arrival in the UK that she or he intended to stay for at least 3 years.

An individual is *domiciled* in the UK if:
- she or he chooses to remain in the UK permanently or indefinitely (which makes the UK the 'domicile of choice' *or*
- her or his father was domiciled in the UK at the time of her or his birth (which makes the UK the 'domicile of origin').

If an individual is resident, ordinarily resident or domiciled in the UK, she or he will have to pay Income Tax on overseas property income, whether or not the income is brought into the UK. This is known as the 'arising basis' of the assessment.

If an individual is resident, but is either not ordinarily resident or not domiciled in the UK, she or he can claim to be taxed only on the income received in the UK. This is known as the 'remittance basis'.

Individuals who have already paid foreign tax on property income from overseas can – subject to some restrictions – claim credit against any UK Income Tax liability.

Note: In the July 2015 Budget, the Chancellor of the Exchequer announced that as from April 2017 permanent non-domiciled tax status will be available to individuals who have lived in the UK for 15 of the past 20 years.

Multiple occupation

If a property is let to several tenants who are not members of the same family, it may be regarded as a House in Multiple Occupation (HMO). A property would be a House in Multiple Occupation if both of the following apply:
- at least three tenants live in the property (forming more than one household) *and*
- toilet, bathroom or kitchen facilities are shared facilities.

Note: A household consists of either a single person or members of the same family who live together. This includes people who are married or living together as partners.

A local authority licence is required if both the following apply:
- the house in multiple occupation is three or more storeys high *and*
- the house in multiple occupation is occupied by five or more people.

5.10 Income from trusts

A trust is a legal vehicle through which assets – money, investments (shares and securities), land and buildings – can be held on behalf of a beneficiary (or beneficiaries). There are three parties to a trust: the settlor, the trustees, and the beneficiary (or beneficiaries).

The settlor sets out how the assets in a trust should be used, usually in a trust deed. (In some instances, the settlor can also benefit from the assets in a trust – such a trust is called a 'settlor-interested' trust.) The trustees are the legal owners of the assets held in a trust. The role of the trustees is to manage the trust assets in accordance with the trust deed or the settlor's will; to decide how to invest or use the trust's assets; and to pay any tax due. The beneficiary (or beneficiaries) benefit from the trust – this benefit may be income-based, capital-based or asset-based, or a combination of these.

There are many different types of trusts, including for example:
- a bare trust
- an interest-in-possession trust
- a discretionary trust

- an accumulation trust
- a mixed trust
- a settlor-interested trust.

Bare trusts

A bare trust is a trust where assets are held in the name of a trustee, but the beneficiary has the right to all of the capital and income for the trust (if 18 or over).

An example would be a 'will trust', where the beneficiaries have an immediate right to income and capital (the underlying assets). The trustee is simply a nominee – the executor of a will – who has a duty to distribute the estate of the deceased within as short a timescale as possible.

Payments made to beneficiaries of a bare trust are paid gross – the beneficiaries are responsible for declaring and paying any Income Tax on its income.

Interest-in-possession trusts

An interest-in-possession trust (a life-interest trust) is a trust where the trustee must pass on all trust income to the beneficiary (often called the life tenant), as it arises – less any expenses. Payments made to beneficiaries out of a trust's non-savings income or savings income are paid net of 20% Income Tax. If the beneficiaries are not taxpayers, the Income Tax deducted can be reclaimed. If the beneficiaries are basic-rate taxpayers, no additional Income Tax is payable. If the beneficiaries are higher-rate taxpayers or additional-rate taxpayers, additional Income Tax will be payable.

If income from an interest-in-possession trust is paid out of dividend income, it is paid to beneficiaries net of 10% Income Tax. If beneficiaries are not taxpayers, the Income Tax deducted cannot be reclaimed. If beneficiaries are basic-rate, higher-rate or additional-rate taxpayers, additional Income Tax will be payable.

Discretionary trusts

A discretionary trust is a trust where the trustees can make decisions about what is paid to the beneficiaries (income or capital), which beneficiaries are paid, how often payments are made, and what (if any) conditions to impose on the beneficiaries. With a discretionary trust, income is distributed at the discretion of the trustees. Income for a discretionary trust is paid to the beneficiaries net of 45% Income Tax.

If beneficiaries are additional-rate taxpayers, there will be no additional Income Tax to pay. If the beneficiaries are non-taxpayers, basic-rate taxpayers or higher-rate taxpayers, any excess Income Tax paid can be reclaimed.

Accumulation trusts

An accumulation trust is a trust where the trustees can accumulate income within the trust and add it to the trust's capital (and where necessary pay out income).

Note: In general, beneficiaries of such trusts are usually:

- minors, for whom the trust is created because of the death of a parent *or*
- vulnerable beneficiaries, for whom the trust is created because they possess an incapacity.

Income for an accumulation trust is paid to the beneficiaries net of 45% Income Tax.

As with discretionary trusts, if beneficiaries are additional-rate taxpayers there will be no more tax to pay. If the beneficiaries are non-taxpayers, basic-rate taxpayers or higher-rate taxpayers, any Income Tax paid can be reclaimed.

Mixed trusts

A mixed trust is a trust that is a combination of more than one type of trust. Each different part of the trust is taxed according to the tax rules that apply to that part of the trust.

Settlor-interested trusts

A settlor-interested trust is a trust where the settlor (or the settlor's spouse or civil partner) benefits from the trust. The settlor-interested trust can be in the form of an interest-in-possession trust, or an accumulation trust, or a discretionary trust.

If, for example, a settlor-interested trust is a discretionary trust, payments made to the settlor's spouse or civil partner are deemed to have been taxed at 45%. Whilst no additional Income Tax is payable, tax deducted cannot be reclaimed.

5.11 Income from savings and investment

Savings income

Savings income is interest received on funds invested in interest-bearing bank or building society accounts, Government securities, or other loan-based securities.

Savings income received gross

The following savings and investments income is received gross – that is, before the deduction of Income Tax:

- interest on National Savings and Investments (NS&I) accounts
- interest on loan-based stock from companies listed on a recognised stock exchange
- interest on Government securities (Gilts).

Savings income received net

The following savings and investments income is received net – that is, after the deduction of (20%) Income Tax:

- interest on bank accounts
- interest on building society accounts
- interest on loan-based stock from companies not listed on a recognised stock exchange
- savings income from non-discretionary trusts.[34]

Savings income starting rate

There is a tax rate of 10% on savings income up to £5,000 (called the 'savings income starting rate limit'). This only applies where the savings income falls wholly or partly below the starting rate limit. Given that Income Tax is charged on non-savings income first (see below), the savings income starting rate is rarely available to use.

Note: In the March 2015 Budget, the Chancellor of the Exchequer announced Government proposals to introduce a new Personal Savings Allowance of £1,000 (or £500 for higher-rate taxpayers) from April 2016.

Dividends on UK shares

Dividends on UK shares are received after the deduction of a Tax Credit. When a company pays a dividend, the shareholder receives a Tax Credit worth one-ninth of the dividend amount, which can be offset against any tax owed by the shareholder.

Note: What the shareholder owes depends on their overall income.

Whilst the Tax Credit can be deducted in the computation of overall tax payable, it cannot be repaid.

How dividends are taxed

What Income Tax is payable on dividends depends on the recipient's income.

Table 5.2 Tax on dividends

Rate of Income Tax	Dividend tax rate (2015/2016)
Basic-rate tax payer (20%)	10.0%
Higher-rate tax payer (40%)	32.5%
Additional-rate tax payer (45%)	37.5%

Source: Data from http://www.hl.co.uk/tools/tax-facts.

Non-taxpayers Non-taxpayers do not have to pay any additional Income Tax, but cannot claim a repayment of the Tax Credit.

Basic-rate taxpayers Basic-rate taxpayers do not need to pay any additional Income Tax. The Tax Credit is automatically offset against the dividend tax owed (10%).

Higher-rate or additional-rate taxpayers Higher-rate or additional-rate taxpayers will need to pay extra tax. Since they have received a Tax Credit, the amount of Income Tax they owe is reduced.

Table 5.3 Higher-rate or additional-rate taxpayers

Rate of Income Tax	Dividend tax rate (2015/2016)	Additional-rate to pay
Higher-rate tax payer (40%)	32.50%	25.00%
Additional-rate tax payer (45%)	37.50%	30.56%

To calculate the amount of additional tax payable, add up all net dividends received (do not include the Tax Credit) and deduct the adjusted rate percentage from the total amount of net dividends received. The deducted amount is the tax owed.

Note: As from April 2016, the dividend Tax Credit is being abolished, and in its place a £5,000 tax-free allowance is being introduced.

In addition, Income Tax rates on dividend income will also change. As from April 2016:
- basic-rate taxpayers (who currently pay 10%) will pay 7.5%
- higher-rate taxpayers will pay 32.5%
- additional-rate taxpayers will pay 38.1%.

Activity 4

James is a higher rate (40%) taxpayer. In July 2015 he received a dividend of £2,700. What additional tax will James have to pay?

5.12 Income from social or welfare benefits

The most common taxable social and welfare benefits include:
- Bereavement Allowance
- Carer's Allowance
- contribution-based Employment and Support Allowance
- Incapacity Benefit (from the 29th week only)
- Jobseeker's Allowance
- State Pension
- Widowed Parent's Allowance.

For further information on other taxable social and welfare benefits, see: www.gov.uk/income-tax/taxfree-and-taxable-state-benefits.

Note: By 2017, contribution-based Employment and Support Allowance and Jobseeker's Allowance will both be replaced by Universal Credit.

5.13 Miscellaneous income

Other types of income that are taxable include:
- casual earnings
- freelance income
- profits from isolated literary or artistic activities
- rental income from (owned) leasing equipment
- sales of patent rights
- receipts under covenants.

There are many others.

5.14 Child Benefit and Income Tax

An Income Tax charge applies (to recover Child Benefit) if the recipient or his or her partner[35] has an adjusted net income of over £50,000 in a tax year.

If a taxpayer has an adjusted net income of between £50,000 and £60,000, the charge is 1% of the amount of Child Benefit received for each £100 of adjusted net income above £50,000. If a taxpayer has an adjusted net income of over £60,000, the charge is equal to the full amount of Child Benefit received. If both partners have adjusted net incomes above £50,000, the partner with the higher adjusted net income is liable for the charge.

Note: The Child Benefit Income Tax charge is collected through the self-assessment scheme.

5.15 National Insurance

National Insurance is paid by both the employed and self-employed, with those out of work able to choose to make voluntary contributions so that they are eligible for the various benefits associated with the payment of National Insurance contributions.

For example, a full State Pension is payable to those who have an appropriate National Insurance contribution record; currently this is 30 years' National Insurance contributions, but from April 2016 it will be 35 years' National Insurance contributions.

National Insurance contributions are divided into four classes:

- Class 1
  - Primary: paid by employees.
  - Secondary: Class 1A and Class 1B, which are paid by employers.
- Class 2: paid by the self-employed.
- Class 3: voluntary contributions.
- Class 4: paid by the self-employed.

National Insurance contributions are only payable by those who are:

- 16 years old or older *and*
- an employee earning more than £156 a week *and/or*
- self-employed and making a profit of over £8,060 a year (unless exempted).

Note: National Insurance is no longer payable once the State Pension age has been reached.

National Insurance contributions: Class 1

Employees pay Class 1 (or primary) National Insurance contributions on employment income[36] received from an employer.

National Insurance is calculated on gross earnings (before tax or pension deductions) above the earnings threshold.

For 2015/2016, the National Insurance threshold is £156 per week. For earnings between £156.00 per week and £815.00 per week, employees' National Insurance contributions are 12%. For earnings above £815.00 per week, employees' National Insurance contributions are 2%.

Employers pay Class 1 (or secondary) National Insurance contributions on employment income paid by the employer. For earnings above £156.00 per week, employers' National Insurance contributions are 13.8%.

Employers pay Class 1A and 1B National Insurance once a year on expenses and benefits paid to, or provided for, employees. For 2015/2016, employers' National Insurance contributions are 13.8%.

National Insurance contributions: Class 2

Class 2 National Insurance contributions are paid by the self-employed. For 2015/2016, Class 2 National Insurance contributions are £2.80 per week on profits (earnings less allowable expenses) over £5,965. National Insurance contributions can be paid monthly, or six-monthly, or on demand. Those with lower profits can apply for 'small earnings' exemptions.[37]

The self-employed must register with HM Revenue and Customs as soon as they become self-employed, and in any case by 31 January following the year they became self-employed. Failure to do so can result in a late notification penalty or a fine.

Note: In the March 2015 Budget, the Chancellor of the Exchequer announced Government proposals to abolish Class 2 National Insurance during the next Parliament.[38]

National Insurance contributions: Class 3

Class 3 National Insurance contributions are voluntary contributions, which can be paid if:
- an individual is not working
- an individual is not liable for, or is exempt from, Class 1 or Class 2 contributions
- an individual's contributions (for a year) are insufficient for State benefit purposes *or*
- an individual lives or is employed overseas.

The 2015/2016 Class 3 National Insurance contribution rate is £14.10 per week.

National Insurance contributions: Class 3A

Class 3A National Insurance contributions represent a voluntary one-off lump-sum payment or contribution available from October 2015 for those who will have reached State Pension age by 6 April 2016. Class 3A National Insurance contributions allow an individual to increase their potential State Pension by up to a maximum extra of £25 per week.

For those aged 65, an extra £1 per week (£52 per year) of State Pension income will cost £890. An extra £25 per week (£1,300 per year), the maximum increase possible, will cost £22,250. For those aged 70, an extra £1 per week (£52 per year) of State Pension income will cost £779. For those aged 75, an extra £1 per week (£52 per year) of State Pension income will cost £674. For those aged 80, an extra £1 per week (£52 per year) of State Pension income will cost £544. The additional pension purchased with Class 3A National Insurance contributions:
- will be index-linked (using the Consumer Prices Index)
- will be inheritable on death (for example, a surviving spouse will be entitled to at least 50% of the additional pension)
- will be taxable
- will be taken into account in the assessment of income-related means-tested benefits.

National Insurance contributions: Class 4

Class 4 National Insurance contributions are payable by self-employed people whose profits are in excess of £8,060 p.a.

For 2015/2016, for profits above £8,060 p.a. but below £42,385 p.a., the National Insurance contributions are 9%. For profits above £42,385 p.a., the National Insurance contributions are 2%.

Activity 5

A sole trader made profits of £18,450 in 2015/2016. What would the sole trader's Class 4 National Insurance contributions be?

Employment Allowance

From April 2014 employers can reduce the National Insurance contributions they pay for their employees, up to a maximum of £2,000. That is, employers do not have to pay any employer National Insurance contributions if they are usually less than £2,000 a year. (This will increase to £3,000 from April 2016.) The Employment Allowance[39] is available for nearly all employers who pay Class 1 National Insurance contributions on employees' and directors' earnings.

National Insurance credits

Those not in paid employment because of:
- childcare commitments
- carer's commitments
- unemployment *and/or*
- illness

may receive National Insurance credits to help them maintain their National Insurance record, and build up the 'qualifying years' that count towards their entitlement to some benefits (including the State Pension).

Childcare

Parents (aged over 16) who receive Child Benefit and who are caring for a child under the age of 12, automatically receive National Insurance credits, known as Class 3 National Insurance credits. Grandparents and other family members aged over 16 but under State Pension age who provide care for a child aged under 12 may be able to get Class 3 Specified Adult National Insurance credits.

Carers

Registered carers and those who care for 20 hours a week or more for someone who is sick or disabled can receive Class 3 National Insurance credits if the person they care for receives a Disability Living Allowance or an Attendance Allowance, or both.

Unemployment

The unemployed may qualify for Class 1 National Insurance credits. To qualify, an individual must be unemployed and receiving Jobseeker's Allowance.

Note: Class 1 National Insurance credits are not credited automatically, but need to be applied for.

Illness and disability

If an individual is unable to work due to illness or disability, that individual may receive National Insurance credits if she or he receives Employment and Support Allowance (or Universal Credit, from April 2017).

Note: In this case, National Insurance credits are credited automatically.

5.16 Tax relief

The effect of a tax relief[40] is that an individual will either pay less tax or receive a tax refund or rebate. Whereas some types of tax relief are received automatically, others must be applied for.

Tax relief applies to some employment- or business-related expenses or allowable deductions (see above). It also applies to:

- pension contributions
- charity donations
- maintenance payments
- time spent working on a ship outside the UK (Seafarers' Earnings Deduction).

Pension contributions

Tax relief is available on private pension contributions,[41] up to 100% of an individual's annual earnings. In general it is not necessary to claim this, as tax relief on pension contributions is automatic if:

- the individual is in a workplace pension scheme and his or her employer deducts pension contributions out of his or her pay before deducting Income Tax *or*
- an individual's pension provider claims 'relief at source' – that is, tax relief at a rate of 20%, which is then added to their pension savings.

Note: Relief at source is available on all personal and stakeholder pensions, and some workplace pensions.

An individual may, however, need to claim tax relief on pension contributions if:

- he or she pays Income Tax at a rate above 20% and the pension provider claims the first 20% (relief at source)
- his or her pension scheme is not set up for automatic tax relief
- someone else pays into his or her pension.

Donations using Gift Aid

Donations made to a charity by an individual are tax-free, and attract tax relief if they are donated using Gift Aid or donated using payroll-giving (that is, deducted from an individual's wage, salary or pension).

Charities and community amateur sports clubs can register with HM Revenue and Customs to be part of the Gift Aid scheme.

When registered, the charities and community amateur sports clubs can claim back the Income Tax already paid on the donation. If an individual pays a higher rate of Income Tax (40%) or the additional rate of Income Tax (45%), they can claim back the difference between the Income Tax paid on the donation and the Income Tax claimed back by the charity or community amateur sports club.

Donations using payroll-giving

If an employer or pension provider offers a payroll-giving scheme, any charity donations made through the scheme are deducted before any Income Tax is taken off.

Note: National Insurance contributions are still payable on the full amount of the donation.

Maintenance payments

Maintenance Payments Relief[42] reduces an individual's Income Tax liability if she or he makes maintenance payments to an ex-spouse or a civil partner. Maintenance Payments Relief is only available if *all* of the following apply:

- both the payer and the payee were born before 6 April 1935 *and*

- the maintenance payments are being made under a court order after the relationship has ended *and*
- the payments are for the maintenance of an ex-spouse or former civil partner (provided that she or he is not now remarried or in a new civil partnership) or for children who are under 21.

Maintenance Payments Relief is 10% of the maintenance paid, up to a maximum of £314 p.a. (that is 10% of £3,140).

Seafarers' earnings

An individual who works at sea may be able to reduce his or her Income Tax liability bill by claiming a Seafarers' Earnings Deduction.[43] To receive the deduction, the individual must have:
- worked on a ship *and*
- performed all (or most) of his or her duties on a ship *and*
- worked outside of the UK long enough to qualify for the deduction (that is, for more than 183 days in a year) *and*
- been resident in the UK or resident for tax purposes in an EU state other than the UK.

The deduction is not available, however, if an individual is (or was during the period):
- a Crown employee (for example, a member of the Royal Navy)
- not a UK resident
- not a resident of an EU state other than the UK.

5.17 Tax reducers

Tax reducers limit or reduce the amount of Income Tax payable at a set rate of relief – they do not affect income. Tax reducers are:
- investments in a Venture Capital Trust[44] (VCT)
- investments in an Enterprise Investment Scheme[45] (EIS)
- investments in a Seed Enterprise Investment Scheme[46] (SEIS).

Investments in the above may qualify for a tax reduction up to the lower of the percentage of the amount subscribed and the individual's tax liability.

For investments in VCTs and under the EIS, the percentage is 30%. For investments under the SEIS, the percentage is 50%.

5.18 Calculating taxable personal income and Income Tax liability

There are a number of steps in calculating Income Tax payable:
- Identify non-savings income, savings income, and dividend income.
- Calculate the total income.
- Deduct any allowable expenses.
- Deduct the Personal Allowance.
- Calculate the Income Tax on non-savings income, savings income, and dividend income.
- Deduct any available tax reducers.
- Calculate tax liability.

- Deduct Tax Credit on dividends.
- Deduct any Tax Credit on interest.
- Deduct tax paid at source (via PAYE).
- Calculate the tax payable.

Taxable personal income and Income Tax liability: an example

Samuel (born in 1957) had a rental income of £65,300. He received savings income (Building Society interest) of £2,300, and net dividends of £7,290. Samuel paid allowable interest of £2,500, and made an investment in a Venture Capital Trust of £2,500.

How much Income Tax is payable?

	Non-savings income £	Savings income £	Dividend income £	Total £
Rental Income	65,300			65,300
Interest (£2,300 * 100/80)		2,875		2,875
Dividends (£7,290 * 100/90)			8,100	8,100
Total Income	65,300	2,875	8,100	76,275
Less Interest paid	−2,500			
	62,800			
Personal Allowance	−10,600			
Taxable income	52,200	2,875	8,100	63,175
Non-savings income				
£31,785 * 20%				6,357
£20,415 * 40%				8,166
				14,523
Savings income				
£2,875 * 40%				1,150
Dividend income				
£8,100 * 32.5%				2,633
				18,306
Tax reducer				
£2,500 * 30%				−750
Tax Liability				17,556
Tax Credit on dividends				−810
Tax Credit on interest				−575
Tax Payable				16,171

5.19 Concluding comments

Unlike National Insurance contributions, Income Tax is a blunt 'political' instrument – a progressive tax for which there is no minimum age requirement. What matters is income: the residual income after the deduction of personal allowances, tax reliefs and deductible expenses. Put simply, the higher the income, the greater the Income Tax.

5.20 Suggested further reading

For further information on the following topics, see the references given.
Income Tax and dividends:
- www.gov.uk/tax-on-dividends

Income Tax and property rental income:
- www.gov.uk/renting-out-a-property/paying-tax

Income Tax and savings interest:
- www.gov.uk/apply-tax-free-interest-on-savings

Taxable and non-taxable benefits:
- www.gov.uk/income-tax/taxfree-and-taxable-state-benefits

Key points

- Income Tax is the principal form of direct personal taxation in the UK.
- The main types of taxable income are:
  - income from employment
  - income from pensions
  - profits from trades, professions and vocations
  - profits from properties
  - income from (some) social and welfare benefits
  - income from savings and investments
  - other miscellaneous income.
- Whereas employment involves a contract *of* services, self-employment involves a contract *for* services.
- Benefits in kind are taxable benefits that an employee or director receives from her or his employment.
- 'Badges of trade' are a collection of principles established by case law to determine whether a person is trading.
- There are two methods of recording income and expenses and of assessing and calculating taxable profits for a tax year: the cash basis and the accruals basis.
- To be allowable (or deductible), an expense must be wholly, exclusively and necessarily incurred.
- A tax relief can either reduce the amount of Income Tax that is payable or increase the amount of Income Tax to be refunded or the rebate that is receivable.
- Tax reducers limit or reduce the amount of Income Tax that is payable at a set rate of relief, but do not affect income.

Self-review questions

1. Describe the main types of *taxable income* and *non-taxable income*.
2. Distinguish between the main types of rental income; and briefly describe the main types of expenses that are – for Income Tax purposes – deductible from rental income.
3. What are the main classes of National Insurance contributions?
4. What are the main factors that determine whether someone is: *resident, ordinarily resident*, or *domiciled*?
5. Distinguish between a *general partnership*, a *limited partnership*, and a *limited liability partnership*.

Case study discussion questions

1. Briefly explain to Claire Carter the implications of not paying National Insurance contributions.
2. Both Stuart Carter and Mary Carter have an unadjusted Income Tax Personal Allowance for 2015/2016. Advise each of them of their individual Income Tax and National Insurance liabilities for the salary, bonus and dividends they received during the year ending 31 March 2016.

Suggested answers to chapter activities

Activity 1

The taxable benefit would be:

$$[(£4{,}870 - £340) + ((£106{,}400 - £75{,}000) * 3\%)] = £5{,}472.$$

Activity 2

For Reece Charlton, the Income Tax implications would be as follows:

1. Income Tax and National Insurance would be payable on the salary.
2. Income Tax and National Insurance would be payable on the performance bonus.
3. The allowance for general travelling and entertainment expenses would be included in earnings for the year, and would be subject to Income Tax and National Insurance. A deduction could however be claimed for actual allowable expenses incurred.
4. The interest-free loan, the company car, and the medical health insurance are benefits in kind and would be subject to Income Tax and National Insurance.

Activity 3

If Suzanne elects *not* to use the Rent-A-Room scheme, her Income Tax would be:

$$£6{,}000 - £2{,}900 = £3{,}100 * 20\% = £620.$$

If Suzanne elects to *use* the Rent-A-Room scheme, her Income Tax would be:

$$£6{,}000 - £4{,}250 = £1{,}750 * 20\% = £350.$$

Suzanne could therefore minimise her Income Tax by making use of the Rent-A-Room scheme.

Activity 4

This can be calculated in two ways (using Table 5.3).
Either:

$$\text{Dividend} = £2{,}700 * 100/90 = £3{,}000$$
$$\text{Tax credit} = £3{,}000 - £2{,}700 = £300$$
$$\text{Tax payable} = £3{,}000 * 32.5\% = £975 - £300 = £675.$$

Or:

$$£2{,}700 * 25\% = £675.$$

Activity 5

Profits:

$$£18,450 - £8,060 \text{ [Class 4 lower limit]} = £10,390.$$

Class 4 National Insurance contributions:

$$£10,390 * 9\% = £935.10.$$

Notes

1. Including Industrial Injuries Disablement Benefit, Reduced Earnings Allowance, Constant Attendance Allowance, and Severe Disablement Allowance.
2. Including budgeting loans, funeral expenses payments, and Sure Start Maternity Grants.
3. Such payments are limited to 25% of the total pension.
4. See the *Income Tax (Trading and Other Income) Act 2005.*
5. Such income includes interest and dividends.
6. Income Tax for employees is collected under the *Income Tax (Earnings and Pensions) Act 2003.*
7. 'Material interest' is defined as control of more than 5% of the ordinary share capital.
8. This includes all earnings and benefits (less any contributions to registered pension schemes and payroll-giving) that would be taxable if the employee were *not* an excluded employee.
9. A P11D is a form completed by an employer for an employee, and details all expenses and benefits.
10. For non-taxable benefits, see: www.gov.uk/government/uploads/system/uploads/attachment_data/file/323555/hs207.pdf.
11. If these limits are exceeded, *all* of the expense is taxable, not just the excess.
12. This does not apply to facilities available to the general public.
13. If the accommodation does not have a rateable value, the value will be estimated by HM Revenue and Customs.
14. This is announced on an annual basis. For 2015/2016, HM Revenue and Customs announced that the official rate of interest would be 3%.
15. The annual value of such furniture and fittings is 20% of the cost.
16. A pool car is one shared by a number of employees and not normally kept overnight at or near an employee's home. In addition, any private use is minor and incidental to business use.
17. This does not include the cost of adaptations and equipment required by a disabled driver.
18. If a car is at least 15 years old (from the date of its first registration) and its market value (at the end of the tax year) is £15,000 or greater than the list price, then the current market price can be used.
19. See: www.gov.uk/expenses-and-benefits-company-cars/whats-exempt.
20. See: www.gov.uk/government/publications/tax-and-tax-credit-rates-and-thresholds-for-2015-16/tax-and-tax-credit-rates-and-thresholds-for-2015-16.
21. See: www.gov.uk/government/publications/tax-and-tax-credit-rates-and-thresholds-for-2015-16/tax-and-tax-credit-rates-and-thresholds-for-2015-16.
22. There are two methods of calculating the interest benefit:
    - the average method, which calculates interest on an annual basis (and is normally used by HM Revenue and Customs)
    - the strict method, which calculates interest on a daily basis.
23. See: https://www.gov.uk/government/uploads/system/uploads/attachment_data/file/323775/hs340.pdf.
24. A company is a 'close company' if it is a UK-resident company and 5 or fewer participants, or any number of participants who are directors (www.practicallaw.com/9-107-6117), either:
    - have control of the company *or*
    - together possess, or are entitled to acquire, rights to receive the greater part of the assets of the company available for distribution among participants on a notional winding up.
25. For the calculation of 'adjusted net income', see: https://www.gov.uk/adjusted-net-income.
26. See: www.gov.uk/expenses-and-benefits-mobile-phones/overview.

27. See: www.gov.uk/expenses-benefits-scholarship-family-employee/overview.
28. If an individual pays for childcare herself or himself, such costs cannot be used to claim relief against tax.
29. Post-April 2011, under the Employer Supported Childcare Vouchers scheme.
30. In the July 2015 Budget, the Chancellor of the Exchequer announced that as from April 2017 landlords would no longer be able to claim tax reliefs worth 40% or 45% of the interest payments on buy-to-let mortgages. From that date, the maximum tax relief will be 20%, although the change will be introduced over a four-year period.
31. For lets of a year or less, or for the renewing of a lease of less than 50 years.
32. For example the cost of telephone calls, and fees for advertising for new tenants.
33. For example: Business Asset Rollover Relief, Entrepreneurs' Relief, Relief for Gifts of Business Assets, and Relief for Loans to Traders.
34. A non-discretionary trust is one in which the trustee is directed to invest only in specifically named securities and to diversify the investments among certain types of securities.
35. 'Partner' means a spouse, a civil partner, or an unmarried partner where the couple are living together as if they were married or are civil partners.
36. This includes salaries, wages, overtime payments, any commission and any bonuses received, as well as Sick Pay, Maternity Pay, Paternity Pay and Adoption Pay.
37. See:www.gov.uk/government/publications/national-insurance-application-for-exception-to-pay-class-2-contributions-cf10.
38. See: www.ft.com/cms/s/0/ecf1dd40-cd81-11e4-a15a-00144feab7de.html#axzz3WhrFN6sH.
39. See: www.gov.uk/employment-allowance.
40. See: www.gov.uk/income-tax-reliefs/overview.
41. See: www.gov.uk/tax-on-your-private-pension/pension-tax-relief.
42. See: www.gov.uk/income-tax-reliefs/maintenance-payments-tax-relief.
43. See: www.gov.uk/government/publications/seafarers-earnings-deduction-hs205-self-assessment-help sheet.
44. A Venture Capital Trust (VCT) is a listed company that is managed by a fund manager and invests mainly in smaller companies that are not quoted on stock exchanges.
45. The Enterprise Investment Scheme (EIS) was launched in 1994 to encourage investments in small unquoted companies carrying on a qualifying trade in the UK.
46. The Seed Enterprise Investment Scheme (SEIS) was launched in 2012 to stimulate entrepreneurship and to kickstart investment in small and early-stage start-up businesses in the UK. See: www.seis .co.uk/.

6

Business tax

Learning outcomes

By the end of this chapter, you should be able to:

- define the key badges of trade
- explain how businesses are taxed
- describe the main types of capital allowance businesses can claim
- describe the factors that determine the choice of a business medium.

6.1 Introduction

An ever-expanding web of interconnected wealth-creating entities, which helps to sustain the fabric of modern life through the taxes it pays, the business sector is now a key feature of contemporary society. This chapter explores how tax is levied on small entities within the business sector, and by means of two taxes in particular:

- Income Tax, which is paid by unincorporated businesses
- Corporation Tax, which is paid by incorporated businesses.

6.2 Types of businesses

For taxation purposes in the UK, there are two types of business arrangements:

- unincorporated businesses, which includes sole traders and partnerships (in their various forms)
- incorporated businesses (or companies).

Note: A 'company' is any corporate body, whether limited, unlimited, or an unincorporated association.

Unincorporated businesses pay Income Tax on any taxable profits, and Capital Gains Tax on any chargeable gains.[1] Incorporated businesses pay Corporation Tax on any taxable profit *and* on any chargeable gains.

Note: Income Tax is collected from unincorporated businesses (self-employed sole traders and individual partners within a partnership) under the *Income Tax (Trading and other Income) Act 2005.* Corporation Tax is collected from companies under the *Corporation Tax Act 2009.*

6.3 Income Tax and unincorporated businesses – profits from trades, professions and vocations

A *trade* may be defined as work requiring manual skills and special training, a *profession* may be defined as a paid occupation involving lengthy training and a formal qualification, and a *vocation* may be defined as a calling or a personal mission. Despite these distinctions, for taxation purposes profits from trades, professions and vocations are taxed in the same way. They are all taxed as *trading businesses* – more specifically, they are all taxed as *unincorporated* trading businesses, whose profits are subject to Income Tax.

Badges of trade

The term 'badges of trade' denotes a collection of principles established by case law to determine whether or not a person is trading, and if so whether the trading constitutes a business. Such badges of trade include:

- a profit-seeking motive
- the organisation of the activity
- the frequency of transactions
- the period of ownership
- the method of finance
- the existence of similar trading transactions
- the nature of the asset
- changes to the asset
- the method of acquisition.

Profit-seeking motive

If the intention of a transaction (or group of transactions) is to generate a profit, then that is an indication of trading activity.

The organisation of the activity

An 'adventure in trade' may be inferred if the transactions are undertaken in the same manner as those undertaken by another individual who is clearly trading.

The frequency of transactions

Although a single transaction can indicate trading activity, such activity is more strongly indicated if there are frequent, repeated and systematic transactions.

The period of ownership

If a commodity or an asset is purchased and then sold soon afterwards, then an adventure in trade may be inferred. Conversely, the longer the period of ownership, the greater the possibility that the transaction occurred as an investment rather than as trade.

The method of finance

If an individual has to borrow money to finance the purchase of an asset and then sells that asset to repay the loan, it may be inferred that trading is taking place.

The existence of similar trading transactions

If a transaction has similarities to an existing trade, then an adventure in trade may be inferred.

The nature of the asset

Trading can be determined by the nature of the asset or, more specifically, by the subject matter of the transaction. Where the subject matter of the transaction is such that it would not be held for investment purposes, then any profit from such a transaction is presumed to be a trading profit.

Changes to the asset

Where changes or modifications are made to an asset to make the asset more marketable, then an adventure in trade may be inferred.

The method of acquisition

If an asset was not purchased but inherited or acquired as a gift, the sale of such an asset would *not* necessarily indicate an adventure in trade.

Activity 1

Briefly describe the main badges of trade.

Assessing profits from a trade

There are two methods of recording income (money received) and expenses (money paid out), and of assessing and calculating taxable profits for a tax year:

- a cash basis
- an accruals basis.

Note: Unless an individual elects to use the cash basis, the accruals basis is automatically applied.

Cash basis

With the cash basis of accounting, income and expenses are recorded when they actually come in or go out of the business. Cash-basis accounting can only be used by an unincorporated business (that is, a self-employed sole trader or a partnership) that has a turnover of less than £81,000 for the year. If an individual has more than one business, he or she must use the cash basis for *all* of these businesses, and the combined turnover from all the businesses must be less than £81,000.

Note: Limited liability partnerships (see below) cannot use cash-basis accounting .

Proper and accurate business records must be maintained, detailing all money received (income), all money paid out (expenses), and the amount of debtors, creditors and stock within the business. Whilst the cash basis is a simpler way of calculating a business profit or loss, there are some restrictions on the treatment of financial expenses and capital allowances (see below), and on the treatment and use of trading losses.

Accruals basis

With accruals-based accounting, income and expenses are recorded when an invoice is issued or a bill received – this method is often called the 'traditional' accounting basis. Proper and accurate business records must be maintained, detailing *all* business-related transactions.

Allowable business expenses

For Income Tax purposes, the following are allowable business expenses:

- accountancy, legal and other professional fees
- advertising and marketing costs
- financial charges, including interest on bank and other business loans[2]
- vehicle expenses
- travel expenses
- telephone, stationery, office costs and business-specific insurance costs
- in the construction industry, payments to subcontractors
- the cost of goods (goods to be sold and goods used in providing a service
- the profit or loss on the sale of an asset
- irrecoverable (bad) debts that are written off
- rent, rates, power and utility costs
- repairs and renewals for property and equipment
- wages, salaries and other staff costs
- other business expenses.

Activity 2

For an unincorporated business, what expenses are generally regarded as allowable business expenses?

Non-deductible business expenses

Expenses may be non-deductible if the expense is not for the purpose of the trade or business (the 'remoteness' test) or if the expense reflects more than one purpose (the 'duality' test); for example, the private proportion of motoring expenses, heating and lighting, rent, and telephone costs would not be deductible. Also, any accounting adjustment or allocation of cost related to non-current assets (for example, depreciation on buildings, plant and machinery, and cars) is non-deductible.

Simplified expenses rules

From April 2013, new rules were introduced (for both the cash basis and the accruals basis) to simplify the calculation of some business expenses by using a flat-rate allowance (instead of assessing and calculating the actual expense). This change applies in three areas:

- expenditure on motor vehicles
- use of the home for business purposes
- premises used both as a home and for business purposes.

Expenditure on motor vehicles Subject to some exceptions, the flat-rate expenses for business miles are:

- for cars: 45p per business mile for the first 10,000 miles
- for cars: 25p per business mile after the first 10,000 miles
- for motorcycles: 24p per business mile.

Use of the home for business purposes If a business is managed from home, a standard allowance (to cover utility and communication costs) can be used. The amounts allowable each month are:
- 25–50 hours per month: £10 per month
- 51–100 hours per month: £18 per month
- 101 hours or more per month: £26 per month.

Premises used both as a home and for business purposes If an individual lives on his or her business premises, he or she can claim a flat-rate allowance which is then deducted from the business's actual costs.

Note: The flat rate does not include costs such as rent, mortgage payments and Council Tax.

The fixed-rate adjustment is based on the number of occupants at the business dwelling:
- 1 occupant: £350 per month
- 2 occupants: £500 per month
- 3 or more occupants: £650 per month.

Excluded income

Only income from trading activities is included: all other (non-trading) income is excluded. For example, any interest received is excluded and assessed using the appropriate rules for that type of income (such as income on savings and investments – see below).

Capital allowances

A sole trader or partnership can claim capital allowances when they purchase assets to retain and use within a business.

(Capital allowances are discussed in more detail later in this chapter.)

Taxable trading profit

Taxable trading profits can be calculated as shown in Figure 6.1.

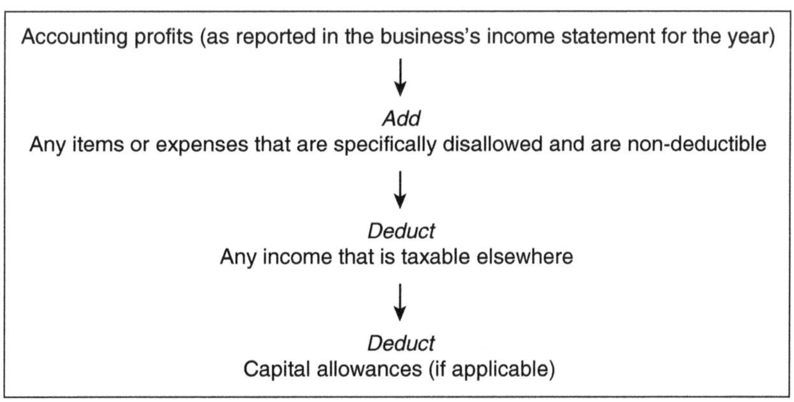

Figure 6.1 Taxable trading profits: unincorporated business

Note: Costs and expenses incurred in the 7 years immediately before a business commences trading can also be claimed as business expenses for Income Tax purposes, and can be claimed as if incurred on the first day of trading.[3]

Payment of Income Tax

Income Tax is payable in three instalments:
- 31 January (on account, based on an estimate) in the current fiscal year[4]
- 31 July (second payment on account)
- 31 January in the following fiscal year (final balancing payment).

Activity 3

Joe Mann has a business with a year-end of 31 March 2016. When would he pay his Income Tax?

Income from a partnership

There are three types of partnership: a general partnership,[5] a limited partnership,[6] and a limited liability partnership.[7]

General partnership

A general partnership is a partnership of two or more individuals co-operating in business with a view to making profits; the number is usually limited to a maximum of 20. Partners not only share responsibility for the business, but also share any profits or debts. Each partner pays tax on his or her own share of the profits.

Note: A 'partner' need not be an actual person. For example, a limited company is a 'legal person' and can therefore be a partner in a partnership.

Limited partnership

A limited partnership is a partnership similar to a general partnership, except that in addition to there being one or more *general* partners there are one or more *limited* partners. In a limited partnership, at least one partner is required to be a general partner.

The liabilities for debts differ between partners:
- general partners are liable for all the partnership's debts (or for their share of the debts)
- limited partners are liable only for partnership debts up to the amount they initially invest in the business.

General partners are also responsible for managing the business.

Limited liability partnerships

In a limited liability partnership, the partners are only liable for partnership debts up to the amount they have invested in the business, with partners' responsibilities and profit shares normally detailed in a limited liability partnership agreement.

Income Tax liability

A partnership is not treated as an entity separate from the individual partners; general partnerships, limited partnerships, limited liability partnerships *and* the partners themselves are all taxed on the same basis.

The profits of a partnership are calculated in the same way as a sole trader (see above), except that partners' drawings (the amounts taken out of, or withdrawn from, the partnership), partners' salaries and interest on partners' capital (their investment in the partnership) are non-deductible expenses and are added back to the partnership's profits. The profits are then shared between the individual partners in accordance with the partnership's profit-sharing agreement for the year, after taking into account any changes in the partnerships or the partnership agreement.

For each active year, a partnership must submit a partnership self-assessment Income Tax return to HM Revenue and Customs. In addition, each partner must:

- submit a personal self-assessment Income Tax return to HM Revenue and Customs
- pay (by the due date) any Income Tax on her or his own share of the partnership's profits
- pay (by the due date) any National Insurance on her or his own share of the partnership's profits.

Activity 4

Anthony Jacobs owns a small electrical retail business. For the year ending 31 March 2016, his income statement was as shown.

	£	£
Sales		68,210
Cost of Sales		38,465
Gross Profit		29,745
Less:		
Wages and Salaries	3,500	
Rent	1,750	
Rates	2,355	
Heating	1,650	
Lighting	2,120	
Advertising	550	
General Expenses	1,525	
Depreciation	2,450	
		15,900
Net Profit		13,845
Less:		
Drawings	11,560	
Profits retained for the year	2,285	

Notes:

1. Sales include £1,650 of electrical equipment (valued at its retail price) which Anthony took for his own personal use.
2. Capital allowances for 2015/2016 are £2,200.
3. General Expenses includes telephone costs of £605, of which £346 related to private use.

Calculate Anthony's taxable profit for the year.

6.4 Corporation Tax and small or medium-sized incorporated businesses

There are many different types of company, including for example:
- companies limited by share capital (private limited companies and public limited companies)
- companies limited by guarantee
- unlimited companies.

By far the most common, and certainly the most popular, type of company used by small and medium-sized businesses in the UK is the private limited company.[8]

Note: In legal terms, a company is a separate 'person'. It can be born (or be created); it can make contracts (make legally binding agreements); it can die (or be dissolved); and, most importantly, whilst it is 'alive' a company *must* pay taxes on any profits it earns.

Corporation Tax and accounting periods

Corporation Tax is paid by companies resident in the UK. It is charged on total taxable profits (income and gains, less allowable losses and qualifying charitable donations) for each accounting period.

An *accounting period* is different from a *period of account*. A period of account is the period over which the company prepares its accounts (usually 12 months), whereas an accounting period commences when a company starts trading, or becomes liable for Corporation Tax, and ends at the earlier of:[9]
- 12 months after its start *or*
- the end of a company's period of account.

Note: An accounting period (based on the periods of account) can never be longer than 12 months. If the period of account is longer than 12 months, there will be two accounting periods: an accounting period of 12 months *and* an accounting period for the remainder.

Taxable trading profits

The taxable trading profits of a company can be calculated as shown in Figure 6.2.

Trading income

For Corporation Tax purposes, trading income is calculated as shown in Figure 6.3.

Note: Costs and expenses incurred in the 7 years immediately before a company commences trading can also be claimed as business expenses for Corporation Tax purposes, and can be claimed as if incurred on the first day of trading.[10]

Property business income

All UK rental income is treated as a single source of income after the deduction of all allowable property-related expenses.

Interest income

A company can have two types of loan relationships:
- a debtor relationship, where the company borrows money or issues securities (for example, company bonds) *and/or*
- a creditor relationship, where the company lends money or invests in securities.

Trading income

↓

Add
Property business income

↓

Add
Interest income from non-trading loans

↓

Add
Miscellaneous income

↓

Add
Chargeable gains

↓

Deduct
Allowable losses

↓

Deduct
Qualifying charitable donations

↓

Equals
Taxable total profits for the accounting period

Figure 6.2 Taxable trading profits: incorporated business

If a company engages in a loan relationship that is for trading purposes (that is, if it borrows money to purchase plant and machinery), then any income or costs can be regarded as trade-related and included in trading income or trading expenses.

If a company engages in a loan relationship that is for non-trading purposes (that is, if it borrows money to invest in non-trade-related assets), then any income or costs must

Profit before taxation (as reported in the company's income statement for the year)

↓

Add
Any items or expenses that are specifically disallowed and are non-deductible

↓

Deduct
Any income that is taxable elsewhere

↓

Deduct
Capital allowances (if applicable)

Figure 6.3 Trading income

be pooled – they cannot be included in trading income or trading expenses, but must be shown separately.

Note: Unlike individuals, UK companies usually receive interest without the deduction of tax.

Miscellaneous income

Miscellaneous income is other income arising from non-trade, non-property-related and non-investment-related activities – for example, the ownership of intellectual property rights or goodwill.

Qualifying charitable donations

Qualifying charitable donations are deductible from total profits. In general, almost all donations to charities qualify, whether single one-off donations or regular periodic donations.

Activity 5

LYG Ltd is a small Manchester-based retailer of garden gnomes. For the year ending 31 January 2016, the company's (abbreviated) income statement was as shown.

	£	£
Sales		125,265
Cost of Sales		(68,840)
Gross Profit		56,425
Administration Costs	(8,500)	
Marketing Costs	(9,825)	
Distribution Costs	(6,500)	
Finance Costs	(3,760)	
		(28,585)
		27,840
Property Income		5,900
Investment Income		3,252
Profit before tax		36,992

Notes:

1. The following items are not allowable for Corporation Tax purposes:
   - In Administration Costs: parking fines (£1,204) and depreciation charges (£1,500).
   - In Marketing Costs: clients' gifts (£850) and entertainment costs (£1,306).
   - In Distribution Costs: stamp duty (£1,500).
   - In Finance Costs: political donations (£500).
2. LYG Ltd has capital allowances of £5,670.

Calculate the company's taxable trading income for the year.

6.5 Chargeable gains for companies

Unlike an individual, a company does not pay Capital Gains Tax on chargeable gains. Any chargeable gains are included in the total taxable profit (see Figure 6.2) and are subject to Corporation Tax.

Note: Although capital gains (less any allowable losses) are calculated in a similar way to those of an individual (see Chapter 7), there are three key differences:

- a company is *not* entitled to, and cannot claim, an annual exemption
- a company can claim an Indexation Allowance *and*
- different matching rules apply if the shareholder (whether buying or selling the shares) is a company.

Indexation Allowance

The Indexation Allowance provides relief for the inflation element of any chargeable gain – that is, its purpose is to eliminate the impact of inflation on any chargeable gain.

A company is entitled to an Indexation Allowance (based on the movement of the Retail Prices Index or RPI) from:

- the date of acquisition (the date when the asset was purchased) to
- the date of disposal (the date when the asset was sold).

The Indexation Allowance is calculated as follows:

$$\frac{RPI_{\text{month of disposal}} - RPI_{\text{month of acquisition}}}{RPI_{\text{month of acquisition}}}$$

The Indexation Allowance is available on the allowable cost of the asset and on any enhancement costs (from the date the work was undertaken). It is not available on any costs of disposal.

Note: The Indexation Allowance cannot create a loss or increase an allowable loss. Any gain before indexation can only be reduced to 0.

Activity 6

CJB Ltd purchased an asset on 1 February 2012 for £23,500 (RPI 239.9). The asset was sold for £31,200 on 1 February 2015 (RPI 256.7). What was the chargeable gain?

Disposal of shares

There are special rules for the matching of shares sold with those purchased. For a company, any shares sold are matched with purchases in the following order:

- shares acquired on the same day
- shares acquired in the previous 9 days[11]
- shares from the FA 1985 share pool.[12]

Rollover Relief

Rollover Relief allows a company to defer the payment of Corporation Tax if the company sells (or disposes of) company assets, and then uses all, or part, of the sale proceeds to purchase new company assets. Corporation Tax is payable when the new company assets are sold (or disposed of).

Rollover Relief can be claimed on a variety of business assets, including land, buildings, plant or machinery.

Note: Rollover Relief must be claimed within 4 years of the end of the tax year in which the new assets were purchased (or the year in which the old assets were sold, if that happened after).

Disincorporation Relief

Disincorporation Relief allows a company to transfer its business to its shareholders without any taxable gains or profits on land, buildings or goodwill arising.

Disincorporation Relief applies where:

- a company transfers its business to some or all of its shareholders *and*
- the transfer is a 'qualifying business transfer'[13] *and*
- the business transfer occurs between 1 April 2013 and 1 April 2018.

6.6 Corporation Tax

For 2015/2016, the rate of Corporation Tax is 20% for all UK resident companies.

Note: In the July 2015 Budget, the Chancellor of the Exchequer announced that for 2017/2018 the rate of Corporation Tax would be 19% for all companies, and that the rate of Corporation Tax would be reduced to 18% for all companies by 2020.

The deadline for the payment of Corporation Tax depends on the company's taxable profits.

Taxable profits of less than £1.5 million

For companies with a taxable profit of less than £1.5 million, the payment of Corporation Tax is due 9 months and 1 day *after* the end of the company's accounting period.

Taxable profits of more than £1.5 million

For companies with a taxable profit of more than £1.5 million, the payment of Corporation Tax must normally be made in four equal instalments, as follows:

- payment 1: due 6 months and 13 days after the first day of the accounting period
- payment 2: due 3 months after the first instalment
- payment 3: due 3 months after the second instalment (14 days after the last day of the accounting period)
- payment 4: due 3 months and 14 days after the last day of the accounting period.

Note: A company does not have to pay by instalments for an accounting period, if either:

- the company's total liability for the accounting period is less than £10,000 *or*
- the company's taxable profits for the accounting period are less than £10 million.[14]

Note: In the July 2015 Budget, the Chancellor of the Exchequer announced proposals to accelerate the payment of Corporation Tax.

6.7 Capital allowances

Both unincorporated businesses (sole traders or partnerships) and incorporated businesses (companies) can claim capital allowances when they buy assets that are retained in the business for use in the business – these are collectively referred to as 'plant and machinery'.

In most cases the value of the asset will be the value paid for the asset. However, if the asset was owned before the business commenced, or if the asset was a gift to the business, the value will be the current realisable value – that is, the market value at which it could be sold 'at arm's length'.[15]

In arriving at taxable trade profits, capital allowances are treated as trading expenses and are deducted. For unincorporated businesses, capital allowances are calculated on periods of account – the periods over which the business chooses to prepare its accounts. For incorporated businesses (or companies), capital allowances are calculated for accounting periods.

Note: If an unincorporated business (a sole trader or a partnership) uses the cash basis (see above), they cannot claim capital allowances on assets purchased, except for cars.[16]

What can capital allowances be claimed for?

Capital allowances can be claimed on plant and machinery, including:
- assets retained in the business for use in the business
- the cost of demolishing plant and machinery
- fixtures (for example, fitted kitchens, bathroom suites, fire alarm and CCTV systems)
- alterations and adaptations (but not repairs)
- integral features, such as:
  - lifts, escalators and moving walkways
  - space- and water-heating systems
  - air-conditioning and air cooling systems
  - hot and cold water systems (but not toilet and kitchen facilities)
  - electrical systems, including lighting systems
  - internal solar shading.

In addition, a business can also claim capital allowances on the following:
- renovations to business premises (in disadvantaged areas of the UK)
- extraction of minerals
- research and development
- knowhow (or intellectual property)
- patents
- dredging.

Capital allowances cannot be claimed on the following:
- lease assets
- buildings (including doors, gates, shutters, mains water and gas systems)
- land and structures
- items used primarily for business entertainment.

Main pool

With a few exceptions (see below), all expenditure on plant and machinery (including cars) is placed into a pool of assets (often referred to as the 'main pool'), on which capital allowances can be claimed. Additions increase the value of the pool, and disposals reduce the value of the pool of assets. Assets *not* placed in the main pool of assets include:

- assets placed in a special pool
- assets used by the business owner for private purposes
- assets placed in a short-life assets pool.

Different types of capital allowances

There are currently four types of capital allowances:

- an Annual Investment Allowance
- the First Year Allowance
- an Enhanced Capital Allowance
- a Writing Down Allowance.

Initially, any asset purchased by a business must be categorised as expenditure, qualifying for:

- the Annual Investment Allowance
- a First Year Allowance *or*
- an Enhanced Capital Allowance

or placed in:

- a main pool of assets
- a special-rate pool of assets
- a short-life asset pool
- a private-use asset pool

and subject, where appropriate, to either a standard or a reduced Writing Down Allowance.

Annual Investment Allowance (AIA)

A business can deduct the full value of an asset that qualifies for the Annual Investment Allowance (AIA). The allowance can only be claimed when the asset is purchased; and it cannot be claimed on cars, assets pre-owned before they were used in the business, and assets gifted (or transferred) to the business.

For 2015/2016, for a 12-month period of account, the maximum total AIA claimable was £500,000.

Note: Where a period of account is *less* than 12 months, then only a proportionate amount can be claimed.

If the asset is sold after having claimed AIA, tax may be payable on any income received from the sale – this is often referred to as a balancing charge.

Note: In the July 2015 Budget, the Chancellor of the Exchequer announced that from January 2016 the Annual Investment Allowance was set permanently at £200,000.

First Year Allowance (FYA)

If a business purchases assets that qualify for First Year Allowances, it can deduct the full cost of the asset (100%) from its profits before tax.

Note: The business can claim First Year Allowances in addition to the Annual Investment Allowance.

Enhanced Capital Allowances (ECA)

Enhanced Capital Allowances are available on green technologies – new energy-saving and water-saving plant and machinery may qualify for 100% Enhanced Capital Allowances. To qualify for Enhanced Capital Allowances, the energy-saving and water-saving plant and machinery must be included in, or meet the criteria stipulated within, either the Energy Technology List (ETL)[17] or the Water Technology List (WTL).[18]

Writing Down Allowance (WDA)

A Writing Down Allowance is given on main pool expenditure at the rate of 18% a year (on a reducing balance basis), after adjusting for additions and disposals during the year. Where an asset is sold, the proceeds of the sale (limited to a maximum of the original cost of the asset) are deducted from the main pool. As long as the business continues, the remaining pool balance can be written down in future years, even if no assets remain.

Activity 7

On 6 April 2015, Elle May had a main pool of assets of £17,500. During the year to 5 April 2016, Elle May purchased machinery for £6,000 and sold machinery for £4,500 (which originally cost £3,800). Calculate the maximum capital allowances her business can claim for 2015/2016.

Special-rate asset pool

A special-rate pool of assets contains expenditure on:

- thermal insulation
- solar panels
- long-life assets
- features integral to the business building (see above)
- cars with CO_2 emissions of over 130 g/km.

The Annual Investment Allowance can apply to the above (except expenditure on cars), but the Writing Down Allowance is only 8% (on a reducing balance basis) for a year.

Short-life asset pool

A business owner (or company director) can elect to have a specific asset that is expected to have only a short or limited life kept in a separate single-asset pool. This choice is known as a 'de-pooling' election.

Note: Specific rules apply to the disposal of short-life assets.

Private-use asset pool

An asset that is used privately by a business owner is placed in a separate single-asset pool. Capital allowances are calculated on the full cost of the asset, but the amount that can be deducted from trading profits is the proportion related to business use only. This restriction applies to the Annual Investment Allowance, First Year Allowances and Writing Down Allowances.

Note: If an asset is used privately by an employee (rather than the business owner), no such restriction applies.

6.8 Selecting a business medium

Whilst there are a number of important factors to consider when starting a business, one key factor is the selection of the business medium – that is, whether to trade as an unincorporated business (a sole trader) or as an incorporated business (a company).

Note: Some professionals – such as solicitors, accountants or architects – may not offer their services and trade through a limited company, although they may be able to do so through an unlimited company or a limited liability partnership.

Sole trader

The advantages of selecting 'sole trader' as the business medium are that:
- this is simple and easy to do
- there are no legalistic formalities
- there are no requirements to publish performance information
- as the business owner, the sole trader retains all profits.

The disadvantages of selecting 'sole trader' as the business medium are that:
- there is no limited liability: the business owner bears legal and financial responsibility for *all* the debts of the business
- there is often only limited access to external business finance.

Company

The advantages of selecting 'company' as the business medium are that:
- the company is a separate legal entity (that is, separate from its owner or owners)
- there is limited liability for the debts of the company
- there is often greater access to business finance.

The disadvantages of selecting a 'company' as the business medium are that:
- the setting-up process (especially for a plc) can be costly and time-consuming
- there are strict, and costly, administrative and financial reporting requirements.

Taxation and the selection of a business medium

Although taxation is by no means the most important factor in the selection of business medium, it can nonetheless have a major impact on why an individual actually chooses a particular business medium. It should be noted, however, that any fiscal benefit (of incorporation or otherwise) would depend on a variety of factors, such as:

- the rate of Income Tax payable on earnings as a sole trader
- the Income Tax personal allowances available as a sole trader
- the National Insurance contributions payable as a company or as a sole trader
- the rate of Corporation Tax payable on earnings as a company
- the type of remuneration paid by the company (for example, a salary, dividends, or a salary plus dividends).

Consider the following example.

Taxation and the selection of a business medium: an example

Bella Jacobs is starting a new business. She expects to make an annual taxable profit of £38,000 before tax and National Insurance, and is considering whether to start her business as a sole trader or as a company.

If Bella starts her business as a company, she has decided that she will pay herself a salary of £20,000. All remaining profits will be paid to Bella in the form of a company dividend.

Using tax rates and allowances for 2015/2016, calculate Bella's net income if:

- she starts her business as a sole trader *or*
- she starts her business as a company.

Note: See Chapter 4 for details of Income Tax rates, Income Tax allowances, National Insurance rates, and Corporation Tax rates.

Business as a sole trader If Bella Jacobs started her business as a sole trader, her net income would be as shown.

	£
Profits	38,000
Personal Allowance	(10,600)
Taxable income	27,400
Income Tax	
£27,400 @ 20%	5,480
National Insurance	
Class 2 (52 * £2.80)	146
Class 4 (£38,000 − £8,060) * 9%	2,695
Net income for the year	£29,679

Business as a company If Bella Jacobs started her business as a company, her net income would be as shown.

Choice of business medium These two sets of accounts, which use tax rates and allowances for 2015/2016, show that Bella's net income would be £29,679 as a sole trader and £31,093 as a company. Her profit would therefore be £1,414 (£31,093 − £29,679) more as a company than as a sole trader, and she would be advised to choose 'company' as her business medium.

	£	£
Profits		38,000
Less: Salary		(20,000)
		18,000
Employer's National Insurance		
(£20,000 − £8,112) * 13.8%	(1,641)	
Employment Allowance		
(below maximum £2,000)	1,641	
		0
Taxable profits		18,000
Less: Corporation Tax @ 20%		(3,600)
Net profits after tax		£14,400

Note: A dividend of £14,400 can be paid.

	Non-savings income £	Dividend income £	Total £
Earned income	20,000		20,000
Dividends (14,400 * 100/90)		16,000	16,000
			36,000
Personal Allowance	(10,600)		(10,600)
Taxable income	9,400	16,000	25,400
Non-savings income (£9,400 * 20%)			1,880
Dividend income (£16,000 * 10%)			1,600
Less: Tax suffered			(1,600)
Income Tax payable			1,880

Bella's net income would be:

	£	£
Salary		20,000
Dividends		14,400
Less: Income Tax	1,880	
Employee's National Insurance		
(£20,000 − £8,112) * 12%	1,427	
		(3,307)
Net income for the year		31,093

6.9 Concluding comments

There are significant differences in the ways in which individual Income Tax or Corporation Tax liabilities are assessed and paid. Even so, all businesses, whether unincorporated (a sole trader or a partnership) or incorporated (as a company), pay tax – either Income Tax or Corporation Tax – on *all* assessable income and earnings.

6.10 Suggested further reading

For further information on capital allowances, see:
- www.gov.uk/capital-allowances
- www.gov.uk/business-tax/capital-allowances.

Key points

- Unincorporated businesses pay Income Tax on any taxable profits and Capital Gains Tax on any chargeable gains.
- Incorporated businesses pay Corporation Tax on any taxable profit and on any chargeable gains.
- 'Badges of trade' represent a collection of principles established by case law to determine whether a person is trading, and if so whether the trading constitutes a business.
- For an unincorporated business, there are two methods of recording income (money received) and expenses (money paid out), and of assessing and calculating taxable profits for a tax year: a cash basis and an accruals basis.
- There are three types of partnership: a general partnership, a limited partnership, and a limited liability partnership.
- For a company, the indexation allowance provides relief for the impact of inflation on any chargeable gain.
- The deadline for the payment of Corporation Tax depends on the company's taxable profits.
- There are four types of capital allowances:
  - an Annual Investment Allowance
  - the First Year Allowance
  - an Enhanced Capital Allowance
  - a Writing Down Allowance.

Self-review questions

1. Distinguish between a general partnership, a limited partnership, and a limited liability partnership.
2. For Corporation Tax purposes, when does an accounting period end?
3. What is an indexation allowance?
4. Distinguish between the Annual Investment Allowance, the First Year Allowance, and the Writing Down Allowance.
5. What is a 'de-pooling' election, and why would a business make such an election?

Case study discussion questions

1. Advise Claire Carter on the legitimacy of Image 20's staff remuneration procedures.
2. Based on the income and benefits she received from Image 20 for the year ending 31 March 2016, advise Claire Carter on her tax liability.

Suggested answers to chapter activities

Activity 1

The main badges of trade include:
- a profit-seeking motive

- the organisation of the activity
- the frequency of transactions
- the period of ownership
- the method of finance
- the existence of similar trading transactions
- the nature of the asset traded
- changes to the asset traded
- the method of acquisition of the asset traded.

Activity 2

For Income Tax purposes, the following are allowable business expenses:
- accountancy, legal and other professional fees
- advertising and marketing costs
- financial charges including interest on bank and other business loans[19]
- vehicle expenses
- travel expenses
- telephone, stationery, office costs and business specific insurance costs,
- in the construction industry, payments to subcontractors
- the cost of goods (goods to be sold and goods used in providing a service)
- the profit or loss on the sale of an asset
- irrecoverable (bad) debts that are written off
- rent, rates, power and utility costs
- repairs and renewals for property and equipment
- wages, salaries and other staff costs
- other business expenses.

Activity 3

For the fiscal year 2015/2016, the Income Tax due on Joe's trading income for the year ended 31 March 2016 would be as follows:
- 1st payment on account: 31 January 2016
- 2nd payment on account: 31 July 2016
- Final balancing payment: 31 January 2017.

Activity 4

Anthony's taxable profit for the year would be as shown.

	£	£
Profit for the year		2,285
Add:		
Depreciation	2,450	
Drawings	11,560	
Sales	1,650	
General Expenses	346	
		16,006
		18,291
Less:		
Capital Allowances		(2,200)
Taxable profit for the year		16,091

Activity 5

LYG Ltd's taxable profit for the year would be as shown.

	£	£
Profit before tax		36,992
Disallowed expenses:		
Parking fines	(1,204)	
Depreciation charges	(1,500)	
Clients' gifts	(850)	
Entertainment costs	(1,306)	
Stamp duty costs	(1,500)	
Political donations	(500)	
		(6,860)
		43,852
Non-trading income:		
Property income		(5,900)
Investment income		(3,252)
		34,700
Capital allowances		(5,670)
Taxable trading profit		29,030

Activity 6

The Indexation Allowance would be: ((256.7 − 239.9)/239.9) = 0.07.

	£
Proceeds	31,200
Cost	(23,500)
Unindexed gain	7,700
Indexation allowance	
(£23,500 * 0.07)	(1,645)
Indexed gain	6,055

The chargeable gain was £6,055.

Activity 7

The maximum capital allowances for 2015/2016 that Elle May can claim would be:

	Main pool of assets
	£
Balance (brought forward)	17,500
Additions	6,000
Disposal (limited to original cost)	(3,800)
Balance	19,700
Writing Down Allowance for	
2015/2016 = £19,700 * 18%	(3,546)
Balance (carried forward)	16,154

Notes

1. With a partnership, any tax liability is a liability of the individual partner.
2. Using the cash basis, there is a maximum limit of £500.
3. This is only the case if the expenses would have qualified as an allowable expense had they actually been incurred on the date when the business commenced trading.
4. The 'fiscal year' is a period used by a company, or by Government, for accounting purposes and for preparing financial statements.
5. See: *Partnerships Act 1890.*
6. See: *Limited Partnerships Act 1907.*
7. See: *Limited Liability Partnerships Act 2000* (and also *Companies Act 2006*).
8. A private limited company is simple to create and to register (registration only costs around £25), and there are no minimum requirements in relation to initial share capital or the number of initial shareholders.
9. The accounting period can also end at other times:
   - if the company ceases trading
   - if the company is wound up
   - if the company ceases to be resident in the UK or
   - if the company ceases to be liable for Corporation Tax.
10. See: *Corporation Tax Act 2009 s.61* and *HM Revenue and Customs BIM 46355.*
11. If there are a number of acquisitions, they are matched on a 'first in, first out' (FIFO) basis.
12. Each year, a Finance Act enacts the requirements of the Government's annual budget. The share pooling requirements included in the *Finance Act 1985* relate to shares (of the same class) that were acquired between 6 April 1982 and 5 April 1998.
13. A 'qualifying business transfer' is a transfer where:
   - the business is transferred as a going concern
   - all of the assets of the business are transferred (except cash)
   - the total market value of the land, buildings and goodwill is less than £100,000 *and*
   - all the shareholders to whom the business is being transferred are individuals and have been shareholders for the previous 12 months.
14. See: www.gov.uk/corporation-tax-paying-in-instalments.
15. The term 'at arm's length' refers to a transaction in which the buyers and sellers of an asset act independently and have no relationship to each other. This is to ensure that both parties in the deal are acting in their own self-interest and are not subject to any pressure from the other party.
16. See: https://online.hmrc.gov.uk/information/help?helpcategory=selfAssessmentFiling1314&affinitygroup=&helpid=hasCashBasisAccountingPTR.
17. ETL products and assets include:
   - air-to-air energy recovery
   - automatic monitoring and targeting
   - boiler equipment
   - combined heat and power
   - compact heat exchangers
   - compressed-air equipment
   - heat pumps
   - heating ventilation and air-conditioning equipment
   - high-speed hand air dryers
   - lighting
   - motors and drives
   - pipework insulation
   - radiant and warm-air heaters
   - refrigeration equipment
   - solar thermal systems
   - uninterruptable power supplies.

   For further detailed information, see: www.gov.uk/government/publications/enhanced-capital-allowance-scheme-energy-technology-product-list.

18. WTL products and assets include:
    - 'cleaning in place' equipment (which delivers and uses water efficiently)
    - efficient showers
    - efficient taps
    - efficient toilets
    - efficient washing machines
    - flow controllers
    - leakage detection equipment
    - meters and monitoring equipment
    - rainwater-harvesting equipment
    - small-scale slurry and sludge dewatering equipment
    - vehicle-wash water reclaim units
    - water-efficient industrial cleaning equipment
    - water-management equipment for mechanical seals
    - water-reuse systems.

    For further detailed information, see: www.gov.uk/government/publications/water-efficient-enhanced-capital-allowances.
19. Using the cash basis, there is a maximum limit of £500.

7

Capital Gains Tax

Learning outcomes

By the end of this chapter, you should be able to:

- describe the key characteristics of Capital Gains Tax
- explain the impact of Capital Gains Tax on personal possessions, property, shares and investments
- describe the reliefs available to individuals and businesses.

7.1 Introduction

As a tax on the profit or gain realised on the sale (or disposal[1]) of an asset, Capital Gains Tax is a fiscal relic of the 1960s. It is a complex personal tax, dependent on an ever-expanding labyrinth of rules, reliefs, exemptions, and allowances.

This chapter explores the scope of the Capital Gains Tax and considers basic elementary calculations for individuals. The basic legislation is in the *Taxation on Chargeable Capital Gains Act 1992* (often referred to as 'TGCA 1992'). For further information, see: http://www.legislation.gov.uk/ukpga/1992/12/contents/enacted.

7.2 A brief history of Capital Gains Tax

There have been many changes to Capital Gains Tax since it was first introduced. Here is a very brief and very selective timeline:

- April 1965: Capital Gains Tax was introduced.
- April 1965–April 1977: Gains were taxed at 30%. There was no annual exemption, and there was no indexation.
- April 1977–April 1980: Relief was extended to gains of up to £9,500.
- April 1980: An annual allowance of £3,000 was introduced.
- April 1982–April 1988: Indexation[2] Relief was introduced.
- April 1988: Relief was reduced to £5,000.
- April 1988–April 2008: The 30% rate of Capital Gains Tax was abolished – capital gains were taxed at the same rate as an individual's highest rate of Income Tax. Also, indexation was replaced by Taper Relief.[3]
- April 2002: Relief was increased to £7,700.

- April 2008: Taper Relief was abolished and a single rate of Capital Gains Tax of 18% was introduced. Entrepreneurs' Relief was introduced.
- April 2009: Relief was increased to £10,100.
- June 2010: A higher rate of Capital Gains Tax (28%) was introduced.

7.3 The nature and scope of Capital Gains Tax

A 'capital gain' is a gain that arises when a person sells (or disposes of) an asset and realises a profit. For Capital Gains Tax to apply – that is, for a chargeable gain to arise – there has to be:
- a chargeable person
- a chargeable disposal *and*
- a chargeable asset.

Chargeable person

For Capital Gains Tax purposes, a 'chargeable person' is one of the following:
- an individual
- a partnership
- a company *or*
- a trustee.

Note: A person who is not resident in the UK is exempt.

Chargeable disposal

For Capital Gains Tax purposes, a 'chargeable disposal' may be any of the following:
- the sale of an asset
- the sale of part of an asset
- the gift of an asset
- the gift of part of an asset
- the receipt of money (a capital sum) on the transfer of legal title to an asset
- the loss or destruction of an asset.

Note: Transfers of assets on death are exempt disposals and are not subject to Capital Gains Tax.

Chargeable assets

Unless specifically designated as exempt, all property and assets are chargeable assets for Capital Gains Tax purposes, wherever they are located in the UK or overseas.

The following assets are exempt from Capital Gains Tax:
- motor vehicles (for private use)
- NS&I certificates and premiums
- foreign currencies and foreign-currency bank accounts (held by individuals, trustees, and personal representatives)
- life insurance policies

- awards and decorations for bravery (that have been purchased)
- damages awarded for personal or professional injury
- UK government Gilts
- works of art
- qualifying Corporate Bonds[4]
- some chattels (see below)
- dwelling houses ('principal private residences')
- the first £50,000 worth of employee shareholder shares
- shares in employer's Share Incentive Plans (SIPs)
- debts (but not debts on securities)
- gambling, betting and lottery winnings
- money or shares held in an ISA
- gifts under £100
- investments in a Venture Capital Trust (VCT), an Enterprise Investment Scheme (EIS), or a Seed Enterprise Investment Scheme (SEIS).

Gifts to a spouse, a civil partner or a charity

Capital Gains Tax is not usually payable if assets are given as a gift to a husband or wife, to a civil partner, or to a charity.

Gifts to a spouse or a civil partner

Capital Gains Tax is not payable on assets given as a gift to a husband or wife or to a civil partner, unless the husband and wife or the civil partners were separated and did not live together for the whole of the tax year, or the gift was a gift of assets for sale in a business owned by them.

Note: If the asset is sold at a later date by the receiving spouse or civil partner, Capital Gains Tax is payable then.

Gifts to a charity

Capital Gains Tax is not payable on assets given as a gift to a charity; but it *is* payable if an asset is sold to a charity both for more than the cost of acquisition (the price paid for the asset) and for less than its market value.

7.4 Rates of Capital Gains Tax and annual exemptions

For 2015/2016, Capital Gains Tax is only payable on gains above the annual exemption threshold of £11,100.[5] For trusts, the annual exemption threshold is £5,550. For standard-rate taxpayers – that is, those paying Income Tax at 20% – capital gains are taxed at a standard rate of 18%. For higher-rate taxpayers – those paying Income Tax at 40% – capital gains are taxed at a higher rate of 28% (Hargreaves & Lansdown 2015). Capital Gains Tax is payable on the taxable gains arising in a tax year: that is, on the net gains made during that tax year (for each asset, the 'disposal consideration' – that is, the money received from the sale of the asset – less any allowable costs), less any allowable losses made in that tax year.

Note: There is also a 10% rate for those who claim Entrepreneurs' Relief (see below).

Activity 1

Steve Clark is a basic-rate Income Tax payer. During 2015/2016 he made a capital gain of £35,950 and had allowable losses of £18,200. What Capital Gains Tax would be payable for 2015/2016?

If the total taxable gain is greater than the annual exemption, Capital Gains Tax will be payable unless there are unused losses from previous tax years. Where losses from previous tax years exceed the capital gain (after the deduction of the annual allowance), no Capital Gains Tax is payable.

Activity 2

Anne Smith is a basic-rate Income Tax payer. During 2015/2016 she made a capital gain of £27,000, but she had unused allowable losses from previous years of £20,500. What Capital Gains Tax would be payable for 2015/2016?

Connected persons

Losses from giving, selling or disposing of an asset to a family member (unless this is done to offset a gain from the same person) or to a connected person cannot be used. For Capital Gains Tax purposes, HM Revenue and Customs define a 'connected person' as a brother or sister, a parent, a grandparent, a son or daughter, a grandson or granddaughter (and their husbands, wives or civil partners), a business partner, or a trustee of a trust of which the individual giving, selling or disposing of the asset is the settlor.[6]

Connected persons and series of transactions

Where a person sells (or disposes of) a large asset (for example, shares in a company) to one or more connected persons in a series of small transactions within 6 years of each other, and this is done primarily to avoid Capital Gains Tax, the disposal proceeds of *all* of the transactions are linked together as if they were a single disposal.

Partnerships

When a partnership sells (or disposes of) an asset, any chargeable gain or allowable loss that may arise is apportioned to the individual partners on the basis of their existing capital or profit-sharing ratio.

7.5 Exempt organisations

For Capital Gains Tax purposes, the following organisations are exempt:
- charities
- housing associations
- friendly societies

- local authorities
- pension funds
- trade unions.

7.6 Computing gains and losses

A gain or loss is calculated by deducting the cost of an asset from the proceeds of a sale or disposal. Any incidental costs related either to the acquisition of the assets or to the disposal of the asset can be deducted, as can any expenditure on enhancing the asset before its disposal.

For Capital Gains Tax purposes, the proceeds of a sale of an asset are usually the consideration (the money) received. However, where:
- the disposal was a gift *or*
- the disposal was not negotiated or undertaken 'at arm's length' *or*
- the disposal was made for a consideration that cannot be valued,

the disposal is assumed to have taken place at market value – although special valuation rules apply to the disposal of shares. Incidental costs related to the disposal of an asset can include valuation fees, advertising fees, solicitors' fees (legal costs), and estate agents' fees. Allowable costs related to the disposal of an asset can include the original cost of acquisition, other incidental costs related to the acquisition, and any expenditure incurred on enhancing the asset (prior to disposal).

Note: Enhancement expenditure would include any spending that increases the value of an asset at the time of the disposal, or expenditure incurred in establishing, preserving or defending title (that is, the right) to an asset. It does *not* include costs of repair and maintenance, costs of insurance, or expenditure paid for by public funds.

7.7 Collection of Capital Gains Tax

HM Revenue and Customs collects Capital Gains Tax through the self-assessment system.

Capital Gains Tax is payable on or before 31 January following the tax year of disposal – that is, the tax year in which the taxable gain was made. For example, for a gain made during the 2015/2016 tax year, any Capital Gains Tax liability arising from that gain would be payable, at the latest, by 31 January 2017.

7.8 Property

A gain made on the disposal of an individual's only and main private residence[7] – often referred to as the person's 'principal private residence' – is exempt from Capital Gains Tax because it qualifies for Private Residence Relief (PRR). There are, however, some exceptions. Part or all of any gain may be taxable if:
- part of the residence is used exclusively for business purposes (see below)
- part or all of the residence is let (see below)
- the residence is converted for alternative use (for example, converted into apartments)
- part of the land or grounds (attached to and belonging to the residence) is sold and the total area is over half a hectare

- the residence was purchased (or improved) partly or wholly for the purposes of making a profit
- occupation of the residence has been on a temporary basis and there have been extended periods of non-occupation.

Note: The final 18 months of ownership are always treated as a period of occupancy, and therefore exempt for Capital Gains Tax purposes.

(For further information, see: https://www.gov.uk/government/publications/private-residence-relief-hs283-self-assessment-helpsheet/hs283-private-residence-relief.)

Business use

Where part of a private residence is used exclusively for business purposes throughout a period of ownership, any gain attributable to that part of the residence is a taxable gain and is therefore subject to Capital Gains Tax.

Activity 3

Carol Grant is a higher-rate Income Tax payer. She bought her house 12 years ago for £85,000. In May 2015 she sold the house for £278,000. During the 12 years of ownership, she used 40% of the house for her accountancy practice. What Capital Gains Tax would be payable on the disposal, and when would the Capital Gains Tax be payable?

Letting relief

Where all or part of a private residence is let, a proportion of any gain realised when the private residence is sold is subject to Capital Gains Tax, except where:
- the owner is absent from the residence and lets the property for residential use *or*
- the owner lets part of the property while occupying the remainder of the residence.

The relief available is limited to the lowest of:
- the total gain available under the PPR provision (including the 18-month exemption) *or*
- the gain related to the letting period *or*
- £40,000.

Note: Private Residence Relief and Letting Relief cannot be claimed for the same period.

Activity 4

Jessica Charlton has owned a property for 13 years (156 months). The property was her main residence for 8 years (96 months). She then used it as a second home for 2 years (24 months), and then rented out the property for the final 3 years (36 months) of ownership, before selling the property and making a profit of £90,000.

Jessica is a lower-rate Income Tax payer and has no allowable losses. What Capital Gains Tax would be payable on the disposal?

More than one private residence

An individual who has more than one private residence (either rented or owned) may elect for one of the properties to be regarded as her or his main, or primary, residence. This is known as Private Residence Relief. HM Revenue and Customs must be notified within 2 years of obtaining the second property.

As the property elected need not be the property currently occupied or the property occupied more, it is generally sensible to elect the property that would provide the largest gain should it be sold.

Note: Whereas married couples and civil partners can have only one primary private residence between them, unmarried couples can each nominate a different home.

Primary private residence rules are relaxed where an individual needs to occupy a work-related property but still own a private residence of his or her own.

Deemed occupation

The period of occupation is deemed to include periods of absence, provided that an individual has no other exempt residence and that the period of absence was preceded by, and followed by, a period of occupation.

Note: For the purposes of Capital Gains Tax, a 'deemed' occupation that did not entail actual occupation during the last 18 months of ownership does not count.

The following are periods of deemed occupation:

- any period (or periods) of absence up to 3 years
- any period (or periods) where the residence owner was required by his or her employment to live overseas
- any period (or periods), up to 4 years, in which the residence owner was required to live elsewhere (whether employed or self-employed).

7.9 Chattels and wasting assets

Gains on most chattels and wasting assets are exempt from Capital Gains Tax, and losses on them are therefore not allowable. For Capital Gains Tax purposes, a 'wasting asset' is an asset with an estimated remaining useful life of 50 years or less.

Note: Special rules apply to assets eligible for capital allowances.

Chattels

The word 'chattel' is a legal term meaning an item of tangible, *moveable* property. It includes:

- personal possessions such as items of household furniture, paintings or antiques
- items of crockery and china, plate and silverware
- motor cars, lorries, and motorcycles
- items of plant and machinery that are not permanently fixed to a building.

Wasting chattels

Wasting chattels (chattels with a predicted life of 50 years or less) are exempt from Capital Gains Tax, provided they were not eligible for business-related capital allowances.

Note: Private cars are always exempt from Capital Gains Tax, even if they are used for business purposes.

Non-wasting chattels

Even if a chattel is not exempt under the 'wasting chattels' rule, any gain on disposal will still be exempt if the chattel was sold for £6,000 or less. If the chattel was sold for between £6,000 and £15,000, the taxable gain will be the lower of *either* the actual gain *or* the amount received (less £6,000) * 5/3.

> **Activity 5**
>
> Kevin Short recently sold for £8,200 a set of antique chairs that had originally been bought for £4,460.
>
> What is the taxable gain?

If the chattel were sold for more than £15,000, the taxable gain would be calculated in the normal way.

Sets of chattels

A 'set of chattels' is a number of chattels that are similar or complementary to each other, and worth more together than separately.

The disposal of chattels in a set is treated as a number of separate disposals, unless they are sold to the same person or to persons who are connected. In that case, the £6,000 limit applies to the whole set collectively, and not to each member individually.

Wasting assets

A wasting asset is an asset (other than a chattel) that has:

- an estimated remaining useful life of 50 years or less *and*
- an original value that will depreciate over time.

Note: Freehold land is never a wasting asset.

Wasting assets are exempt from Capital Gains Tax unless they were eligible for business-related capital allowances, in which case the excess is subject to Capital Gains Tax.

7.10 Damage or destruction of assets

Damaged assets

If an asset is damaged and compensation or insurance money is received, then this situation will normally be treated as a part disposal. However, by election an individual may deduct the compensation received from the cost of the asset, provided that the capital sum received is small.

Destroyed assets

If an asset is completely destroyed and compensation or insurance money is received, the asset will be deemed to have been disposed of. The date of disposal is the date when the insurance proceeds were received, not the date when the asset was destroyed.

Negligible value claims

Sometimes the value of a chargeable asset becomes negligible, which HM Revenue and Customs interprets as meaning 'next to nothing' or virtually worthless. Subject to approval from HM Revenue and Customs, the chargeable asset in this case can be treated as if it had been sold and then repurchased at its (negligible) market value, thereby realising a loss for Capital Gains Tax purposes – a loss that can be set against other taxable gains.

A claim for negligible value can be made retrospectively for up to 2 years, providing it can be shown that the asset was owned at the time that its value became negligible. If an asset deemed to be of negligible value is subsequently sold, the whole of the sale proceeds will be subject to Capital Gains Tax.

One of the most common assets to be assigned a negligible value is a shareholding in a limited company.

7.11 Shares and other investment securities

Capital Gains Tax is payable on any profit or gain realised on the disposal of shares or other investment securities. These include:

- shares that are not included in an Individual Savings Account (ISA) or a Personal Equity Plan (PEP)
- units in a unit trust
- some bonds (see below).

Capital Gains Tax is not usually payable if shares or other investment securities are given as a gift to a husband or wife, a civil partner, or a charity. In addition, it is not payable on any profit or gain realised on the sale or disposal of:

- shares included in an ISA or PEP
- the first £50,000 of employee shareholder shares
- shares in employers' Share Incentive Plans (SIPs)
- UK government Gilts (including Premium Bonds)
- qualifying Corporate Bonds.[8]

Matching and pooling

There are special rules for the matching of shares and other investment securities sold with shares and securities purchased. For an individual, share and other investment securities sold are matched with purchases in the following order:

- acquisitions on the same day as the disposal (the 'same day' rule) *then*
- acquisitions within the following 30 days (the 'bed and breakfasting' rule)[9] *then*
- any shares in the share pool (using average cost).

Note: Some costs incurred when buying or selling shares can be deducted from any gain: such costs include stockbrokers' costs and fees, and Stamp Duty Reserve Tax (SDRT) incurred when the shares were purchased.

> ## Activity 6
>
> In July 2009 David Trent purchased 6,500 shares in Tuckman plc at a cost of £22,750. In September 2015, David Trent sold 4,200 shares in Tuckman for £25,200. Calculate the gain and the value of the share pool following the disposal.

Note: The share pooling and matching rules do not apply to employee shareholder shares (see below).

Using market value

In some situations, the *market value* of the shares or investment securities is used. This is done when the shares or investment securities were:

- given as a gift to someone other than a spouse, a civil partner, or a charity
- sold for less than they were worth
- inherited
- owned before April 1982
- acquired through an employee share scheme.

Special circumstances

There are special rules for calculating the cost of shares if an individual:

- sells shares in the same company that were purchased at different times and at different prices
- sells shares through an investment club
- sells shares in a company after a merger or takeover
- sells shares in an employee share scheme.

Selling shares in the same company

If shares in the same company are sold that were purchased at different times and at different prices, the gain is calculated by deducting from the sale proceeds the *average cost* of the shares.

> ## Activity 7
>
> Over the past year, Ellie Charlton bought shares in FTA plc as follows:
>
> - 100 shares for £180
> - 300 shares for £460
> - 200 shares for £320.
>
> Then 4 months ago Eli sold 350 shares for £800. What was his gain on the sale of these shares?

Selling shares through an investment club

An investment club is a collective of individuals who buy and sell shares together. Annually the investment club will provide individual investors in the club with a statement – an investment club certificate – detailing any gains and losses.

Leaving the investment club

If an individual investor leaves an investment club and the club buys back his or her shares, any taxable gain or allowable loss would be:

- the amount received from the investment club
- *less* the investor's share of any net gains
- *plus* any funds (including dividends) received
- *less* any amounts paid in.

Transferring shares into the investment club

If an individual investor transfers into the club shares that she or he already owns, the shares are deemed to have been sold to the investment club on the date of the transfer.

Selling shares in a company after a merger or takeover

Where an individual holds shares in a company and that company is acquired by another company,[10] the most common forms of compensation are shares, cash or securities, or any combination of these.

Shares

If the acquiring company issues shares, no Capital Gains Tax is payable when the shares are received. When the shares are sold, however, they are deemed to have been bought at the same time and at the same cost as the original shares.

Shares and cash

If the acquiring company issues shares as well as paying some cash, Capital Gains Tax may be payable on the cash received. Capital Gains Tax is payable if the cash is less than £3,000 (or less than 5% of the value of the shares in the company) *and* if the cash received is less than the cost of the original shares. When the shares are sold, the allowable cost is the cost of the original shares less the amount of cash received.

Where the cash received is more than £3,000 (or equal to or more than 5% of the value of the shares in the company) *and* the cash received is more than the cost of the original shares, alternative rules apply.

Securities

If the acquiring company issues securities and the securities are qualifying Corporate Bonds, the gain is calculated as if the original shares had been sold at their market value immediately before the takeover, and the gain is not chargeable to Capital Gains Tax until the securities are sold. If the securities are not qualifying Corporate Bonds, they are treated in the same way as shares issued in a merger or takeover.

Selling shares in an employee share scheme

If a company employer offers an employee shares in the company, possible tax advantages – Income Tax, National Insurance, and Capital Gains Tax – may arise. However, such tax advantages only apply if the shares are offered through:

- a Share Incentive Plan (SIP)
- a Save As You Earn (SAYE) scheme
- a Company Share Option Plan (CSOP) *or*
- an Enterprise Management Incentive (EMI).

Some tax advantages are also available to employee shareholders.

Note: Before April 2014 all Share Incentive Plans, Save As You Earn schemes and Company Share Option Plans had to be approved by HM Revenue and Customs. From April 2014, however, all Share Incentive Plans, Save As You Earn schemes and Company Share Option Plan must be registered but can be self-certified.

Share Incentive Plans (SIP)

Launched in July 2000, a Share Incentive Plan (SIP) provides a company with the opportunity to give or sell to its employees shares in the company that also offer attractive tax breaks.

Note: Shares in a Share Incentive Plan must be fully-paid irredeemable ordinary shares in a company, and the company must be either listed in a recognised stock exchange (or in a subsidiary) or at least not controlled by another company.

If an employee receives shares through, or purchases shares in, a company Share Incentive Plan, no Capital Gains Tax is payable provided that the employee:
- sells the shares immediately or
- keeps the shares in the Share Incentive Plan until they are sold.

A third possibility, in which case a Capital Gains Tax charge may arise, is for the employee to take shares out of the plan, but keep them and sell them at a later date. For Capital Gains Tax purposes, the cost of the shares would then be the market value of the shares at the date they were withdrawn from the Share Incentive Plan, and a gain would arise only if there had been a subsequent increase in the market value of the shares.

Acquiring shares in a Share Incentive Plan There are four ways in which an employee can acquire shares in a Share Incentive Plan:
- Free shares: an employer gives employees shares free of charge. (This is limited to £3,600 of free shares in any tax year.)
- Partnership shares: an employee purchases shares which are usually funded through a deduction out of the employee's pre-tax salary. (This is limited to the lower of £1,800 or 10% of the employee's salary for the tax year.)
- Matching shares: an employer awards an employee up to two free matching shares for each partnership share he or she purchases.
- Dividend shares: an employee uses dividends received from shares in a Share Incentive Plan to purchase additional shares in the Plan.

Note: For free shares and matching shares, there is no Income Tax and National Insurance liability provided that shares are retained in the Plan for at least 3 years. However, if an employee withdraws shares after 3 years, there is an Income Tax and National Insurance charge based on the market value of the shares when they are withdrawn. Once shares have been held within a Share Incentive Plan for 5 years, there is no Income Tax or National Insurance charge when they are withdrawn.

Save As You Earn (SAYE) scheme

A Save As You Earn (SAYE) scheme must be open to all full-time and part-time employees, and to full-time directors.

The scheme allows employees and directors to make a monthly investment (between £5 and £500 a month) into a sharesave account. The investment period is usually 3, 5 or 7 years, during which a tax-free bonus is added to the sharesave account by way of interest. At the end of the investment period, the employee or director can either withdraw the funds in cash or use the funds to purchase ordinary shares in the company (or its parent or holding company). If shares are purchased and subsequently sold, any taxable gain or loss would be based on the sale price less the price[11] at which the employee acquired the shares under the scheme purchase option.

Note: Any (interest) bonus is tax-free, and there is no Income Tax or National Insurance liability on the difference between what the employee pays for the shares and the market value of the shares on the date they were purchased.

Transferring shares to an ISA

When an employee withdraws shares from a Share Incentive Plan or a Save As You Earn scheme, any gain or increase in value can be ignored if they are transferred (within 90 days) to a share ISA. This transfer is, however, limited to a maximum of £15,000 in any tax year.

Company Share Option Plans (CSOPs)

A Company Share Option Plan (CSOP), which need not be open to all employees, provides selected employees and full-time directors with the option to purchase shares in the company at a future date at a set price. Any option must be exercised within 3–10 years from the date the option is granted, and can be up to a value of £30,000.

Note: The set price cannot be less than the market value of the shares on the date the option is granted.

If the option is exercised and the shares are subsequently sold, any taxable gain or loss would be based on the sale price less the option price at which the shares were acquired.

Note: There is no Income Tax or National Insurance liability on the granting of the option, nor on the sale of shares acquired under a Company Share Option Plan. However, this exemption is lost if the shares are sold in less than 3 years or more than 10 years.

Enterprise Management Incentives (EMIs)

Launched in 2000, Enterprise Management Incentives (EMIs) are tax-advantaged share options designed to help small or medium-sized higher-risk companies to recruit and retain employees. To qualify, a company must have maximum gross assets of no more than £30 million, and at least 250 full-time equivalent employees.

Companies that undertake excluded activities are not allowed to offer Enterprise Management Incentives. Such activities include:

- the provision of legal services
- the provision of banking services
- property development
- farming-related activities
- shipbuilding.

Enterprise Management Incentives are very similar to company share option schemes, inasmuch as an employee is granted an option to purchase shares in the company.

The shares to which the option relates *must be* fully paid-up irredeemable ordinary shares. The scheme need not be open to all employees; to qualify an employee must:
- be employed by the company (or a subsidiary) whose shares are the subject of the option *and*
- spend at least 25 hours a week (or at least 75% of her or his working time) working for the company (or for other subsidiary companies within the group).

Share options with a market value of up to £250,000 may be granted to a qualifying employee. This is subject to a total share value of £3 million for all share options granted by a company under the scheme.

If the option is exercised and the shares are subsequently sold, any taxable gain or loss would be based on the sale price less the option price of the shares.

Note: The grant of the option is tax-free and there is normally no Income Tax or National Insurance liability when the option is exercised, provided that the option is exercised within 10 years of the granting of the option and that the exercise price is at least equal to the market value of the shares on the date when the option was granted. However, if the option was granted at a price less than the market value of the shares on that date, Income Tax may be payable when the option is exercised.

Employee shareholder shares

An 'employee shareholder' is an employee who is employed under an 'employee shareholder employment contract'. In exchange for giving up certain employment rights, the employee is given shares in the employer's company (or parent company) which must have a minimum value of £2,000. (There is no maximum.)

If the total value of the shares acquired is less than £50,000, any gain on the disposal of employee shareholder shares by the employee shareholder is exempt from Capital Gains Tax. If the total value of the shares acquired is greater than £50,000, only the first £50,000 is exempt from Capital Gains Tax. If a loss arises, the loss is not an allowable loss for Capital Gains Tax purposes.

Note: If £2,000 worth of shares are provided to an employee shareholder, there is no Income Tax or National Insurance liability (the employee shareholder is deemed to have made a payment of £2,000 for the shares). If more than £2,000 worth of shares are provided to an employee shareholder, the excess over £2,000 is subject to Income Tax or National Insurance.

(For further details on employee shareholders, see: www.gov.uk/employee-shareholders.)

7.12 Capital Gains Tax Relief

In addition to the reliefs discussed above, the following reliefs may also be available:
- Rollover Relief
- Gift Hold-Over Relief
- Entrepreneurs' Relief
- Incorporation Relief.

Rollover Relief

Rollover Relief allows a business to defer the payment of Capital Gains Tax if the business sells (or disposes of) business assets, and to use all or part of the sale proceeds to purchase new business assets. Capital Gains Tax is then payable when the new business assets are sold (or disposed of).

To qualify for Rollover Relief:

- the business must have been trading when the old business assets were sold (or disposed of) and the new business assets were purchased
- the business must purchase the new assets:
  - up to 1 year before the new business assets are purchased *or*
  - within 3 years of selling (or disposing of) the old business assets

    and
- the old assets and the new assets must be used wholly and exclusively for the business.

Rollover Relief can be claimed on a variety of business assets, including land, buildings, plant or machinery; and, in some cases, goodwill.

Amended rules apply if only part of the sale proceeds are reinvested in new business assets; or if the assets sold are only partly used in the business; or if the sale proceeds are used to purchase depreciating assets.

Note: Rollover Relief must be claimed within 4 years of the end of the tax year in which the new assets were purchased (or the old ones sold, if that happened after).

Gift Hold-Over Relief

Gift Hold-Over Relief is available when an individual:

- gives away qualifying business assets (including some shares) *or*
- sells qualifying business assets for less than their current value.

With Gift Hold-Over Relief, no Capital Gains Tax is paid when the business assets are given away; but Capital Gains Tax is payable when the new owner sells (or disposes of) the business assets. A claim for Gift Hold-Over Relief requires confirmation of the transfer from both parties in the transfer.

Note: Capital Gains Tax is not usually payable on gifts to a husband or wife, a civil partner, or a charity.

Gift Hold-Over Relief can be claimed on the gift or the sale (at lower than the current value) of a variety of assets, including business assets used in a trade, profession or vocation, agricultural property, and shares and securities in a trading company.

Entrepreneurs' Relief

Entrepreneurs' Relief reduces the rate of Capital Gains Tax on the disposal of qualifying assets from 18% (or 28%) to 10%. It is a lifetime allowance of £10 million. To be eligible, a shareholder must have a 5% shareholding or greater, and must have been involved for a year or more with the company as an employee or a director.

There are three types of qualifying disposals:

- the disposal of all or part of a business
- the disposal of assets used in a business that is no longer trading
- the disposal of shares or securities.

Disposal of all or part of a business

To qualify:

- the business must be a trade, profession or vocation that is conducted on a commercial basis

- the business must have been conducted with the aim of realising a profit
- the business must have been owned (or partly owned) by the individual claiming Entrepreneurs' Relief (that is, a sole trader or a partnership)
- the individual must have owned the business for at least 1 year before the date of sale or the date of closure *and*
- the sale (or disposal) of any business assets must occur within 3 years of selling or closing the business.

Disposal of assets used in a business that is no longer trading

To qualify:

- the individual must have owned the business for at least 1 year before the date of sale or the date of closure *and*
- the sale (or disposal) of any business assets must occur within 3 years of selling or closing the business.

Disposal of shares or securities

To qualify:

- the main activities of the company to which the shares (or securities) relate must be of a trading nature
- the individual claiming Entrepreneurs' Relief must have at least 5% of the shares and voting rights in the company *and*
- the individual claiming Entrepreneurs' Relief must be an employee or a director of the company (or a company in the same group).

Incorporation Relief

Unlike many other reliefs, Incorporation Relief is automatic – it does not have to be claimed. It applies when a business, whether operating as a sole trader or as a partnership, is incorporated – that is, converted into a company. Incorporation Relief allows individuals to delay the payment of Capital Gains Tax if they transfer their business to a company in return for shares. Capital Gains Tax becomes payable when the shares in the company are sold (or disposed of).

Note: The transfer of the business and all its assets (except cash) *must* be in exchange for shares in the company. If cash is received, Incorporation Relief is only available for the proportion of the business exchanged for shares; and Capital Gains Tax will be payable for the proportion of the business exchanged for cash.

7.13 Divorce and separation

For Capital Gains Tax purposes, an individual and her or his spouse or civil partner are separate individuals. Although they may be regarded as 'connected' (see above), they each pay Capital Gains Tax on their own gains and they each receive relief for their own losses.

Living together

If an individual and her or his spouse or civil partner are living together, any transfer of assets between them does not give rise to either a gain or a loss for the person transferring it. Any amount actually paid is ignored; and if the transferee (the spouse or civil partner receiving the asset) subsequently sells (or disposes of) the asset, the transferee is treated as if she or he had paid an amount equal to the total of the transferor's costs.

Note: An individual and her or his spouse or civil partner are treated as living together unless they are separated under a court order, or by a deed of separation executed under seal, or in such circumstances that the separation is likely to be permanent. In each case, the marriage or civil partnership is deemed to have broken down.[12]

If an individual and her or his spouse or civil partner are *not* living together, any asset transferred between them is treated as having been transferred at its market value at the time of the transfer, in which case the transferor may make a chargeable gain or an allowable loss.

Permanent separation

If an individual and her or his spouse or civil partner were living together at some time during a tax year, they can transfer assets between themselves at any time in that tax year without realising any gain or loss.

Note: There is no requirement that an individual and her or his spouse or civil partner should be living together at the time of the transfer.

If a transfer occurs between an individual and her or his spouse or civil partner *after* the end of the tax year in which they ceased to live together, a chargeable gain or allowable loss may arise (depending on the date of disposal and the value of the assets at the time of disposal).

Note: On permanent separation, Capital Gains Tax issues may also arise in relation to a property on which Private Residence Relief has previously been claimed.

7.14 Trusts

A trust is a way of managing assets. There are many different types of trusts (see Chapter 5), and they are created for a variety of reasons, including:

- to control family assets
- to protect family assets
- to manage the assets and affairs of a minor
- to manage the assets and affairs of someone who is unable to manage his or her assets or affairs (because of a physical or mental incapacity) *and/or*
- to transfer assets when an individual dies (a will trust).

The trustees of any trust are responsible for paying any Capital Gains Tax due on trust assets that are sold (or disposed of), given away, exchanged, or transferred. In 2015/2016, the Capital Gains Tax rate for trustees is 28%; with trusts receiving an annual exemption of £5,500 (or £11,100 if the beneficiary, or one of the beneficiaries, is disabled).

Note: Where a settlor creates several trusts, the annual exemption is divided equally between them, subject to a minimum exemption of £1,090 for each trust. (See: http://www.wgn.co.uk/tax-data/789-capital-gains-tax.html.)

Assets placed into a trust

When assets are placed into a trust, Capital Gains Tax is payable by:

- the person selling the asset (although she or he can claim Hold-Over Relief – see above) *or*
- the person transferring the asset (the settlor).

Assets taken out of a trust

The trustees usually have to pay Capital Gains Tax if they sell or transfer assets on behalf of the trust beneficiary (or beneficiaries). There is no tax to pay in a bare trust when the assets are transferred to the beneficiary (or beneficiaries)

Note: In calculating a taxable gain or an allowable loss, trustees can deduct costs to reduce the gains, including the cost of improving property or land to increase its value (but not repairs or regular maintenance) and professional fees.

Tax reliefs

Trustees may be able to reduce the amount of Capital Gains Tax payable, or to delay the payment of Capital Gains Tax, if eligible for the following tax reliefs:

- Private Residence Relief
- Entrepreneurs' Relief
- Hold-Over Relief.

Private Residence Relief

Trustees do not pay Capital Gains Tax when they sell (or dispose of) a property or residence owned by the trust – but in order to be exempt, the property or residence *must* become the main residence of the individual whom the trust has authorised or allowed to live there.

Entrepreneurs' Relief

Trustees pay 10% Capital Gains Tax on gains made if they sell (or dispose of) assets used in a business that was owned by the beneficiary of the trust and that has now ceased trading; and if they sell (or dispose of) shares in a company of which the beneficiary of the trust owned at least 5% of the shares and voting rights.

Hold-Over Relief

Trustees pay no Capital Gains Tax if they transfer assets to beneficiaries (or to trustees of other trusts, in some cases). The recipient pays tax when she or he sells or disposes of the assets, unless of course she or he also claims relief.

7.15 Concluding comments

Capital Gains Tax is often viewed as a 'voluntary' tax, because of the sheer number of exemptions, reliefs and allowances, yet it is does raise valuable tax revenue for the government. Nevertheless, it is frequently criticised not only for discouraging entrepreneurship, savings and investment, but more importantly for adversely affecting economic growth. There seems little doubt that the future of Capital Gains Tax as a personal tax, whilst unclear and uncertain, is definitely limited.

7.16 Suggested further reading

For further reading on the following topics, see the references given.
Capital Gains Tax:
- www.gov.uk/capital-gains-tax

Employee share schemes:
- www.gov.uk/tax-employee-share-schemes

Entrepreneurs' Relief:
- www.gov.uk/entrepreneurs-relief

Gift Hold-Over Relief:
- www.gov.uk/gift-holdover-relief

Private Residence Relief:
- www.gov.uk/tax-sell-home/private-residence-relief

Key points

- Capital Gains Tax can only arise where there is a chargeable person, a chargeable disposal, and a chargeable asset, and is only payable on gains above the annual exemption threshold.
- For basic-rate Income Tax payers, capital gains are taxed at a standard rate of 18%, and for higher-rate Income Tax payers, capital gains are taxed at a higher rate of 28%.
- Capital Gains Tax is not usually payable if assets are given as a gift to a husband (or wife), to a civil partner or to a charity.
- A gain made on the disposal of an individual's only and main private residence (often referred to as their principle private residence) is exempt from Capital Gains Tax.
- Gains on most chattels and wasting assets are exempt from Capital Gains Tax.
- Capital Gains Tax is payable on any profit/gain realised on the disposal of shares and/or other investment securities, with special rules for the matching of shares and other investment securities sold with those purchased.
- There are special rules for calculating the cost of shares if an individual sells shares purchased at different times and at different prices in the same company, shares through an investment club, shares in a company after merger or takeover, and shares in an employee share scheme.

Self-review questions

1. Which assets are subject to Capital Gains Tax?
2. What losses cannot be offset against a taxable gain?
3. Define a *chattel* and a *wasting asset*, and distinguish between them.
4. Distinguish between a *Share Incentive Plan* (SIP) and a *Company Share Option Plan* (CSOP).
5. In terms of shares and securities, explain the terms *matching* and *pooling*.

Case study discussion questions

1. Advise Stuart and Mary Carter on the Capital Gains Tax implications of selling their apartment in Bath.
2. Briefly describe the possible advantages and disadvantages of their proposed Share Incentive Plan for the company and its employees.

Suggested answers to chapter activities

Activity 1

The Capital Gains Tax payable by Steve Clark for 2015/2016 would be calculated as follows:

	£
Capital gain	35,950
Allowable loss	(18,200)
	17,750
Annual allowance	(11,100)
Taxable gain	6,650
Capital Gains Tax rate	18%
Capital Gains Tax payable: £6,650 * 18% = £1,197	

Activity 2

The Capital Gains Tax payable by Anne Smith for 2015/2016 would be calculated as follows:

	£
Capital gain	27,000
Annual allowance	(11,100)
	15,900
Unused allowable losses	(20,500)
Allowable losses carried forward	(4,600)
Capital Gains Tax rate	18%
Capital Gains Tax payable: £0 * 18% = £0	

Activity 3

The Capital Gains Tax payable by Carol Grant for 2015/2016 would be calculated as follows:

	£
Sale proceeds	278,000
Cost	(85,000)
Gain before PPR exemption	193,000
PPR exemption (60%)	(115,800)
Gain	77,200
Annual allowance	(11,100)
Gain	66,100
Capital Gains Tax payable: £66,100 * 28% = £18,508	

The Capital Gains Tax would be payable on or before 31 January 2017.

Activity 4

The Capital Gains Tax payable by Jessica Charlton for 2015/2016 would be calculated as follows:

1. Private Residence Relief can be claimed for 96 months, plus 18 months for the final period of ownership, a total of 114 months. That is 73% (114/156), which means that £65,700 of the £90,000 gain (£90,000 * 73%) is tax-free and the taxable gain is £24,300.
2. From the remaining £24,300 gain, Letting Relief for 18 months would be available (36 months' letting period – 18 months' primary private residence). The gain attributable to the letting period is 11.5% (18/156): 11.5% * £90,000 = £10,350.
3. The amount of Letting Relief is the lowest of the attributable gain (£10,350) *or* the Private Residence Relief claimed (£65,700) *or* £40,000. The taxable gain is therefore £24,300 − £10,350 = £13,950.

Capital Gains Tax payable would therefore be: (£13,950 − £11,100) * 18% = £2,850 * 18% = £513.

Activity 5

The taxable gain is the lower of the actual gain of *either* (£8,200 − £4,460) = £3,740 *or* (£8,200 − £6,000) * 5/3 = £3,667.

Since £3,667 is the lower figure, that would be the taxable gain.

Activity 6

The gain and the value of the share pool following the disposal by David Trent would be calculated as follows:

	£	
Proceeds of sale	25,200	
Less: cost	(14,700)†	
Gain	10,500	
Share pool		
	Number	Value
		£
Acquisition (July 2009)	6,500	22,750
Disposal (Sept. 2015)	4,200	14,700
	2,300	8,050

† (4,200/6,500) * £22,750 = £14,700.

Activity 7

The average cost of Ellie Charlton's shares is (£180+£460+£320)/(100+300+200) = £960/600) = £1.60.

	£
Sale proceeds	800
less: Cost (350*£1.60)	560
Gain	240

Eli's gain on the sale of these shares would therefore be £240.

Notes

1. In general, the word 'sale' is used to denote a transaction carried out 'at arm's length' – a transaction in which one asset is exchanged for another: money. The word 'disposal' is used to denote a situation in which there is no *exchange*, because the asset has no value.
2. Indexation changes the acquisition cost of an asset by the increase in RPI between acquisition and disposal. This method is still used for gains made by companies.
3. Taper Relief reduced the percentage of the gain subject to Capital Gains Tax according to how long the asset had been owned.
4. A qualifying Corporate Bond is a security that:
   - represents a normal commercial loan
   - is expressed in sterling
   - does not have a redemption value dependent on a published index of share prices *and*
   - was acquired (after 13 March 1984) by the individual disposing of it.
5. The exemption cannot be carried forward to future tax years if it is not fully utilised in the current tax year.
6. The settlor is the person who puts assets into a trust for the benefit of the trust beneficiaries.
7. The exemptions cover both house and grounds (up to half a hectare).
8. A qualifying Corporate Bond is a debt security that satisfies all of the following criteria:
   - the Bond is a sterling currency bond
   - the Bond has no rights of conversion into a currency other than sterling
   - the Bond has no rights of redemption in a currency other than sterling
   - the Bond has no rights of conversion to shares or other securities
   - the interest paid on the Bond must not exceed a reasonable commercial return
   - the interest paid on the Bond must not depend on the results of all or part of the bond issuer's business
   - the Bond is redeemable at par (or on terms comparable with other similar listed debt securities).
9. If there is more than one acquisition, they are matched on a 'first in, first out' (FIFO) basis.
10. See: www.gov.uk/capital-gains-tax-share-reorganisation-takeover-or-merger.
11. The price of the shares must be at least 80% of the market value of the shares on the date on which the (purchase) option is granted.
12. For Capital Gains Tax purposes, if the marriage or civil partnership has not broken down but an individual and his or her spouse or civil partner do not live in the same residence, they are still treated as living together.

8

Inheritance Tax

Learning outcomes

By the end of this chapter, you should be able to:

- describe the key characteristics of Inheritance Tax
- distinguish between different types of Inheritance Tax exemptions
- describe the Inheritance Tax reliefs available to individuals
- explain the main measures taken to avoid Inheritance Tax.

8.1 Introduction

Unlike many other taxes, Inheritance Tax (IHT) is an avoidable tax. Indeed, relatively few estates are actually liable for Inheritance Tax,[1] which is why many refer to Inheritance Tax as a 'voluntary' tax – good tax planning and forward-thinking financial management can, in the majority of cases, totally eliminate any Inheritance Tax liability.

This chapter explores:

- the scope and nature of Inheritance Tax as a wealth tax
- the exemptions from the *Inheritance Tax Act 1985* (as amended)
- how Inheritance Tax can be avoided through careful planning.

Note: Provisions are amended and updated as required by the Government's annual *Finance Act.*

8.2 A brief history of Inheritance Tax (IHT)

Inheritance Tax (IHT) is essentially a transfer tax. Its history can be traced back to the late 18th century and to the introduction in 1796 of Legacy, Estate and Succession Duties, which were imposed on *all* estates. In 1857, Legacy, Estate and Succession Duties were restricted to estates valued at more than £20, although in practice it proved difficult to administer and was only collected on estates valued at more than £1,500.

Death Duties were introduced in 1894 and remained in place until 1975, when they were replaced by Capital Transfer Tax. In 1986 Capital Transfer Tax was in turn replaced by Inheritance Tax.

8.3 The nature and scope of Inheritance Tax

Inheritance Tax is a tax on gifts – or, more specifically, a tax on the transfer of assets (of value) made by chargeable persons. It is a tax on the transfer of assets, worldwide, made by persons who are domiciled (or who are deemed to be domiciled[2]) in the UK.

Chargeable persons

For Inheritance Tax purposes, chargeable persons include individuals (spouses and civil partners are taxed separately) and trustees of settled property. Companies are not chargeable persons.

Note: For individuals *not* domiciled in the UK, only transfers of UK assets are subject to Inheritance Tax.

Chargeable transfers

Inheritance Tax can only arise were there has been a chargeable transfer of value (or gift) – that is, a transfer that results in the transferor (or the transferor's estate) suffering a reduction in wealth. There are two types of chargeable transfers:

- transfers of value (or gifts) made during the lifetime of the transferor (chargeable lifetime transfers) *and*
- transfers of value (or gifts) made on the death of the transferor (as a bequest made in a will – estate transfers at death).

Note: For Inheritance Tax purposes, the value of the transfer (or gift) is measured by the loss suffered by the transferor, and not the amount gained by the transferee.

8.4 Basic principles

Inheritance Tax thresholds

For 2015/2016, individuals have a tax-free inheritance allowance of £325,000 (see: https://www.gov.uk/inheritance-tax).

Note: The amount below £325,000 is often referred to as the 'Nil' band.

Subject to some exceptions,[3] this individual tax-free allowance is transferable. A surviving spouse or civil partner is allowed not only to use his or her own tax-free allowance but also to use any *unused* tax-free allowance from the deceased spouse or civil partner (even if the surviving spouse or civil partner remarries or enters into a new civil partnership). This transfer of tax-free allowance is actioned when the surviving spouse or civil partner dies.

Note: In the July 2015 Budget, the Chancellor of the Exchequer announced Government proposals to add a tapered[4] Family Home Allowance of £175,000 per person to the existing £325,000 tax-free allowance from April 2017.

Rates of Inheritance Tax

For 2015/2016, an estate worth more than £325,000 (after deducting allowable debts and expenses) is subject to an Inheritance Tax charge of 40%. For example, an estate worth £700,000 would be subject to an Inheritance Tax charge of £150,000 – that is, (£700,000 − £325,000) * 40%.

If, however, the estate were that of an individual whose deceased spouse or civil partner had died without using any of her or his tax-free allowance, the estate would be subject to an Inheritance Tax charge of £20,000 – that is: (£700,000 − (£325,000 + £325,000)) * 40%.

Note: If 10% or more of the net value[5] of the estate is left to a registered charity, an estate can pay Inheritance Tax at a reduced rate of 36% on some assets (instead of 40%). See: https://www.gov.uk/inheritance-tax/giving-to-charity-to-reduce-an-inheritance-tax-bill.

Activity 1

In terms of Inheritance Tax, distinguish between the two main types of chargeable transfers.

Payment of Inheritance Tax

Inheritance Tax that becomes due on money, possessions or assets transferred when an individual dies is usually paid from the deceased's estate. If Inheritance Tax becomes due on transfers of value (or gifts) made during the last 7 years before the transferor's death, it is the individual who receives the gift or gifts (the transferee) who must pay the Inheritance Tax.[6]

Note: Inheritance Tax would become due only if the deceased gave away gifts worth more than £325,000 in that period.

Any Inheritance Tax must be paid by the end of the sixth month after the death of the transferor; if not, interest charges may be imposed. (The due dates are different for payments on a trust.) Payments can be made from:

- the transferee's bank account
- the transferor's bank account
- a joint bank account of which the transferor (the deceased) was one of the account holders *and/or*
- government savings and investments owned by the transferor (for example, NS&I or government Gilts).

In some cases, Inheritance Tax payments can be made by transferring national heritage property[7] to the Crown.

Note: Inheritance Tax can be paid in annual instalments (equal amounts) over a maximum period of 10 years.

Exceptions to Inheritance Tax

For Inheritance Tax purposes, the following transfers are not regarded as chargeable transfers:

- expenditure on family maintenance (such as the payment of education fees or charges)
- transfers made in the course of a trade, profession or vocation (such as birthday or Christmas gifts to employees)

- transfers where there is no gratuitous intent (made 'at arm's length' and between unconnected individuals)
- waivers of remuneration
- waivers of dividends (if made within the 12 months before the dividend is declared)
- transfers of excluded property (see below)
- transfers that are exempt from Inheritance Tax.

Exemptions from Inheritance Tax

Exemptions are available that can reduce or even eliminate the chargeable amount of Inheritance Tax:
- lifetime transfers (including potentially exempt transfers: see below)
- a transfer on the transferor's death.

Some exemptions apply to lifetime transfers only; some apply to both lifetime transfers and to transfers on death.

Exemptions that apply to lifetime transfers

Annual exemption All individuals have an annual exemption of £3,000. Any unused annual exemption can be carried forward for 1 year only. Spouses and civil partners each have their own individual annual exemption.

Note: The annual exemption cannot be combined with the small gift exemption (see below).

Small gift exemption There is no Inheritance Tax on gifts (to any individual) of up to £250, unless in the same tax year the deceased gave the same individual more than £250 worth of gifts or other gifts that were free from Inheritance Tax.

Gifts in consideration of a marriage or civil partnership There is no Inheritance Tax on a gift in consideration of a wedding or civil partnership, up to these limits:
- £5,000 from each parent of the couple
- £2,500 from each grandparent (or more remote relative) of the couple
- £2,500 from the bridegroom to the bride, or from the bride to the bridegroom
- £1,000 from anyone else.

Note: The gift must be given on or shortly before the date of the wedding or the civil partnership ceremony.

Normal expenditure out of income Transfers of value (or gifts) made as part of normal expenditure are exempt from Inheritance Tax, providing that the gift does not reduce the transferor's standard of living.

Note: Inheritance Tax is a tax on transfers of capital, not income.

Exemptions that apply to lifetime transfers and to transfers on death

Gifts between spouses or civil partners Transfers of value (or gifts) between spouses and civil partners who are both domiciled (or deemed to be domiciled) in the UK are exempt from Inheritance Tax. The exemption covers both lifetime transfers and property or assets transferred under a will or through intestacy (that is, because the deceased person had not made a will).

Note: Where the transfer is from a party domiciled in the UK to a partner domiciled abroad, only gifts up to £55,000 are exempt.

Other exempt transfers Transfers of value (or gifts) to the National Trust and to charities, museums, universities, registered housing associations and community amateur sports clubs in the UK are exempt from Inheritance Tax. In addition, there is no Inheritance Tax on transfers of value (or gifts) to political parties, provided that the political party has:

- at least two members elected to the House of Commons *or*
- one member elected to the House of Commons who received at least 150,000 votes in a general election.

Potentially exempt transfers (PETs)

A potentially exempt transfer (PET) is a lifetime transfer made by a chargeable person. Such transfers are exempt from Inheritance Tax when the transfer occurs, and remain exempt if the transferor survives for more than 7 years (calendar years, not tax years) after making the chargeable transfer. If the transferor dies within 7 years of making the transfer, however, the transfer becomes chargeable to Inheritance Tax.

Tapering relief

When a transferor dies, any potentially exempt transfers are reassessed and (if within 7 calendar years of the transfer) added to any other transfers of value made by the deceased prior to her or his death. If Inheritance Tax does become payable on what had been a potentially exempt transfer (as indicated above), the individual receiving the transfer of value (the transferee) will be required to pay the Inheritance Tax. However, the Inheritance Tax due may be reduced as shown in Table 8.1.

Table 8.1 Tapering Relief

Number of years between the transfer and the transferor's death	% reduction in Inheritance Tax
Less than 3 years	0
More than 3 but less than 4 years	20
More than 4 but less than 5 years	40
More than 5 but less than 6 years	60
More than 6 but less than 7 years	80
More than 7 years	100

Note: If the total of taxable transfers of value (or gifts) and potentially exempt transfers during the 7-year period is less than the tax-free allowance (at the date of death), no tax will be due on the transfers that had been treated as potentially exempt .

Activity 2

What are the main 'exceptions' to Inheritance Tax?

Gifts with reservation

A 'gift with reservation' arises when an individual makes a gift of property or assets to another person while retaining some or all of the *benefit* of owning the property or asset for herself or himself. Examples of such gifts include:

- the transfer of legal ownership of a property in which the transferor continues to reside (as, for example, when an elderly parent transfers title to the house to a son or daughter, but continues to live in it).
- the transfer of a rented property where the transferor continues to receive the rental income
- the transfer of a caravan, boat or holiday home that the transferor continues to use regularly for holidays
- the transfer of a work of art that the transferor continues to display in his or her home
- the transfer of shares in a company for which the transferor continues to receive the dividend
- the transfer of shares in a company where the transferor retains an option to buy back the shares.

Such gifts do not qualify as potentially exempt transfers if the reservation still existed at the time of the transferor's death. If the reservation ceased 7 or more years before the transferor's death, however, the gift is treated as a potentially exempt transfer.

Activity 3

In January 2002 Margaret Lamb, a widowed mother of two, purchased a detached cottage in Grassington, North Yorkshire, for £220,000. In March 2003 she 'gifted' the house to her daughters, but she continued to live in the cottage rent-free. The cottage is now worth £655,000.

What are the Inheritance Tax implications?

Excluded property

The rules determining whether property can be regarded as 'excluded property' for Inheritance Tax purposes are complicated, and generally take account of the following:

- the title to the property
- the nature of the property
- the geographical location of the property
- the identity and domicile of the person or persons entitled to the property *and*
- for property held in trust, the settlor's domicile when he or she made the settlement.

For example, property situated outside the UK, that is held in trust, and settled by someone who was permanently living outside the UK at the time of making the settlement could be regarded as excluded property.

Activity 4

In January 2009 Jon Andrews made a significant gift to a family friend. For Inheritance Tax purposes, when will the gift become exempt?

8.5 Valuation of assets

When an individual dies and leaves assets as part of his or her estate, there are detailed rules on how to value such assets. A starting point is the market value or selling price of the assets at the time of the individual's death. For Inheritance Tax purposes, assets include:

- bank accounts and building society accounts
- property
- personal assets
- shares, securities and investments
- assets held in trust
- pensions that include a lump-sum payment on death
- life insurance and life assurance policies
- jointly-owned assets.

Bank accounts and building society accounts

Where money is held in a bank account or building society account, its value is the balance of funds (with any accrued interest) at the time of death. Where the account is held in another currency, the funds should be converted into sterling using whichever of the 'buy' or 'sell' exchange rates provides the *lower* valuation.

Note: For joint accounts, if the person who died provided all the money in the account, all the funds should be included. If, however, the joint account holder provided some of the funds held in the account, then only the money provided by the deceased (with any accrued interest) should be included.

Property

There are special rules for valuing particular types of property. For Inheritance Tax purposes, the value of any property is the price for which the property might reasonably be sold on the open market.

Overseas property

The basis of valuation for overseas property is the same as for UK property, but the value of the overseas property is converted into sterling using whichever of the 'buy' or 'sell' exchange rates provides the *lower* valuation.

Note: Any overseas debts are deductible.

Related property

Related property must be valued as a proportion of the value of the related property if this produces a higher value than the stand-alone value.

Personal assets and belongings

For Inheritance Tax purposes, the value of any personal assets would be the price for which those assets might reasonably be sold on the open market, often referred to as the 'net realisable value' of the assets. Such assets would include jewellery, furniture and motor vehicles, for example.

Shares, securities and investments

Quoted shares and securities

For quoted shares and securities, the Stock Exchange bid and offer prices are used (the bid price being the highest price in the market, and the offer price the lowest price for which a seller of a particular stock is willing to sell a share of that stock). The valuation takes the lower of:

- the value on the 'quarter-up' basis[8] *and*
- the average of the highest and the lowest marked bargains (specially priced offers) for the day.

Note: If a transfer occurs on a day when the Stock Market is closed, the valuation is based on the prices or bargains on the most recent day of trading or the next day of trading. Of all the alternative valuations, the lowest is taken.

Unquoted shares and securities

As there is no open market price for unquoted shares and securities,valuations are undertaken on a negotiated basis with HM Revenue and Customs' SAV (Share and Assets Valuation) service.[9]

Note: If an agreement cannot be reached, an appeal can be made to the Tax Tribunal.

Unit trusts

Units in authorised trusts are valued at the trust manager's bid price.

Assets held in trust

Where assets are held in trust, it is necessary to clarify whether any of the assets held by the trustee count as part of the estate for Inheritance Tax purposes; to determine the value of any assets that do; and to decide who is liable for any Inheritance Tax that may be due.

Pensions

If the deceased had a pension other than the State Pension, it is necessary to determine (usually with the pension provider):

- what part of the pension (if any) counts as part of the estate, for Inheritance Tax purposes *and*
- the value of any part of the pension that does count as part of the estate.

Life insurance and life assurance policies

For Inheritance Tax purposes, if an individual dies and the estate includes a life assurance policy that matures on her or his death, the proceeds of that policy payable to the deceased's personal representatives *must* be included in the estate.

Note: Where an individual writes an assurance policy in trust or makes a declaration of trust at a later date, the life assurance policy proceeds are paid to the trustees for the trust beneficiaries. In this case, they are *not* required to be included in the deceased's estate.

Jointly owned assets

Where an asset is jointly owned, it is necessary to value the whole of the asset and then to calculate the portion owned by the deceased.

8.6 Debts and liabilities

When an individual dies there are detailed rules on what debts and liabilities can be deducted from the value of that person's estate. The following are generally deductible:
- unpaid household bills
- outstanding property mortgages or secured loans
- loans, overdrafts, and credit card debts
- debts owed to close friends or family (but only if they are legally enforceable)
- gambling debts (but again, only if they are legally enforceable)
- funeral expenses (such as the cost of flowers, refreshments for mourners, funeral arrangement expenses, and the grave headstone).

8.7 Inheritance Tax reliefs

Inheritance Tax reliefs allow some assets to be transferred either free of Inheritance Tax or subject to a reduced rate of Inheritance Tax. The main types of Inheritance Tax reliefs are:
- Business Relief
- Agricultural Relief
- Woodland Relief
- Heritage Assets Relief
- Quick Succession Relief
- Double Taxation Relief.

Business Relief

Inheritance Tax Business Relief can reduce the value of assets by 50% or 100%, and can be applied to lifetime transfers of value as well as to transfers on the death of the owner. It can only be applied to relevant business assets.

Qualifying assets

Business Relief at 100% is available on:
- a business or an interest in a business *and*
- shares or securities (or both) in an unlisted or unquoted company.

Business Relief at 50% is available on:
- shares controlling more than 50% of the voting rights of a listed company
- land, buildings or machinery owned by the deceased and used in a business in which she or he was a partner or possessed a controlling interest
- land, buildings or machinery held in a trust but used in the business.

Note: Business Relief is only available if the deceased owned the business or asset for at least 2 years before she or he died.

Non-qualifying assets

Business Relief is *not* available on an asset if:
- the asset also qualifies for Agricultural Relief (see below)
- the asset was not used in the business in the 2 years before it was transferred
- the asset is not required for future use in the business.

Note: If only part of a qualifying asset is used in the business, that part may qualify for Business Relief.

Non-qualifying businesses

Business Relief is not available if the company:
- mainly deals with shares or securities, or both
- mainly deals with land or buildings
- mainly deals with the making or holding of investments
- is a not-for-profit organisation
- is being sold[10]
- is being wound up.[11]

Agricultural Relief

Inheritance Tax Agricultural Relief can be applied to lifetime transfers of value as well as to transfers on the death of the owner, and can allow agricultural property to be transferred free of Inheritance Tax.

Qualifying assets

Agricultural property that qualifies for Agricultural Relief includes:
- land for growing crops
- farms for breeding and rearing horses
- grazing pasture
- trees that are planted and harvested at least every 10 years
- land not currently being farmed under the Habitat Scheme[12]
- land not currently being farmed under a crop-rotation scheme[13]
  the value of the milk quota associated with the land
- some agricultural shares and securities
- farm buildings, farm cottages and farmhouses.

Note: To qualify, agricultural property must be part of a working farm and located in the UK, the Channel Islands, the Isle of Man, or the EU. In addition, the property must have been owned and used for agricultural purposes or activities immediately before its transfer.[14]

Non-qualifying assets

Agricultural property that does *not* qualify for Agricultural Relief includes:
- farm equipment and machinery
- derelict buildings
- harvested crops
- livestock
- property under a contract for sale.

Woodland Relief

Once a popular relief, Woodland Relief has become less important since the introduction of Business Relief.[15] Also, in certain circumstances woodlands may also qualify for the conditional exemption as National Heritage Property, using Heritage Assets Relief.

When a woodland (located in the UK) is transferred on death, the individual liable for the Inheritance Tax can elect to have the value of the timber (the trees and the underwood), but not the underlying land, excluded from the deceased's estate. If the timber is later disposed of, its value at that time will be subject to Inheritance Tax.

Note: The Woodland Relief is not available for:

- an outright lifetime transfer
- a transfer by a close company
- woodlands held on discretionary trust[16]
- woodlands that are on agricultural property.

Activity 5

In the context of Inheritance Tax, distinguish between *Agricultural Relief* and *Woodland Relief.*

Heritage Assets Relief

Some buildings, land, works of art and other assets can be exempt from Inheritance Tax when they are transferred to a new owner either as a lifetime transfer or as a gift on death.

Qualifying conditions

To qualify for Heritage Assets Relief, the assets must be one of the following:

- buildings, estates or parklands of outstanding historical or architectural interest
- land of outstanding natural beauty and spectacular views
- land of outstanding scientific interest, including special areas for the conservation of wildlife, plants and trees
- objects with national scientific, historic or artistic interest, either in their own right or due to a connection with historical buildings.

In addition, the transferee must agree:

- to maintain the asset or item
- to make it available to the general public *and*
- to retain the asset or item in the UK.

If the transferee does not keep to this agreement or sells the asset, the Inheritance Tax exemption is withdrawn and any outstanding liability must be paid.

Quick Succession Relief

If an individual inherits an asset (on the death of another person) and then dies within a short space of time, there is a possibility that the asset would suffer Inheritance Tax twice. Quick Succession Relief reduces any possible double taxation by providing a reduction to the Inheritance Tax payable on the asset at the *transferee's* death (that is, the second death) – see Table 8.2.

Table 8.2 Quick Succession Relief

Number of years between the transferor's death and the transferee's death	% reduction in Inheritance Tax
1 year or less	100
1 year to 2 years	80
2 years to 3 years	60
3 years to 4 years	40
4 years to 5 years	20

Double Taxation Relief

Double taxation conventions are treaties (agreements) that help to prevent an individual from being taxed in two different countries. This possibility could arise, for example, if an individual died in a country other than the country in which she or he was domiciled, especially if the country where the individual was living also charges Inheritance Tax on the same property (or the same transfers of value) that HM Revenue and Customs would be taxing. To minimise this, the UK has a number of bilateral double tax treaties for taxes on estates, gifts and inheritances.

Note: If a transfer is liable to Inheritance Tax and to a similar tax imposed by another country with which there is *no* double taxation treaty, relief may still be available under HM Revenue and Customs unilateral relief provisions. (See: https://www.gov.uk/guidance/inheritance-tax-double-taxation-relief.)

8.8 Minimising Inheritance Tax

A variety of measures can be used to minimise any possible Inheritance Tax liability. These include:

- writing a will
- using a deed of variation
- using a trust
- using lifetime transfers of value
- taking advantage of Inheritance Tax exemptions and reliefs
- making gifts out of excess income
- using life assurance or life cover
- preserving access to income
- making a charitable donation
- using equity release.

Writing a will

Writing a will may not eliminate any Inheritance Tax liability, but it will avoid having to rely on the intestacy rules (whereby the law decides what happens to assets left in an estate for which no will has been written).

Using a deed of variation

A deed of variation allows the beneficiaries of an estate to alter the deceased's will (after her or his death) so that part or all of the inheritance is redirected to one or more other individuals (for example, to children) or to a charity. When granted, a deed of variation is treated as though the variation had been made to the will by the deceased, rather than by the beneficiary. A deed of variation must be drawn up within 2 years of the death, and all beneficiaries under the will must agree to the variation.

Using a trust

Placing assets in trust means that they are no longer part of the estate and are therefore not subject to Inheritance Tax.

Lifetime transfers of value

One of the simplest ways to avoid Inheritance Tax is to make lifetime transfers of value (or gifts). There are several types of gifts that are completely free of Inheritance Tax, and several other types of gift that are potentially free of Inheritance Tax.

Making gifts out of excess income

Transfers of value (or gifts) out of income are free from Inheritance Tax. To qualify, such transfers of value must form part of normal expenditure, be made out of income, and not such as to reduce the transferor's standard of living.

Using life assurance or life cover

One of the simplest ways of providing funds to pay any possible Inheritance Tax liability is to establish a life assurance policy. Payable on death, this is designed to pay into trust a sum equal to any possible Inheritance Tax liability. Because it is written in trust, the money is exempt from Inheritance Tax, and it will therefore be available to beneficiaries to pay the tax due.

Usually the death benefit is paid immediately on the death of the person assured, with the funds then being available to pay any Inheritance Tax due.

Making a charitable donation

Gifts to charities are exempt from Inheritance Tax; but in addition, if a donation of 10% of a net estate is made, the rate of Inheritance Tax applied to the remainder of the estate falls to 36%.

Using equity release

With an equity release scheme, a property owner can:

- borrow money against the value of her or his home (known as a lifetime mortgage) *or*
- sell part of the home, at a reduced market rate, but remain living there throughout the rest of her or his life (a home reversion scheme).

The owner can then use any money released to make a potentially exempt lifetime transfer of value.

> **Activity 6**
>
> Identify six strategies an individual could use to minimise any possible Inheritance Tax liability.

8.9 Concluding comments

Like many of its predecessors, Inheritance Tax has always been a politically and socially unpopular tax. Whilst Labour peer Lord Glasman notably joked 'It's good to tax the dead as they don't vote',[17] there is little doubt that the future of this so-called 'voluntary tax' will be shaped by the UK's future political landscape.

8.10 Suggested further reading

For further reading on the following topics, see the references given.
Inheritance Tax:
- www.gov.uk/inheritance-tax

Paying Inheritance Tax:
- www.gov.uk/paying-inheritance-tax

Key points

- Inheritance Tax arises were there have been chargeable lifetime transfers or estate transfers at death, or both.
- For 2015/2016, individuals have a tax-free inheritance allowance of £325,000.
- The current rate of Inheritance Tax is 40%.
- A 'potentially exempt transfer' is a lifetime transfer, made by a chargeable person, that becomes exempt if the transferor survives for more than 7 years after making the transfer.
- A 'gift with reservation' arises when an individual makes a gift of property or assets to another person while retaining some or all of the *benefit* of owning the property or asset.
- The main types of Inheritance Tax reliefs are Business Relief, Agricultural Relief, Woodland Relief, Heritage Assets Relief, Quick Succession Relief, and Double Taxation Relief.

Self-review questions

1. Which assets are subject to Inheritance Tax?
2. What types of transfers of value by an individual are *potentially exempt transfers*?
3. What gifts in consideration of marriage or civil partnership are exempt from Inheritance Tax?
4. With examples, brief explain the term *gift with reservation*.
5. Briefly explain *Quick Succession Relief*.

Case study discussion question

1. Stuart and Mary Carter have decided to retire on 30 November 2016, and have decided to:
   - o transfer part-ownership of CLB Ltd to their children
   - o dispose of property assets and place the proceeds in trust for the benefit of their grandchildren
   - o restructure their portfolio of investments.

Advise Stuart and Mary Carter on the possible Inheritance Tax consequences of these decisions.

Suggested answers to chapter activities

Activity 1

The two types of chargeable transfers are:
- transfers of value (or gifts) made during the lifetime of the transferor (chargeable lifetime transfers) *and*
- transfers of value (or gifts) made on the death of the transferor (as bequests made in a will, which become estate transfers at death).

Activity 2

For Inheritance Tax purposes, the following transfers are not regarded as chargeable transfers: expenditure on family maintenance; transfers made in the course of a trade, profession or vocation; transfers where there is no gratuitous intent; waivers of remuneration; waivers of dividends; transfers of excluded property; and transfers exempt from Inheritance Tax.

Activity 3

Because Margaret Lamb continues to live in the cottage rent-free, the gift of the cottage to her daughters is a 'gift with reservation'. For Inheritance Tax purposes, therefore, it would still be considered as part of Margaret Lamb's estate.

Activity 4

For Inheritance Tax purposes, gifts become free from Inheritance Tax 7 years (calendar years, not tax years) after the gift is made. For example, a gift made in January 2009 would become exempt in January 2016.

Activity 5

Agricultural Relief can be applied to lifetime transfers of value as well as to transfers on the death of the owner, and relates to, for example: land for growing crops; farms for breeding and rearing horses; grazing pasture; and farm buildings, farm cottages and farmhouses.

Woodland Relief is available when a woodland (located in the UK) is transferred on death. The individual liable for the Inheritance Tax can elect to have the value of the timber (the trees and the underwood) excluded from the deceased's estate.

Activity 6

Measures that could be used to minimise any possible Inheritance Tax liability would include, for example: writing a will; using a deed of variation; using a trust; using lifetime transfers of value; taking advantage of Inheritance Tax exemptions and reliefs; and making gifts out of excess income.

Notes

1. See: S. Adam and C. Emmerson (2014): 'Should IHT be abolished or reformed?' (FT Advisor). Available at: www.ftadviser.com/2014/05/22/ifa-industry/tax-planning/iht-abolition-or-reform-CxWJpqMJrhQnrvw9mWJDbJ/article.html.
2. For Inheritance Tax purposes, an individual is deemed 'domiciled' if she or he has been either:
   - resident in the UK within the last 3 years *or*
   - resident in the UK for 17 out of the last 20 tax years.
3. For example:
   - if the estate of the deceased spouse or civil partner qualified for Woodland Relief or Heritage Assets Relief *or*
   - if the deceased spouse or civil partner died before 1975.
4. The additional allowance is to be gradually withdrawn for estates worth more than £2m.
5. The 'net value' of an estate is the total value of all the assets, less any debts and liabilities, any reliefs, any exemptions, and anything below the Inheritance Tax threshold of £325,000.
6. However, if the transferee cannot pay the Inheritance Tax due, the tax becomes payable out of the transferor's (the deceased's) estate.
7. National Heritage Property includes:
   - buildings or land of historic, architectural, scenic or scientific interest
   - artworks, books, manuscripts, or collections of historic, scenic or scientific interest.

   For the purpose of settling Inheritance Tax, its value is determined by HMRC.
8. The 'quarter-up price' (QUP) is the lower of the two prices shown in the quotations for the shares or securities in the Stock Exchange daily official list on the relevant date, plus one-quarter of the difference between the two prices.
9. See: www.gov.uk/government/publications/hmrc-shares-and-assets-valuations-sav/hmrc-shares-and-assets-valuations-sav.
10. Unless the sale is to a company that will continue the business *and* the deceased's estate will be paid mainly in shares in the company.
11. Unless being wound up is part of a process to allow the business of the company to continue. (For example, the business could be transferred to another company; or to another trading entity, such as a partnership or sole trader.)
12. A number of 'habitat' schemes have been introduced throughout the UK to help to preserve the nature of the countryside and to maintain a habitat for wild animals and birds.
13. Agricultural Relief is available only if crop rotation is practised, with dissimilar crops being grown in the same location in sequenced years.
14. It must have been owned and occupied for 2 years, if occupied by the owner, a company controlled by the owner, or the owner's spouse or civil partner; or 7 years, if occupied by someone else.
15. This is because if an estate includes woodlands as part of a business, Business Relief may be available if the ordinary conditions for that relief are satisfied.
16. A discretionary trust is one in which the number of shares of each beneficiary is not fixed by the settlor in the trust deed, but is at the discretion of the trustees.
17. See: 'It's good to tax the dead, they don't vote, jokes Ed Miliband's guru friend Lord Glasman'. Available at: www.dailymail.co.uk/news/article-2711351/It-s-good-tax-dead-don-t-vote-jokes-Ed-Miliband-s-guru-friend-Lord-Glasman.html.

Part 3 Investments, pensions, and insurance

Overview

Chapter 9 explores the types of investments a personal portfolio might contain: from cash-related investments, through bonds and bills (debt-related investments), shares (equity-related investments), property (asset-related investments), and pensions and endowments, to investments in commodities or venture capital trusts. It also considers the risks and uncertainty associated with each type of investment, the factors to consider when selecting an investment, and the merits of a balanced portfolio.

Chapter 10 explores the nature of State-related pensions and the range of alternative pension schemes, from private occupational pensions, through self employed pensions or personal pension plans (PPP) and stakeholder pensions, to self-invested personal pensions (SIPPs).

Chapter 11 explores the range of insurance products and schemes now available: from life policies, through health-related policies and asset-protection policies, to activity- or travel-related policies.

9

Savings and investments

> **Learning outcomes**
>
> By the end of this chapter, you should be able to:
>
> - distinguish between different types of cash-related investments
> - identify the key characteristics of different types of market-based investments
> - appreciate the risks and returns associated with different types of investments.

9.1 Introduction

For many people, the only way to become financially secure is to work, to save and to invest. Unfortunately, the variety of savings and investments now available to investors is almost endless: some are merely cash-related savings products, while others are very complex highly structured investment vehicles; some have very little or no associated risk, while others have a high potential risk; some provide a predictable fixed return, while others provide an unpredictable variable return; and some have a substantial associated tax benefit, while others do not.

This chapter explores the most popular types of savings accounts and investment products, and considers the risks associated with each.

9.2 Are you ready to invest?

If you find that you have surplus funds – for example, from an inheritance, from a divorce settlement, from the sale of a major personal asset, from a Lottery win, or simply from years of thrift and prudence – you may wonder about investing. Before you do, there are four simple questions you need to ask yourself.

Have you paid off all your debts?

Generally, the cost of servicing a debt will be greater than the return you may receive from any equivalent investment. More importantly, losing money on a speculative investment may significantly affect your ability to service your outstanding debt.

Do you have any savings?

Before introducing additional investment risk, you need to ensure that you have some easily accessible 'core' savings that can act as an emergency fund (sufficient savings to pay for 6 months of average budgeted monthly expenses) to cover any unforeseen issues and events that may arise. If you do need to draw on this fund at any point, be sure to reinstate the fund as soon as you can.

Do you have insurance protection?

Before investing, you should ensure that you and your earnings are protected. For example, are you entitled to sickness pay from your employer if you are ill? If not (or if you are self-employed), you should have an income protection insurance policy. Are you covered in the event of a longer-term illness? If not, you should have a critical illness insurance policy. Do you have a partner and family? If so, you should have a life insurance policy in place.

Do you contribute to a pension?

If you are employed, you should be contributing to an employee pension scheme. If an employee pension scheme is not available or if you are self-employed, then you should consider contributing to a private pension. (We will discuss and explore alternative pensions in more detail in Chapter 10.)

If the answer to each of these four key questions is 'Yes', then you are ready!

9.3 Establishing an investment profile

Before selecting an investment strategy and making an investment choice, it is important to determine your investor profile. Again, there are four simple questions.

What are your underlying investment objectives?

What are your goals? Consider your short-term goals (for the next 5 years); your medium-term goals (for the next 5–10 years); and your longer-term goals (for 10 years or more). Why are you going to make the investment? Is the investment required for capital growth purposes, or is it required for an ongoing income-based return; or is it for a combination of both?

What is your investment timeframe?

For how long do you expect to hold the investment? Will it be a short-term investment (1–5 years), a medium-term investment (5–10 years), or a long-term investment (over 10 years)?

What type of investment do you prefer?

Whilst it is important to determine what level of investment risk you are prepared to accept and what minimum rate of return you will consider, it is also important to decide what type of investment you prefer. Would you like:

- an asset-based investment (for example, shares or property)
- a debt-based investment (for example, bonds or Gilts)
- a pooled investment (for example, a mutual fund or a unit trust).

In addition, before selecting an investment it is important to ensure that:

- there is a readily assessable market available for the disposal of any investment

- the investment is affordable (either as a single lump-sum investment or as a regular top-up investment)
- the tax implications of the investment are clear
- information about the investment and the investment market is readily available.

9.4 Types of savings and investments

An enormous variety of savings and investments are available: some that offer investment growth, some that offer an income-based return, and some that offer a combination of both. Some of the more common types of savings and investments are the following:
- Low-risk savings and investments: these include cash-related savings and investments (including ISAs), cash bonds, Premium Bonds, Savings Certificates, Children's Bonds, Pensioner Bonds, Investment Bonds, Gilts, and pensions.
- Medium-risk investments: these include endowments and Friendly Society tax-exempt savings plans, Company Bonds, shares, property, offshore savings accounts, and pooled investment funds.
- Higher-risk investments: these include peer-to-peer lending, commodities, structured products, Venture Capital Trusts, spread betting, Contracts for Difference, land banking, and other unregulated collective investment schemes.

Note: Before investing in any savings or investment product, always consult an independent financial adviser.

9.5 International Securities Identification Number (ISIN)

A standard numbering system, the International Securities Identification Number (ISIN), is used worldwide to identify specific securities such as bonds, shares and other tradable securities. There are three parts to an ISIN:
- a two-letter country code (XS is used for international securities)
- a nine-digit numeric identifier, called the National Securities Identifying Number (NSIN)
- a single check-digit based upon the preceding 11 characters.

For example:
- the ISIN for shares in the US-based technology company Apple Inc. is US0378331005
- the ISIN for shares in the UK-based retailer Tesco plc is GB0008847096
- the ISIN for GBP bonds issued by the European Investment Bank is XS0434040167.

9.6 Cash-related savings and investments

Current accounts

Also called an instant access account, a select account, a flexible account, or a flex plus account, and available from a wide range of high street banks and building societies and increasingly from credit unions, a current account is merely a simple, convenient and flexible way of storing funds temporarily. Current accounts are increasingly accessible through a range of web-enabled devices. There are many different types of current account, including:

- a standard current account
- a current account with extras (such as travel insurance, roadside assistance and medical support – all for a monthly fee)
- a student current account (usually with a free limited overdraft)
- a graduate current account (usually with low-interest loans or borrowing)
- a foreign currency account (allowing regular foreign currency transactions to be undertaken)
- a special current account to cater for specific religious beliefs (for example, an Islamic, or Sharia-compliant, current account).

Subject to certain conditions and restrictions, all of these provide immediate and unrestricted access to funds held in the account. Although often linked to an overdraft facility, a current account, whatever the type, generally earns no interest (or very little interest) and is in essence a flexible purse for day-to-day use rather than a wealth-creating investment vehicle.

Note: In September 2013 the Payments Council launched a free-to-use current account switching service (backed by a new Current Account Switch Guarantee), designed to make the process of switching current accounts from one bank or building society to another simpler and more reliable.[1]

Basic bank account

'Basic bank accounts' were launched in 2015, following agreement between the UK Government and all of the major UK banks. The new basic bank account is only available to those with a low credit score or a poor credit history (or both). Basic bank accounts have three key features:

- no interest is earned on any surplus balances
- no charges are imposed for late or failed payments
- no overdraft facility is available.

Instant-access savings accounts

Although rates of return do tend to be lower than those on fixed-term saving accounts, or notice savings accounts, instant-access savings accounts nonetheless provide an opportunity to save and to obtain at least a small rate of return, while also providing the flexibility and freedom of unrestricted and immediate access to savings on demand and without penalties.

Available from many high street banks, building societies and a range of credit unions, many of which now provide online access, instant access savings accounts can usually be opened and kept open with a small minimal balance (which may vary between providers from £1 to £1,000). Interest rates may be fixed or variable, and may vary enormously between different banks and building societies. Some offer instant access savings accounts with tiered interest rates depending on the amount invested; others offer 'new saver' interest rates designed to attract new customers.

Although some instant access savings accounts offer monthly interest payments (usually at a reduced rate), interest on instant access savings accounts is usually paid annually, either on the anniversary of opening the account or on a pre-specified fixed date.

Notice savings accounts

Notice savings accounts are available from a wide range of high street banks and building societies, and usually offer better interest rates than instant access savings accounts. This kind of account is essentially an investment account in which money is deposited for an indefinite period of time, and from which any withdrawal of savings is subject to a period of notice – for example, a 30-day notice savings account would require 30 days' advance notice of the intention to withdraw savings.

In general, the longer the notice period, the higher the rate of interest. There are notice savings accounts available with notice periods as short as 1 day and as long as 180 days, although 30-day, 60-day and 90-day notice savings accounts appear to be the norm for most banks and building societies.[2]

Many notice savings accounts require a minimum opening balance, which might vary from £100 to £5,000. Interest rates also vary enormously between banks and building societies. Many only offer fixed-rate notice savings accounts; although variable-rate notice savings accounts are available, with tiered interest rates dependent on the amount invested.

ISAs (Individual Savings Accounts)

Originally introduced in April 1999, Individual Savings Accounts (ISAs)[3] have undergone a number of cosmetic changes over the last few years. One, which took effect on 1 July 2014, was the rebranding of all ISAs as 'new ISAs'. As this rebranding was purely political and as many banks and building societies continue to use the term 'ISAs', we too will use the term 'ISAs'.

For 2015/2016, savers and investors have an annual allowance of £15,240 that can be used in any combination of cash and investments.

From 2015/2016 (unlike previous tax years), savers can withdraw as often as they wish and invest as often as they wish within the same tax year, without losing the ISA tax benefit – although the maximum balance cannot exceed £15,240.

Note: An ISA cannot be opened as a joint account, and cannot be opened on behalf of someone else.

Cash ISA

A Cash ISA is simply a savings account on which the interest is not taxed. Cash savings that stay within the Cash ISA earn a tax-free return until the cash is withdrawn. Such ISAs are available from most, if not all, high street banks and building societies, and also from National Savings and Investments (NS&I)[4]. For basic-rate Income Tax payers, investing in a Cash ISA increases their return by 20%; this figure increases to 40% or even 50% for those taxed at a higher rate of Income Tax.

Cash ISAs are available to all UK residents over the age of 16.

As with other savings accounts, there is a wide variety of Cash ISAs available, from instant access ISAs to fixed-rate ISAs, and access is determined by the type of account –for example, with an instant-access ISA, cash can be withdrawn on demand, whereas with a fixed-rate Cash ISA some restrictions may apply and there may be an interest penalty imposed for early withdrawal.

Investment ISA (Stocks and Shares ISA)

An Investment ISA (also called a Stocks and Shares ISA) is a tax-efficient investment account that allows a saver or an investor[5] to invest money into different types of investments, including unit trusts, open-ended investment companies (OEICs), investment trusts, Government bonds, and Corporate Bonds, as well as individual company shares.

Investment ISAs are provided by a range of financial institutions, including banks, building societies and fund-management companies, all of whom will normally charge a fee. Some Stocks and Shares ISA providers may also allow investors to hold some of their annual allowance as cash within the same ISA.

Investing in stocks and shares using an ISA account does not mean that the ISA is tax-free, but it does mean that no Capital Gains Tax is paid on profits made, should the share price increase; that no Income Tax is paid on interest earned on bonds; and that there is a 10% Income Tax cap on income (dividends) earned from any shares.

Investment ISAs are available to all UK residents over the age of 18.

Peer-to-peer (P2P) ISA

In October 2014,[6] the UK Government launched a consultation that outlined proposals for a third ISA – a Peer to Peer ISA (P2P ISA) that would complement the traditional Cash and Investment ISAs. The aims would be:

- to increase lending to small and medium-sized companies *and*
- to provide opportunities for investors seeking higher rates of return.

Note: Peer-to-peer lending (P2P lending) is the practice of lending money to unrelated individuals ('peers') without using a traditional financial intermediary such as a bank or other financial institution.

The exact details of the P2P ISA have yet to be confirmed. It should be noted, though, that unlike traditional savings accounts, peer-to-peer lending is considered an investment, and is therefore *not* covered by the Financial Services Compensation Scheme.

Help to Buy ISA

In the autumn of 2015, the government launched a new Help to Buy ISA targeted at first-time buyers. Available from both banks and building societies, Help to Buy ISAs are available for 4 years, with savers (who must be over 16 years of age) able to deposit up to £200 a month. Together with the normal ISA tax benefit (that interest is tax-free), with a Help to Buy ISA the Government will also provide a bonus of 25% to savers (with a minimum of £400 and a maximum of £3,000), this bonus being payable when the first home is purchased. The bonus is only available to first-time buyers purchasing UK properties and only for home purchases costing up to £450,000 in London or £250,000 outside London.

Note: Help to Buy ISAs are limited to one per person.

Switching ISA providers

There are few restrictions on switching from one ISA provider to another. Because it is a technical process, however, for the transfer to be official it should be completed by the new provider, who will (once the saver or investor has completed the appropriate transfer documents) ensure that all the savings are transferred correctly.

Note: Remember that you should never withdraw cash from an ISA yourself in order to reinvest it in another ISA– not only would this count as a new deposit and be deducted from your overall annual allowance, but you could also lose your tax-free status.

Limits on active ISAs An active ISA is one that has had funds transferred into it during the current tax year. A saver or an investor may transfer funds between different ISA providers as often as they wish, but they may only have two active ISAs open at a time – one Cash ISA and one Investment ISA (Stocks and Shares ISA). A saver or an investor may transfer all the funds from an active ISA to a different provider, but she or he may not split these funds between different providers. However, funds from an *inactive* ISA (that is, an ISA from a previous tax year) can be divided between more than one ISA provider.

Note: Not all ISA providers will accept transfers of previous years' allowances.

Switching ISAs

Currently a saver or an investor can transfer all of the savings in a Cash ISA to an Investment ISA (Stocks and Shares ISA) or vice versa, provided they do not have more than one active ISA of each kind open at a time.

Note: Following an Office of Fair Trade ruling (1 January 2011) the transfer of funds from a Cash ISA should take no more than 15 business days and the transfer of funds from an Investment ISA (Stocks and Shares ISA) should take no more than 30 business days.

Junior ISAs

A Junior ISA allows a saver or an investor to save tax-free or tax-efficiently on behalf of her or his child. In general, a Junior ISA has an annual allowance (in 2015/2016) of up to £4,080. The annual allowance can be divided between a Cash ISA and an Investment ISA (Stocks and Shares ISA) in any proportions, and is held in the child's name. The child cannot have access to the ISA until 18 years old, although she or he can take control of the ISA when 16 years old. The Junior ISA must be held with a single provider.

Junior ISAs replaced Child Trust Funds, which were withdrawn (for new savers) on 3 January 2011. Junior ISAs are available only to children born on or after that day and to children under 18 years of age but born before 1 September 2002 (the date when Child Trust Funds were introduced).

Note: A young person who is 16 or 17 is entitled to two ISA allowances: the Junior ISA annual allowance of £4,000 *and* the adult Cash ISA annual allowance of £15,000.

Activity 1

Distinguish between a *Cash ISA* and an *Investment ISA*.

Index-linked savings accounts

Index-linked savings accounts are also fixed-term deposits, and are offered by a range of high street banks and building societies. They are also known as inflation-linked savings accounts. They represent a low-risk non-transferable investment, usually for a fixed term of between 3 and 5 years, which provides an index-linked return.

Most providers require a minimum investment deposit of £500 and do not allow early withdrawal of savings without imposing high penalty charges.

Offshore savings accounts

Offshore savings accounts are savings accounts located outside an account holder's country of residence[7] and allow account holders to save in different currencies. The accounts are offered by many high street banks and building societies and can be opened by anyone over the age of 18. Whilst some account providers require a minimum initial deposit of at least £5,000, some offshore accounts can be opened with as little as £1.

Offshore accounts are useful for those savers and investors who live or work overseas, who travel overseas regularly, who hope to retire to another country, or who simply wish to gain from currency exchange-rate movements. Some offshore accounts offer variable interest rates, with easy access to savings; others offer fixed-interest rates and require fixed-period savings for up to 5 years. All offshore accounts charge fees for cash withdrawals, and interest is paid gross (that is, without deduction of Income Tax).

Note: Unlike UK-based savings accounts, offshore savings accounts are *not* protected by the Financial Services Compensation Scheme.

9.7 Bonds

There are many different types of bonds, some of which are marketed as bonds but are merely fixed-term savings accounts. The most common are: cash bonds (or savings bonds), Savings Certificates (index-linked or fixed-interest), Premium Bonds, Children's Bonds, Pensioner Bonds, Investment Bonds, Gilts (Government bonds), supranational bonds, local authority bonds, Company Bonds (including retail bonds and mini-bonds), and Permanent Interest Bearing Shares (PIBS).

Note: Gilts and company or retail bonds can be bought directly or as part of a pooled fund.

Cash bond (or savings bond)

Cash bonds (or savings bonds) are essentially long-term savings accounts, and are also known as fixed-rate bonds or fixed-term deposits. A cash bond is a long-term interest-bearing savings account, generally for a fixed term of between 1 and 5 years. Offered by a range of high street banks, building societies, investment funds and (occasionally) National Savings and Investments (NS&I), cash bonds represent a low-risk non-transferable investment, provide only a limited return (although the return is generally higher than that for an instant savings account or a notice deposit account, for example), and provide no capital growth.

Most providers require a minimum investment deposit (between £500 and £1,000) and set a maximum of £500,000, with their interest rates sometimes being tiered, depending on the amount invested or deposited.

There are a number of different types of cash bonds, the most common being:

- a fixed-rate savings bond that provides a guaranteed fixed-interest rate over the life of the bond
- a variable-rate (or tracker) savings bond that provides a variable interest rate linked to a particular index or rate (for example, the Consumer Prices Index or CPI), with the interest rate on the bond being reviewed at set intervals (for example, every 3 months) over the life of the bond.

Note: Cash bonds are long-term savings account. Most providers do not allow early withdrawal of savings, with those that do imposing high penalty charges.

Index-linked Savings Certificates

Index-linked Savings Certificates are issued by National Savings and Investments (NS&I) and are very similar to the index-linked savings accounts above. They are generally issued for a fixed term of between 3 and 5 years, with a guaranteed return linked to the Retail Prices Index (RPI). Index-linked Savings Certificates are free from UK Income Tax and can be redeemed at any time, although there is a penalty and loss of index-linking for cashing-in early (a penalty equivalent to 90 days' interest on the amount cashed in) and also the loss of index-linking on the whole of the certificate balance for the investment year in which the withdrawal is made.

There is a minimum balance of £100 and a maximum balance of £15,000 (with a maximum balance of £30,000 for a joint account). Index-linked Savings Certificates are available to those over the age of 16.

Fixed-interest Savings Certificates

Fixed-interest Savings Certificates are also issued by National Savings and Investments (NS&I). Again, they are generally issued for a fixed term of between 3 and 5 years, and provide a guaranteed fixed return. Fixed-interest Savings Certificates are free from UK Income Tax and can be redeemed at any time, although there is a penalty loss equivalent to 90 days' interest on the amount cashed in. As with index-linked Savings Certificates, there is a minimum balance of £100 and a maximum balance of £15,000 (with a maximum balance of £30,000 for a joint account). Fixed-interest Savings Certificates are available to those over the age of 16.

Premium Bonds

Issued by National Savings and Investments (NS&I), Premium Bonds do not pay interest – instead, they are entered into a monthly draw for tax-free prizes. Each Premium Bond has a unique bond number. The winning bond numbers are chosen completely at random by ERNIE (Electronic Random Number Indicator Equipment), with prizes ranging from £25 to £1 million. All prizes are tax-free and may, if desired, be reinvested (up to the current maximum holding).

Note: All issued Premium Bonds have an equal chance of winning.

Anyone aged 16 or over can purchase Premium Bonds. Premium Bonds can also be purchased and held by a parent, a guardian, a grandparent or a great-grandparent on behalf of a child. They cannot, however, be held jointly with anyone else.

The minimum investment is £100 (or £50 if purchased with a Standing Order or bank transfer). In 2015, the maximum holding is £50,000. To be eligible for the prize draw, the Premium Bond must be held for one full calendar month following the month in which it was purchased. Premium Bonds can be redeemed (cashed in) for their face value at any time, without prior notice.

Children's Bonds

Children's Bonds (previously known as Children's Bonus Bonds) are 5-year renewable bonds issued by National Savings and Investments (NS&I). They offer a tax-free fixed-interest payment annually.

Note: Interest on Children's Bonds is free of UK Income Tax and Capital Gains Tax for the child and also for the parent, guardian, grandparent or great-grandparent.

Only parents, guardians, grandparents and great-grandparents can purchase Children's Bonds, and only on behalf of someone under 16 years of age. The investment is in the child's name, although the parent or guardian retains control until the child's 16th birthday (or the first 5-year anniversary after the child's 16th birthday). On maturity, the bond can be redeemed (cashed in) or reinvested in another 5-year bond at a new tax-free interest rate; and this can continue until the child's 16th birthday.

The bond finally matures on the first 5-year anniversary after the child's 16th birthday, after which it stops earning interest. There is a minimum investment of £25 and a maximum investment of £3,000 per bond issue, per child. Children's bonds can be redeemed at any time, although there is a penalty equivalent to 90 days' interest on the amount cashed in.

Pensioner Bonds

Introduced in January 2015, Pensioner Bonds offer fixed rates of interest and are available from National Savings and Investments (NS&I) to all UK residents aged 65 and over. There are two versions, a 1-year bond and a 3-year bond, both with interest paid annually. The minimum investment is £500 and the maximum investment is £10,000 per person, per bond. Any interest earned is subject to UK Income Tax.

Interest rates were 2.8% for the 1-year bond and 4.0% for the 3-year bond. Interest is paid in full at the end of the investment period.

Investment Bonds

Some financial products are designed to be both long-term investments and life-related insurance policies. If purchased by the payment of regular (usually monthly) premiums, they are called endowments plans or investment plans. If purchased by the payment of one or more lump sums, they are called Investment Bonds or single Premium Bonds.

(We will discuss endowment plans and investment plans later in this chapter.)

Investment bonds are also known as insurance bonds, with-profit bonds, and unit-linked bonds. They vary greatly between different issuers: some are issued for a minimum term; some are issued for a fixed term (usually 5 years or more); some are issued with no fixed term; and some are issued as lifetime bonds (repayable only at death). Most have a minimum investment level, which may vary between £1,000 and £10,000; and all have early cashing-in penalties and charges (although some Investment Bonds do allow investors to make regular annual withdrawals, up to a specified limit).

Funds invested by the investor are allocated to a selected investment fund – either a with-profits fund or a unit-linked fund, with any Investment Bond redemption or surrender value or early cashing-in value depending on how well or how badly the investment fund has performed. The end value of the Investment Bond may in fact be less than the amount initially invested. (Some Investment Bonds may guarantee to return the amount initially invested, but a charge or fee will be payable for this guarantee.)

Note: Tax is payable on both the growth and the income accrued.

Investment Bonds can be purchased through a financial adviser or directly from an insurance company.

Gilts

Gilts[8] are bonds, or units of debt, issued by the Government to raise money. Since April 1998, Gilts have been issued by the Debt Management Office (DMO; see: www.dmo.gov.uk)

on behalf of HM Treasury. Gilts are issued with a nominal value (or face value) of £100. In terms of maturity, the convention is to divide Gilts into three categories:

- shorts: Gilts with a maturity of between 1 and 7 years
- mediums: Gilts with a maturity of between 7 and 15 years
- longs: Gilts with a maturity of over 15 years (including undated perpetuities).

There are essentially three types of Gilts: a conventional gilt-edged security; an index-linked gilt-edged security; and a zero-coupon gilt-edged security (often referred to as a strip[9]).

Conventional gilt-edged security

A conventional gilt-edged security is the simplest and oldest form of Government bond. The bond pays a fixed-percentage coupon (interest) every six months until the maturity date. On redemption, the final coupon payment and the principal (the initial investment) are paid to the holder in full.

A conventional gilt-edged security is denoted by its coupon rate and its maturity date, for example: 3% Treasury Gilt 2020.

Index-linked gilt-edged security Unlike a conventional gilt-edged security, an index-linked gilt-edged security provides a fixed return that is inflation-adjusted – that is, both the principal and the coupon are adjusted in value for inflation. The adjustment factor, which is lagged by 3 months (older issues, prior to September 2005, were lagged by 8 months), is calculated by reference to the original nominal value of the gilt-edged security and to the change in the Retail Prices Index (RPI) since the time of issue. The coupon is calculated and paid on the adjusted value.

On redemption, both the coupon and the principal are adjusted to account for accrued inflation from the date the gilt-edged security was issued.[10]

Zero-coupon gilt-edged security

A zero-coupon gilt-edged security (or strip) is a bond that is issued at a discount – that is at a price below the nominal value of the gilt-edged security. They are separately traded non-interest-bearing bonds. Any return is derived from the capital appreciation that may result as the bond reaches maturity.[11]

Other types of gilt-edged security

Double-dated conventional gilt-edged security A double-dated gilt-edged security was a conventional gilt-edged security that is issued with a band of maturity dates. Such securities can be redeemed (in whole or in part) on any day between the first and the last maturity dates, subject to a notice period of 3 months.

The final double-dated gilt-edged security (12% Exchequer Stock 2013–17) was redeemed on 12 December 2013.

Undated gilt-edged security An undated gilt-edged security is a conventional gilt-edged security that has no redemption date but can be redeemed at the discretion of the Government. Because such securities carry very low coupon rates, redemption is very unlikely.

Note: With the exception of 3½% War Loan, undated gilt-edged securities are referred to as 'rumps'.

Buying and selling gilt-edged securities

With the exception of zero-coupon gilt-edged securities, Gilts are issued at par (that is, at face value) and then traded on the open market, where gilt-edged securities can be bought and sold up to their redemption date. Market prices fluctuate with changes in interest rates and of course with market demand.

New issues of Gilts can be purchased directly from the DMO at a Gilt auction (a new issue of Gilts), either through a Gilt-Edged Market Maker (GEMM) or by direct application to the DMO. (To be able to do this, however, the bidder must be a member of the DMO's approved group of investors.) Gilts can also be purchased on the secondary market, using a bank, a stockbroker, or the DMO's purchase and sale service.[12]

Gilts can be bought by anyone. Although pension funds are by far the largest buyers of Gilts, Gilts are also used by individual investors who are looking for a secure, low-risk investment.

Note: Gilts can also be bought as part of a Gilt fund (an investment fund specialising only in gilt-edged securities), but annual fees and management charges reduce the overall returns. There are two types of Gilt funds available to investors:
- gilt funds that must have 80% invested in UK Gilts
- index-linked gilt funds that must have 80% invested in UK index-linked Gilts.

Supranational bonds

Supranational bonds are issued by institutions such as the European Investment Bank (EIB) and the World Bank, and are available on both the local markets of member countries and the Eurobond market. As with Government bonds (Gilts), they are regarded as very low-risk investments with a high credit rating.

Local authority bonds

Local authority bonds are issued by local governments such as borough councils. They are generally of a slightly lower credit rating than sovereign debt because they are not backed by the central Government. Local authority bonds are not as liquid as Government bonds and are not so easily traded in the secondary markets.

Company Bonds

Company Bonds are debt securities: they are negotiable, tradable, and often exchange-listed[13] financial securities issued by a company. They represent a formal agreement between a company (the bond issuer) and a lender (the bondholder), with the bondholder in effect extending a loan to the bond issuer. Company Bonds usually have a nominal (face) value of £100; generally pay a coupon (interest) annually (although some Company Bonds pay twice a year); and are usually issued for fixed periods of greater than 1 year,[14] after which time the bonds are redeemed. At redemption, the nominal value of the bond is paid back to the investor. (It is also possible to issue bonds that have no redemption date.) The yield to maturity of a Company Bond is the rate of return on a bond expressed as an annual rate.[15]

The main risks associated with Company Bonds are:
- the default risk (or issuer risk): the risk that the bond issuer may not be able to meet its obligations in terms of coupon payments or that it may not be able at maturity to pay the principal amount back to the bondholder

- the market risk: the risk that the market price of the bond may fluctuate away from the market price at which the bond was bought.

Note: Company Bonds are generally considered to represent a higher risk than Government bonds (Gilts), but a lower risk than company shares or equities.

Note: Remember that Company Bonds and retail bonds can form part of an ISA.

Types of bonds

There are many alternative types of Company Bonds, of which the most common are:

- Fixed-rate bonds: these have a coupon (interest) rate that remains the same for the life of the bond.
- Variable-rate bonds (sometimes known as floating-rate bonds or roll-over bonds): these have a coupon (interest) rate that is revised at regular intervals over the life of the bond according to a particular reference rate, usually LIBOR (London Interbank Offered Rate) or EURIBOR (Euro Interbank Offered Rate).
- Index-linked bonds: these have a coupon (interest) rate that is linked to a reference index (for example, inflation-linked bonds are linked to a consumer Retail Prices Index).
- Zero-coupon bonds: these do not pay any coupon (interest) for the life of the bond, but are issued at a deep discount (at a price below the nominal value of the bond).
- Convertible bonds: these have the option, during the life of the bond, to be converted into shares at a pre-agreed conversion rate.

There is an active market for the issue, the buying and the selling of Company Bonds. Although other market-related factors can and do have an impact on the market prices of Company Bonds, in general the market prices of Company Bonds are determined principally by movements in interest rates – that is, if interest rates rise, bond prices fall, and if interest rate fall, bond prices rise.[16]

For current bond prices, see: www.fixedincomeinvestor.co.uk.

Grades of bonds

Investment-grade Company Bonds generally provide a low level of return because there is a low risk of the issuing company defaulting. Non-investment grade Company Bonds (often called junk bonds) provide a more generous level of return because there is a higher risk of the issuing company defaulting.

Credit rating agencies such as Standard & Poor's and Moody's rate Company Bonds – from the very secure Company Bonds, rated 'AAA' level, to the very unsecure junk Company Bonds, rated 'D'.

Retail bonds

Because of the high minimum investment requirements, historically the Corporate Bond market was beyond the reach of individual investors, apart from the very wealthy. In 2010, however, the London Stock Exchange (LSE) launched the Order book for Retail Bonds[17] (ORB). Approximately 80 bonds were moved onto ORB. Although trading was initially restricted to the secondary market (that is, for bonds already in issue), new issues have been added since 2010 with more than 20 of these issues now being made available to individuals and private investors.

Retail bonds are specifically targeted at small individual investors and are separate from the far larger Corporate Bond market, which is dominated by the large institutional investors. The minimum investment requirement depends on the bond issuer, but typically Corporate Bonds have a minimum investment requirement as low as £1,000.

Individual investors can invest in Company Bonds by:

- investing in a managed fund that includes Company Bonds as part of its investment strategy
- investing in an exchange-traded fund that tracks the Company Bond market
- buying Company Bonds directly through a retail broker who is a member of the Order book for Retail Bonds or through an online trading platform.

Note: Although some Company Bonds may appear similar to a fixed-rate savings account or a savings bond, a Company Bond is an investment and not a savings product, and so is *not* covered by the Financial Services Compensation Scheme's £85,000 individual savings protection cover.

Mini-bonds

Mini-bonds[18] are unlisted financial securities. They are non-transferable debt securities. As with a traditional bond, the bondholder is paid a coupon (interest) until the bond reaches maturity, when the nominal value is repaid in full. Unlike a traditional bond, mini-bonds are unlisted – they cannot be traded on the ORB market. Once bought, a mini-bond has to be held to maturity.

Permanent Interest Bearing Shares (PIBS)

Permanent Interest Bearing Shares (PIBS)[19] are market-based fixed-interest loan securities issued by Building Societies. They share the features of both preference shares (see below) and Company Bonds. They are exchange-tradable shares; they usually have a fixed coupon (interest) rate (though variable-rate PIBS are also possible); and they are permanent or long-life securities, although they are callable, when the issuer may redeem the securities.

Interest is payable annually (or biannually), with coupon (interest) rates generally marginally higher than returns on Government bonds (Gilts). Interest is paid gross but is subject to Income Tax.

PIBS are relatively illiquid – that is, they cannot easily be converted to cash as the number in issue is relatively small and there is only a small demand for them. As with Company Bonds or retail bonds, PIBS can form part of an ISA.

Note: PIBS are *not* covered by the Financial Services Compensation Scheme.

Activity 2

Distinguish between the following types of bonds: *Premium Bonds, Pensioner Bonds, Gilts,* and *mini-bonds.*

9.8 Shares

Shares are securities (usually irredeemable) that represent an ownership interest in a company limited by shares (or sometimes by guarantee). There are two types of shares: ordinary shares and preference shares, and different classes of shares can exist for each type of share.

Ordinary shares provide the shareholder with an entitlement to receive a dividend (but only after other demands have been met, including those of preference shareholders), a legal right to receive any residual share of the company's assets in the event of the company's liquidation, and a voting right.[20] Preference shares provide the shareholder with a preferential entitlement to receive a fixed dividend[21] before any payments are made to ordinary shareholders, and a legal right to receive a share of the company's assets in the event of the company's liquidation.

Note: The vast majority of companies limited by shares in the UK are *private* limited companies, but only shares in *public* limited companies can be sold to the public and listed on an exchange such as the London Stock Exchange. Shares in a private limited company can only be sold by private invitation.

Shares in companies listed on the London Stock Exchange can be classified as follows:

- by index: for example, company shares in the FTSE 100, the FTSE 250, the FTSE Small Cap, the FTSE Fledgling, and the FTSE AIM (Alternative Investment Market)
- by sector: for example, company shares in the banking sector, the retail sector, or the leisure sector
- by type: for example, *defensive* company shares (shares that generate returns that vary by a smaller proportion than overall market returns), *aggressive* company shares (shares that generate returns that vary by a larger proportion than overall market returns), or *neutral* company shares (shares that generate returns that vary in the same proportion as overall market returns).

Why invest in company shares?

The value of company share prices can go down as well as up, due to:

- the supply of and demand for the shares
- the underlying inherent value of the shares
- other less direct influences (for example, Government policy).

Investing in company shares is not without risk, but over the longer term company shares can generate very good returns. Indeed, many studies have shown that over the longer term (10 years or more), company shares tend to outperform Government bonds, Corporate Bonds, property, and many other types of asset.

Company shares can provide investors with two types of return: an annual income and long-term capital growth. Most company shares offer income in the form of dividends (usually paid every 6 months) when a company is profitable and has cash in the bank after it has satisfied all its obligations. Generally, the more profitable the company, the higher the dividend payments will be. Long-term capital growth occurs when a company share price increases over a period of time.

Investing in company shares

For the individual investor, an investment in company shares can be made either by investing directly in the company or by investing indirectly using a pooled investment vehicle.

Investing directly

Investing directly in company shares generally means buying such shares using broker services. Some brokers offer bespoke services with tailored advice; others merely provide an execution-only share-dealing service, whereby investors can buy and sell shares independently through a share-dealing account without being offered advice. Many high street banks also offer online execution-only share-dealing services for account holders. In addition, shares can be acquired through a Company Share Option Plan.

Investing indirectly

Investing indirectly in company shares is a more common way of accessing shares, as it spreads risk by investing in a number of companies, This can be done through a pooled investment vehicle, such as an open-ended fund (an open-ended investment company or a unit trust) an investment trust, or an exchange-traded fund (ETF).

Risks of investing in company shares

The main risks associated with company shares are:

- risk due to the under-performance of the company (sometimes referred to as unsystematic risk, inherent risk, or diversifiable risk)
- risk due to the volatility of the overall market (sometimes referred to as systematic risk, market risk, or non-diversifiable risk).

Either kind of risk could result in low dividends (or even no dividends), share price volatility, and a possible reduction in the market value of the shares.

Whilst unsystematic risk can be eliminated, or at least reduced, by diversification (see later in the chapter), risk due to the volatility of the overall market (non-diversifiable risk) cannot. Consequently, for an investor, only systematic risk (or market risk) is relevant. A measure of such systematic risk is beta (β), which measures the relationship between the returns on a particular share and the return on the market as a whole. In general:

- a share with a β of greater than 1.0 is *aggressive* (that is, it is more volatile and potentially more risky than the market)
- a share with a β of less than 1.0 is *defensive* (that is, it is less volatile and potentially less risky than the market)
- a share with a β equal to 1.0 is *neutral* (that is, it is equally as volatile and potentially equally as risky as the market).

Note: Remember that shares can also form part of an Investment ISA.

9.9 Investment funds

Investment funds pool the funds provided by many different investors and use the pool to hold a wide range of shares, bonds and other assets. Investment funds generally provide a broader selection of investment opportunities, for a management fee.

There are many different types of investment funds, of which some of the most common are: unit trusts, open-ended investment companies (OEICs), investment trusts, exchange-traded funds, money-market funds, hedge funds, and pension funds.

Unit trusts

Unit trusts are managed trusts, formed (under deed) to manage a portfolio of assets or securities, or both, of which small investors can buy units. These are open-ended investments: the trust can issue or redeem units in the trust, allowing investors to buy into the trust or to sell their existing stake.

Open-ended investment companies (OEICs)

Open-ended investment companies (OEICs) – or investment companies with variable capital (ICVCs) – are open-ended collective investments formed as a company under the *Open-Ended Investment Company Regulations 2001*. They represent a popular way of investing in the stock market. Investors hold shares in an OEIC: money invested by each investor is pooled with that of other investors and invested in a variety of investments, for example equities, fixed-interest securities, and property. OEIC funds are medium- to long-term investments (at least 5–10 years).

Investment trusts

Investment trusts are a form of collective investment. They are closed-ended funds, incorporated as listed public limited companies. Shares in an investment trust are traded marketable securities. Investors' money, gathered from the sale of a fixed number of shares issued by the investment trust when launched, is pooled together and then invested in the stocks and shares of a wide range of companies.

Exchange-traded funds (ETFs)

Exchange-traded funds (ETFs) are listed investment companies whose share price is linked to the underlying value of their investments. When investing in an ETF, the investor is purchasing a portfolio that tracks the yield and return of a specific index – for example, the FTSE 100, commodity prices, or even property values.

Money-market funds

Money-market funds (or money-market mutual funds) are open-ended mutual funds that invest in short-term debt securities. They generally provide greater returns than traditional bank deposits.

Hedge funds

Hedge funds are investment vehicles. They are also known as 'absolute return funds'. They invest in a range of traditional financial market products – shares, bonds, commodities, currencies, derivatives,[22] and many others – and may apply non-traditional portfolio management techniques, such as shorting, leveraging, arbitrage, and swaps.

Hedge funds are typically limited partnerships and charge performance-related fees, have high minimum investment requirements, restrict the types and numbers of investor, and impose entry and exit conditions.

Pension funds

Pension funds are pooled contributions from pension plans set up by employers, unions, or other organisations to provide employees' or members' retirement benefits.

9.10 Property

There are two types of property: residential property and commercial property. Both can be used as investment vehicles, to produce either:

- rental income (by letting out property to tenants) *or*
- capital profits (by buying property and selling it at a higher price).

Investors can invest directly in individual properties; or alternatively they can invest in a property fund or a property maintenance and management service company.

Note: Investing in property can be very risky – property prices can fluctuate, and the demand for rental properties can vary considerably.

Direct investment in property

There are several issues that should be considered before investing in or buying property directly, whether for yourself or as a buy-to-let investment (that is, investing in property specifically for its rental value). The most important issues to note are these:

- It is important to clarify what the investment represents: is it freehold or leasehold?
- Unlike shares or bonds, an investment in property cannot be converted to cash very quickly – properties can take many months to sell.
- An investment in property usually represents a substantial financial commitment.
- There are a range of additional costs associated with buying and selling properties, including estate agents' costs, surveyors' fees, stamp duty, solicitors' and conveyancing fees, and any land tax.
- If the property investment is specifically for the generation of rental income, costs will also be incurred in maintaining the property and in managing the tenants.

Indirect investment in property

An indirect investment in property involves using a pooled (or collective) managed property fund. There many types of pooled property funds, the most common being:

- real estate investment trusts (often called REITs)
- property investment trusts
- insurance company property funds
- property unit trusts.

Fees will normally be charged for using a pooled managed property fund, and these will of course affect any earnings.

> **Activity 3**
>
> List the ways in which an investor can invest in property.

9.11 Pensions

A pension is a form of savings plan, designed to provide an income during retirement. There are many different types of pension arrangements and many different types of pension schemes. In terms of pension arrangements, there are:

- money-purchase pensions
- defined-benefits pensions
- cash-balance pensions
- hybrid pensions.

In terms of pension schemes, there are:
- occupational (or workplace) pension schemes
- contract-based pension schemes.

There is also the State Pension scheme. We will discuss pensions fully in Chapter 10.

9.12 Peer-to-peer lending

Peer-to-peer (P2P) lending enables savers to lend or invest funds (usually through an online account) and to achieve rates of returns higher than those offered by the more traditional investments through banks or building societies.

Peer-to-peer lending essentially matches savers or investors, who want a better return on their money, with borrowers (individuals or small businesses), who want to borrow at competitive rates. Currently, the main consumer peer-to-peer lenders are:
- Zopa (see: www.zopa.com)
- RateSetter (see: www.ratesetter.com)
- Funding Circle (see: www.fundingcircle.com)
- Relendex (see: www.relendex.com).

Whilst these lenders do offer very attractive rates of return, and the peer-to-peer lending sector is (as of April 2014) regulated by the Financial Conduct Authority, there are nonetheless risks and costs to lending in this way. The following are the most noteworthy:
- peer-to-peer schemes are *not* protected under the Financial Services Compensation Scheme (FSCS)
- peer-to-peer lenders are for-profit businesses and as such impose very high annual service charges
- peer-to-peer lending schemes are often fixed-term investments, so any early withdrawal of funds from a scheme can result in very high penalty charges.

9.13 Commodities

There are two main types of commodities: *soft* commodities (commodities that are grown) and *hard* commodities (commodities that are extracted). They are divided into four categories of traded commodities: energy (for example, crude oil and natural gas); metals (for example, gold, silver, platinum and copper); livestock; and agricultural (for example, corn, wheat, rice, cocoa, coffee, cotton and sugar).

There are a number of different ways in which an investor can invest in commodities or take advantage of (and potentially profit from) fluctuations in commodity prices. Some, if not all, of these alternatives are now open even to the average investor. Possible alternatives include:
- using a futures contract
- buying options on futures contracts
- buying shares in commodity companies
- buying share options
- using exchange-traded funds and exchange-traded notes.

A futures contract is a binding obligation to buy or sell an asset at a specified exercise price on the contract maturity date. Futures are exchange-traded instruments.

An option is a contract that gives the holder the right to buy (a 'call' option) or to sell (a 'put' option) an asset at a pre-agreed price (the 'strike' price).

Exchange-traded funds and exchange-traded notes are exchange-tradable instruments that can be traded like shares and can allow investors to participate in commodity price fluctuations without investing directly in futures contracts.

Call option: an example

Jonathan Neil purchases a call option to buy 1,000 shares in ABC plc at a strike price of £50. The option expiration date is 5 November 2016. He pays a premium of £5 per share for the call option. The current price of a share in ABC plc is £40.

Assuming that the share price (or the spot price) rises and peaks at £60 on the strike date (5 November 2015), Jonathan could exercise the option – that is, he could buy the shares in ABC plc from the counterparty at £50 each – and could then sell them on the open market at the market price of £60. For each share, he would have made a profit of £10 (that is, £60−£50) less £5 (the premium paid for the option) – a net profit of £5 per share or in total, for 1000 shares, £5000. (The 'counterparty' is the opposite party in a contract or financial transaction.)

Note: This figure excludes any commission that may be payable.

Put option: an example

Matthew Shaw purchased a put option to sell 1000 shares of XYZ plc for £50 per share. The current price is £55. He pays a premium of £5 per share. The put option expiration date is 1 December 2016.

Assuming that the share price of XYZ plc's shares falls to £40 per share before the expiration date, Matthew could exercise the put option by buying 1000 shares for £40,000, and then selling these to a put writer for £50,000. (The 'put writer' is the seller of an option who collects the premium payment from the buyer.)

His total profit would be £5,000 (£50,000 from the put writer – £40,000 for buying the stock – £5,000 for buying the put contract of 1000 shares at £5 per share).

Note: This figure excludes any commission that may be payable.

9.14 Endowment plans

An endowment (or an endowment plan) is a savings plan – a fixed long-term investment plan with life cover. Regular (usually monthly) fixed payments (premiums) are paid: part of the premium is for life assurance; the remainder (usually less an administration charge) is invested in an investment fund.

Most plans have a fixed maturity date. On maturity, a cash lump sum is paid. In addition, because the plan includes life cover, a cash lump sum is also paid if the investor dies during the period of the plan – either the sum assured (see below) or the value of the investment fund, whichever is the greater at the time.

When the plan matures, the proceeds are tax-free, provided that the savings plan is a 'qualifying' savings plan. An endowment plan is a 'qualifying' savings plan[23] if:

- the plan is for 10 years or more *and*
- the premiums are paid yearly or more frequently (usually monthly) *and*
- the sum assured is not less than 75% of the total premiums to be paid.

Historically, endowment plans were also used as a repayment vehicle for interest-only mortgages (also known as endowment mortgages), the cash lump sum on maturity being designed to pay off the outstanding mortgage loan. Although some still exist, the popularity of endowment mortgages has diminished considerably since the 1980s and 1990s.

Note: We briefly discussed endowment mortgages in Chapter 3.

Unit-linked or with-profits?

An endowment plan can be unit-linked or with-profits. Unit-linked means that savings paid into the plan are used to buy units in a fund[24] (similar to a unit trust). Endowment providers will normally offer a range of funds from which to choose, with the final value of the endowment plan dependent on how well the underlying unit fund has performed. Remember, however, that the value of unit-linked investments can go down as well as up, so the final value may be less than invested.

With-profits means that any savings paid into the plan are pooled with other investors' money and invested by the insurance company in a range of different investments, typically including shares, fixed-interest investments, and property. Bonuses are generally paid annually, based on how well the fund has performed.[25]

When the plan matures, the investor receives the annual bonuses plus a terminal bonus based on the overall performance of the investments during the period of the plan. Terminal bonuses are not guaranteed and can vary enormously.

Access and charges

As indicated above, an administration charge will usually be deducted from any regular premiums paid into the endowment plan. In addition, if the endowment plan is unit-linked, a variety of charges will be deducted by each fund. If the endowment plan is with-profits, various costs and charges will be deducted from the investment fund before bonuses are calculated.

Finally, once money is invested in an endowment plan, the funds are not easily accessible until the end of the plan. Although endowment plans can be terminated before maturity, high exit charges and penalties will normally be incurred, reducing the early redemption value of the plan.

So – are endowments safe?

Endowment plans can be purchased through a financial adviser or directly from an endowment provider – for example, an insurance company. If the endowment provider fails, compensation will normally be available via the Financial Services Compensation Scheme, providing the endowment provider was authorised by the Financial Conduct Authority and has been declared in default.

Note: You cannot claim compensation simply because the value of an endowment plan decreases.

9.15 Tax-exempt savings plans

Tax-exempt savings plans are provided by Friendly Societies – mutual associations that provide sickness benefits, life assurance, and pensions. They allow an investor to save up to £25 a month or £270 a year and to build up a tax-free lump sum. The minimum investment period is 10 years, after which any investment growth or gain is free of Capital Gains Tax.

Tax-exempt savings plans are available to UK residents only, who must be over the age of 16. Some Friendly Societies provide life insurance as part of the savings plan, with most providing a guaranteed minimum lump sum.

Fees and charges apply, but these differ considerably between Friendly Societies.

Activity 4

List the following savings and investments in terms of risk and return: *Company Bonds, property, current account, pensions, unit trusts, government Gilts,* and *company shares.*

9.16 High-risk investment products

There is a wide variety of high-risk investment products, some of which are closer to financial gambling than to traditional financial investments. The most common are structured products, Venture Capital Trusts, spread betting, Contracts for Difference (CFDs), land banking, and unregulated collective investment schemes.

Structured products

Structured products are fixed-term (usually 3–6 years) lump-sum investment products that offer returns based on the performance of an underlying investment, commodity, or index. There are two main types of structured product: structured investments and structured deposits.

Structured investments

Structured investments are investment products offered by banks and insurance companies. The return on the investment product (usually invested through a counterparty) is dependent on how an underlying investment or index performs (for example, the FTSE 100). If the underlying investment or index performs poorly, or if the company or firm providing the underlying investment fails, some or all of the original money invested could be lost.

Structured investment product providers must provide potential investors with key facts and information. They should explain what the investment is, how the investment works, the key risks (including the risk of capital loss and counterparty risks), charges and fees, rights to access to the Financial Ombudsman service, and the cover (if any) provided by the Financial Services Compensation Scheme.

Structured deposits

Structured deposits are savings accounts offered by banks, some building societies and NS&I. The return on the investment product is also dependent on how an underlying investment or index performs (for example, the FTSE 100), but – unlike structured investments – the money originally invested has the same protection as any other type of savings account.

Structured deposit providers are not required to provide a 'key facts' document, although they must provide sufficient information to allow an investor to make an informed choice.

Note: Counterparties are not used, as the invested capital is deposited with a bank, building society or credit union, and such deposits are protected, up to £75,000, under the Financial Services Compensation Scheme.

Structured investments and deposits are sold under many different names, including, for example, guaranteed equity bonds, guaranteed income bonds, structured Cash ISAs, growth deposit plans, guaranteed capital plans, guaranteed stock market bonds, and protected investment funds.[26]

Venture Capital Trusts (VCTs)

Venture Capital Trusts are managed investment companies that provide private equity investment capital for small start-up companies. VCTs normally invest in small, new, growing companies whose shares are not currently bought or sold on a recognised stock exchange. Investing funds in a Venture Capital Trust can be very risky. Any gains or losses will be totally dependent upon the success or otherwise of the Venture Capital Trust's fund manager and on the selection of up-and-coming companies.

Note: An investment in a Venture Capital Trust should be regarded as a long-term investment (over 5 years).

Spread betting

Spread betting is essentially financial gambling – it is more like placing a bet than making a financial investment, and carries a very high level of risk. The potential loss or gain could far exceed the original money wagered. In the UK, spread betting is regulated by the Financial Conduct Authority.

A spread is essentially a range of outcomes: the bet is whether the outcome will be above or below the spread. Supposedly invented by a US academic in the 1940s, spread betting became popular in the UK in the 1980s. Although betting on sporting events and financial markets (those dealing with shares, bonds and derivatives) has long been the most popular form of spread betting, spread betting today covers a wide range of markets and indices.

Spread betting: an example

INT plc is a UK-based spread-betting company. For a single trading period in August 2016, INT plc is quoting 6050–6250 for the UK FTSE 100 index. That is, it is quoting:

- 6250 to place a 'buy' or 'up' bet *and*
- 6050 to place a 'sell' or 'down' bet.

If an investor believes that the FTSE 100 index is going to *rise* over the single trading period in August 2016, she or he could place a 'buy' or 'up' bet – for example, buying £100 per point at 6250.

If the FTSE 100 index rose to 6430 within the specified trading period, the investor would earn a profit of £18,000 (6430–6250 * £100). If, however, the FTSE 100 index fell to 6070 within the specified period, the investor would lose £18,000 (6250–6070 * £100).

Alternatively, if an investor believes that the FTSE 100 is going to *fall* over the single trading period in August 2015, they could place a 'sell' or 'down' bet – for example, buying £100 per point at 6050.

Now, if the FTSE 100 index fell to 5870 within the specified trading period they would make a profit of £18,000. If, however, the FTSE 100 rose to 6230 within the specified period, they would lose £18,000.

Note: For obvious reasons, HM Revenue and Customs designates financial spread betting as gambling and not investing, and as such any profits or gains made from spread betting are not liable to UK tax.

Contracts for Difference (CFDs)

Contracts for Difference (CFDs) can be referenced to equities, FOREX, commodities, market indices or EFTs, with the contract being an agreement between a broker and an investor in which the investor agrees to exchange the difference in value between what an asset costs at the beginning of the contract and what it costs at the end of the contract. CFDs are very similar to spread bets (see above), inasmuch as the investor needs to predict whether the value of a particular asset, commodity, index or fund will go up or down; but with CFDs the investor purchases an interest in the price movement, rather than just betting on it.

CFDs carry a very high risk so, as with spread bets, it is possible to incur substantial losses very quickly.

Land banking

Land banking is an investment in land whereby an investor purchases land that has yet to be granted planning or development permission in anticipation that approval will be granted and the value of the land will increase.

Unregulated collective investment schemes (UCIS)

A collective investment scheme (or pooled investment) is a fund to which several people contribute, their pooled funds being invested in one or more types of assets or investment products, such as stocks, bonds or property. Many of these schemes are authorised and regulated by the Financial Conduct Authority.

If an investment scheme is not authorised or recognised by the Financial Conduct Authority, it is considered to be an unregulated collective investment scheme (UCIS). Such schemes are not subject to the same restrictions in terms of their management and their investment powers.

Restrictions imposed on the marketing of these unregulated schemes (from January 2014) mean that they cannot be promoted to the general public in the UK, but can be offered to certain limited categories of investors, including high net worth investors and existing investors in UCIS.

UCIS are by their nature very complex, very opaque, and very risky. More importantly, they are not covered by the Financial Services Compensation Scheme (FSCS).

9.17 Fund supermarkets

Also referred to as fund platforms or fund wrappers, fund supermarkets are online platforms that allow investors to buy and hold a range of investment products from a host of fund management companies together in one portfolio. Some fund supermarkets also enable clients to buy and sell individual shares. There are a wide range of fund supermarkets, the main ones being:

- InvestorProfile.co.uk (see: www.investorprofile.co.uk)
- Fidelity Funds Network (see: www.fidelity.co.uk)
- BestInvest (see: www.bestinvest.co.uk)
- Interactive Investor (see: www.iii.co.uk)
- Hargreaves Lansdown (see: www.h-l.co.uk)
- Chelsea Financial Services (see: www.chelseafs.co.uk).

The main advantage of using a fund supermarket is cost – the availability of heavily discounted fees and administrative charges, with an investor's portfolio of investments being managed and held by single provider.

The main disadvantage of a fund supermarket is the limited range of funds or investments available from some.

9.18 Investment risk and diversification

It is important to remember that *all* savings and investment products have some associated risk, however small that risk might appear to be. There are many different types of investment risk, the most common being:

- capital risk: the risk of losing some or all of the invested money
- inflation risk: the risk that inflation may erode the value of an investment
- business risk (or unsystematic risk): the risk that the company or organisation invested in performs badly
- market risk (or systematic risk): the risk of a fall in a particular market
- currency risk: the risk of adverse currency fluctuations
- social risk: the risk associated with unexpected social change
- political risk: the risk associated with unfavourable Government action.

Exposure to investment risk cannot be totally eliminated, but it can be reduced by diversification – that is, by holding a combination of investments. To create a balanced collection or a 'safe' portfolio of investments, it is important to remember (and follow) the old maxim, 'Don't put all your eggs in one basket.' Where possible, therefore:

- invest in a variety of investment types (shares, Gilts, Company Bonds, property and cash)
- invest in a range of different and unrelated companies and organisations
- invest in different (preferably unrelated) market sectors *and*
- invest in different markets, regions, or countries.

Note: Remember also that it is possible to *over-diversify* – holding too many investments could be detrimental to the overall return on the portfolio of investments.

> ### Activity 5
>
> Last week you bought your first National Lottery ticket ... and won ... along with three other lucky gamblers. You have won £3,346,000. Where would you invest your winnings?

9.19 Your rights as an investor

The Financial Ombudsman Service (FOS) and the Financial Services Compensation Scheme (FSCS) provide a significant umbrella of financial protection for savers and investors who have a genuine complaint against a financial adviser or a provider of financial products or services.

Details of the services provided by the Financial Ombudsman Service and the Financial Services Compensation Scheme are discussed in Chapter 13.

9.20 Concluding comments

The perfect 'one size fits all' investment, or indeed portfolio, does not exist – the appropriateness of any investment or collection of investments is very much dependent on the requirements of the investor, and the risk/return profile of the investment (see Figure 9.1).

As well as considering the investment risk and the expected yield or financial return, it is important before making any financial commitment to obtain information and advice – preferably *independent* information and advice – about the suitability of any given savings account or investment product. Even more crucially, it is essential to ensure that any investment made – whether in a simple cash-based savings account, or in a complex, highly structured, market-based investment product – is protected by the Financial Services Compensation Scheme.

9.21 Suggested further reading

For further reading on the following topics, see the references given.

Cash bonds or savings bonds (comparison):
- www.money.co.uk/savings-accounts/best-savings-accounts-2014.htm

Cash ISAs (comparison):
- www.money.co.uk/savings-accounts/cash-isas.htm

Children's Bonds:
- www.nsandi.com/savings-childrens-bonds

Current accounts (comparison):
- www.money.co.uk/current-accounts.htm

Instant access savings accounts (comparison):
- www.money.co.uk/savings-accounts/instant-access-savings.htm

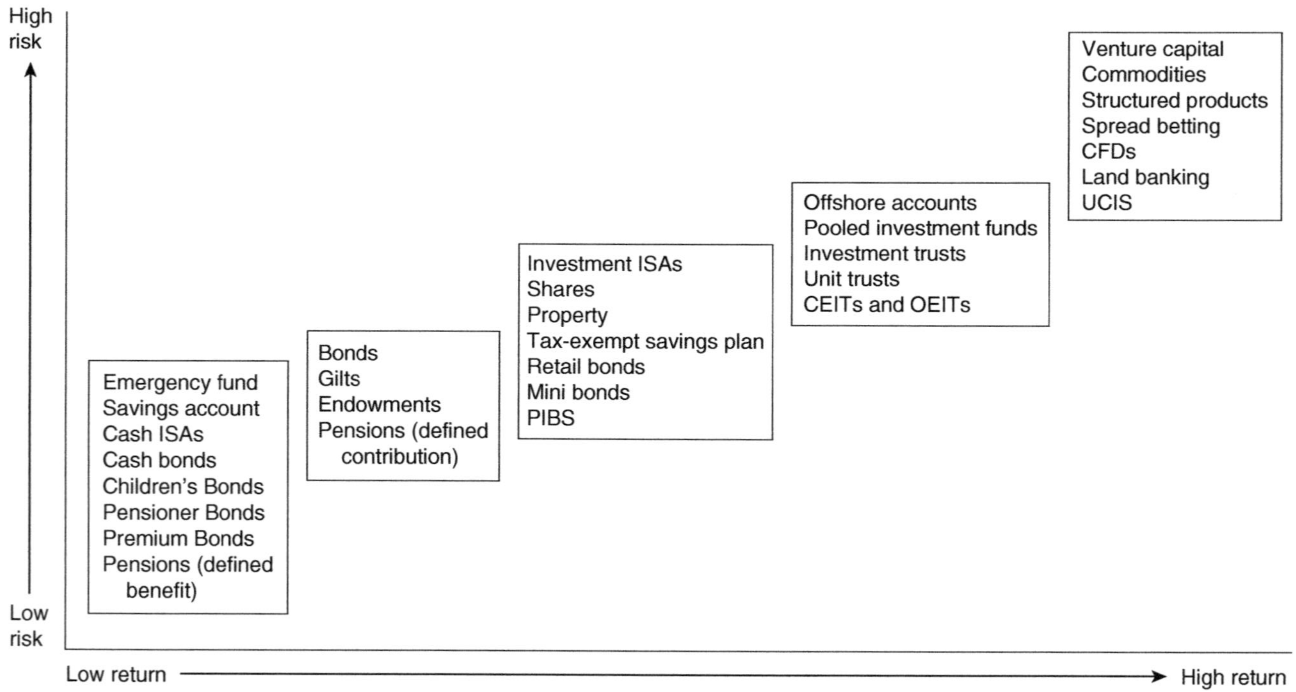

Figure 9.1 Risk and return

Investment ISAs or Stocks and Shares ISAs (comparison):
- www.money.co.uk/savings-accounts/investment-isas.htm

Notice deposit accounts (comparison):
- www.money.co.uk/savings-accounts/notice-savings.htm

Premium Bonds:
- www.nsandi.com/savings-premium-bonds

Key points

- ISIN is a standard numbering system that is used worldwide to identify specific securities such as bonds, shares and other tradable securities.
- Low-risk savings and investments include cash-related savings and investments (including ISAs), cash bonds, Premium Bonds, Savings Certificates, Children's Bonds, Pensioner Bonds, Investment Bonds, Gilts, pensions.
- Medium-risk investments include endowments plans, Friendly Society tax-exempt savings plans, Company Bonds, shares, property, offshore savings accounts, and pooled investment funds.
- Higher-risk investments include commodities, structured products, venture capital trusts, spread betting, contracts for difference, land banking, and unregulated collective investment schemes.
- Gilts are bonds issued by the UK Government to raise money.
- Premium Bonds are issued by National Savings and Investments (NS&I). They do not pay interest, but instead are entered into a monthly draw for tax-free prizes.
- Pensions are a form of investment or savings plan designed to provide an income during retirement.
- Investment funds pool the funds provided by many different investors. The most common are: unit trusts, open-ended investment companies (OEICs), investment trusts, exchange-traded funds, money-market funds, hedge funds, and pension funds.
- Shares are securities that represent an ownership interest in a company limited by shares.
- Shares can be purchased directly, using a broker or an online platform, or indirectly, using a pooled investment vehicle.

Self-review questions

1. What factors should be considered before making an investment?
2. What is *investment risk*? How can overall investment risk be reduced?
3. Distinguish between the following types of Company Bonds: *fixed-rate bond*, *variable-rate bonds*, and *convertible bonds*.
4. 'Investing in commodities can be very risky.' Discuss.
5. Explain the four key ways in which an investor can buy shares.

Case study discussion questions

1. Stuart and Mary Carter have decided to liquidate their UK Gilts and Commercial Bonds, and to invest the total amount in a diversified portfolio of UK-based FTSE 100 equities. Briefly outline the benefits of diversification, and advise them on an investment strategy for their 'post-retirement' portfolio.
2. Michelle Carter has decided to invest her Lottery winnings. Advise her on a possible investment strategy.

Suggested answers to chapter activities

Activity 1

A Cash ISA is simply a savings account on which the interest is not taxed. Any cash savings that stay within a Cash ISA will earn a tax-free return until the cash is withdrawn. Cash ISAs are available to all UK residents over the age of 16.

An Investment ISA (Stocks and Shares ISA) is a tax-efficient investment account that allows a saver or an investor to invest money into different types of investments, including unit trusts, open-ended investment companies (OEICs), investment trusts, government bonds, and Corporate Bonds, as well as individual company shares. Investment ISAs are available to all UK residents over the age of 18.

Activity 2

Premium Bonds are issued by National Savings and Investments (NS&I). They do not pay interest. Anyone aged 16 or over can purchase Premium Bonds.

Pensioner Bonds were launched in January 2015 and are available to all UK residents aged 65 and over. There are two versions: a 1-year bond and a 3-year bond, both with interest paid annually.

Gilts are bonds, or units of debt, issued by the Government to raise money. Since April 1998, Gilts have been issued by the Debt Management Office (DMO). Gilts are issued with a nominal value (face value) of £100.

Mini-bonds are unlisted non-transferable debt securities. The bondholder is paid a coupon (interest) until the bond reaches maturity, when the nominal value is repaid in full.

Activity 3

Investors can invest directly in individual properties, in a property fund, or in a property maintenance and management service company.

Activity 4

Using Figure 9.1, an example prioritisation (low-risk to high-risk) would be as follows: current account; government Gilts; pensions; property; Company Bonds; company shares unit trusts; and company shares.

Activity 5

There is no single solution to this question. Much would depend on the lucky winner's risk profile, his or her current level of debt, and his or her family, since most Lottery winners tend to give away some portion of their winnings to close family members (after they have returned from that 'holiday of a lifetime' they always promised themselves).

In general, and where possible, lucky winners should ensure they diversify their portfolios and that they:

- invest in a variety of investment types (shares, Gilts, Company Bonds, property and cash)
- invest in a range of different and unrelated companies and organisations
- invest in different (preferably unrelated) market sectors *and*
- invest in different markets, regions and countries.

Notes

1. For further information, see: http://www.paymentscouncil.org.uk/switch_service/overview_of_account_switching/.

2. Some banks and building societies *do* allow immediate access, but only in exceptional circumstances and usually with significant financial penalties.
3. ISAs were introduced on 6 April 1999, replacing the Personal Equity Plan (PEP) with the Investment ISA (Stocks and Shares ISA), and the Tax Exempt Special Savings Account (TESSA) with the Cash ISA.
4. National Savings and Investments (NS&I) is a UK-based Government-owned savings bank. It offers a wide range of savings accounts and investment products, some of which are tax-free. Taxable accounts include: direct saver accounts, investment accounts, guaranteed bonds, income bonds, and Pensioner Bonds. Tax-free accounts include: Premium Bonds, ISAs, Children's Bonds, index-linked Savings Certificates, and fixed-interest Savings Certificates.
5. A 'saver' invests in cash-based products, which usually show no capital growth. An 'investor' invests in other types of investments (such as shares or property), which may indeed yield capital growth – or capital losses.
6. For further information, see: http://www.ft.com/cms/s/0/3ae23438-55d6-11e4-93b3-00144feab7de.html#axzz3JXhxJuui.
7. Most of the offshore accounts available to UK savers are based in the Channel Islands or the Isle of Man.
8. Historically, the term 'Gilts' referred to debt securities that had a gilt (or gilded) edge.
9. The term 'strip' stands for 'Separate Trading of Registered Interest and Principal Securities'. Strips were first issued by the UK Government in 1997.
10. For higher-rate taxpayers, there may be some advantage in holding index-linked gilt-edged securities rather than conventional gilt-edged securities, because tax is only payable on the coupon payment, which is based on nominal value (and not the inflation-protection element of the coupon).
11. All gains from zero-coupon gilt-edged securities are, in effect, taxed as income on an annual basis. Bondholders are deemed to have 'bed and breakfasted' the strip if they hold it from one year to the next, and any resulting gain (or loss) is taxed as income.
12. The DMO's purchase and sale service is operated by Computershare Investor Services plc (see: www.computershare.com/uk), which is also responsible for maintaining the register of Gilt holdings.
13. The Order book for Retail Bonds (ORB) is an EU-regulated market. All bonds admitted to the market must comply with the requirements both of ORB and of the UK Listing Authority.
14. Corporate debt that matures in less than 1 year is typically called 'commercial paper'.
15. The yield to maturity takes into account the current market price of the bond, the nominal value of the bond, the coupon rate, and the time to maturity.
16. Consider the following: A UK irredeemable bond pays a coupon of £10 p.a. What would the (theoretical) price of the bond be today if interest rates were at 6%, and what would the (theoretical) value of the bond be if interest rates were to increase to 9%?

    'Irredeemable' means that the bond will never be paid back (or redeemed), which in turn means that the bond in effect provides the bondholder with a future stream of income (the coupon) forever. The (theoretical) price of such an irredeemable bond today can be calculated as: (coupon/r), where r is the interest rate (expressed as a decimal).

    If interest rates were at 6%, the (theoretical) price of the irredeemable bond today would be £10/0.06 = £166.66. If interest rates were at 9%, the (theoretical) price of the irredeemable bond today would be £10/0.09 = £111.11.
17. The word 'retail' means that the bonds are available to retail buyers – or, more appropriately, to individual or private investors, as opposed to the big financial institutions.
18. Because of lower regulatory costs (mini-bonds are not subject to the same scrutiny as listed bonds), they are cheaper to issue and are being used increasingly by smaller high-risk companies to raise finance.
19. PIBS are regarded as subordinated debt – in the event of the issuer (the building society) being forced into liquidation, PIBS rank lower than deposits and bonds.
20. It is possible to issue non-voting ordinary shares, and such shares are sometimes used as part of employee remuneration packages.
21. Some preference shares are 'cumulative preference' shares: this means that dividends not paid in one year must be paid in a subsequent year (before any ordinary share dividend is paid).
22. A derivative is an arrangement or a product (such as a future, an option, or a warrant) whose value derives from, and is dependent on, the value of an underlying asset such as a commodity, a currency, or a security.

23. See: IPTM2020, 'Qualifying policies and life assurance premium relief: outline of qualifying policy rules'. Available at: www.hmrc.gov.uk/manuals/iptm/iptm2020.htm.
24. It may be a fund managed by the endowment provider, by another unit trust, or by an open-ended investment company (OEIC).
25. If the fund has performed very well, some of the bonuses may be set aside to boost bonuses in later years, when the fund may not perform so well. This process is called 'smoothing' and is designed to smooth out stock-market volatility.
26. The word 'guaranteed' means that the capital is guaranteed only if the company providing the guarantee can meet its obligations *or* is covered by the Financial Services Compensation Scheme.

10

Pensions

Learning outcomes

By the end of this chapter, you should be able to:

- describe the different types of pension schemes available in the UK
- explain the alternative types of pension arrangements
- describe the forthcoming changes to the State Pension
- explain the advantages and disadvantages of an occupational (or workplace) pension
- describe alternative types of contract-based pensions.

10.1 Introduction

The State Pension scheme in the UK is changing – forever. Not only will the State Pension age increase to 66 by 2020 and to 68 by 2028, but the amount of the State Pension payable under the new simplified State Pension scheme was set at £148.40 per week per person for those over the pension age after 6 April 2016.[1] As a consequence, contributing to a private pension – an occupational pension, a workplace pension, or an individual contract-based pension – has become an absolute necessity for those concerned about their future financial security and their well-being in retirement.

This chapter explores a range of topics related to the State Pension, occupational pensions, and alternative individual contract-based pensions.

10.2 Understanding pensions

Although a pension is merely a type of savings plan, there are many different types of pension arrangements and many different types of pension schemes and pension plans.

Types of pension arrangements

There are four different types of pension arrangements:

- money-purchase arrangements
- defined benefits arrangements
- cash-balance arrangements
- hybrid arrangements.

Money-purchase arrangements

In money-purchase arrangements, the pension that will be payable on retirement is unknown – the final value of the pension (and thus the amount payable on retirement) will depend both on how much money has been contributed and how well the funds have been invested.

Defined benefits arrangements

In defined benefits arrangements, the amount of pension payable on retirement is based on an individual's pay and length of service, rather than on the value of her or his contributions. Examples of defined benefits arrangements include:

- a *final salary* arrangement, in which the pension is based on the member's final salary and number of years' service
- a *career-average* arrangement, in which the pension is based on the member's average earnings over her or his period of employment
- a *lump-sum-only* arrangement, which only provides a lump-sum payment, the size of which is based on the member's final salary and number of years' service.

Cash-balance arrangements

In cash-balance arrangements, the amount of pension payable on retirement depends on how much members' promised pension pots (the accumulated contributions) can buy when they start to take their pension on retirement. A cash-balance arrangement is a form of defined benefits arrangement under which an individual is promised not a defined amount of pension on retirement but a defined lump sum, which is generally defined as a proportion of her or his salary income.

Note: Because an individual's final pension is not readily predictable as a proportion of his or her income before retirement, cash-balance arrangements may be regarded as being much closer to money-purchase arrangements.

Hybrid arrangements

Hybrid arrangements are defined benefits arrangements that include elements of a money-purchase arrangement. The two most common types of hybrid arrangements are:

- a sequential hybrid arrangement (or 'nursery arrangement'), where pension benefits are accumulated first in one pension arrangement (for example, a defined benefits arrangement), and then in a second pension arrangement (for example, a money-purchase arrangement)
- a combination hybrid pension scheme, where pension benefits are accumulated in both a defined benefits arrangement and a money-purchase arrangement at the same time.

Activity 1

Distinguish between a *money-purchase pension arrangement* and a *defined benefits pension arrangement.*

Types of pension schemes

There are three different types of pension schemes:

- the State Pension scheme
- occupational (or workplace) pension schemes
- contract-based pension schemes.

The State Pension (also known as the 'old-age pension' or the 'Government pension') is the UK Government's pension scheme. It is dependent on the amount of National Insurance contributions made by the individual before reaching the State Pension age.

Occupational pensions (also known as company pensions) are workplace-related pension schemes managed by an individual's employer, with both the employee and the employer contributing to the pension scheme.

Contract-based pension schemes are effectively savings or investment contracts between an individual and a pension provider.

There are other pension schemes too, which can be categorised as being either an occupational pension scheme or a contract-based pension scheme. They include:

- small self-administered schemes (SSAS)
- employer-financed retirement benefits schemes (EFRBS).

10.3 The State Pension scheme

The State Pension scheme is changing. Those who reach the State Pension age *before* 6 April 2016 will receive their State Pension in accordance with the pre-April 2016 State Pension scheme. Those who reach the State Pension age *after* 6 April 2016 will receive their State Pension in accordance with the post-April 2016 simplified State Pension scheme.

The pre-April 2016 two-tier State Pension scheme

The pre-April 2016 two-tier State Pension scheme comprises:

- the basic State Pension *and*
- (if eligible) an additional State Pension (currently known as the State Second Pension or S2P).

Basic State Pension

Providing sufficient National Insurance contributions (NICs) have been paid (up to a maximum of 30 qualifying years[2]), women receive the basic State Pension from between 60 and 65 (for women born after 5 April 1950 and before 6 December 1953) and men receive the basic State Pension from 65 (for men born before 6 December 1953). The basic State Pension is still claimable even if the man or woman, having reached the State Pension age, chooses to continue to work, whether on a paid or on a voluntary basis. (However, any money earned may, of course, affect any entitlement to other benefits or allowances.)

Note: The basic State Pension does not *have* to be claimed at the State Pension age: it can instead be deferred, with the deferred pension (and accrued interest) paid at a later date either as a lump sum or as an increased weekly pension.

For 2014/2015, the maximum basic State Pension was £113.10 per week per person (or £5,881 per annum). For a married couple (both of whom receive the State Pension), if both have the maximum number of State Pension qualifying years, the combined State Pension will be £226.20 per week for the couple. For a married couple where only one partner has the maximum number of State Pension qualifying years, an additional top-up allowance is claimable up to a maximum of £67.80 per week, making the total State Pension of £180.90 per couple per week.

Prior to April 2016, the basic State Pension was increased annually, by the highest of the average percentage growth in earnings *or* the percentage growth in UK prices, as measured by the Consumer Prices Index (CPI) *or* 2.5%.

Additional State Pension

There have been three different schemes that have existed to provide an additional pension (extra to the basic State Pension) to employees paying National Insurance contributions (and some exempted groups, but not including the self-employed). These three schemes are:

- Graduated Retirement Benefit scheme: from 1961 and 1975
- SERPS (State Earnings-Related Pension Scheme): from 1978 to 2002
- S2P (State Second Pension Scheme): from 2002 to 2016.

This additional State Pension was a top-up to the basic State Pension. Made available by paying extra National Insurance contributions, the additional State Pension was only accessible to those who had not 'opted out' or 'contracted out' and who belonged to an occupational pension scheme. They must also have been:

- employed and earning over £5,824 (in 2015/2016), from any one employment *or*
- caring for children under 12 years old and claiming Child Benefit *or*
- caring for a sick or disabled person for more than 20 hours a week and claiming Carer's Credit *or*
- registered as a foster carer and claiming Carer's Credit *or*
- receiving benefits due to illness or disability.

The amount of additional State Pension receivable depends on a range of factors, and (unlike the basic State Pension) there is no fixed or minimum payable amount.

Note: For those who are eligible (that is, those who have not 'contracted out'), the additional State Pension is paid automatically with the basic State Pension.

The single-tier State Pension scheme

Following the *Pension Act 2014*, a simplified and streamlined State Pension scheme was introduced from 6 April 2016, replacing both the current basic State Pension *and* the State Second Pension.

So why the change? Pension arrangements are being changed partly for economic and political reasons and partly for social reasons, in particular the demographic changes taking place within the UK population. People are living longer; couples are having fewer children; and people are spending more time in retirement. For example:[3]

- There are 9,000 people over 100 years old in the UK: by 2051 there are expected to be 160,000 centenarians.
- In 1950 life expectancy for a man at 65 was another 12 years: it is now closer to 20 years, and by 2051 it is expected to be 25.9 years.
- In the 1940s 1 in 10 women remained childless: the figure now is 1 in 5.
- In 1964, at the peak of the 'baby boom', the birth rate was almost 3 children per woman: in 2010 the figure has fallen to 2 children per woman.
- In 1901 there were 10 working people for every pensioner: the figure is now 3.2 working people for every pensioner, and by 2051 it is expected to be 2.9 working people for every pensioner.
- In 2007 there were more people over the State Pension age than there were under 16.
- Around 56 per cent of people of working age are not saving in a personal pension.

Under the post-April 2016 pension scheme, all women born on or after 6 April 1953 and all men born on or after 6 April 1951 will receive the post-April 2016 single-tier State

Pension; while those who have already reached the State Pension age by 6 April 2016 will continue to receive their State Pension in accordance with the pre-6 April 2016 scheme.

Currently expected to be £148.40 per week per person (in 2015/2016 terms), the post-April 2016 single-tier State Pension (like the basic State Pension prior to 6 April 2015) will be increased annually by the highest of the average percentage growth in earnings *or* the percentage growth in UK prices as measured by the CPI *or* 2.5%.

To receive the post-April 2016 single-tier State Pension, a minimum qualifying period of at least 10 years' National Insurance contributions (or credits) will normally be required, with a qualifying period of 35 years' National Insurance contributions (or credits) required to receive the full single-tier State Pension. Those with fewer than 35 years' contributions (or credits), but not less than 10 years' National Insurance contributions (or credits), will receive an adjusted reduced amount.

As a consequence of the post-April 2016 single-tier pension scheme:

- means-tested Pension Credit (and in particular the Savings Credit element of Pension Credit), the State Second Pension, and other top-up pension arrangements will be stopped
- pension eligibility will have an individual basis, and married women who do not have enough qualifying years themselves will no longer receive a proportion of their husband's entitlement after his death.

Understanding 'foundation amount'

National Insurance contributions paid (or credits received) in relation to the pre-6 April 2016 State Pension scheme will be converted into a foundation amount for the single-tier State Pension scheme. This foundation amount will be the higher of:

- the amount that would have been received under the pre-6 April 2016 system (including basic and additional State Pension) *or*
- the amount that would have been received had the post-April 2016 State Pension system been in place at the start of the individual's working life.

Note: If an individual's foundation amount is *more* than the level of the post-April 2016 single-tier State Pension (because of any basic and additional pension already accumulated), any excess will be protected and paid in addition to the single-tier pension when they reach the State Pension age. If the foundation amount is *less* than the level of the post-April 2016 single-tier State Pension, an individual will be able to build up more pension during the period from 6 April 2016 and when they reach State Pension age.

Implications of 'contracting out'

Where necessary, a deduction will be made from the foundation amount if an individual has been in a 'contracted out' personal or workplace pension scheme. This is because those who have been in a 'contracted out' pension scheme will have paid lower National Insurance contributions.

Top-up scheme for those on the pre-6 April 2016 State Pension scheme

For existing pensioners and for those who reach the State Pension age before 6 April 2016, a top-up scheme was introduced from October 2015. Under this scheme, individuals will be able to pay a lump-sum National Insurance contribution (depending on their age) to increase the amount of weekly State Pension they receive by up to an additional £25 a week.

Note: The State Pension top-up can be inherited by a surviving husband or wife or by a civil partner.

10.4 Pensions and tax relief

All contributions paid into occupational pension schemes and contract-based pension schemes, and those paid into overseas pension schemes that qualify for UK tax relief, are tax-free subject to both an Annual Allowance and a Lifetime Allowance.

Note: In some instances tax may be payable if a pension provider does not invest pension savings according to HMRC prescribed rules.

Annual Allowance

Tax relief is available on contributions paid into a pension scheme up to 100% of an individual's UK earnings (salary and other earned income), providing the total is below the Annual Allowance of £40,000 (for 2015/2016). In essence, the Annual Allowance limits the amount of tax-advantaged pension saving an individual can accumulate in a single year.

The Annual Allowance can be topped up with any unused Annual Allowance from the previous three tax years, but any contributions above the Annual Allowance will be subject to a tax charge. What counts towards the Annual Allowance depends on the type of pension scheme arrangement.

Note: An Annual Allowance is not available if an individual takes a pension using flexible drawdown[4] – tax is payable on all new pension savings.

In the July 2015 Budget, the Chancellor of the Exchequer announced plans to limit pension tax relief for those earning more than £150,000. Currently, individuals paying into a pension are entitled to tax relief on contributions of up to £40,000 p.a. From April 2016 this will be gradually reduced at a rate of £1 for every £2 earned over £150,000, until the tax-free limit has been reduced to £10,000 p.a.

Lifetime Allowance

For 2015/2016, the Lifetime Allowance is £1.25 million. The Lifetime Allowance restricts the tax-advantaged pension savings that individuals can accumulate over their entire career. The Lifetime Allowance applies to any pension savings in a registered pension scheme, and to any overseas pension scheme that qualifies for UK tax relief.

10.5 Personal pensions: changes from 6 April 2015

As from April 2015, some individuals are able to access and use their accumulated pension pot in any way they wish once they reach 55 years of age. This so-called 'pension revolution' applies both to occupational pensions and to contract-based pensions – but only to those based in the private sector. Public sector pension schemes are not eligible.

Those individuals eligible to take advantage of the changes can:

- withdraw a lump sum of up to 25%, free of Income Tax *and/or*

- convert some or all of the remaining accumulated pension pot into a regular retirement income (known as an annuity) *and/or*
- withdraw the remaining cash in stages or as a single lump sum which would be subject to Income Tax (at the highest rate currently paid by the individual).

For further information on current and forthcoming changes, see: www.pensionwise.gov.uk/.

10.6 Occupational pension schemes

Occupational pension schemes are set up by employers to provide pensions for their employees. There are two different types of occupational pensions:

- money-purchase arrangements
- defined benefits arrangements.

Money-purchase arrangements

Money-purchase arrangements are also called defined-contribution arrangements.

The money paid by individuals into an occupational pension scheme of this kind is invested, usually in a portfolio of investments, with the aim of providing an amount of money when they retire. An individual will normally pay a percentage of his or her salary (each month) into the scheme. The money paid in is normally increased (but not always) by an additional contribution from the employer. On retirement, the individual's pension will be based on the total amount of money paid into the scheme and how the investments have performed.

Defined benefits arrangements

Defined benefits arrangements are also called final salary arrangements or career-average arrangements. In defined benefits arrangements, an individual's pension is linked to her or his salary while working, so the pension automatically increases as the individual's pay increases.

An individual pays a percentage of his or her salary (each month) towards the pension fund. The employer will also contribute to the pension fund.

On retirement, the pension is based on the individual's final salary at retirement (or, increasingly, on the individual's career-average salary), together with the number of years for which the individual has been a member of the occupational pension scheme. An individual's pension entitlement does not depend on the performance of a portfolio of equities, bonds, or other investments.

Note: Final salary arrangements are becoming less common, with most defined benefits arrangements now being career-average arrangements.

Other benefits of occupational pension schemes

In addition to a pension when they retire, occupational pension schemes may offer individuals other related benefits, for example:

- a pension if the individual has to retire early because of ill-health *and*
- a life insurance which pays a lump sum and a pension to an individual's dependants if the individual dies while still employed.

Automatic enrolment into a workplace pension

From October 2012 (to April 2017), employers *must* enrol all eligible employees into their occupational (workplace) pension scheme. Employees with more than 3 months' service are eligible for automatic enrolment[5] if they:

- are aged 22 or over
- are under State Pension age
- earn more than £10,000 a year
- work (or usually work) in the UK *and*
- are not already in an occupational (workplace) pension scheme.

If you are automatically enrolled into an occupational pension scheme, your employer *must* make a minimum level of contributions.

Note: For employees, the monthly contributions are 0.8% of their qualifying earnings until September 2017, rising to 2.4% from October 2017 to September 2018, and then rising to 4.0% from October 2018. For employers, the monthly contributions are 1.0% of an employee's qualifying earnings until September 2017, rising to 2.0% from October 2017 to September 2018, and then rising to 3.0% from October 2018.[6]

Choosing to join an occupational pension scheme

If you are an eligible employee, before deciding whether or not to join an occupational (workplace) pension scheme, it is important that you clarify the following:

- What type of pension arrangement is it: defined-contribution or money-purchase?
- Is it an occupational pension or a personal pension scheme? (See below.)
- How much would your contributions be?
- What contributions would your employer make?
- If it is a money-purchase arrangement, how will the money you pay in be invested?

Note: Once you have decided to join an occupational pension scheme, it is best to join as early as possible to get the maximum benefit from your contributions.

If you already have a pension, what should you do?

There is no limit to the number of pension schemes to which an individual may contribute. This means that an individual may join an occupational (workplace) pension scheme, even if she or he has another pension fund (from a previous employer) or is currently contributing to another fund (such as a personal pension). However, there *is* a limit on how much tax relief an individual can claim.

For 2015/2016, the maximum tax relief on pension contributions that a UK taxpayer can claim is *either* 100% of their earnings *or* an annual allowance of £40,000, whichever is lower.

Changing employment

Although some rules and restrictions do exist regarding some occupational (workplace) pensions, in general when changing employment and moving employers individuals can choose to:

- leave their pension in their previous employer's pension scheme, and have any accumulated pension paid when they retire
- transfer their pension to a new occupational pension scheme *or*
- transfer their pension to a contract-based personal pension scheme.

Group personal pensions and stakeholder pensions through the workplace

Group personal pensions and stakeholder pensions are options for any individual who is not eligible for automatic enrolment into an occupational (workplace) pension. They work in a similar way to individually arranged contract-based pension schemes inasmuch as money paid into the pension scheme by the individual (together with any contribution made by the employer) is invested, usually in a portfolio of investments, with the aim of providing an amount of money on retirement.

Although the employer may select the pension provider and retain some amount of control over how the money paid into the fund is invested, the pension is still an individual savings contract with the pension provider.

Note: We will discuss group personal pensions and stakeholder pensions in more detail later in this chapter.

National Employment Savings Trust (NEST)

The National Employment Savings Trust (NEST) is an independently-run Government-backed pension scheme. It is a pension scheme based on a money purchase arrangement. It is designed for employees who are eligible for auto-enrolment into a pension scheme, who earn (for 2015/2016) above the qualifying earnings minimum of £5,824 but below the qualifying earnings maximum of £42,385, but whose employer does not offer its own company-based pension scheme.

Contributions to NEST are as follows:

- between October 2012 and September 2017 there will be a minimum contribution of 2% (of which the employee must pay 1%)
- between October 2017 and September 2018 there will be a minimum contribution of 5% (of which the employee must pay 2%) *and*
- from October 2018 there will be a minimum contribution of 8% (of which the employee must pay 3%).

Tax relief is available on all NEST contributions, although (as at September 2015) there is a limit of £3,600 p.a. on what can be paid into a NEST pension.

Note: For further information on NEST pensions, see: www.nestpensions.org.uk.

Activity 2

What is the purpose of NEST?

10.7 Contract-based pension schemes

Contract-based pension schemes are in effect savings or investment contracts between an individual and the pension provider. Contract-based pensions are money-purchase arrangements, with the value of any pension determined by:

- the amount of contributions made into the fund
- the period over which the contributions have been invested
- the investment growth of the underlying investments in the fund over the investment period *and*
- the level of charges imposed by the pension provider.

There are many different types of contract-based pension schemes, the most common being:
- personal pension schemes
- self-invested personal pensions (SIPPs)
- stakeholder pension schemes.

Personal pension schemes (or insured personal pensions) are pension plans managed by a regulated pension provider. Self-invested personal pensions are pension schemes managed by the pension holder, who can select and manage the investments made. Stakeholder pensions are personal pension schemes which satisfy certain other conditions. Contract-based pension schemes may also be offered by employers.

In addition to the above, older contract-based pension schemes include:
- retirement annuity contracts
- buyout policies (or deferred-annuity contracts).

Personal pension schemes

Personal pension schemes, also known as personal pension plans or insured personal pensions, are tax-privileged individual investment vehicles. They replaced retirement annuity plans (see below) in July 1988, and are available from and provided by a wide variety of insurance companies, banks and building societies.

Note: Pension providers *must* be regulated financial institutions.

How do personal pensions work?

Personal pensions are defined-contribution arrangements, the primary purpose of which is to accumulate a capital sum to provide financial benefits on retirement, and (usually) financial benefits to named beneficiaries on the death of the scheme member or plan holder.

Once an individual has selected a pension provider and a suitable personal pension scheme, she or he will make regular contributions (usually monthly) into the scheme. The selected pension provider will then invest the contributions in one or more funds, the aim being to maximise the value of the final pension pot.

Note: With personal pensions, the pension provider (as trustee) has ownership and control of the assets and investment portfolio.

The size of the accumulated pension pot and the amount of income available on retirement will depend on:
- how much is paid into the pension scheme
- the period over which contributions are paid into the pension scheme
- how well the pension fund investments perform
- the charges made and fees imposed by the pension provider
- any tax reliefs received *and*
- the annuity rate used to convert the accumulated pension pot (or the amount remaining, if a lump sum has been withdrawn on retirement) into a guaranteed monthly income payable for the duration of retirement (that is, until death).

Note: Personal pension schemes are sometimes available through an employee's workplace via his or her employer (see 'Group personal pension schemes', below).

Who should arrange a personal pension?

Personal pensions are a good way of saving for retirement, and should be considered by those who do not have an occupational pension (because they do not qualify for a workplace pension) and those who are self-employed. Not only are personal pension schemes a tax-efficient way of saving, but they are also:

- portable, and can be kept irrespective of employment status, allowing a larger pension pot to be accumulated *and*
- flexible, with many personal pension schemes allowing members to vary their contributions, paying in more when they can and taking a 'contribution holiday' when they cannot.

Disadvantages of personal pensions

There are of course a number of disadvantages to personal pensions, the main drawbacks being these:

- Most personal pensions are self-funded, with no employer contribution to boost the accumulated pension pot.
- Fees and charges can be high: often much higher than those paid in occupational schemes, group personal pension schemes (see below), or stakeholder pension plans (which have their annual fees capped).
- Many personal pension plans offer only a limited choice of investments, often far more limited than (for example) a self-invested personal pension (SIPP; see below).

Choosing a personal pension

There is a wide variety personal pension schemes available. Before selecting a personal pension scheme:

- Shop around and compare plans and schemes from as wide a range of pension providers as possible.
- Get as much independent information and advice as possible.
- Make sure that the pension contributions are affordable.
- Check what charges or fees (if any) are payable to the pension provider.
- Check what investment choices are available.
- Clarify how and where the pension contributions are going to be invested.

> **Activity 3**
>
> Briefly describe the main disadvantages of a personal pension.

Group personal pension schemes

Like other personal pension schemes, group personal pension schemes are also based on money-purchase (defined-contribution) arrangements. They are offered by some employers to their workers. As with other pension schemes based on money-purchase arrangements, members in a group personal pension scheme accumulate a personal pension pot, which can then be converted into an income on retirement.

In a group personal pension scheme, the scheme is run by a pension provider selected by the employer, but the pension arrangement is still an individual contract between the employee and the pension provider.

Note: If an employer offers a personal pension scheme, confirm whether it is a personal pension or an occupational pension scheme (as this may affect the portability of the pension should an employee later change employer).

An individual employee's accumulated pension pot will be built up using:
- personal contributions made by the employee
- additional contributions (if any) made by the employer
- returns made on the investment portfolios in which the pension contributions are invested *and*
- tax relief claimed by the pension provider.

Note: All personal pensions and all group personal pensions based on money-purchase (defined-contribution) arrangements are protected by the Financial Services Compensation Service (FSCS). However, the Financial Services Compensation Service does not pay compensation for poor investment performance.

Self-invested personal pensions (SIPPs)

Self-invested personal pensions (SIPPs) are a type of UK Government-approved personal pension scheme, which allow individuals to make their own investment decisions from the full range of investments approved by HMRC.

In common with personal pension schemes, self-invested personal pensions are tax 'wrappers',[7] which allow tax rebates on pension contributions in exchange for limits on accessibility.

Self-invested personal pensions are established under a trust. However, unlike conventional personal pensions where the *pension provider* (as trustee) has ownership and control of the assets or investments, in self-invested personal pensions the *member* can have ownership of the assets or investments. This allows individual plan holders much greater freedom in deciding what to invest in – although they can, if they wish, appoint a fund manager to manage the investments.[8]

What can self-invested personal pension schemes invest in?

Self-invested personal pensions funds can be invested in a range of assets or investments, including stocks and shares, investment trusts listed on any stock exchange, Government bonds (both UK and overseas), open-ended investment companies (if recognised by the FCA), company bonds, traded options, exchange-traded funds, bank deposit accounts (including foreign currency accounts), commercial property, real estate investment trusts (if listed), and offshore funds. In addition, self-invested personal pension funds can also invest in tangible property, including residential property and exotic assets such as wine, art, and vintage motor vehicles, although such investments may be subject to heavy tax penalties.

Types of self-invested personal pensions

There are essentially three types of self-invested personal pensions:
- a low-cost self-invested personal pension
- a full self-invested personal pension
- a hybrid (or deferred) self-invested personal pension.

Low-cost self-invested personal pension Low-cost self-invested personal pensions are designed for the majority of individuals, and are generally suitable for people with smaller pension savings to invest. They offer access to a wide range of funds at reduced charges, with the more flexible low-cost self-invested personal pensions also allowing individuals to invest in shares, bonds and cash. Low-cost self-invested personal pensions, however, do not generally allow direct investments in property offshore funds or in unquoted shares.

Low-cost self-invested personal pensions tend to impose an annual fee, either a fixed charge or a percentage fee (based on the value of the investment portfolio). Charges (dealing fees) can also be imposed for the buying and selling of shares.

Note: Low-cost self-invested personal pensions are normally execution-only, and charges tend to be lower than charges on other types of self-invested personal pension.

Full self-invested personal pension Full self-invested personal pensions offer the widest choice of investments, allowing investments in everything from cash, through investment funds and commercial property, to assets traded on any recognised exchanges, structured products, derivatives, and hedge funds. Some full self-invested personal pensions may also allow traded options, endowments, gold bullion, commercial property, and unlisted shares.

Full self-invested personal pensions tend to impose initial set-up fees and an annual management fee, which is usually a percentage fee based on the value of the investment portfolio.

Note: For full self-invested personal pensions, providers will also request a minimum contribution per month.

Hybrid self-invested personal pension Hybrid self-invested personal pensions are usually personal pensions with the option of using additional self-investment facilities. They are offered by insurance companies.

Note: Individuals who simply want a choice of funds or shares into which they can invest their pension should select a low-cost self-invested personal pension. Individuals who want the opportunity to own their own complex portfolio from the widest possible range of assets, including commercial property, should select a full self-invested personal pension.

For whom are self-invested personal pensions suitable?

Self-invested personal pension plans could be suitable for individuals who want greater control over their pension savings *and* who want to create a uniquely blended pension portfolio from their preferred funds, shares, commercial property, cash, National Savings products, and traditional insured funds – that is, individuals who do not want a pension company deciding how their pension savings are invested, but wish to control personally where their money is invested. Such people might be, for example:

- people who are comfortable with their own investment decisions and want a wider range of investments
- people who have a larger pension 'pot' or who will be making significant pension contributions
- people who have a financial adviser making decisions on their behalf
- people who are looking to consolidate all of their pensions into one place
- people who want to keep their money invested after they retire so that they have more access and control and can drawdown an income.

Fees and charges

The size of the fees and charges will obviously depend on many factors (including the type of self-invested personal pension and the pension provider), but in general initial set-up fees can vary between £0 and £1,000, and annual management charges can vary from 0.50% to 0.75%, with additional fund fees between 0.50% and 0.75%. Exit fees may also apply.

> **Activity 4**
>
> What is a SIPP? What are the main types of SIPPs?

Group self-invested personal pensions (GSIPPs)

Group self-invested personal pensions (GSIPPs) operate like other occupational pension schemes, but generally offer a wider range of investment choices and provide individuals with greater control over investment choices.

Stakeholder pensions (SHPs)

Stakeholder pensions (SHPs) were introduced in 2001 as a consequence of the *Welfare Reform and Pensions Act 1999.* They are defined-contribution personal pensions and are generally more flexible than personal pensions.

Note: Although stakeholder pensions are individually based pensions, some employers also offer them. Such stakeholder pensions are referred to as group stakeholder pensions (see below).

Stakeholder pensions must meet minimum standards, which include:
- charges are limited (no more than 1.5% of the fund's value for the first 10 years, and 1% after that)
- low minimum contributions can be made (as low as £20)
- flexible contributions can be made (that is, payments can be irregular and can be stopped and started as and when required, which makes SHPs particularly useful for the self-employed)
- lump-sum contributions can be made *and*
- transfers are penalty-free.

Note: There is no limit to the amount that can be paid into a stakeholder pension.

How stakeholder pensions work

The individual makes contributions into the chosen stakeholder pension. The selected pension provider then invests the contributions in one or more funds, the primary purpose being to accumulate a capital sum to provide financial benefits on retirement.

Note: All stakeholder pension schemes must be registered with the Pensions Regulator.

As with personal pensions, the size of the accumulated pension pot and the amount of income available on retirement will depend on:
- how much is paid into the pension scheme
- the period over which contributions are paid into the pension scheme

- how well the pension fund investments perform
- the charges made or fees imposed by the pension provider
- any tax reliefs received *and*
- the annuity rate used to convert the accumulated pension pot (or the amount remaining, if a lump sum has been withdrawn on retirement) into a guaranteed income payable for the duration of retirement (that is, until death).

Group stakeholder pension schemes

Employers can offer stakeholder pensions to employees, although since October 2012 employers are not *obliged* to offer them. SHPs can also be used for auto-enrolment purposes.

The pension provider will be chosen by the employer. The employer will also arrange for contributions to be paid (as a deduction from an employee's salary), and may even contribute to the employee's pension.

Stakeholder pensions offered through an employer are usually referred to as group stakeholder pensions.

Retirement annuity contracts

Retirement annuities contracts (RACs) were a type of pension scheme that was available to the self-employed, or employees not in an occupational pension scheme, before July 1988.

They were also known as s.226 pensions (after s.226 of the *Income and Corporation Taxes Act 1970*) or self-employed retirement annuities.

Although retirement annuities contracts were replaced by personal pension schemes, many retirement annuities contracts arranged and approved before July 1988 remain in existence.

Note: In April 2006 HMRC changed the rules that applied to retirement annuities contracts to align them with those applying to personal pension schemes. In particular, HMRC restricted the maximum tax-free lump sum payable to 25% of the value of the benefits coming into payment.

Buyout policies (deferred annuity contracts)

Buyout policies (deferred annuity contracts) were introduced in the early 1980s and were also known as s.32 buyout policies or s.32 buyouts (after s.32 of the *Finance Act 1981*). Although buyout policies were largely superseded by the arrival of personal pension schemes in July 1988, some s.32 buyout policies remain in existence.

Buyout policies were generally used to transfer pension benefits from, for example, statutory schemes, money-purchase occupational pension schemes, final salary-related occupational pension schemes, and other s.32 buyout plans; and were used:

- if the occupational pension scheme was about to wind up *and/or*
- if a pension scheme member had moved employment and wished to transfer to a deferred annuity contract rather than another employer's scheme, personal pension, or stakeholder pension.

Note: No additional pension contributions can be paid into an s.32 buyout plan – these plans can only accept pension transfers from other pension schemes.

10.8 Transferring a personal pension

A personal pension can be transferred to another registered pension scheme, an overseas pension scheme (providing it is a qualifying recognised pension scheme), or the Pension Protection Fund.[9] There are many valid reasons why an individual would consider transferring their personal pension, for example:

- their current pension scheme may be being closed
- they may want to move to a less expensive pension scheme
- they may want greater investment choice (and may want to move their personal pension into a self-invested personal pension)
- they may currently contribute to a number of different pension schemes and want to consolidate them into a single, more manageable pension scheme.

Such a course of action is, however, not without cost or risk. These would include:

- the possible imposition of exit penalties or costs
- the loss of possible guaranteed benefits
- the increased risk, especially where a pension is transferred from an occupational pension to a personal pension
- the loss of time-related bonuses *and*
- the loss of rights to lump sums free from Income Tax.

Where possible, independent specialist advice should be obtained before any decision to transfer a personal pension is taken. Generally, however, there is no financial benefit to be gained by transferring out of an occupational pension scheme (either a defined benefits arrangement or a money-purchase arrangement) to a personal pension scheme. This is mainly because of:

- the benefits accrued from the additional 'top-up' contributions made by employers *and*
- the generous retirement packages and benefits (including death benefits) associated with some pension schemes, especially benefit-based occupational pension schemes.

Activity 5

Briefly describe the main reasons why an individual might want to transfer his or her pension.

10.9 Other pension schemes

Small self-administered schemes (SSAS)

Small self-administered schemes (SSAS) are a type of UK occupational pension scheme. They are trust-based pension schemes established by organisations such as family businesses, partnerships and companies for specified groups of individuals, usually employees. The maximum membership of a small self-administered scheme is 12, with such schemes generally suited to groups of individuals who run a common business and wish to:

- retain control over their pension benefits
- use the self-investment facility to help the company's development *and*
- have greater control over the pension fund.

Note: Because all small self-administered scheme members must be trustees, they must also be at least 18 years old.

Small self-administered schemes give the managing trustees wide investment powers. For example, they can:
- loan funds to the company to allow business expansion
- purchase the company's premises, with the trustees then acting as landlords *and/or*
- purchase equity capital in the company to allow business expansion (which might avoid partial surrender of control to external interests).

If registered with HMRC, the scheme can enjoy tax-exempt status, with all contributions made by scheme members and the sponsoring employer or organisation attracting tax relief. For scheme members, contributions are limited to the Annual Allowance of £40,000 (for 2015/2016), providing the scheme member does not also contribute to another pension scheme.

Small self-administered schemes can invest their funds in a variety of investment and assets, including stocks and shares, investment trusts listed on any stock exchange, Government bonds (both UK and overseas), open-ended investment companies (if recognised by the Financial Conduct Authority), company bonds, traded options, exchange-traded funds, bank deposit accounts (including foreign currency accounts), commercial property, real estate investment trusts (if listed), and offshore funds. In addition, self-invested personal pension funds can also invest in tangible property, including residential property and exotic assets such as wine, art, and vintage motor vehicles, although such investments can be subject to heavy tax penalties.

Pension benefits generally include a tax-free cash sum from age 50 or 55 and an annual pension income paid from the pension scheme. When a scheme member dies, the benefits may be paid to beneficiaries, although special rules apply if the death occurs after age 75.

Employer-financed retirement benefits schemes (EFRBS)

Employer-financed retirement benefits schemes (EFRBS) are unapproved pension schemes with few if any tax benefits. They are often located offshore, and are generally suitable for non-domiciled employees or workers who are living or are thinking of retiring abroad.

Historically considered as an alternative to a formal UK-registered pension scheme or employee benefit trust as a way of providing benefits – for example, a lump sum or a gratuity or other benefit on retirement or at death – employer-financed retirement benefits schemes are now seldom used.

Pension schemes for the Armed Forces and their families

There are a number of different pension schemes available to former members of the Armed Forces and their families. The pension scheme applicable depends on an individual's type of service, dates of service, and length of service. The pension schemes available as at September 2015 include:
- the Armed Forces Pension Scheme 1975 (AFPS 1975)
- the Armed Forces Pension Scheme 2005 (AFPS 2005)
- the Reserve Forces Pension Scheme 2005 (RFPS 2005)
- the War Widow's/War Widower's Pension.

Note: The Armed Forces Pension Scheme does not affect an individual's entitlement to the State Pension.

Armed Forces Pension Scheme 1975

The Armed Forces Pension Scheme 1975 (AFPS 1975) is a work-related pension scheme that commenced in 1975 and ceased in 2005. It is applicable to all individuals who joined the Armed Forces after 2005 (AFPS 2005). The amount of pension receivable depends on an individual's rank and length of service, and the age at which the individual commenced service in the armed forces.

Armed Forces Pension Scheme 2005

The Armed Forces Pension Scheme 2005 (AFPS 2005) is a work-related pension scheme that commenced in 2005 and replaced AFPS 1975. It is applicable to all individuals who joined the Armed Forces between 1975 and 2005, unless they elected transfer to the Armed Forces Pension Scheme 2005 (AFPS 2005). The amount of pension receivable depends on an individual's length of service, their final salary, their age when leaving the armed forces, and whether service was terminated due to illness or injury.

Reserve Forces Pension Scheme 2005

The Reserve Forces Pension Scheme 2005 (RFPS 2005) is available to all individuals who joined or rejoined full-time service in the reserve forces from 2005 onwards, unless they elected to opt out of the scheme. Individuals qualify if they have served in the following:

- the Territorial Army
- the Royal Naval Reserve
- the Royal Marines Reserve
- the Royal Air Force Volunteer Reserve.

War Widow's/War Widower's Pension

Where a husband or wife or a civil partner has died as a result of serving in any of the UK armed forces, the surviving partner may be entitled to a War Widow's/War Widower's pension, based on the pay and age of the deceased husband, wife or civil partner.

In addition, if the deceased person served in the UK armed forces after 6 April 2005, the surviving partner may be able to claim from the Armed Forces Compensation Scheme. For more information, see: www.veterans-uk.info.

10.10 Alternatives to a pension

Whilst many people now contribute regularly either to an occupational pension scheme or to a contract-based pension scheme, there are many who do not or whose accumulated pension pot will be insufficient to meet their retirement needs.

So what are the alternatives to contributing regularly to a pension? The main ones are:

- investing in property to accumulate value, and either selling the property to release any capital value or generating a regular income by renting out the property
- using an ISA to save towards retirement
- investing in stocks and shares
- investing in a Venture Capital Trust
- investing in art or antiques.

10.11 Concluding comments

There are many ways in which an individual can save for the future, but only pensions – and in particular occupational pensions and contract-based pensions – are designed specifically for retirement. More importantly, such pensions are some of the most tax-efficient ways to save for the future.

10.12 Suggested further reading

For further reading on the following topics, see the references given.
Occupational and contract-based pensions:
– http://www.pensionsadvisoryservice.org.uk/

Post-6 April 2016 single-tier State Pension:
– www.thepensionsregulator.gov.uk/

Key points

- There are four different types of pension arrangements: money purchase arrangements, defined benefits arrangements, cash balance arrangements, and hybrid arrangements.
- There are three different types of pension schemes: the State Pension scheme, occupational (or workplace) pension schemes, and contract-based pension schemes.
- The existing two-tier State Pension scheme was replaced with a single-tier State Pension from 6 April 2016.
- Tax relief of up to 100% of an individual's UK earnings is available on contributions paid into a pension scheme, providing the total is below the Annual Allowance of £40,000 (for 2015/2016).
- Occupational pension schemes are set up by employers to provide pensions for their employees.
- From October 2012 employers must enrol all eligible employees into their occupational (workplace) pension scheme.
- Contract-based pension schemes are effectively savings or investment contracts between an individual and the pension provider.
- There are many different types of contract-based pension schemes, the most common being: personal pension schemes, self-invested personal pensions (SIPPs), and stakeholder pension schemes.
- A personal pension can be transferred: to another registered pension scheme, to an overseas pension scheme (providing it is a qualifying recognised pension scheme), or to the Pension Protection Fund.
- Small self-administered schemes are trust-based pension schemes established by organisations. The maximum membership of a small self-administered scheme is 12.

Self-review questions

1. Briefly explain the key characteristics of the post-April 2016 single-tier State Pension scheme.
2. What are the requirements for auto-enrolment in an occupational pension scheme?
3. Compare and contrast *self-invested personal pensions* and *stakeholder pensions*.

4. Compare and contrast the following: a *low-cost self-invested personal pension*, a *full self-invested personal pension*, and a *hybrid (or deferred) self-invested personal pension*.
5. What is a *small self-administered scheme*? Why would a company want to establish such a scheme?

Case study discussion questions

1. Advise Jonathan Carter on the adequacy of his current pension provision and the problems he may face in retirement.
2. Claire Carter does not currently contribute to a pension scheme. Prepare a brief report for her, detailing the alternative types of individual contract-based pension schemes currently available.

Suggested answers to chapter activities

Activity 1

A money-purchase arrangement is one where the pension payable on retirement is unknown – the final value of the pension (and therefore the amount payable on retirement) depends on how much money is contributed and how well the funds are invested.

A defined benefits arrangement is one where the amount of pension payable on retirement is based on an individual's pay and length of service, rather than on the value of their contributions.

Activity 2

The National Employment Savings Trust (NEST) is an independently-run Government-backed pension scheme. It is a money-purchase pension scheme, designed for employees who are eligible for auto-enrolment into a pension scheme, who earn (for 2015/2016) more than the qualifying earnings minimum of £5,824 but less than the qualifying earnings maximum of £42,385, but whose employer does not offer a company-based pension scheme.

Activity 3

The main disadvantages of personal pensions are that most personal pensions are self-funded, with no employer contributions to boost the accumulated pension pot; that the fees and charges can be high (often much higher than those paid in occupational schemes, group personal pension schemes and stakeholder pension plans); and that many personal pension plans offer only a limited choice of investments.

Activity 4

Self-invested personal pensions are a type of UK Government-approved personal pension scheme and allow individuals to make their own investment decisions from the full range of investments approved by HMRC.

There are essentially three types of self-invested personal pensions: a low-cost SIPP, a full SIPP, and a hybrid (or deferred) SIPP.

Activity 5

Individuals might consider transferring their personal pensions if, for example, their current pension scheme is being closed; if they wish to move to a less expensive pension scheme; if they want more investment choice (and perhaps to move their personal pension into a self-invested personal pension); or if they currently contribute to a number of different pension schemes and wish to consolidate them into a single, more manageable pension scheme.

Notes

1. The full new State Pension will be no less than £148.40 per week. (The actual amount was set in autumn 2015.) See: www.gov.uk/new-state-pension/overview.
2. The amount payable as the basic State Pension is dependent on the amount of National Insurance contributions paid. To receive the full basic State Pension, an individual must have accumulated 30 qualifying years of National Insurance contributions. However, those not in employment can claim National Insurance credits towards their basic State Pension if, for example, they claim benefits or allowances such as Jobseeker's Allowance or Carer's Allowance.
3. See: www.ons.gov.uk/ons/rel/pensions/pension-trends/chapter-2--population-change--2012-edition-/bkd-pt2012ch2.pdf.
4. Flexible drawdown is a form of 'income withdrawal' whereby a pension is paid direct from a pension scheme. There is no limit on the amount that a pension scheme can pay in any year. All payments of flexible drawdown are taxed under PAYE.
5. For further information on automatic enrolment, see: Department for Work and Pensions 2014: 'Automatic enrolment in to a workplace pension: key facts'. Available at: www.gov.uk/government/uploads/system/uploads/attachment_data/file/299886/auto-key-facts-enrolment-booklet.pdf.
6. See: www.pensionsadvisoryservice.org.uk/about-pensions/pensions-basics/automatic-enrolment/how-much-do-i-and-my-employer-have-to-pay.
7. Tax wrappers are tax breaks that investors can 'wrap' around their investments, so that these can be sheltered so that the investor pays only some or no tax on them. The most common tax wrappers are ISAs and pensions.
8. The Association of Member-directed Pension Schemes (AMPS) is the trade body for self-invested personal pension providers and managers. See: www.ampsonline.co.uk.
9. See: www.pensionprotectionfund.org.uk/.

11

Insurance, assurance, and protecting what you have

Learning outcomes

By the end of this chapter, you should be able to:

- distinguish between insurance and assurance
- explain the main uses of insurance
- describe the different types of insurance available.

11.1 Introduction

From home insurance to vehicle insurance, from health insurance to critical illness insurance, from travel insurance to life insurance, income protection insurance and insurance-related investments, there can be little doubt insurance has, in one form or another, become an important part of our daily lives. And yet, whilst many people have some form of insurance, few people actually understand what insurance is or indeed how it works, even though possessing the correct types of insurance and the correct level of insurance cover needs to be a critical part of any person's wealth-management and risk-management plan.

This chapter explores a range of topics related to the fundamentals of insurance, the main uses of insurance, and the alternative types of insurance that are available.

11.2 What is insurance?

Insurance is a contractual agreement where in exchange for payments (called premiums), an insurer agrees to pay to the insured (the policyholder) a sum of money should a specific event or financial loss occur. The *insurer* may be a person or an organisation, but is usually an insurance company; and in exchange for regular payments the insurer accepts the risk of loss and compensates the insured in the event of loss. The *insured* is the person or organisation that takes out the insurance: in doing so, the insured is paying premiums to transfer to the insurer the risk of loss under a contractual agreement (the insurance policy) that will provide compensation for any insured loss. Details of the coverage, features, conditions and limitations of the insurance policy are specified in the contractual agreement, the insurance policy, which is a legal document.

It is important to understand that insurance is a form of risk management whereby, in return for the payment of agreed premiums, the insured transfers the cost of a potential loss to the insurer. Insurance therefore allows people and businesses to protect themselves against the risk of possible financial hardship.

Note: Insurance is only really appropriate where protection is required against a *significant* monetary loss: that is, where the loss could be high but the likely frequency of this occurrence may be low. Insurance is generally not appropriate where the loss is small but the likely frequency of the occurrence is high: in such cases, the cost of transferring (or insuring) the risk would be excessive when compared to the possible financial loss.

Excesses

A policy 'excess' is a deduction made by the insurer from payment in settlement of a claim. A *compulsory* excess is one that is applied to every claim; a *voluntary* excess is an additional fixed amount (for example, the first £100) agreed by the insured.

By accepting a voluntary excess, the insured is also accepting a proportion of the risk, and in return the insurer will charge reduced premiums. In taking out the insurance, the insured can then make a choice about whether to pay lower premiums and accept more of the risk or to pay higher premiums and accept less of the risk.

11.3 How insurance works

The UK has the largest insurance industry in Europe and the third largest in the world (Association of British Insurers 2014). With 387 authorised life insurance companies, and 911 authorised general insurance companies, the UK insurance industry in 2014 managed investments of £1.8 trillion, employed approximately 314,400 people, and received worldwide net premiums of £50.2 billion (ibid.).

There are three key aspects to insurance:

- underwriting
- pooling
- reinsurance.

Underwriting

Before offering insurance, an insurer (insurance company) will first seek to determine:

- how likely it is that a possible loss will occur
- how much the loss could be
- how much should be paid to insure against the risk.

This is known as 'underwriting' and is essentially a process of evaluating the risk and exposure of a potential client or applicant. Each insurance company will have its own underwriting procedures and guidelines to help determine whether or not the company should accept a given risk; and many insurance companies now employ computer-based risk evaluation and profiling systems to inform these decisions. Underwriting is especially relevant to life-related insurances, because of the possibility of a claim being made.

Pooling

The law of large numbers[1] suggests that the greater the number of people individually exposed to an event, the greater the likelihood that the actual results of that exposure will equal the expected results. That is, although individuals may face uncertainty, groups may face approximate certainty.

Insurance companies use the law of large numbers to lessen their own risk of loss by pooling a large enough number of people together in an 'insured group' to ensure that the size of the pool corresponds to their prediction of the likelihood of possible losses – the idea being that not all of the insured individuals within the insured group will suffer losses at the same time, or at all. In theory, this allows an insurance company to operate profitably and to pay for claims as and when they may arise.

Reinsurance

'Reinsurance' is a method of spreading risk. In this case, insurance companies share risk mutually by purchasing insurance policies from each other. This has two key benefits:

- it can limit the total possible loss that the original insurer would experience in case of disaster *and*
- it can increase the insurance coverage that an individual insurance company can offer.

When reinsurance occurs, the premiums paid by the insured are usually shared by all of the insurance companies involved.

11.4 Insurance or assurance – what is the difference?

Although the terms 'insurance' and 'assurance' are often used interchangeably, they do have distinct and separate meanings.[2]

As suggested above, *insurance* is a promise of full or partial compensation, in exchange for the regular payment of a premium and during a specific time period, for an identifiable future event that *might* happen. Some forms of insurance are required by law, others are optional. Common types of insurance include home insurance, vehicle insurance, health insurance, illness insurance, and travel insurance.

Assurance is a promise of compensation, in exchange for a regular payment of a premium, for an identifiable future event that *will* happen. It is cover against an eventuality that *will* occur: that is, the event is 'assured' – it is certain to happen.

In essence, insurance protects policyholders from events that *might* happen (sometimes within a specified time period), whereas assurance protects policyholders from events that are *certain* to happen. For example, in terms of a life policy, a life insurance policy would pay out *if* the insured dies (during a specific time period), whereas a life assurance policy would pay out *when* the insured dies.

11.5 Buying insurance

In general, insurance can be bought:[3]

- from an insurer
- from a bank, a building society, a travel agent, or a high street retailer

- through a comparison website (though these may not list all insurers)
- through an insurance agent.[4]

Before buying insurance (or even accepting an insurance quote), it is important to compare the offer with those from other possible insurers or insurance retailers. Consider:
- the suitability of the insurance policy
- the cost of the insurance (the premiums)
- the restrictions or exclusions imposed by the insurer
- the cover offered by the insurance *and*
- the overall benefit available under the insurance.

Note: Although some insurance is compulsory (for example, vehicle insurance), it is also important to consider whether other insurance is actually necessary. For example, buying additional (and often very costly) *product insurance* from a high street retailer may be an unnecessary additional expense, since many products are likely to be covered by a *home contents insurance* policy.

Applying for insurance

Information you must give an insurer

When buying insurance it is of course necessary to complete an application. When the application is completed in person – face-to-face, perhaps with a broker or an agent – it is known as a proposal form. Where the application is completed online or over the phone, it is known as a statement of facts.

Note: The *Consumer Insurance (Disclosure and Representations) Act 2012* provides that it is the *insurer's* responsibility to ask all relevant questions when considering a new application or an application to change or renew an insurance policy. This applies to all personal insurance, including buildings insurance, contents insurance, vehicle insurance, travel insurance, and health and life cover.

All questions must be answered honestly, responsibly, and as accurately as possible. An insurer cannot refuse to pay a claim if the information provided was unknowingly incorrect or merely incomplete, but problems can still arise:
- If a careless mistake was made (which the insurer must prove) and the insurer would not otherwise have entered into the insurance agreement, the insurer can terminate the contract,[5] refuse all claims, and return the premiums paid.
- If a careless mistake was made and the insurer would still have entered into the insurance agreement, but on different terms, the insurer can treat the agreement as if it *had* been agreed on those different terms.
- If a careless mistake is made and the insurer would have charged a higher premium, the insurer can reduce the amount paid on a claim by an amount commensurate with the reduced premiums that have been paid.

If the information provided is deliberately deceitful or carelessly withheld with the intention of misleading the insurer (as for example by deliberately failing to disclose, when requested, a known medical condition), the insurer can cancel the insurance[6] and refuse to pay any claim, providing that the insurer can prove that deception or dishonesty had occurred.

Information an insurer must give you

When you request an insurance quotation, the insurer *must* provide a summary document which contains certain key facts about the insurance it is offering. The summary document must include the following:

- details of the insurer
- the key features of the insurance
- the main benefits of the insurance
- significant (or unusual exclusions) from the insurance
- the period of cover provided by the insurance *and*
- details of any cancellation rights.

When insurance is purchased, the insurer *must* provide an insurance policy that contains the terms of agreement with the insurer, and must also provide a schedule that includes the following:

- personal details of the insured
- details of the insurance policy
- details of exclusions and excesses *and*
- details of additional risks covered by the policy.

> **Activity 1**
>
> Where can insurance be purchased and what key factors should be considered before purchasing insurance?

11.6 Cost of insurance

The cost of insurance will depend on a range of factors, including:

- geographical location
- personal lifestyle and activities
- demographics and personal circumstances *and*
- the history of previous claims.

Geographical location

Where you live can have a dramatic impact on the cost of insurance: living in a high-crime area could affect the cost of household contents insurance or vehicle insurance, for example, whereas living in a high flood-risk area could affect the cost of buildings insurance.

Personal lifestyle and activities

Undertaking dangerous activities (for example, paragliding, mountaineering, or high-speed motor sports), travelling to unsafe high-risk destinations (for example, war zones or countries in political turmoil), or being employed in a high-risk occupation (for example, being in the armed forces or working in the oil or gas industry) can all affect the cost of insurance.

Demographics and personal circumstances

Factors such as age, gender, pre-existing health conditions, family health history, excessive alcohol consumption and smoking can all affect insurance premiums.

History of previous claims

The number of times insurance claims have been made in the past can also affect insurance premiums – the fewer the claims, the cheaper the insurance.

In addition, the cost of insurance may also depend on:

- how the cost of insurance is paid: in a single lump sum, or in equal instalments over the insurance period (usually a calendar year)[7] *and*
- whether there is a compulsory excess or an agreed voluntary excess (usually between £50 and £100, but it can be up to £400 for some insurance), or both.

11.7 Cancelling insurance

Although some insurers may offer longer, all insurers are legally obliged to offer a minimum 14-day cooling-off period. During this time, the individual can cancel the insurance policy for any reason. There are two exceptions: the right to cancel during a cooling-off period does not apply to travel insurance lasting less than 1 month, and for life insurance the cooling-off period is 30 days.

Note: The cooling-off period commences when the policy begins or when the policy documents are received – whichever is later. Premiums paid must be refunded, less the cost of insurance for the days on which the insurance was in place, together with any administration fee.

Cancelling an insurance policy *after* the cooling-off period can be more complex, and the ability to do so depends on the specifics of the insurance policy. Some insurers may provide a refund as long as no claims have been made during the policy period, though they are likely to charge an administration fees. Others may not, in which case it will be necessary to wait until the policy is due to be renewed and then not renew it.

Note: Cancelling a direct debit does not cancel your insurance policy (and could damage your credit history). To cancel an insurance policy, you must contact the insurer and arrange cancellation.

Finally, it is possible for the *insurer* to cancel an insurance policy. Although fairly rare – most insurers would simply wait out the insured period and then decline to renew the policy – an insurer would cancel an insurance policy if it had reason to believe that the insured had not complied with the terms of the insurance policy, and had thereby increased the likelihood of making a claim.

11.8 Types of insurance

There are many types of insurance, covering a wide range of risks. Insurance can be classified into three groups, as shown in Figure 11.1.

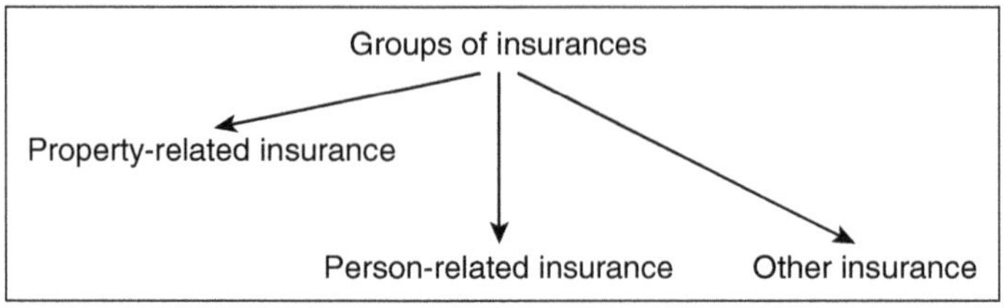

Figure 11.1 Groups of insurances

Within these three groups of insurances, some of the more common types are as follows:

- Property-related insurance:
  - o Buildings insurance, contents insurance, vehicle (motorcar or motorcycle) insurance; and vehicle repair insurance, breakdown insurance, and breakdown repair insurance.
- Person-related insurance:
  - o Healthcare-related insurance – for example, private medical insurance and dental insurance.
  - o Illness-related insurance – for example, critical illness insurance, payment protection insurance, mortgage payment protection insurance, and income protection insurance.
  - o Life insurance (including whole-of-life assurance).
- Other types of insurance:
  - o Professional indemnity (liability) insurance, travel insurance, and pet insurance.

11.9 Property-related insurance

Buildings insurance

Buildings insurance covers the cost of repairing damage to the physical fabric of a building.[8] It usually covers losses resulting from:

- damage caused by fire, explosion, storms or floods
- destruction caused by earthquakes and subsidence
- theft and vandalism
- damage due to burst water pipes
- damage due to oil leaks from a faulty heating system
- damage caused by fallen trees, lamp-posts, aerials or satellite dishes
- vehicle collision damage.

In addition, most buildings insurance covers costs resulting from:

- the replacement of glass and sanitary ware
- the repairing of underground services (pipes and cables)
- the clearing of sewerage blockages
- the tracing and repairing of water leaks.

Note: Most buildings insurance covers not only the primary building (the house) but also associated structures such as garages, sheds, fences, outside walls, and driveways.

Common exclusions

In general, buildings insurance does *not* cover:

- damage from ageing or wear and tear
- self-inflicted damage (for example, DIY projects gone wrong)
- intentional damage and wilful neglect
- damage and destruction due to war or terrorism
- damage due to pollution.

Is buildings insurance necessary?

Put simply ... yes, it is! For those with a mortgage, buildings insurance will often be a condition of the mortgage. In general, most mortgage providers require that the value of the buildings insurance cover be sufficient to cover the outstanding mortgage.

For those without a mortgage, buildings insurance is optional – given the large cost of rebuilding a badly damaged property, however, it is certainly advisable. For those who rent, buildings insurance will normally be the responsibility of the landlord or property owner.

Activity 2

Buildings insurance covers the cost of repairing damage to the physical fabric of a building. Describe the types of damage or losses covered by buildings insurance.

Types of buildings insurance

Whilst the cost of buildings insurance can vary enormously, premiums are primarily determined by the insured value of the buildings. This insured sum can be either limited or unlimited.

Limited-sum buildings insurance With limited-sum buildings insurance cover, insurers offer buildings insurance based on an assessment of the property, bearing in mind, for example, the type of property, its age, its size and structure, and its geographical location. There are two approaches: a bedroom-rated approach and a sum-insured approach.

Using a bedroom-rated approach, insurers estimate the cost of rebuilding a property based on the number of bedrooms: this generally provides a high buildings value. Using a sum-insured approach, the insurers estimate the full cost of completely rebuilding a property.

Unlimited-sum buildings insurance With unlimited-sum buildings insurance, insurers offer unlimited insurance cover, irrespective of any predetermined or pre-assessed building cost.

Buying buildings insurance

When buying buildings insurance it is important to ensure, as minimum requirements, that:

- the sum insured (if limited) is sufficient to cover *all* the possible rebuilding cost of the buildings
- the sum insured is inflation-protected (index-linked)
- personal liability cover[9] is included *and*
- cover includes a provision for alternative accommodation.

It is also important to clarify:
- how long the building may be left unoccupied before the insurer restricts or removes insurance cover
- what accidental damage cover is provided, if any
- what excess is payable
- what cover is available for legal expenses
- what repair guarantees are provided *and*
- whether an emergency helpline is provided.

Contents insurance

Contents insurance covers losses (above the insurance policy excess) that result from damage (due to fire, floods or storms), theft, or the loss of insured personal possessions (usually including those of close family members living with the insured[10]). It can also cover, perhaps for an additional charge:
- accidental loss or damage *and*
- loss or damage to personal possessions located away from the insured home.

Note: Although some contents insurance policies only offer to cover the *net current value* of the items lost, stolen or damaged, many – indeed most – now offer 'new for old' cover, such that the insurance policy covers the *full replacement cost* of items that are lost, stolen or damaged.

Common exclusions

In general, contents insurance does *not* cover:
- damage due to excessive wear and tear *or*
- intentional damage or wilful neglect.

In addition, contents insurance does *not* cover personal possessions in properties left unoccupied for lengthy periods (usually for more than 60 days continuously).

Types of contents insurance

Contents insurance can be provided using a bedroom-rated approach or a sum-insured approach. Using a bedroom-rated approach, insurers estimate the value of contents based on the number of bedrooms in the insured's property. Using a sum-insured approach, the insurers calculate the full value of contents.

Note: Whilst the cost of insurance (the premiums) can be higher using a bedroom-rated approach, those insurance policies tend to offer greater cover.

The cost of contents insurance

The geographical location (the postcode of a property) can have a significant impact on the cost of contents insurance. Personal possessions located in a high-risk area (for example, an area at high risk from theft, flooding or subsidence) will have a higher insurance cost then personal possessions located in a low-risk area.

The cost of contents insurance can be reduced, however, by:
- increasing property security and improving door and window locks *and*
- installing protection systems such as smoke alarms and burglar alarms.

In addition, insurance costs can be reduced further by:
- increasing the excess on the contents insurance policy
- buying buildings and contents insurance together (as most insurers would offer a discount) *and*
- paying the premiums annually, and so eliminating any interest charges.

Buying contents insurance

When buying contents insurance, it is important to ensure, as minimum requirements, that:
- the sum insured is inflation-protected (index-linked) *and*
- any value limit for single items is clearly identified.

In addition, it is important to identify:
- what value of cash is insured against theft
- whether fridge and freezer contents are covered
- what contents left outside the main building but within the boundaries of the property are covered, if any (for example, garden tools)
- whether theft of property from outbuildings or a garage is covered *and*
- what personal liability cover is included.

It is also important to clarify:
- what accidental damage cover is provided
- what excess is payable, if any
- what cover is available for legal expenses
- what replacement guarantees are provided *and*
- whether an emergency helpline is provided.

Vehicle insurance

Unlike other kinds of insurance, vehicle insurance – that is, motorcar insurance and motorcycle insurance – is mandatory. UK law specifies that a driver or motorcyclist must have at least third-party motor insurance before driving a motorcar or riding a motorcycle on a public road.

Note: Any vehicle can be spot-checked against the UK Motor Insurance Database, and any uninsured motorcar or motorcycle found to be uninsured (even if it is parked on a private driveway) can be seized by the police and if necessary disposed of.

Types of vehicle insurance

There are three main types of policy, for both motorcars and motorcycles:
- third-party insurance
- third-party, fire and theft insurance
- comprehensive insurance.

Third-party insurance Third-party insurance is the minimum legal requirement: it covers the insured (the policyholder) for damage to someone else's vehicle or property and for injury to someone else in an accident. This cover also includes accidents caused by a passenger in the motorcar or on the motorcycle. Third-party insurance does not cover repairs to the insured's own vehicle.

Third-party, fire and theft insurance Third-party, fire and theft insurance includes third-party cover (as above), and also damage or loss to the insured's own car as a result of fire or theft.

Comprehensive insurance Comprehensive insurance includes third-party, fire and theft (as above), and also repairs to the insured motorcar or motorcycle. In addition, comprehensive insurance may also cover (subject to the insurer):
- death or injury of the insured or a family member
- personal possessions stolen from the insured's motorcar or motorcycle
- medical or legal expenses *and*
- hiring a replacement motorcar or motorcycle.

Note: Vehicle insurance purchased from an EU-based insurer will give the insured third-party insurance cover to drive in any EU country (and some non-EU countries).

When is vehicle insurance not required?

It is important to note that vehicle insurance is *not* required if certain conditions have been reported to the Driver and Vehicle Licensing Agency (DVLA):
- a valid Statutory Off Road Notification (SORN) has been issued for the vehicle by the DVLA
- the vehicle has been scrapped, stolen or exported (but the DVLA must have been formally notified of this) *or*
- the vehicle is between registered keepers or is registered with the DVLA as 'in trade'.

However, as part of the Continuous Insurance Enforcement (CIE) process, the Motor Insurers' Bureau (MIB) and the DVLA work in partnership to identify uninsured vehicles. Where the registered keeper of an uninsured vehicle fails to comply with an Insurance Advisory Letter (IAL), she or he faces these possible penalties:
- a fixed penalty notice of £100
- the vehicle could be clamped, seized and disposed of *and*
- there could be a court prosecution with a maximum fine of £1,000.

Note: These insurance enforcement measures are in addition to the ordinary powers of the police to seize an uninsured vehicle and to fine the driver.

Common exclusions

In general, vehicle insurance does not cover:
- a vehicle that is deemed not to be roadworthy *or*
- a vehicle that has previously been recorded or registered as stolen.

In addition, vehicle insurance will not cover any damage caused by someone who is not covered by that vehicle insurance policy, which would include anyone who drives without a valid driving licence.

Buying vehicle insurance

Because the cost of vehicle insurance can vary enormously, it is important to compare and contrast vehicle insurance policies from a range of insurers, In particular, it is important to identify:
- what the insurance covers

- what exclusions are applicable, if any
- what excess is payable, if any
- any discounts offered
- what no claims discounts are available (see below) *and*
- what restrictions apply.

The cost of vehicle insurance

There are many factors that affect the cost of vehicle insurance. They include:

- the age of the vehicle user or owner (those aged between 17 and 25 generally face the highest premiums)
- the occupation of the vehicle user or owner
- the type, age, engine size, and value of the vehicle
- the security features installed on the vehicle
- the geographical location of the vehicle
- where the vehicle is kept when not in use (such as in a garage, on a private driveway or at the roadside)
- how the vehicle is mostly used (business commuting or private personal use only)
- the driving record of the vehicle user or owner
- the availability of no claims discounts (see below)
- any insurance policy excess (in general, the higher the voluntary excess, the lower the cost of insurance)
- the type of vehicle insurance (third-party; third-party, fire and theft; or comprehensive) *and*
- the addition of other named drivers authorised to use the vehicle (as well as the vehicle's owner).

No claims discount Vehicle insurance premiums tend to rise each year, in part because of a general increase in claims made year by year. However, this increase is often offset by a reduction offered to a particular policyholder who has not made any claim in the past year, the so-called 'no claims discount'. The size of this discount may rise with each year in which no claims are made; and some insurers offer to protect the discount at an additional cost.

Note: The cost of vehicle insurance (in particular motorcar insurance) is no longer gender-sensitive. Following a ruling by the European Court of Justice, a ban on gender-related pricing came into effect on 21 December 2012.

Making a claim

If an accident occurs, you should if possible:

- exchange names and other details with the other driver (or drivers) involved
- get details of any independent witnesses
- take photographs, for use later as evidence in a claim *and*
- inform your insurer as soon as possible after the accident.

Note: On no account should you admit responsibility for the accident.

If you have a comprehensive policy, you can claim from your own insurer; but you may lose any no claims discount if the insurer cannot recover the costs from the other party's insurer. If you have third-party insurance, you can claim against the other party and allow the insurer to decide who is responsible for the accident. If the insurer says that you yourself are responsible, you will have to pay for repairs to your own vehicle.

Note: Any repairs can only be carried out with the insurer's permission, and usually only at an approved repairer. If the insurer decides that, following the accident, the vehicle is uneconomical to repair, the insurer will – subject to the vehicle insurance policy – offer appropriate recompense (usually equivalent to the vehicle's market value).

> ### Activity 3
>
> Describe the main factors that can affect the cost of vehicle insurance.

Making a claim if the insured vehicle is stolen

If your vehicle is stolen, you should inform the police and get an incident number, and then inform the insurer and make a claim. The insurer will normally wait to see whether the vehicle is found, and then settle the claim in accordance with the insurance policy.

Making a claim if personal possessions are stolen

If your possessions are stolen from your vehicle, you may be able to claim either on property contents insurance or on vehicle insurance (but not both).

Note: If claiming on your vehicle insurance would affect any no claims discount, you should claim on your property contents insurance.

Vehicle repair insurance

Vehicle repair insurance (also known as vehicle warranty) covers the cost of all mechanical and electrical repairs, including parts and labour, and can be used to manage the cost of unexpected failure and potentially expensive repair bills.

Whilst vehicle repair insurance is often provided when buying a new car (usually in the form of a manufacturer's or dealer's warranty), and to a limited extent when buying a secondhand used car through a dealership (usually limited to 1 year), such insurance can also be purchased independently from a specialist warranty provider. The benefits of independently purchased vehicle repair insurance (or a stand-alone warranty) are that:

- it can be attached to a privately purchased secondhand used car *or*
- it can be used to extend the cover offered by a manufacturer's or dealer's warranty.

Leading providers of new and used car warranties (and vehicle repair insurance) include:

- Warranty Direct: see www.warrantydirect.co.uk
- Click4Warranty: see www.click4warranty.co.uk
- Warrantywise: see www.warrantywise.co.uk.

Breakdown insurance

Breakdown insurance (or breakdown cover) is an insurance policy that provides breakdown assistance 24 hours a day, 7 days a week, anywhere in the UK. If a vehicle develops a fault and leaves the driver stranded, the insurance policy provides an experienced roadside mechanic, dispatched to the stranded driver's location, to diagnose the problem and if possible repair the vehicle.

There are different levels of cover available. For example, the AA provides four alternatives levels of breakdown insurance (AA 2015a):

- Roadside assistance: this provides cover for breakdowns more than a quarter of a mile away from home, including if necessary towing to a nearby garage.
- At home: this provides cover for breakdowns on your driveway or within a quarter of a mile from home.
- National recovery: this provides transport to any single UK destination if your vehicle breaks down and cannot be repaired at the roadside.
- Onward travel: this provides car hire, public transport and if necessary a hotel room if your vehicle breaks down and cannot be repaired at the roadside.

Note: It is important to realise, however, that no matter which level of breakdown insurance is selected, it does *not* include the cost of replacement parts used by the mechanic to repair the vehicle.

Breakdown repair insurance

Breakdown repair insurance can be purchased as an add-on element to breakdown insurance, and can be used together with any of the above options (roadside assistance, at home, national recovery, or onward travel cover).

Whilst most breakdown repair insurance covers the cost of replacement parts – including battery, starter motor, alternator, clutch, head gasket, radiator, and cam belt – insurers often impose a limit on the number of repairs covered. For example, the AA 'parts and garage' cover only covers up to five claims a year, each of up to £500 and with a £35 excess per claim (AA 2015b).

11.10 Person-related insurance

Healthcare-related insurance

Private medical insurance

Private medical insurance provides access to a complementary healthcare provision. It does not replace the healthcare provision provided by the National Health Service (NHS), which offers free automatic healthcare for all UK residents.

What does private medical insurance cover? Private medical insurance covers the cost of private medical treatment for a range of diseases, illnesses or injuries. It is intended for short-term or acute conditions that can be cured or managed without lengthy medical intervention. Although policy coverage can vary, in general such policies cover the cost of private day-patient surgery, tests and hospital accommodation, out-patient treatment, diagnostic procedures, radiotherapy and chemotherapy, physiotherapy, annual check-ups, and home nursing. Some policies also cover alternative treatment such as homoeopathy and acupuncture.

Common exclusions In general, private medical insurance does *not* cover private treatment for:

- pre-existing medical conditions
- chronic illnesses[11]
- pregnancy and childbirth costs

- organ transplants
- injuries related to dangerous sporting activities
- injuries arising from war-related hostilities
- cosmetic surgery to improve your appearance.

Why do people buy private medical insurance? People buy private medical insurance for three reasons:
- choice: policyholders can choose where and how they are treated
- speed: policyholders can avoid NHS waiting lists, avoid standard waiting periods, and receive faster consultations
- quality of facilities: policyholders can select from a range of private facilities.

Note: Many people have private medical insurance as part of their employment remuneration package.

Advantages and disadvantages of private medical insurance The advantages of private medical insurance include:
- medical treatment, including specialist referrals on demand
- reduced waiting times
- the use of private facilities
- personal selection of facilities, hospitals and surgeons or specialists *and*
- the use and availability of specialist drugs and treatments.

The disadvantages of private medical insurance include:
- better medical healthcare may be available on the NHS, especially for serious chronic conditions
- the overall expense and the cost of premiums, which tend to increase year by year
- local treatment options may not be available
- cover does not include pre-existing conditions
- some treatments are not covered.

The cost of private medical insurance There are many factors that can affect the cost of private medical insurance. In particular:
- age: older people are generally charged higher premiums than younger people
- geographic location
- the level of enrolment: whether this is an individual policy or a family policy *and*
- the nature of the insurance plan cover: that is, which treatments and medical conditions, illnesses and diseases are covered.

The cost of private medical insurance can be reduced by:
- electing to pay an excess
- limiting the choice of treatments and hospitals *or*
- self-insuring (using a high-interest savings account and paying for private healthcare on a pay-as-you-go basis).

Dental insurance

Dental insurance covers a range of dental treatments and is an alternative to receiving dental care either through the NHS or privately on a pay-as-you-go basis. Most dental insurance policies cover dental maintenance (for example, check-ups and polishing) and dental treatments (for example, fillings, crowns and root-canal work), but not dental cosmetics (for example, whitening teeth).

Whereas NHS-only dental insurance provides unlimited maintenance and treatment on the NHS per policy year, private-only dental insurance provides only limited cover, which is usually capped at a maximum benefit amount per policy year.

Note: Most dental insurance policies impose a minimum period (usually between 3 and 6 months) before a claim can be made, with reimbursement only occurring *after* dental treatment has been received and paid for.

> ## Activity 4
>
> Briefly explain the advantages and disadvantages of private medical insurance.

Illness-related insurance

Illness-related insurance is designed to protect an insured person's income if he or she is unable to work because of an accident, long-term ill-health, or disability. There are several different kinds of illness insurance, the most common being:

- critical illness insurance
- income protection insurance
- payment protection insurance (PPI)
- mortgage payment protection insurance.

Critical illness insurance

Critical illness insurance is an inexpensive way of easing the financial pressures of possible illness or disability. It provides a tax-free lump-sum payment, or payment of income if the policyholder is diagnosed with a serious long-term condition, illness or disability. Policies usually cover conditions such as a heart attack or a stroke, diseases or illnesses such as cancer, multiple sclerosis or Parkinson's disease, and permanent disability due to, for example, the permanent loss of one or both arms or legs.

Common exclusions

Critical illness insurance does *not* cover illnesses related to, or conditions or injuries arising from:

- drug abuse
- hazardous sports and pastimes
- war, civil commotion, or terrorism
- criminal acts *or*
- HIV/AIDS.

In addition, it does not cover conditions or injuries that are deemed to have been self-inflicted.

The cost of critical illness insurance

There are many providers of critical illness insurance, and many different types and versions of critical illness insurance. The cost of such insurance (whether premiums are guaranteed or variable and index-linked) can be affected by many factors, including:

- age: increasing age can increase the risk of illness

- gender: men generally claim more often than women, so their premiums tend to be greater
- health: regular exercise, a low alcohol intake, and not smoking can significantly reduce premiums
- occupation, hobbies and lifestyle: a risky occupation or dangerous hobbies can increase the possibility of injury and therefore the cost of insurance cover.

Payment protection insurance

Payment protection insurance covers the repayment of car finance, personal loans, credit cards, store cards, catalogue payments and mortgages if the insured is unable to work due to an accident, illness or unemployment.

Payment protection insurance only covers loan or credit repayments for a limited period of time, usually between 12 and 24 months, with the amount covered depending on the type of payment protection insurance. For example:

- for mortgages and loans, repayments are usually covered in full for the agreed period of time *whereas*
- for credit and store cards, repayments are often covered only for the interest on the outstanding balance or the minimum payment (whichever is the lower).

Some payment protection insurance policies also provide a life insurance benefit which pays off the outstanding balance on a loan or card if the insured person dies.

Note: Most payment protection insurance has a deferral period (or waiting period) of 30 days before payment is made.

Types of payment protection insurance

There are three types of payment protection insurance:

- unemployment only
- accident and sickness only
- accident, sickness and unemployment.

An unemployment-only policy covers the insured if she or he is made redundant. An accident and sickness policy covers the insured against accidental injury, long-term (medically certified) illness, or both. An accident, sickness and unemployment policy covers the insured against redundancy, accidental injury or long-term (medically certified) illness.

Common exclusions

Payment protection insurance generally excludes some or all of the following conditions:

- illness due to a pre-existing medical condition
- self-inflicted or deliberate injury (injury from high-risk activities)
- conditions arising from alcohol or drug abuse *and*
- unemployment (but unemployment due to foreseeable redundancy, voluntary redundancy or termination due to misconduct are *not* covered).

Note: Most payment protection insurance policies exclude the self-employed, or at least impose significant restrictions.

The payment protection insurance scandal

For many years payment protection insurance was offered by banks, lenders and other credit providers at the same time as a loan or credit facility was arranged – indeed, some providers made its purchase a condition of the finance facility. In recent years, however, many banks, lenders and credit providers have been severely criticised, prosecuted, and fined for the mis-selling of payment protection insurance to customers who either:

- did not realise they were making payments for payment protection insurance *or*
- agreed to pay for payment protection insurance (usually under pressure from the bank, lender or credit provider) but would in fact never be able to make a claim, because of policy exclusions and exemptions.

As a consequence, the popularity of payment protection insurance has declined substantially, although it is still available.

Mortgage payment protection insurance

Mortgage payment protection insurance covers the insured's mortgage payments for a defined period (usually between 12 and 24 months), if she or he is unable to work due to an accident, illness, or unemployment. The maximum amount that can be claimed per month will depend on the type of cover purchased (see below) and on the insurer, but payments can be up to £2,000 per month or 65% of the insured monthly income, whichever is the lower. Some policies also allow the amount insured to cover other monthly payments (for example, Council Tax payments or utility payments), up to 125% of monthly mortgage payments.

Types of mortgage payment protection insurance

As with payment protection insurance, there are three types of mortgage payment protection insurance:

- unemployment only
- accident and sickness only
- accident, sickness and unemployment.

An unemployment-only policy covers the insured if he or she is made redundant. An accident and sickness policy covers the insured against accidental injury and long-term (medically certified) illness. An accident, sickness and unemployment policy covers the insured against redundancy, accidental injury, and long-term (medically certified) illness.

Common exclusions

Mortgage payment protection insurance does *not* cover:

- pre-existing medical conditions
- redundancy, if such redundancy was foreseeable at the time the policy was taken out
- redundancy, if the redundancy was voluntary
- self-inflicted or deliberate injury (resulting from high-risk activities)
- conditions arising from childbirth.

In addition, this kind of insurance is generally not available to those who are self-employed, who are on a temporary contract, who work as independent contractors, or who are retired or unemployed.

The cost of mortgage payment protection insurance

The cost of mortgage payment protection insurance can vary, depending an individual circumstances and on the policy excess period (sometimes called a deferral period). The excess period is the period the insured has to wait between lodging a claim with the insurer and the insurance payments commencing. These can vary from a minimum of 30 days to a maximum of 90 days.

Note: In general, the longer the excess period, the lower the cost of the insurance.

Income protection insurance

Income protection insurance covers the loss of income suffered by the insured if he or she is unable to work because of illness or injury. Insurance payments are usually based on a percentage of the insured earnings – between 50% and 70% of net earnings (earnings after tax). Payments are tax-free and are usually paid until the insured's retirement, death, or return to employment.

Note: Income protection insurance payments are normally paid following an agreed excess or deferral period – usually 4 weeks, but it can be much longer.

Types of income protection

There are three types of insurance to protect your income:
- long-term income protection insurance
- short-term income protection insurance
- accident, sickness and unemployment insurance protection.

Long-term income protection insurance Long-term income protection insurance is fully underwritten (so there is certainty for any legitimate claim) and pays out until a fixed age (usually the State retirement age), the insured's death, or his or her return to work.

Short-term income protection insurance Short-term income insurance protection is also fully underwritten, but only pays out for a fixed maximum period – usually between 1 and 5 years.

Accident, sickness and unemployment insurance protection Accident, sickness and unemployment insurance protection is *not* underwritten. The cost of insurance therefore tends to be less than that of the long-term income protection insurance option above, but there is less certainty regarding the acceptance of any claim.

The cost of income protection insurance

Whilst a long agreed excess or deferral period – that is, the period the insured is willing to wait before payment begins – can reduce the cost of insurance, the cost of income protection insurance is primarily affected by the following:
- age: age can affect the risk of illness
- gender: men generally claim more often than women, so their premiums tend to be greater
- health: regular exercise, low alcohol intake, and not smoking can significantly reduce premiums
- hobbies and lifestyle: dangerous hobbies can increase the possibility of injury and therefore the cost of cover
- occupation: the riskier the occupation, the greater the cost of insurance (see below).

Income protection occupation groups Many insurers group occupations into risk categories – the higher the risk category (or class), the higher the cost of insurance. A typical occupation risk classification would be:
- Class 1: professionally qualified workers
- Class 2: skilled workers
- Class 3: semi-skilled workers
- Class 4: unskilled workers and manual workers.

Premiums Premiums can be either guaranteed or reviewable. Guaranteed premiums are fixed for the life of the insurance policy: premiums will only change if the policy cover changes. Reviewable premiums are variable and often index-linked, and are renewed (and usually increased) after an agreed period (usually every 5 years).

Common exclusions

Common exclusions can include one or more of the following:
- pre-existing medical conditions
- self-inflicted or deliberate injury (resulting from high-risk activities)
- conditions arising from childbirth
- disabilities, injuries or illnesses arising from criminal acts
- illnesses and disabilities arising from drug or alcohol abuse
- disabilities or illnesses resulting from war, civil commotion or terrorism.

Activity 5

Distinguish between the following types of illness insurance: *critical illness insurance, income protection insurance,* and *payment protection insurance* (PPI).

Life insurance (term insurance)

Life insurance is often known as 'term insurance'. These insurance policies pay out an agreed amount – called 'the sum assured' when the insured (the policyholder) dies within a fixed period of time. Most life insurance policies are underwritten and are arranged for periods of between 10 and 25 years, but there is no predetermined time limit – periods can be much longer or much shorter.

Note: If the insured lives beyond the term of the policy, the cover ends: there is no terminal value or investment element.

Types of life insurance

There are three main types of life insurance:
- level term insurance
- decreasing term insurance
- increasing term insurance.

Level term insurance

With level term insurance, the sum assured remains the same throughout the life of the policy.

Decreasing term insurance

With decreasing term insurance, the sum assured decreases throughout the life of the policy, so the potential payout reduces over the life of the policy. This type of life insurance is often associated with repayment mortgages.

Increasing term insurance

With increasing term insurance, the sum assured increases throughout the life of the policy, so the potential payout increases over the life of the policy, whether by an agreed fixed percentage amount each year or in line with the Retail Prices Index (RPI). For example, if you have children or if your income increases, a greater payout will be required to provide a suitable level of protection for your dependants. The benefits your dependants will receive upon your death, within the term of your life insurance policy, increase in return for paying higher premiums.

Alternatives to life insurance

Whilst life insurance is a popular form of life cover, there are alternatives that can also provide financial protection, the most common being:

- family income benefit
- guaranteed whole-of-life cover (also known as life assurance)
- over-50s life cover.

Family income benefit Unlike the standard life insurances above, which pay out a single lump sum if the insured dies during the term of the policy, a family income benefit policy provides a monthly tax-free income (either fixed or index-linked), which is paid over the remainder of the policy term.

The disadvantage of a family income benefit policy is that the monthly tax-free income payments cease at the end of the agreed term or policy period.

Guaranteed whole-of-life cover Unlike the standard life insurances above, which provide a payout within a specified period, guaranteed whole-of-life cover (also known as life assurance) provides payment only when the insured (the policyholder) dies – there is no pre-agreed policy end date. Also, when the insured dies, the policy ends.

(We will discuss this type of insurance in more detail later.)

Over-50s life cover Whilst only available to those who are over 50, with over-50s life insurance anyone at or over the minimum age is guaranteed to be accepted, without the need for a medical and despite any pre-existing medical conditions or current illness issues. Most policies have a maximum age limit (usually 75), and no claim may be made during a minimum policy period of 12 months (some policies impose a minimum policy period of 24 months).[12]

The disadvantage of an over-50s life policy is that although premium payments may be fairly inexpensive, they may be paid for a long time.

The cost of life insurance

The cost of life insurance can vary significantly, and whilst insurers generally do not take into account geographical location (or postcodes) when pricing life insurance, there are a number of factors that do influence the cost of life insurance, including health, hobbies and lifestyle, occupation, age, and relationship status.

Health Health plays a major part in the pricing of life insurance – the applicant's current health profile (including height, weight, exercise regime, and whether she or he smokes), any current or pre-existing medical conditions and treatments, and the individual's family history can all impact on the cost of life insurance.

Hobbies and lifestyle Adventurous hobbies or pastimes, such as mountaineering, car racing, skydiving or scuba diving, can all have a significant impact on the cost of life insurance, because they are inherently risky. Excessive alcohol consumption and drug abuse can also impact on premiums. Similarly, travelling to dangerous places (such as war zones, areas of terrorism, or countries in political turmoil), whether on vacation or because of one's occupation, can also increase life insurance premiums.

Occupation For those whose occupations are deemed to be dangerous and which therefore present a higher risk of injury, the cost of life insurance will generally be higher.

Such occupations would include, for example, miners, pilots, police officers, fire service officers, members of the armed forces, professional sportsmen and sportswomen, steeplejacks, aerial riggers, offshore divers, and offshore riggers.

Age Age naturally impacts on the cost of life insurance – the younger the insured, the greater the number of years ahead (in all likelihood), so the lower the premiums.

Relationship status Unfortunately, marital status can have an impact on the cost of life insurance – some insurers believe that people who are married or in civil partnerships tend to live longer than people who are not married.

Other factors Other factors that affect the cost include:
- the type of cover required (for example, a lump sum or continuing income)
- the amount of cover
- the length of the cover
- the number of persons covered.

Note: As with other insurances, premiums may be guaranteed (fixed) or reviewable (variable). Guaranteed premiums are more expensive at the outset, but tend to be more cost-efficient in the long term.

Single life cover or joint life cover

For married couples and civil partners, it is often natural to consider a joint life insurance policy rather than two single life insurance policies. This may not necessarily be the best decision, however, for three reasons:
- a joint policy is generally only marginally cheaper than two separate single life policies
- a joint policy will only provide one payout, at the first death, which would leave the surviving policyholder without any life insurance (unless he or she arranged a new life insurance policy) *and*
- buying two single life policies may provide more flexibility in terms of the amount of cover and the period of cover for each policyholder.

How much life insurance is sufficient?

How much life insurance is sufficient depends on a range of personal circumstances and financial commitments, and is, of course, partly dictated by how much the policyholder can afford. There is no single 'one-size-fits-all' solution: the amount of cover desired and the period of cover that seems appropriate will differ from person to person. Personal circumstances and financial commitments need to be taken into account when deciding on the amount of life insurance, and especially if the life insurance relates to the main earner within a household. You should consider:

- the cost of monthly mortgage repayments
- the cost of other loan repayments
- the cost of credit card repayments
- the cost of childcare expenses
- the cost of current and future education expenses *and*
- income replacement to meet other day-to-day living expenses.

Life insurance and taxation

For the 2015/2016 tax year, the Inheritance Tax threshold is £325,000 for a single person or £650,000 for a married couple and for registered civil partners. Inheritance Tax (at a rate of 40%) is charged on any estate valued above that threshold. This could potentially mean that any life insurance payout would be subject to Inheritance Tax.

Clearly, no one chooses to give money to HMRC if they can avoid doing so, so to protect any life insurance payout the life insurance policy when arranged should be written 'in trust'. A trust is a legal device that allows individuals to keep some of their assets separate from their estate, thereby avoiding Inheritance Tax.

Note: The reason why there is no Inheritance Tax is that any assets held in trust belong to the trust beneficiaries. In addition, because payment is made to the trustees (and does not form part of the estate), any payment can be made without having to wait for probate to be granted.

Whole-of-life assurance

Whole-of-life assurance is different from life (or term) insurance because there is a guaranteed payout when the insured dies, whenever that might be. As a consequence, it is more expensive than term insurance because for whole-of-life assurance, a claim is inevitable.

Types of whole-of-life assurance

Whole-of-life assurance can be:

- non-profit whole-of-life assurance
- with-profits whole-of-life assurance *or*
- unit-linked whole-of-life assurance.

Non-profit whole-of-life assurance With non-profit whole-of-life assurance, premiums are fixed and there is no investment element to the policy: it simply provides a fixed cash lump sum on the death of the insured.

With-profit whole-of-life assurance With-profit whole-of-life assurance includes an investment element: the payout on the death of the insured will be the sum assured together with any investment profits allocated to the policy.

Unit-linked whole-of-life assurance Unit-linked whole-of-life assurance also includes an investment element: in this case the monthly premiums are used to purchase units in a selected investment fund, and the payout on the death of the insured will be the sum of the values of the units purchased.

The cost of whole-of-life assurance

As with life insurance, the cost of whole-of-life assurance can vary significantly depending on a number of personal factors, such as health, hobbies and lifestyle, occupation, and age. Other factors include:

- the type of cover required (for example, a lump sum or a continuing income)
- the amount of cover
- the length of the cover
- the number of persons covered.

Note: As with other insurances, premiums can be guaranteed (fixed) or reviewable (variable). Guaranteed premiums are more expensive at the outset, but tend to be more cost-efficient in the long term.

Single life cover or joint life cover

With *single* life whole-of-life assurance, an individual can arrange a single life policy for herself or himself, or for another individual (for example, her or his spouse or business partner), provided that there is a provable financial relationship between them.

With *joint* whole-of-life assurance, the policy can be either a 'first death' policy, which pays out at the first death of those whose lives are assured, or a 'last survivor' policy, which pays out on the death of the last of those whose lives are assured.

Note: Whichever cover is selected, if a whole-of-life assurance policy is no longer required, it can be 'cashed in', or surrendered, although the surrender value is often considerably less than the value of the total premiums paid – especially in the early years of the policy.

Whole-of-life assurance 'in trust'

As with life insurance, the proceeds of whole-of-life assurance are not usually subject to Income Tax or Capital Gains Tax, but they could be subject to Inheritance Tax on the payout.

As with life insurance, to protect the whole-of-life assurance payout, the whole-of-life assurance policy when arranged should be written 'in trust'.

How much whole-of-life assurance is sufficient?

How much whole-of-life assurance is sufficient is – as with life insurance (see above) – dependent on a range of personal circumstances and financial commitments, and will differ from person to person.

Endowments

Endowments are savings products – longer-term investments that include a life assurance element. At the end of the investment term, the endowment pays out accumulated returns. If the life-assured policyholder dies before the end of the investment term, the sum assured, together with any accumulated returns, is paid out.

Note: As with whole-of-life assurance, there are unit-linked endowments and with-profits endowments, but the advantage of an endowment is that the proceeds are tax-free.

11.11 Other types of insurance

Professional indemnity (liability) insurance

Professional indemnity insurance, or professional liability insurance, is insurance that covers legal costs and expenses incurred in defence of a compensation claim made by a dissatisfied customer or client. For example, such a claim might be related to:
- professional negligence
- defamation
- loss of confidential information
- loss of customer or client resources
- libel
- breach of copyright
- breach of confidentiality.

Professional indemnity insurance also covers the cost of any damages awarded should the dissatisfied customer's or client's claim be successful.

Note: Whilst there is no *legal* requirement for business-related service professionals to have professional liability insurance, it is often a mandatory part of the regulatory requirements of membership of a professional body (for example, for accountants).

Professional indemnity insurance cover can be purchased on the basis of an individual contract or an agreed period (usually annually). It generally operates on a 'claims made' basis,[13] with the cost of the insurance being dependent upon a range of factors, including:
- the nature of the services offered or work undertaken
- the geographical location of the services offered
- the types of customers or clients serviced
- the amount of professional indemnity cover required.

Travel insurance

Travel insurance is designed to provide insurance cover while travelling, whether nationally or internationally. It may offer cover for:
- medical expenses related accidental personal injuries, illness, and death (including repatriation home, if necessary)
- costs related to travel cancellation (for reasons beyond the insured's control)
- the cost of replacing lost, stolen or damaged luggage, including personal baggage, passports and money
- costs related to departure delays, flight cancellations, and crashes
- costs related to accidental damage or injury caused by the insured to a third party or to a third party's property.

Travel insurance is widely available and can be purchased from travel agents, holiday companies, insurance companies, banks, retailers, and some online comparison websites. Travel insurance policies can be either 'single journey' policies or 'multi-journey' policies covering an unlimited number of journeys within a set time period.

Note: Many high street banks and building societies also offer travel insurance as part of a fee-based suite of current account add-on services.

Common exclusions

Most travel insurance policies do *not* provide insurance cover for:
- pre-existing and pre-diagnosed medical conditions
- high-risk activities
- illness or personal injury caused by alcohol or drug use
- travel to high-risk countries (such as countries at war or affected by natural disasters) *or*
- losses resulting from acts of terrorism.

Nevertheless, some insurers *will* provide insurance cover for risks such as those above on payment of an additional premium.

Note: Many insurers also provide additional help in the form of concierge services (24 hours a day, 7 days a week) and emergency travel assistance.

Buying travel insurance

Travel insurance is essential, especially for people travelling independently. There are many factors that influence the cost of travel insurance, including:
- the type of policy (single journey or multi-journey)
- the age of the traveller
- the destination and activities to be undertaken (risky activities such as scuba diving or skiing will increase the cost)
- the type of travel (independently or on a package holiday)
- the mode of travel.

To reduce the overall cost of travel insurance, shop around for the best deal, choose the policy that provides the most appropriate cover, and, if travelling in Europe, register for an EHIC card (see below).

For a comparison of available travel insurance policies, see: www.money.co.uk/travel-insurance.

European Health Insurance Card (EHIC)

The European Health Insurance Card (EHIC) is available free of charge and allows the holder access to State-provided healthcare in countries in the European Economic Area (EEA), and also in Switzerland, at a reduced cost or free of charge. It covers all treatment until the holder's return to the UK. It includes cover for treatment of pre-existing medical conditions and for routine maternity care.

Note: The European Health Insurance Card does not replace travel insurance. When travelling to or through Europe, it is important to have both an EHIC and a valid private travel insurance policy.

Pet insurance

Originating in Sweden in 1890,[14] the first pet insurance policy was sold in the UK in 1947 (Filofetch 2013). In 2014, the Association of British Insurers estimated that 2.8 million pet owners had their pets insured, with over 95% of pet insurance being for cats and dogs (Association of British Insurers 2014: 8), and with an estimated 25% of domestic pets now being insured.

In general, pet insurance policies only cover medical expenses and veterinary fees related to illness or injury.[15] They do not cover medical expenses related to preventative and routine treatments such as vaccinations, flea and worm control, neutering, and costs related to pregnancy or birth. In addition, they do not cover medical expenses related to pre-existing medical conditions – that is, conditions that existed before the insurance policy commenced.

Note: Pet insurance is a form of property insurance. Reimbursement occurs only *after* the pet has received the required veterinary care and the pet owner (the policyholder) has submitted an insurance claim to the insurer.

There are currently four types of pet insurance:

- lifetime insurance
- non-lifetime maximum-benefit insurance
- non-lifetime time-limited insurance
- accident-only insurance.

Lifetime insurance

Lifetime insurance policies generally offer the most comprehensive and the most expensive level of insurance, covering fees and expenses up to an agreed amount per year. There are two alternatives: a 'per condition per year' lifetime policy provides a maximum cover limit per condition, which resets each year, whereas an 'annual lifetime' cover policy provides a maximum overall cover limit, which again resets each year.

Non-lifetime maximum-benefit insurance

Non-lifetime maximum-benefit insurance policies offer a maximum amount of veterinary fees and medical expenses cover per condition. Once the financial limit has been reached, however, the condition becomes a pre-existing condition and is excluded from future claims.

Non-lifetime time-limited insurance

Non-lifetime time-limited insurance policies have both a 'per condition' limit and a time limit (usually 12 months) before the condition is excluded. Whilst these policies are often the cheapest, they tend to offer the lowest level of insurance cover.

Accident-only insurance

Accident-only insurance policies only cover fees and expenses related to treating injuries resulting from an accident, although some policies also cover fees and expenses related to illnesses that have occurred as a direct consequence of an accident.

Additional features

Many insurers also offer a variety of supplementary features that can be added to individual pet insurance policies. Although the range and specific nature of these additional features may differ between insurers, most insurers offer some, if not all, of the following add-on policy features:

- insurance cover for dental care
- insurance cover for veterinary fees and medical expenses if the pet is ill overseas
- a lump-sum payment if the insured pet dies
- payment for the cost of advertising if the insured pet goes missing
- third-party liability cover (dog policies only) if the insured pet injures a third party or damages property

- insurance cover for cattery or kennel fees if the insured pet owner is hospitalised
- insurance cover for euthanasia costs if the insured pet is terminally ill
- insurance cover for burial or cremation costs when the insured pet dies.

Buying pet insurance

Because the cost of pet insurance can vary enormously, it is important to find the correct balance between the insurance cover offered (or required) and the annual cost of the insurance.

There are four factors that influence the cost of pet insurance:

- the geographical residence of the policyholder (and the pet)
- the age of the pet being insured
- the type or nature of pet being insured
- the breed or pedigree of the pet being insured (especially for cats and dogs).

To reduce the overall cost of pet insurance, ensure (where appropriate) that pets are regularly inoculated; and for cats and dogs, ensure that they are microchipped. Also, shop around for the best deal – some insurers even offer discounts if more than one pet is insured.

11.12 Making a claim on an insurance policy

Before contacting the insurer and making a claim, it is important to check the following:

- that the event or loss being claimed for is covered (and not specifically excluded) by the insurance policy
- that all conditions imposed by the insurer and detailed in the insurance policy have been complied with
- that the insurance policy was active when the event or loss being claimed for occurred *and*
- that the amount being claimed is greater than the insurance policy excess.

It is also important to retain a detailed record of the events that result in the insurance claim, together with copies of all relevant documentation (for example, expenditure receipts, medical certificates, and valuations or reports from a loss adjuster[16]).

On receiving a claim, an insurer can:

- accept the claim and pay the full amount (less any excess)
- accept the claim but not pay the full amount (less any excess) *or*
- reject a claim and refuse to pay.

Claim accepted and full amount paid (less any excess)

Once an insurer has accepted and validated the claim, and accepted it as legitimate, the time taken to pay the claim can still vary, depending on:

- the nature and type of the insurance
- the value of the insurance claim *and*
- the insurer.

For most insurers, BACS is the preferred method of payment. For very large payments, some insurers will pay using CHAPS (subject to the payment of a small administrative charge).

Claim accepted but less than full amount paid

There are many reasons why an insurer might accept an insurance claim but refuse to pay the full amount (less any excess). The most common are that:

- There is insufficient insurance to cover all the losses.
- The value of the insurance claim is judged (by the insurer) to be overstated and unrealistic.
- There is an imposed limit (or a value restriction) within the insurance policy on the amount the insurer has agreed to pay per claim or per item or per event.
- When the insurance policy was arranged, renewed or amended, information was deliberately or carelessly withheld, or was provided in a way that misled the insurer.

Claim rejected and nothing paid

There are many reasons why an insurer might reject a claim and refuse to pay. The most common are that:

- The insurance policy does not cover the event or item claimed for (which is therefore a so-called 'uninsured loss'), or the event or item is specifically excluded.
- The policy was not active when the event or loss being claimed for occurred.
- The insurance policy was invalid because of a failure to disclose relevant information,[17] or a deliberate attempt to mislead the insurers (another uninsured loss), or a failure to disclose a relevant change in circumstances.
- Insurance premiums have not been paid in full.
- The claims procedure or the insurance policy conditions, or both, have not been correctly adhered to.
- The claim is judged (by the insurer) to be exaggerated.
- The amount claimed is less than the insurance policy excess.

Resolving a claims dispute

If an insurer accepts a claim but refuses to pay the full amount, or rejects a claim and refuses to pay, the insurer must provide a full and reasonable explanation. If you are unhappy with the offer made by the insurer, or disagree with the explanation given, you can seek to resolve the dispute through the insurer's own complaints procedures and, if necessary, refer the dispute to the Financial Ombudsman Service.

The Financial Ombudsman Service is a mediation service. It is a free service, but it is only available once the insurer's own complaints procedures have been exhausted. If mediation fails, the Financial Ombudsman Service can launch a formal investigation. Any final decision is binding on the insurer and the insured, although if the insured is unhappy with the Financial Ombudsman Service's final decision, she or he can, if desired, pursue the matter in the courts.

Note: A referral to the Financial Ombudsman Service must be made within 6 months of receiving a final response from the insurer. The Service is discussed further in Chapter 13.

11.13 Reporting insurance fraud – the Insurance Fraud Bureau

The Association of British Insurers (ABI) estimates that undetected insurance fraud costs the insurance industry over £2 billion each year, with detected fraud costing an additional estimated £1 billion each year (Insurance Fraud Bureau 2015).

The Insurance Fraud Bureau (IFB) is a not-for-profit company established in 2006 to lead the insurance industry's collective fight against insurance fraud. The Bureau acts as an information-sharing and intelligence-gathering service, and aims:

- to assist insurers in identifying fraud
- to support the police, the financial services regulators and other law-enforcement agencies in locating, identifying and prosecuting fraudsters *and*
- to raise public awareness of insurance fraud scams.

The Insurance Fraud Bureau operates a free and confidential 'Cheatline' through which individuals (and companies) can report suspected insurance fraud anonymously. Suspected insurance fraud can be reported online or using a freephone number.[18]

11.14 Concluding comments

As we have seen, insurance is merely a contractual agreement – an agreement whereby, in exchange for payments, an insurer agrees to pay the insured a sum of money should a specific event occur. It is, however, the uncertainties of life and the world in which we live that make insurance important, both as a form of protection and as a form of risk management against the financial consequences of such uncertainties.

11.15 Suggested further reading

For further reading on the following topics, see the references given.

Buildings insurance (comparison):
- www.money.co.uk/home-insurance/building-insurance.htm

Contents insurance (comparison):
- www.money.co.uk/home-insurance/contents-insurance.htm

Breakdown insurance (comparison):
- www.breakdowncover.co.uk

Private medical insurance (comparison):
- www.money.co.uk/health-insurance.htm

Dental insurance (comparison):
- www.money.co.uk/health-insurance/dental-insurance.htm

Professional indemnity insurance (comparison):
- www.money.co.uk/business-insurance/professional-indemnity-insurance.htm

European Health Insurance Card (how to apply):
- www.nhs.uk/NHSEngland/Healthcareabroad/EHIC/Pages/about-the-ehic.aspx

Pet insurance (comparison):
- www.money.co.uk/pet insurance.htm

Key points

- Insurance is a contractual agreement whereby, in exchange for payments (called premiums), an insurer agrees to pay to the insured (the policyholder), a sum of money should a specific event or financial loss occur.

- There are three key aspects to insurance: underwriting, pooling, and reinsurance.
- Insurance is a promise of compensation for an identifiable future event that *might* happen. Assurance is a promise of compensation for an identifiable future event that *will* happen.
- The *Consumer Insurance (Disclosure and Representations) Act 2012* provides that it is the insurer's responsibility to ask all relevant questions when considering an insurance application.
- The cost of insurance can vary depending on a range of factors, including geographical location, personal lifestyle and activities, demographics and personal circumstances, and the individual's history of previous claims.
- The more common types of insurances are property-related insurance, healthcare-related insurance, illness-related insurance, life insurance, whole-of-life assurance, professional liability insurance, travel insurance, and pet insurance.

Self-review questions

1. Distinguish between *life insurance* and *life assurance.*
2. What factors affect the cost of vehicle insurance?
3. Distinguish between *income protection insurance* and *payment protection insurance.*
4. When requesting an insurance quotation, the insurer must provide you with a summary document that contains certain key facts about the insurance being offered. What information *must* the summary document contain?
5. Briefly explain the main reasons why an insurer might reject an insurance claim and refuse to pay.

Case study discussion questions

1. Advise Jonathan Carter on the adequacy of his life insurance provision, and the possible consequences of cancelling his mortgage-related life insurance.
2. Advise Stuart Carter and Mary Carter on the appropriateness of their whole-of-life assurances, neither of which is held 'in trust'.
3. Advise Michelle on her choice of vehicle insurance, and the problems that could arise from her misleading the insurance company regarding her home address.

Suggested answers to chapter activities

Activity 1

Insurance can be purchased from an insurer, a bank, a building society, a travel agent, or a high street retailer; through a comparison website; or through an insurance agent.

Before buying insurance (or even accepting an insurance quote), it is important to consider the suitability of the insurance policy, the cost of the insurance (the premiums), the restrictions or exclusions imposed by the insurer, the cover offered by the insurance, and the overall benefit available under the insurance.

Activity 2

Buildings insurance covers the cost of repairing damage to the physical fabric of a building, and usually covers losses resulting from damage caused by fire, explosion, storms, floods, destruction caused by earthquakes and subsidence, theft and vandalism, damage due to burst water pipes, damage due to oil leaks from a faulty heating system, damage caused by fallen trees, lamp-posts, aerials or satellite dishes, and vehicle collision damage.

Activity 3

The main factors that affect the cost of vehicle insurance include the age of the vehicle's user or owner; the occupation of the vehicle's user or owner; the type, age, engine size, and value of the vehicle; the security features installed on the vehicle; the geographical location of the vehicle; where the vehicle is kept when not in use (in a garage, on a private driveway, or at the roadside); the general use of the vehicle (such as business commuting or for private personal use only); the driving record of the vehicle user or owner; the availability of a no claims discount; the insurance policy excess (in general, the higher the voluntary excess, the lower the cost of insurance); the type of vehicle insurance (third-party; third-party, fire and theft; or comprehensive); and the addition of other named drivers authorised to use the vehicle (as well as the vehicle owner).

Activity 4

The advantages of private medical insurance are medical treatment on demand, reduced waiting times, the use of private facilities, personal selection of the facilities, the hospital and the surgeon or specialist, and the use and availability of specialist drugs and treatments.

The disadvantages of private medical insurance are that better medical healthcare may be available on the NHS (especially for serious chronic illnesses), that the overall cost of private medical insurance is expensive, and that some pre-existing conditions and their treatments are not covered by private medical insurance.

Activity 5

Critical illness insurance provides a tax-free lump-sum payment or a payment of income if the insured (policyholder) is diagnosed with a serious long-term condition, illness or disability (or both).

Payment protection insurance covers the repayment of car finance, personal loans, credit cards, store cards, catalogue payments and mortgages if the insured is unable to work due to an accident, illness or unemployment. Payment protection insurance only covers loan or credit repayments for a limited period of time, usually between 12 and 24 months. There are three types of payment protection insurance: unemployment only; accident and sickness only; and accident, sickness and unemployment.

Income protection insurance covers the loss of income suffered by the insured if she or he is unable to work because of illness or injury. Insurance payments are usually based on a percentage of the insured earnings – between 50% and 70% of net payment. Payments are tax-free and are usually paid until the insured's retirement, death, or return to employment. There are three types of income protection insurance: long-term income protection insurance; short-term income insurance protection; and accident, sickness and unemployment insurance protection.

Notes

1. The law of large numbers states that as the size of a sample size grows, its mean will get closer and closer to the mean for the whole population. In this context, the larger the number of individuals independently exposed to a loss, the greater the probability that *actual* loss will equal *expected* loss.
2. For a list of terminology commonly used in insurance, see: www.biba.org.uk/JargonBuster.aspx.

3. Companies and firms selling insurance in the UK *must* be authorised by the Financial Conduct Authority (FCA) to sell insurance.
4. An insurance agent is usually employed by one insurer through an insurance broker or an independent financial adviser (IFA).
5. This does not apply to life insurance, where the insurer cannot end the contract.
6. The insurer would not have to return the premiums paid, unless this action would be unfair – for example, where an insurance policy was a joint policy and where only one person acted dishonestly.
7. If the cost of insurance is paid in equal instalments throughout the insurance period, insurers will normally increase the premiums to cover interest charges.
8. This will also include all costs related to demolition and site clearance, and consultants' fees (for example, surveyors' fees and architects' fees).
9. 'Personal liability' covers the legal costs which may arise if anyone is injured or killed or if their personal property is damaged at the insured property.
10. Contents insurance may not necessarily cover the possessions of someone staying with the insured temporarily.
11. Including, for example, HIV- and AIDS-related illnesses, diabetes, epilepsy, and hypertension.
12. With some over-50s policies, if the insured dies within this period, any premiums paid to the date of death are refunded to the deceased's estate.
13. A 'claims made' basis of cover is different from the majority of insurance types because the policy provides cover for claims or circumstances notified to the insurer during the period of cover. It can be months or even years after a professional service has been provided to a client that a claim arises, and it will be the policy that was in force *at the time of the claim* that will need to have provided adequate cover.
14. The first pet insurance policy was written in 1890 by Claes Virgin, the founder of Länsförsäkrings Alliance.
15. Pet insurance policies generally pay 100% of veterinary fees and medical expenses, but many insurers offer policy discounts in exchange for imposing an insurance policy excess (usually between £20 and £100).
16. A loss adjuster assesses (on behalf of the insurer) the amount of compensation that should be paid following an insurance claim.
17. For policies taken out, renewed or changed after 6 April 2013.
18. To contact the Insurance Fraud Bureau, online, see www.insurancefraudbureau.org/cheatline/. To telephone (without charge), call 0800 422 0421.

Part 4
Fraud and debt

Overview

Chapter 12 explores the range of 'person-related' frauds and scams, from money-laundering scams, pyramid investment schemes, boiler-room scams and affinity scams, to false-billing frauds, financial (funds) frauds (including ATM- and card-based fraud), advance-fee frauds, identity-theft-related frauds (including phishing and pharming and spoofing-related frauds).

Chapter 13 explores the main regulatory bodies for the finance sector within the UK: the Financial Conduct Authority, the Prudential Regulatory Authority, and the Competitions and Markets Authority. It also explores the role and regulation of Independent Financial Advisers and the use and powers of the Financial Ombudsman Service.

Chapter 14 explores the options available to an individual with debt problems, and offers a practical guide to the advantages and disadvantages of many alternative debt-management strategies now available.

12

Fraud

Learning outcomes

By the end of this chapter, you should be able to:

- distinguish between different types of fraud
- identify and recognise the characteristics of a potential fraud
- explain how people can protect themselves from possible fraud.

12.1 Introduction

Fraud is a deliberate act designed to secure an unfair or unlawful gain. It is both a *civil* offence, which means that a victim of fraud can sue the perpetrator of the fraud to recover monies lost as a consequence of the fraud, and a *criminal* offence, which means that the perpetrator can be prosecuted and imprisoned by the legal authorities.

The term 'fraud' is associated with an array of illegal acts. They include, for example:

- Deception: providing misleading information to others.
- False representation: concealing material facts with the intention of misleading others.
- Bribery: offering others something (usually money) in order to gain an illicit advantage.
- Forgery: making or adapting objects or documents with the intention of deceiving others.
- Extortion: using violence, fear or the pretence of authority to force a person to give up ownership or possession of goods or assets.
- Corruption: unlawful or improper use of influence, power, and other means.
- Conspiracy: making secret undertakings to carry out harmful or illegal acts.
- Embezzlement and misappropriation: appropriation of funds or property entrusted to the fraudster's care but actually owned by someone else.
- Collusion: agreeing with others to defraud someone else of his or her property or rights, or to obtain an object or property forbidden by law.
- Illegal gratuity: an illegal reward to another in exchange for a service.

Although defrauding people (or companies or other organisations) of money or valuable tangible assets is the usual purpose of fraud, in some instances fraud may simply be to acquire an identity – to steal someone's identity and then to enjoy the benefits of that identity, without depriving anyone of any money or tangible assets.

This chapter explores the range of person-related frauds, from money-laundering scams, pyramid investment schemes, boiler-room scams and affinity scams, to false-billing frauds, financial frauds (including ATM- and card-based frauds), advance-fee frauds, and identity-related frauds (including phishing, pharming and spoofing frauds).

12.2 Fraud Act 2006

The word 'fraud' originates from the Latin word *fraus*, meaning 'deceit' or 'injury' (*Oxford English Dictionary* 1991). There are now many other words and phrases commonly used for fraud, including a scam, a confidence trick, a con, a swindle, a sham, a double-cross, a hoax, a cheat, a ruse, and a hoodwink. But what *is* fraud?

Fraud is essentially the use of false representation or criminal deception, or both, either to gain an unjust personal advantage or to avoid a legal or moral obligation. The *Fraud Act 2006* provides a statutory definition of the criminal offence of fraud, and defines three classes of fraud:

- 'fraud by false representation' (s.2)
- 'fraud by failing to disclose information' (s.3)
- 'fraud by abuse of position' (s.4).

Fraud by false representation occurs when a person makes any representation as to fact or law, either express or implied, that they know to be untrue or misleading. Fraud by failing to disclose information occurs when a person fails to disclose any information to a third party that they are under a legal duty to disclose. Fraud by abuse of position occurs when a person who occupies a position of influence or power, in which they are expected to safeguard the financial interests of others, abuse that position for their own benefit. Such abuse includes abuse by omission, as well as abuse by overt act.

For each of the above to constitute an *offence*, the person must have acted dishonestly and with the intent of making a gain or inflicting a loss on another person.

Note: In the context of fraud, a *gain* or a *loss* is considered only in terms of the gain or loss of money or property (including intangible property). A gain or loss can be temporary or permanent. A 'gain' includes gains accrued by keeping existing possessions that do not belong to the fraudster, not just by obtaining new ones. A 'loss' includes losses of expected acquisitions, as well as losses of property that is already held.

12.3 Different types of fraud

Fraud can be loosely categorised into the following groups of corrupt practices:

- an intentional perversion of truth, a misrepresentation, a concealment or an omission of material fact, perpetrated with the intention of deceiving another to the detriment or injury of that person (or both)
- a deceitful practice or device perpetrated with the intention of depriving another of property or other rights
- a dishonest act designed to manipulate another person into giving away something of value.

The most common types of person-related frauds[1] are:

- identity theft

- person-based financial fraud (which includes account takeover fraud; ATM-based fraud; online banking fraud; cash-back fraud; cash-back money-transfer fraud; and card-related fraud, including credit-card fraud)
- false-billing fraud
- advance-fee fraud (which includes dead relative scams and inheritance fraud, competition win scams, current affairs scams, psychic and clairvoyant scams, work-from-home scams, loan scams, fraud recovery scams, rental scams, racing tipster scams, and vehicle-matching scams).

Other types of commonly occurring frauds include:
- money-laundering and money-transfer scams
- pyramid schemes (and Ponzi schemes)
- boiler-room scams (share sale fraud)
- affinity fraud
- dating and romance scams
- door-to-door scams (bogus tradesmen fraud)
- health and medical fraud (including miracle health scams)
- holiday club fraud
- timeshare fraud
- insurance broker fraud
- internet dialler scams
- land banking scams
- pension liberation scams
- property investment scams
- online shopping and auction fraud.

Before looking at some of these different types of fraud, we look briefly at how using a common-sense approach can help you protect yourself against fraud.

12.4 Protecting yourself against fraud

Despite what you might otherwise hear, there are *no* 'get rich quick' schemes, and no shortcuts to fortune and wealth. Therefore, whether it is –
- a letter received through the post advertising a spectacular 'deal of the century' that just cannot be overlooked *or*
- an email selling a miraculous 'get rich' scheme that cannot possibly be ignored *or*
- a 'pop up' website offering branded products at heavily discounted prices that are too good to be true and never to be repeated *or*
- an ingratiating telephone call offering an amazing 'one-off' investment opportunity that is available for a limited period and just cannot be missed

– it is a scam. All such schemes are fakes, shams, cons, ruses ... and all are designed for one simple purpose: to defraud you! In 2014 there were nearly 277,000 recorded frauds in the UK (CIFAS 2015a: 2), an increase of 25% on 2013.

Simple strategies for protecting yourself

There are three simple strategies you can use to help protect yourself against such attempted deceptions.

First, trust your instincts – that goes a long way! Remember, if it *sounds* too good to be true, it probably *is* too good to be true.

Secondly, always be suspicious, always be sceptical, and always be cautious.[2] Use the ABC: *assume* nothing, *believe* no one, *check* everything.

Thirdly, treat your personal details (especially personal credentials, such as debit card, credit card or charge card PINs, bank account usernames, and passwords) as you would treat your cash. Protect them! Never write them down, never leave them lying around for others to view, and never let anyone you do not know or do not trust to gain access to them, copy them, or take them away.

Remember: a scam may not necessarily be about money – it may instead be about stealing personal data or gaining access to confidential information that can then be used for fraudulent purposes. It is therefore ever more important to protect not only your money, but more importantly yourself and your identity.

Here are some simple, easy-to-follow guidelines:

- Never agree to a deal straight away, and especially not with a door-to-door salesman or if the deal involves a large sum of money.
- Never sign an agreement without appropriate independent advice.
- Never hand money over (for either a deposit or a payment in advance) until you have checked the validity of the goods or services, and verified the company or organisation you are dealing with (especially if this is an online transaction).
- Never respond to text messages or missed calls from telephone numbers you do not recognise.
- Never believe glowing testimonials (especially on websites), which can easily be faked or doctored – if in doubt, always get a 'third party' independent opinion.
- Never give your personal details to anyone you do not know or do not trust, especially details of your address, your bank accounts, or your debit cards, credit cards, or charge cards.

In addition to the above:

- Never give anyone access to any PINs, passwords, or usernames you use.
- Never reply to spam emails, not even to stop them. Letters, documents and emails sent by fraudsters are often badly written, so look out for obvious spelling mistakes and poor grammar.
- Never respond to spam text messages.
- Never call a telephone number or use contact details in a spam email or spam text.
- Never use another person's computer for personal or confidential transactions (especially those involving either your bank account or your debit card, credit card or charge card details).
- Never let anyone you do not know or do not trust have access to your phone, your tablet or computer, or your debit cards, credit cards or charge cards.
- Never let anyone (for example, in a shop or a restaurant) take your debit card, credit card or charge cards away from you and out of your sight.
- *Never ever* use your debit card to pay for online purchases! (It is directly linked to your bank account.)

Protecting your bank accounts

To protect your bank account, it is useful to adopt the following measures:

- Regularly check your bank account statements and verify all entries. (If there are any entries you do not recognise, contact your bank immediately.)

- Always ensure that you shred or destroy any paper bank statements you may receive.
- Carefully check your credit score report, and contact your bank or credit score provider if your score has suddenly and unexpectedly changed.
- Always ensure that you use a secure facility for online card payments (for example, AMEX use 'Safekey', Visa use 'Verified by Visa', and Mastercard use 'Securecode').
- Never respond to emails (see the example in Figure 12.1), phone calls or letters that request personal bank details (for example, bank account PIN numbers, debit card or credit card numbers, or card security codes[3]), however legitimate the request may appear.

Protecting your phone

To protect your mobile phone, it is useful to adopt the following measures:

- Use the Telephone Preference Service to discourage unwanted marketing calls.
- Password-protect your mobile phone.
- Always use the most up-to-date software for your mobile phone.
- Never reply to unsolicited text messages, and especially not those requesting personal details or confidential information.

Protecting your tablet or computer

To protect your tablet or computer, take the following measures:

- Always use anti-virus software, and ensure that it is up to date.[4]
- Minimise the amount of personal data and information you store on your tablet or computer.
- Be careful with the type and amount of personal data and information you provide online for social network websites.

Date: Thurs, 8 Jan 2015 07:55:27 -0500
From: Barclays Bank PLC do-not-reply@barclays.co.uk
To: Undisclosed Recipients
Reply-to: do-not-reply@barclays.co.uk
Subject: Reactivate Your Barclays Account Now

Dear Barclays Bank PLC Customer,

The Barclays Bank PLC Online department temporary disabled your account. After three unsuccessful login attempts your account was temporary disabled until further investigations. You must reactivate your account at Barclays Bank PLC immediately. Once you have completed these steps, we will send you an email notifying that your account is available again. The information you provide us is all non-sensitive and anonymous – No part of it is handed down to any third party.

Sorry for any inconvenience this may cause you and thank you for your patience.

To continue please click the link below
http://www.barclays.co.uk/goto/online_update.html
©2015 Barclays Bank PLC

Figure 12.1 Bank account fraud

- Always encrypt or password-protect important documents (and always ensure that you have an up-to-date back-up).
- Minimise the amount of personal and confidential data and information that you store 'in the cloud'.
- Always verify the security and validity of a website before you enter any personal data or confidential information. Look for the padlock symbol and also a green-coloured URL address box.
- Regularly change the passwords you use, and if possible use a reputable password manager (such as LastPass: see https://lastpass.com/). See also: http://lifehacker.com/5529133/five-best-password-managers.

For up-to-date information on the many different types of fraud, information on how to guard and protect yourself against fraud, and news alerts, stories and information on new emerging frauds, see: www.met.police.uk/fraudalert.

12.5 Identity theft

A key part of many person-related frauds is identity theft. This is the deliberate and fraudulent use of details of another person's identity in order to obtain goods or services, to gain access to a source of finance or credit, to assign guilt for a crime, to enable illegal immigration, or to facilitate terrorism, espionage, blackmail, or extortion.

Identity theft is sometimes categorised into the following groups:

- Criminal identity theft: using another person's identity when apprehended for a crime (for example, a road traffic offence such as speeding).
- Financial identity theft: using another person's identity to obtain credit, goods or services.
- Identity cloning: using another person's personal information to assume her or his identity in daily life (for example, to conceal the true identity of an illegal immigrant or convicted criminal).
- Medical identity theft: using another person's identity to obtain medication or pharmaceuticals.
- Child identity theft: using a child's identity to apply for Government benefits, to open bank accounts, to obtain credit cards or charge cards, to apply for loan finance, or to obtain utility services or rented accommodation.
- Synthetic identify theft: a variation on identity theft, in which an identity is completely or partially fabricated, usually using a combination of two or more real identities.

In 2014, 41% of all reported frauds in the UK were related to identity theft (CIFAS 2015b: 2), with a staggering 82% of identify frauds being committed online (CIFAS 2015b: 1).

Obtaining and exploiting personal information

There are many ways of acquiring personal and confidential information about individuals, including the credentials – usernames, PINs, and passwords – they use to authenticate themselves. Some of the most common include:

- Searching through discarded rubbish for personal information (sometimes referred to as 'dumpster diving').

- Retrieving personal data from redundant IT equipment or storage media (for example, PCs, tablets, mobile phones, USB memory sticks or hard drives) that have been disposed of, given away or sold without appropriate sanitisation.[5]
- Stealing debit cards, credit cards, charge cards, identification cards or documents (including employment-related ID cards, birth certificates, or passports).
- Stealing information from debit cards, credit cards or charge cards using compromised card readers (sometimes referred to as 'card skimming'), and using the information to create 'cloned' debit cards, credit cards or charge cards.
- Impersonating trusted companies or organisations in emails,[6] text messages, telephone calls or other forms of communication – for example, on a fake website or online data collection form – to obtain personal information or log-in credentials (sometimes referred to as phishing[7] and/or pharming[8]).
- Stealing personal information from computers or tablets using malware, keystroke-logging programs or other spyware programs.
- Browsing social networking websites for personal details and confidential information for use in social engineering attacks.
- Diverting email or stealing post (for example, credit cards, utility bills, and bank or credit card statements) to obtain personal information and credentials.
- Hacking into a person's computer to obtain personal data.
- Watching people enter log-in credentials (for example, at an ATM) and stealing their user details or credentials (sometimes referred to as 'shoulder surfing').
- Using a brute-force attack to guess at weak user passwords.

Activity 1

Identify and describe the main categories of identity theft.

CIFAS Protective Registration

For people who believe they are at risk, one possible defence against identity theft or identity fraud is CIFAS[9] Protective Registration. Those at particular risk include, for example:

- people who have recently lost personal documents
- people who have recently had personal documents stolen
- customers of organisations that are known to have lost or leaked sensitive data recently
- people who have been advised by the police that they are at potential risk.

Protective Registration is available for people who want to protect themselves, and for companies and organisations that want to protect their customers or their employees.

CIFAS operates a National Fraud Database. If a person requests Protective Registration, CIFAS places a warning flag against that person's name and all related personal details in this Database. This alerts companies and organisations (which include all the main credit reference agencies) to pay special attention if that person's details are used to apply for any products or services. In practical terms this means that companies and organisations will carry out additional extra checks to validate the application and to confirm the identity of the person making it, to ensure that it is not fraudulent.

12.6 Person-based financial fraud

Person-based financial fraud can range from financial theft and the illegal transfer of funds from a person's bank account, to ATM-based fraud and crimes involving credit cards or electronic funds. Normally such fraud involves obtaining goods or services for payment using stolen or illegally obtained financial information. The most common types of person-based financial frauds are card-not-present fraud – in which a stolen or cloned debit card, credit card, or charge card is used to buy goods and services – and cash-back fraud.

Account takeover fraud

An account takeover fraud occurs when a scammer or fraudster takes control of another person's account (usually a bank account, but the same can be done with a credit card or charge card account). Having gathered confidential personal information about the intended victim, the fraudster then contacts the victim's bank or card issuer, impersonates the real account holder, and asks for mail to be redirected to a new address. The fraudster then reports the bank account debit card (or credit card or charge card) as lost and requests that a replacement card be sent.

Once this card has been received, the fraudster validates and activates it, creates a new PIN, and then commences using the card ... This continues until the rightful account holder discovers the deception, usually by trying to use her or his own card and encountering difficulties. By this time, the bank account may have been emptied or the credit card or charge card used up to the spending limit.

ATM-based fraud

Pioneered by Scottish inventor John Shepherd-Barron in the 1960s, ATMs have become an essential part of consumer-related banking services since the mid-1970s, and are now commonplace not only in banks but also in large retail outlets, train stations, bus stations, pubs, clubs, hotels, garages, and many other places. At the end of 2013, there were over 67,000 ATMs in use in the UK (Link 2015), with total ATM cash withdrawals amounting to £2,899 million (ibid.). Of these cash withdrawals, 97% were from 'free to use' ATMs.

Unfortunately, whilst there has been substantial growth in the availability, acceptability and use of ATMs in the UK (for example, between 2003 and 2013 the number of ATMs in the UK increased by approximately 20,000), there has also been an alarming increase in ATM fraud. Between 2003 and 2013, total fraud losses at UK ATMs amounted to £485 million (Financial Fraud Action 2014: 9). Indeed, in 2013 alone, the total fraud losses at UK ATMs amounted to nearly £32 million (ibid.: 29), an increase of 10% on 2012.

ATMs generally use a two-factor authentication process – first an encoded physical card (a debit card, credit card or charge card), which has a magnetic strip and a programmed chip; and secondly a matching PIN. As a consequence, ATM-based fraud essentially involves:

- stealing the physical card *and/or*
- stealing the credentials encoded on the card.

There are a number of ways in which a fraudster can do this, including:

- skimming
- using a hidden camera
- using a card trap
- shoulder surfing.

Skimming

Skimming is essentially the theft of the debit card, credit card or charge card information, which is achieved by attaching a device to an ATM (usually above the slot where the card is inserted) to record the electronic details from the magnetic strip on the card. Often this is done in conjunction with a hidden miniature camera (see below). A small skimming device can swipe and store thousands of card numbers before a fraudster needs to remove it.

Note: Before you insert your debit card, credit card or charge card into an ATM, always check to ensure that there is nothing unusual about the appearance of the ATM. For example, does any part of the machine appear newer or made from a different material than the remainder of the ATM? Are there any scratches, sticky residue, or other signs of tampering near the ATM card slot?

Although skimming is associated with ATM fraud, it is commonly done elsewhere too. For example, skimming may also occur in shops, restaurants or bars, where a member of staff who has possession of a customer's debit card, credit card or charge card may take it out of the cardholder's immediate view to skim it.

Hidden camera

Often used in association with a a card trap or a skimming device, a camera, inconspicuously hidden in a fake panel close to the ATM keypad, may be used by fraudsters to capture either the card details or (perhaps more importantly) the card's PIN. Although such cameras can be difficult to identify, slight variations in colour between panels or small pinholes located in the panel near or above the keypad should be treated with suspicion, and immediately reported to the bank branch where the ATM is situated or, if the ATM is in a store, to the bank's head office.

Card trap

A card trap works by jamming the debit card, credit card or charge card in the ATM. A device attached to the ATM allows the fraudster to capture the card and retrieve it at a later date.

Note: Although there are legitimate reasons why an ATM sometimes retains a card, you should never assume that the retained card is safe. If your card is retained by an ATM, report this to your bank or card issuer immediately, and cancel the card!

Shoulder surfing

Shoulder surfing occurs when a fraudster (or an associate) observes a person entering a PIN at an ATM. It could be someone in a queue behind the ATM user, or someone loitering near the ATM.

The fraudster may then seek to distract the ATM user – perhaps by 'accidentally' dropping or spilling something near the ATM, or by 'innocently' tripping and bumping into the cardholder – in order to steal the card from the ATM. If a group of fraudsters are 'working an ATM together', they may even pickpocket the ATM user once the transaction is complete, especially if the ATM is located in a busy and crowded area.

Using an ATM

To protect your bank account:

- Before you use an ATM, check that the ATM has not been tampered with, and that the card slot and keypad are legitimate.

- When entering your PIN at an ATM, shield the keypad with your hand to prevent shoulder surfing.
- Always use familiar ATMs (as you would be more likely to notice any tampering) and if possible limit the number of visits.
- Do not use ATMs were there are groups of people loitering near the ATM.
- Try not to use ATMs located in dimly lit areas or late at night – these could be more susceptible to fraud.
- Try to use ATMs in public places and if possible under video-surveillance – these are likely to be safer.
- Check your bank balance frequently and confirm any cash withdrawals from your account.

Activity 2

ATM-based fraud essentially involves stealing either the physical card or the encoded credentials on the card, or both. Briefly list the various ways in which a fraudster can do this.

Online banking fraud

Online banking fraud occurs when a fraudster covertly accesses a person's online bank account and transfers funds for the purposes of financial gain. In some cases, people may even be deceived by a fraudster into making fraudulent money transfers themselves (see below).

Between 2004 and 2013, total online banking fraud losses amounted to £366 million (Financial Fraud Action 2014: 9), while the total online banking fraud losses for 2013 amounted to nearly £41 million (ibid.: 37), an increase of 3% on 2012. Whilst there is no single explanation for the increase in online banking fraud, it has primarily been driven by a change in the attack methods used by fraudsters, including the use of phishing, social engineering scams[10] such as vishing,[11] and more sophisticated online attacks such as infecting computers with malicious software (malware).

Cash-back fraud

The starting point for a cash-back fraud is usually a busy retail outlet, and the victim is usually a busy shopper who is paying by debit card – perhaps a housewife with overly mischievous children, or a distracted and remiss elderly couple confused by modern payment technology. The shopper pays for her or his goods and, unknown to the shopper, the cashier adds a cash-back amount; or the shopper requests cash-back, but the cashier processes a larger amount than that requested. In either case, the cashier pockets the extra amount. The fraud is discovered only when the shopper checks his or her receipt, which might be at home some hours or even days later; and by that stage, proving that no cash-back was requested or that the cash-back amount received was less than that identified on the receipt, is very difficult.

Cash-back money-transfer fraud

Although historically they were very popular, cash-back money-transfer frauds are now fairly rare.

A cash-back money-transfer fraud occurs when a person sells goods online and the buyer (usually an overseas buyer) offers to pay by cheque or by banker's draft for *more* money than the asking price – usually offering some fictitious and contrived excuse for doing so.

Alternatively, the buyer may attempt to pay using a stolen payment card (usually a credit card or charge card whose loss has not yet been reported), and then claim to have accidently paid too much.

The person selling the goods will then receive a request from the buyer to send all or some of the difference back to the buyer or to a third party, by way of a money transfer; and to do this irrespective of whether the cheque, banker's draft or card payment has cleared. Typically, the cheque or banker's draft will 'bounce', or the stolen-card payment will not be honoured by the card company, and the seller will lose financially.

Card-related fraud

'Card-related fraud' is an all-encompassing term. It is used to describe the fraud committed using stolen payment cards, such as debit, credit or charge cards, in order to buy goods or services or to obtain unauthorised funds from an account. Increasingly such fraud is the result of deception crimes, identity theft, and online attacks using malware and data hacking to compromise card details. In 2013, the total fraud losses on UK-issued cards amounted to £450 million (Financial Fraud Action 2014: 9). Of these:

- £301 million was related to card-not-present fraud (of which an estimated £163 million was related to eCommerce transactions)
- £43 million was as a result of the use of counterfeit cards
- £59 million was related to lost or stolen cards[12]
- £10 million was due to non-receipt of mail
- £37 million was as a result of card identity theft.

This was an increase of 16% on 2012. Overall, as a proportion of card-related spending in 2013, card fraud losses were 7.4p for every £100. (In 2012, card fraud losses were 7.1p for every £100.)

Card-not-present fraud

Having acquired a person's details electronically (for example, using computer-based malware or spyware) or using a phishing email or a telephone scam, a 'card-not-present' fraud occurs when a fraudster uses the person's debit, credit or charge card credentials to make purchases without the card being physically present[13] – that is, online via a website, over the telephone, or by mail order.[14]

For a retailer, card-not-present transactions are far riskier than card-present transactions, because they must rely on indirect information from the cardholder – or someone purporting to be the cardholder – to verify and validate the transaction. That is why most card issuers charge retailers a higher transaction rate for card-not-present transactions.

To minimise possible fraud, card issuers and retailers use a range of technologies (or more accurately countermeasures), the most common being:

- the use of 3D secure protocols (American Express SafeKey, MasterCard SecureCode and Verified By Visa)
- the use of Address Verification Service (AVS) and card security code (CSC) facilities
- the use of fraud screening and other detection technologies (such as pattern recognition or rule generation)
- the use of payment service-provider security facilities.

Counterfeit card fraud

Counterfeit card fraud relates to the use of either an imitation card or a doctored card, and occurs when a card is created using personal credentials from a compromised debit card, credit card or charge card.[15] The counterfeit card is then used (often overseas) to make ATM withdrawals, shop purchases, or online purchases. Whilst this kind of fraud was historically very popular, the introduction of new security features and new technologies by card issuers (for example, the introduction and use of embossed holograms on payment cards), the effort and cost required in manufacturing fake payment cards or doctoring existing cards, and the risks involved in their eventual use, have together diminished considerably the use of such methods for the illicit accumulation of either funds or goods.

Lost and stolen cards

Distracting people in retail outlets, cafés or restaurants or at ATMs and then stealing their payment cards without their noticing (often called 'distraction theft') is perhaps the most common way in which payment cards are stolen. Of course, some debit, credit or charge cards are simply lost accidently, in a mislaid wallet or a lost purse.

When a payment card is stolen or lost, it may be possible for a fraudster to use the card for illegal purchases – at least until the cardholder notices the loss and notifies the issuing bank, and the bank imposes a block on the account. To limit the window of opportunity, all banks now have free 24-hour telephone numbers to encourage prompt reporting. Even so, given the window of opportunity that could exist (especially if the cardholder is unaware of the loss or theft), the thief or fraudster may be able to make unauthorised purchases on the payment card before either the cardholder or the card issuer realises that the card has been lost or stolen and arranges for it to be cancelled.

Application and intercept fraud

Application fraud Application fraud occurs when a fraudster makes a false application, seeking to acquire another person's debit card, credit card or charge card by using stolen or fake documents.

Intercept fraud This type of fraud occurs when a fraudster intercepts and steals a debit card, credit card or charge card while it is in transit – after the bank or card company has issued and sent out the card, but before the genuine cardholder receives the card. Communal properties with shared letterboxes, such as flats, apartments, sheltered housing and student halls of residence, are particularly vulnerable – and especially so if people do not get their mail redirected when they move away and change their address.

12.7 False billing

False billing is the fraudulent act of invoicing or requesting payment from a person for goods or services that do not exist or were not used (and will never be used). Such fraud also includes charging for goods or services at an overly inflated price.

Historically, false-billing frauds were usually aimed at corporate organisations with large, often automated, payment systems and subsystems. Recently, however, such scams have increasingly been targeted at the elderly. They often involve an attempt to obtain payments for bogus goods or for services that have never been provided.

Note: The submission of incorrect taxation or benefit claims is also a form of false-billing fraud.

12.8 Advance-fee fraud

Advanced-fee frauds often (but not exclusively) used to originate from parts of Africa. In particular, Nigeria was infamous as a source of this type of fraud – indeed, advanced-fee frauds are often referred to as '419 schemes', after section 4:1:9 of the Nigerian Government's penal code.

The common characteristic of advanced-fee frauds is an offer to transfer money into a person's bank account on receipt of confidential details or the payment of an upfront or advance fee. There are many varieties of advance-fee frauds, the most popular being the dead relative scam or inheritance fraud, the competition win scam, and the current affairs scam. Other lesser-known advance-fee frauds include the psychic or clairvoyant scam, the work-from-home scam, the loan scam, the fraud recovery scam, the rental scam, the racing tipster scam, and the vehicle-matching scam.

Dead relative scams and inheritance fraud

There are many alternative scenarios used for the dead relative or inheritance scam: here is one example.

You receive a fraudulent email: someone very rich – perhaps a long-distant relative, or just somebody with the same family name – has died and you are now in line to receive a huge inheritance. The fraudster claims to be an overseas lawyer or legal official administering the inheritance. He has been unable to identify any direct relatives of the deceased person. As a consequence, in accordance with local legal requirements, the inheritance money will be paid to the government and as legal administrator to the deceased he himself will receive no payment of fees. The fraudster suggests that, because you share the same family name as the deceased, he could pay the inheritance to you. The inheritance could then be divided between you and him, rather than handing it over to the government.

Because of the nature of the suggested transaction and the amount of money involved, the fraudster will emphasise the need for secrecy and the need for you to respond and act quickly.

If you respond to the fraudster, you will be asked to pay various upfront fees, such as administration fees, legal fees, banking fees, or transfer fees – so that he can release the (non-existent) inheritance. You may also be told that the inheritance money is locked in an account in a third country – for example, Switzerland – and that because of EU legal requirements, he needs an EU-based bank account into which the inheritance can be transferred.

There is, of course, no inheritance – no one has died, and the person contacting you is not a lawyer or other legal official. Any money you pay will be lost, and any bank account details you provide will be used to steal any money you may have in that account.

Competition win scams

The competition win scam is also known as the fake prize or lottery win scam.[16] It works like this.

The fraudster contacts you (usually by email or through an online social network) to tell you that you have won a large sum of money in an international lottery – the Spanish, Canadian, US and Australian lotteries are among the most common lotteries and competitions used. To claim your winnings, you are asked to contact an official at the lottery company as soon as possible (see the sample email in Figure 12.2), and you will probably be advised to keep your lottery win a secret.

Date: Fri, 26 June 2015 16:26:46 +0100
From: nacenet1 nacenet1@libero.it
To: **********.co.uk

Subject: Call Luke Davies For Your Claim
Claim Ticket Number; CA235676778
S.FC.N: ALC1679087678/2006/TH
Batch Number VCF: 578999008777AAF

We wish to inform you of the yearly sweepstakes program that your e-mail address has won an award sum of a total cash prize of 1,000,000.00 (ONE MILLION Dollars) in the 2nd category. Do contact the PROCESSING DEPARTMENT detail below for your Claim. You are advised to quote your BATCH NUMBER AND TICKET NUMBER for your claim.

DR.LUKE DAVIES.
Promo Claims Manager
Email: ecoworldinterr@gawab.com
ecoworldinterr@aim.com
TEL: +31-610-698-963.
****
Yours faithfully,
MR.JOSS BOUMAN (Mrs.).
TEL/Fax; 0031-610-698-903
INTERNET SWEEPTSTAKES LOTTERY COORDINATOR

Figure 12.2 Competition win fraud

Of course, the lottery does not exist – or if there is a genuine lottery, the fraudster is misusing or misrepresenting it – and there is no prize money to win.

If you contact them, the fraudster will first request proof of your identity – for example, copies of official documents such as your driving licence or passport. This information will then be used for identity-theft purposes. The fraudster will then request the payment of an upfront administration fee (to cover legal and banking costs) and ask for your bank account details so that the (non-existent) winnings can be released and paid into your account. In reality, these details will be used to empty your account.

Current affairs scams

Current affairs scams are also known as natural disaster scams or war and famine scams. There are many alternative scenarios: here is one example.

There has been a natural disaster in South East Asia. Thousands of men, women and children have been killed, and many more thousands have been made homeless and lost all their possessions. You receive an email, a text message, a telephone call or even a link on Facebook, from an overseas, obscurely named, charitable organisation claiming to be collecting funds on behalf of those affected by the recent tragic natural disaster in South East Asia. Providing a graphic description of the problems faced by local people in the disaster area – the pain, the suffering and the loss – the email, message, call or link will seek to appeal to your sense of charity, your conscience and your humanity, and will ask you for a charitable donation … as much as you can give.

Whilst there may well have been a natural disaster in South East Asia that has been widely reported in the media, there is of course no such charity, and any money you donate will be lost. More importantly, by making a donation to the fraudulent charity you will also unknowingly validate your contact details – your email address, your telephone number or your Facebook address – which will then be sold on to other groups of fraudsters.

Psychic and clairvoyant scams

Perhaps one of the more bizarre frauds, psychic and clairvoyant scams also use many alternative scenarios.

In general, you are contacted by a fraudster, by email or telephone call, who informs you that she has seen something wonderful (or something terrible) in your immediate future or your family's immediate future. Unsurprisingly, they ask for an upfront fee to provide a full report of whatever event they claim to have foreseen!

Work-from-home scams

Work-from-home scams are also known as business opportunity frauds.[17] They involve an offer for you to become self-employed and to generate extra income by working at home. The offer may come in a mailshot letter, an advertisement, a 'pop up' website, a spam email, a text message or even a telephone call; in any case, it will ask if you would be interested in earning money and becoming financially independent by setting up a business that would enable you to tailor your work commitments around your personal responsibilities.

To register with the scheme, of couse, an upfront fee will be payable. The scheme will normally involve tedious activities, such as filling envelopes, assembling poorly produced products, or selling goods or services to others. Unfortunately, the fraudsters will always find fault with your work and use this as a reason not to pay you; and any products or services you are asked to sell will usually be of a very poor quality, probably worthless, and for which there is little or no demand.

Many of these schemes are straightforward pyramid schemes (see below), whereby a person will only earn money by introducing other people to the scheme.

Loan scams

A loan scam occurs when a person applies for a loan, usually by replying to an online advert or a spam email. The advert or email offers a fast loan (usually from an obscure and bizarrely named loan company), and claims that all applications will be considered and approved, regardless of the applicant's credit rating and credit history. An upfront administration and insurance fee is payable with the application, and you may also be asked to supply personal and confidential bank account details (in some instances, not only your bank account number but also the PIN).

Once the application is submitted and the upfront fee is paid, you will not hear from the loan company again: the loan will never be received and if you have provided your bank account number and PIN, your account may be emptied of whatever funds it contained.

Fraud-recovery scams

Recovery fraud occurs when *former* fraud victims are advised (for example, by spam email, doorstep cold-calling, or telephone spoofing[18]) that any monies they have recently lost as a result of the fraud can be legitimately recovered. The fraudsters will often pose as a legitimate claims company, and will not only allege that they can identify the fraudster and recover any monies lost (for a fee), but will also claim that they have recovered funds in the past and offer glowing (but nonetheless fake) testimonials as proof.

As with all advanced-fee frauds, if a person responds to the fraudulent offer of help, the fraudsters will ask for immediate payment of an administration fee. They will then periodically request additional 'investigation' fees to be paid as they 'proceed' with their investigations. They may even ask for bank account details, so that they can deposit any recovered monies. No money will ever be returned.

Rental scams

Rental fraud occurs when a prospective tenant is tricked into paying an upfront payment to rent a property. In reality, the property does not exist, or is not habitable, or has already been rented out – possibly to a number of people at the same time. The prospective tenants not only lose the advance payments they have already made, but are also unable to rent the property they thought they had secured.

Rental scammers often target undergraduate students who are looking for university accommodation.

Racing tipster scams

Racing tipster scams involve a victim being offered racing advice and guaranteed winning tips ... for a small subscription fee. Often offered via a professional-looking letter, email or website, the scammers promise that all past subscribers have made a small fortune, and offer as proof an extensive list of previous racing tips (all of which, surprisingly, have won), together with an array of glowing testimonials.

In reality, few if any of the racing tips actually result in wins. The so-called expert racing tipsters are not real, and any money-back guarantees provided are worthless and never honoured.

Vehicle-matching scams

A vehicle-matching scam occurs when a fraudster, usually representing a fake dealership, cold-calls a person who has just placed an advert to sell his or her vehicle. The caller claims to have an immediate buyer for the car, at a price higher than the advertised price, but requires an upfront fee which they say will be refunded if the car is not sold. The car is not sold, and the refund is never paid.

> **Activity 3**
>
> What is advance-fee fraud? What are the main types?

12.9 Other types of fraud

Money-laundering and money-transfer frauds

Money is 'laundered' to disguise where it came from and how it was acquired. Laundering is usually undertaken to make the proceeds of a criminal activity appear legal. Although there are many ways in which fraudsters can launder money – they can, for example, use a virtual payment system, electronic money exchangers or international transfer agents, prepaid cards and vouchers, or even Hawala banking[19] for the non-electronic transfer of funds – one of the most popular ways in which money can be laundered is through the use of a money mule.

A 'money mule' is a person who transfers money, either in person through a courier service (a money-transfer agent) or electronically (online). Mules are often recruited online and are frequently used to launder the proceeds of frauds and scams linked to organised crime, including online frauds such as phishing scams, malware scams and shopping or auction scams associated with websites such as eBay.

Fraudsters often target the young, the naïve and the gullible, people on low incomes (such as students, the unemployed, and those on benefits), or people who have their personal details on a range of social networking websites, recruitment websites, or even in chat rooms. Remember: for a fraudster, using a money mule is a win–win situation – by using a money mule, the fraudsters can not only move vast amounts of money with ease, but can also distance themselves from any of the risks associated with the transfer of the money.

So how does money laundering work? In simple terms, once recruited the mule will receive (on a regular basis) payments into her or his personal bank account. For a small commission, she or he will then be instructed to withdraw the funds (sometimes as physical cash) and to send the funds overseas, using for example a money-transfer service, to accounts that are in reality owned by the fraudsters. Often mules are told that the funds are (for example) charitable donations that require distribution overseas.

Note: Assisting fraudsters to clean 'dirty money' in this way is of course a serious criminal office, and if convicted a person could face a sentence of up to 14 years in prison and an unlimited monetary fine.

Pyramid scheme fraud and Ponzi schemes

Although the terms are used interchangeably, there are in fact slight differences between a Ponzi[20] scheme and a pyramid scheme.

A true *Ponzi scheme* usually promotes what appears to be a real investment opportunity, to which investors are invited to contribute. A *pyramid scheme*, however, usually requires that participants make a payment to the people who recruit them for the right to recruit *other* people into the scheme, at which point they will receive payments from the people they themselves recruit.

Pyramid schemes

In simple terms, a pyramid scheme is an unsustainable business scheme which rewards people for enrolling others into the scheme – a scheme that in fact offers either non-existent or worthless products. Often pyramid schemes are advertised as 'multi-level investment schemes' which offer extraordinary profits for little or no risk. Participants are always required to pay a fee to enter the scheme, and are then required to recruit other participants (such as friends, work colleagues or family members) into the scheme. If successful, participants are paid out of the receipts generated by their recruits – recruits who are themselves required to recruit new participants, in order to keep the chain going.

Whilst the initiator of the pyramid scheme – the fraudster at the top – will collect most of the profits, those entering the scheme later will in all probability lose any funds they have paid into the scheme.

In September 2014, six women from Bristol were convicted of operating a £20m 'pyramid' scheme in which thousands of investors lost money.[21]

Ponzi schemes

A true Ponzi scheme[22] usually promotes what appears to be a real investment opportunity to which investors may contribute. It is essentially a fraudulent investment operation. Investors provide capital to a 'portfolio manager' (the scheme manager), who promises the investors high returns. However, these returns are actually paid to existing investors from new capital paid into the investment scheme by new investors, not from profit earned by the portfolio manager. Of course, to sustain the scheme the continuation of the returns requires an ever-increasing flow of capital from new investors. These new investors are usually enticed into investing by the promise of abnormally high returns. As importantly, these high returns also encourage existing investors to leave their money in the scheme, which results in very little capital outflow from the scheme.[23]

Inevitably, however, it is impossible to sustain the continuing stream of new investors needed to maintain the scheme, so the scheme ultimately collapses and investors lose their investments. For example, in 2009, an American, Bernard Madoff – a former stockbroker, former investment adviser, and former non-executive chairman of the NASDAQ stock market – admitted operating a Ponzi scheme in what is now considered to be the largest financial fraud in US history. On 12 March 2009, Madoff pleaded guilty to 11 federal felonies and admitted having turned his wealth-management business into a Ponzi scheme that defrauded thousands of investors. In total, the amount missing from client accounts, including fabricated gains, was estimated to be almost $65 billion, though this was later revised down to $18 billion. On 29 June 2009, Madoff was sentenced to 150 years in prison – the maximum allowed by US law.

Boiler-room scams (share sale fraud)

A share sale fraud (or a bond fraud, or even a hedge-fund fraud) occurs when fraudsters acting as bogus stockbrokers, usually based overseas, cold-call potential investors and offer worthless, over-priced or even non-existent financial investments. Often operating from so-called 'boiler rooms', the fraudsters will promise potential investors high capital growth and exceptional income yields – all at well above market averages.

Using high-pressure sales tactics and citing spurious research evidence on the financial performance of the financial investments, and perhaps couching these in bogus and often made-up technical jargon, the fraudsters will pressurise potential investors into making a quick, rushed decision that gives them little or no time to consider the true nature of the investment.

'A spectacular deal of the century', 'an investment that just cannot be overlooked' and 'an amazing one-off opportunity' are just a few of the common phrases used by boiler-room fraudsters trying to sell shares, bonds or derivatives in obscure (or unheard of) overseas companies that in all likelihood do not exist. Any investment bought by a potential investor will more than likely turn out to be absolutely valueless.

As with many other fraudulent schemes, the fraudsters may also use mock websites and glossy brochures to provide glowing testimonials to the services they provide.

Affinity fraud

Affinity scams are usually investment-related frauds that target members and associates of a specific identifiable group. The groups could be religious groups, members of ethnic communities, members of language minorities, the elderly, employees of a business, or members of a professional association – any group or association whose members take pride in their commonalities and mutual support.

Affinity scams generally exploit the trust and friendship that exist within such groups, with the fraudster frequently becoming, or at least pretending to become, a member of the group. The fraudster will often convince respected senior members of the group and enlist them to champion the scheme – to spread the word about the scheme, and to convince other members of the group that the (fraudulent) investment is legitimate and worthwhile.

Many affinity frauds involve a Ponzi scheme or a pyramid scheme, in which new investors' money is used to make payments to earlier investors: this not only provides the illusion that the investment is successful and convinces new investors to invest in the scheme, but also reassures existing investors that their investments are safe and secure. The scammers and their collaborators in the fraud almost always steal the money for their personal use; and inevitably as the supply of investors' money dries up, the whole scheme collapses, the sham is exposed, and the investors discover that most or all of their money is gone.

Dating and romance fraud

A romance fraud[24] is a confidence trick,[25] a ruse involving the feigning of romantic intentions towards a person (the victim or target) in order to gain her or his affection, and then to abuse her or his goodwill and trust to commit a fraud. The fraudulent act may involve, for example, gaining access to a person's money, bank account, credit cards, passport or email accounts; or it may involve getting the person to unwittingly commit financial fraud on behalf of the fraudster.

Such frauds are almost invariably online. The scammer (which may often be not a single individual but a criminal group working together) will often post fake profiles on dating websites and social networking websites (such as Facebook), using stolen photographs of attractive people (often models), and asking others to contact them. This is often referred to as 'catfishing'.[26]

Once a person has been lured into the scam, the fraudster will ask him or her to use a more private means of communication, for example a private personal email address, to allow the fraud to be carried out. The fraud will typically involve the fraudster quickly developing a romantic attachment to the victim – they may even fall in love! The communications will become more intimate and the fraudster may even send (fake) intimate photographs of themselves and ask the victim to reciprocate. The fraudster may even ask the victim (particularly if the victim is female) to perform sexual acts in front of a webcam. Once the fraudster is confident that the victim has become emotionally involved and that he or she has the victim's trust, the fraudster will take the opportunity to ask for money and exploit the victim's feelings of embarrassment, shame or fear of exposure if she or he declines the request for money.

There are various ways in which fraudsters may represent their need for money. Here are some common examples:

- they want to visit the victim but need money to pay travel costs, visa costs or passport costs
- they have paid for a plane ticket but this has been stolen and they cannot afford to buy another
- a family member or someone else for whom they are responsible is very ill, and they need money for medical treatment

- they are being held against their will by immigration authorities, who are demanding a bribe for their release which they cannot afford
- they are being held against their will for failure to pay a large bill
- they need the money to pay for the telephone bills in order to continue communicating with the victim
- they need the money to successfully graduate before they can visit the victim.

Note: If the victim has been persuaded to send intimate pictures, or has carried out any sexual acts in front of a webcam, the fraudster may also threaten to send the pictures or recordings to the victim's family, friends or work colleagues if the victim does not accede to their request for money.

Sadly, frauds of this sort are increasingly common. If you believe that you yourself have been a victim a dating or romance fraud, report it to Action Fraud (at www.actionfraud.police.uk), terminate all contact immediately, and report the fraudster to the social network website or chat-room operator. Remember to trust your instincts, protect your money, and guard your privacy ... and *never* send money or give debit card, credit card or charge card details, online account details or access credentials to anyone you do not know in person or do not trust.

Door-to-door scams (bogus tradesmen fraud)

Whilst many honest businesses use legitimate doorstep selling or marketing, door-to-door scams (or bogus tradesmen frauds, or doorstep selling frauds) have become increasingly popular, and involve a fraudster trying to scam a person in their own home after knocking at their door. There are many types of door-to-door frauds, including pressure doorstep selling, the use of unfair contracts, over-priced home maintenance work, and substandard home improvement work.

Such frauds can involve promoting and selling goods or services that are never delivered or are of a very poor quality, or charging and billing for maintenance work or home improvement work that was never agreed to or never undertaken. Invariably they also involve payment in cash, usually before the goods or services have been delivered or the work undertaken.

In addition to the above, other doorstep frauds include counterfeit charity collections, spurious consumer surveys, and utility services maintenance checks or surveys. For these types of scams, the fraudster may seek to gain access to a property in order to steal assets or money.

As a general guide, do not agree to purchase goods or services from doorstep sellers without first checking their identification and confirming their identity.

Also, remember the law of trespass: a tradesperson or seller can be asked to leave your home at any time – if the person refuses, he or she is then trespassing on your property and committing a criminal offence.

Health and medical fraud (including miracle health scams)

There are essentially two types of health and medical frauds: frauds that involve the retail of health-related and medical-related products or services which appear to be a legitimate form of alternative medicine and promise extraordinary results (miracle cures), and frauds that involve the use of fake online pharmacies which offer very cheap conventional drugs and medicines – without prescription.

Website advertisements for such medical products or miracle health cures will often include fake testimonials from apparently satisfied customers, bogus scientific claims about the product's effectiveness, false claims about non-existent clinical tests, and worthless 'money back' guarantees. In reality, it is unlikely that any of the above products will prove medically effective. At the very least, the purchaser will be left out of pocket (sometimes by a considerable sum of money); at the very worst, the purchaser's health and well-being might be irreparably damaged.

Holiday club fraud

Holiday club fraud occurs when you are told that you have won a 'free' holiday, but that to claim your prize you must first attend a presentation (usually at a local five-star hotel) to learn more about the new holiday venture. A slick professional and persuasive presentation, glossy and convincing brochures, together with free champagne and expensive lunches, are all designed to promote an illusion: that those invited to the presentation have a unique 'one-off' opportunity to join an exclusive holiday club offering top-class accommodation all over the world.

Unfortunately, what is said in the presentation and what is then stipulated in the holiday club contract you will be pressurised into signing at the end of the sales pitch are often very different, and it is not until you commit to joining the exclusive holiday club that you discover that your 'free' holiday is not free at all – there are invariably fees to pay for flights, transfers, and other holiday add-ons (for example, additional fees for upgrading accommodation). You may also discover that the holiday destinations advertised in the presentation are neither guaranteed nor available when you want them.

Timeshare fraud

A timeshare is a particular form of property ownership or access, in which different people share rights to the same property, with each sharer allocated a period of time (usually a limited number of weeks, and almost always at the same time every year) in which they may use the property. This kind of arrangement can work well and be beneficial to all concerned.

Timeshare *fraud*, in contrast, occurs when a group of people are persuaded (usually with the promise of an expensive gift) to attend a timeshare presentation at which they are invited (or more accurately pressurised) into buying a share in a property that will allow each of them to use it themselves or to rent it out for a certain number of weeks every year. There will usually be a fee to pay, to cover legal and administrative costs. Sometimes the properties involved do not exist; in other cases they exist but fall well below the standards described in the glossy presentation and sales brochure.

Insurance broker fraud

Insurance broker fraud occurs when a person buys an insurance policy from a fraudster claiming to be an insurance broker. The insurance policy may be related to the person's assets (such as a car or property), the person himself or herself (such as health or travel), the person's earnings (if faced with a critical illness or redundancy), or the person's dependants (a life policy). Insurance broker fraud is often associated with pressurised door-to-door sales, and often to vulnerable elderly people.

Typically, upfront annual fees or premiums must be paid (usually with the offer of a huge discount), and it is not until a claim is made, or the insurance policy is checked, that the fraud is discovered – that the insurance policy is bogus, and the insurance cover paid for is non-existent.

Internet dialler scams

An internet dialler scam occurs when a person's computer settings are changed so that the internet connection is re-routed via an expensive telephone line. This can happen when the person opens a spam email, clicks on a pop-up box or visits a pay-per-view website and unwittingly downloads software that makes this change to their computer.

Land banking scams

Land banking scams occur when small plots of agricultural land are advertised as credible investment opportunities, whether online, via emails, by means of spoof telephone calls, or even at displays at lifestyle or agricultural exhibitions. Often the plots of land are offered close to urban areas where house prices are high, or close to areas of land that have already been allocated for development, and prospective buyers are told that, once planning permission has been granted, the land could be sold to a developer for a substantial profit. In reality, there is often virtually no development potential and little if any profit to be made.

Pension liberation scams

Pension scams can be given a number of labels, including:

- pension loans
- early pension release
- pension selling
- cashing in your pension
- pension liberation.

Pension liberation fraudsters promise to convert a person's pension benefits into cash before she or he reaches the age of 55. Although this is not in itself illegal, there are a number of ways in which fraudsters may seek to exploit the pension liberation process, for example:

- by misrepresenting the tax implications of receiving cash from a pension
- by misrepresenting the full extent of fees to be paid in relation to any onward investment
- by falsely representing any anticipated levels of returns
- by falsely representing anticipated levels of risk.

Pension scammers can use a variety of tricks to entice the unsuspecting. They may offer an upfront cash payment, for example, or a free pension review, or the offer of a so-called one-off investment opportunity.

Never be rushed into making a decision – and remember: savings that may have taken many years to accumulate can be lost in a moment.

A pension scams leaflet, which includes examples of real-life pension scams, is available from the Pensions Advisory Service (see: www.pensionsadvisoryservice.org.uk). In addition, the UK Pensions Regulator (see: www.thepensionsregulator.gov.uk) has produced a range of resources that explore and highlight the consequences of pension liberation schemes.

See also: www.getsafeonline.org/protecting-yourself/pension-liberation-fraud.

Property investment scams

A property investment fraud occurs when people are persuaded to invest in a property development or investment scheme (very often overseas) that ultimately has little or no value.

Unlike other types of frauds, property investment scams are often targeted at specific individuals or groups of individuals (and may also be affinity frauds). The initial contact often starts with a cold-call from a representative of what appears to be a credible property investment company, who offers a 'unique' opportunity with little risk and the possibility of huge future financial gains. The representative will sound very genuine and not in the least bit pushy or harassing, and may even have some personal information about you. The representative will send you glossy brochures about the various property development or investment schemes the company is currently involved in, provide information about past (and very profitable) schemes it has been involved in before, and offer a range of glowing references and 'credible' testimonials from current and past investors. No pressure will be applied. Indeed, the representative may call on a number of occasions, seeking to develop a friendly relationship – a relationship of trust.

Were you to invest in the scheme, you would receive copies of investment agreements, legal deeds, and development contracts – all of which would be worthless. You might also be persuaded to invest further amounts of money. Unfortunately, though, it is all a con: there is no development scheme, there are no huge financial profits to be made, and any monies invested will invariably be lost.

Online shopping and auction fraud

Online shopping and auction fraud rely on the anonymity of the internet. They occur when:

- a buyer does not receive the goods ordered and paid for
- a buyer receives the goods ordered and paid for, but the goods are either less valuable than those advertised or significantly different from the goods described (for example, the goods might be damaged)
- a seller fails to disclose relevant information about a product (for example, health and safety information) or the terms of sale
- a buyer does not pay for goods bought.

Protecting yourself against shopping and auction fraud

When buying online:

- make sure the website's feedback function works (for example, that the feedback received appears valid, and that it is not excessively positive all the time), and be careful when buying things from sellers with little or no selling history
- always check the description of the goods carefully
- beware of people offering deals at prices below the current bid or reserve price
- be aware of phishing emails that appear to come from the online auction or payment site you are registered with
- always check the URL in the web browser
- always read the terms and conditions carefully, including those relating to any dispute resolution procedures offered by the site.

In addition, as a buyer, always use an established online payment facility such as PayPal, and *never* send confidential personal or financial information by email. As a seller, never accept payment by cheque, and do not accept a payment for a higher amount and then refund the difference.

12.10 Reporting a fraud

For urgent fraud matters, for example where an immediate police response is required because a suspect is near or because there is an immediate risk to a victim's well-being due to the scam or fraud, call the police on 999. Where an immediate police response is not required, for example where there is no immediate risk to a victim's well-being, call 101 (or a local police station).

For non-urgent fraud matters,when a suspect is not immediately identifiable and when no one is at immediate risk, use the Action Fraud website, www.actionfraud.police.uk, to report the fraud. Alternatively, if anonymity is required, call Crimestoppers on 0800 555 111 or visit www.crimestoppers-uk.org.

Other useful contacts, for information and advice, include these organisations:

- Citizens Advice Bureaux (CAB): a national charity that provides free, independent and confidential advice. Telephone 08444 111 444 (helpline: 08454 04 05 06). See also: www.adviceguide.org.uk or www.citizensadvice.org.uk.
- Action on Elder Abuse (AEA): a national charity that works to protect vulnerable older adults and to prevent abuse. Telephone: 0208 835 9280; helpline: 0808 808 8141. See also: www.elderabuse.org.uk.
- Age UK: a national charity that provides advice and information for people in later life, through an advice line and various publications. Telephone: 0800 169 6565. See also: www.ageuk.org.uk.
- Think Jessica: a national charity that seeks to protect the elderly and vulnerable people from frauds and scams via the postal system or by telephone. Address: Think Jessica, PO Box 4442, Chesterfield, S44 9AS. See also: www.thinkjessica.com.
- Office of the Public Guardian (OPG): the government agency that is responsible for protecting people who no longer have the capacity to make certain decisions themselves. The OPG:
  - supervises Deputies appointed by the Court of Protection (CoP)
  - registers Enduring Powers of Attorney (EPAs) and Lasting Powers of Attorney (LPAs)
  - maintains a register of Deputies, Enduring Powers of Attorney and Lasting Powers of Attorney
  - investigates allegations of abuse of their roles and powers by Court-appointed Deputies or Attorneys acting under a registered EPA or LPA.
  - Address: Office of the Public Guardian, PO Box 16185, Birmingham B2 2WH. Telephone: 0300 456 0300.

12.11 Concluding comments

The explosion of internet and web-based innovation during the late 20th century and the early 21st century has clearly transformed the way we live our lives. It has changed the way we store personal data and confidential information; it has changed the way we interact socially with each other (using email and other forms of online social media, such as Facebook and Twitter); and it has changed the way we interact economically with each other – the way we buy goods, the way we consume services, the way we pay for the goods and services we buy and consume, and the way we manage our personal finances (including our bank accounts). Unfortunately, this online revolution has come at a heavy price. Not only has it opened up a brave new world of technological interconnectivity – a global virtual network that was once the stuff of science fiction – but it has also, as we have seen, opened up many new opportunities for the dark menace of criminality.

The anonymity offered by the internet and the World Wide Web has been lovingly embraced by today's fraudsters, who are increasingly cyber-connected, online and out there waiting to trap you. Beware of the risks, which are real; but remember also that the single greatest tool available for an individual in combating fraud is ... common sense!

12.12 Suggested further reading

For further reading on the following topics, see the references given.
Dealing with fraud (and up-to-date fraud alerts):
- www.financialfraudaction.org.uk

Protecting yourself and your identity online:
- www.getsafeonline.org/protecting-yourself/safeguarding-identity

Types of fraud:
- www.actionfraud.police.uk

Types of person-related scams:
- Metropolitan Police Service. 'Little book of big scams'. Available at: www.met.police.uk/docs/little_book_scam.pdf

Key points

- The Fraud Act 2006 defines three classes of fraud: fraud by false representation (s.2), fraud by failing to disclose information (s.3), and fraud by abuse of position (s.4).
- Identity theft is the deliberate and fraudulent use of another's identity to obtain goods or services, to gain access to a source of finance or credit, to assign guilt for a crime, to enable illegal immigration, or to facilitate terrorism, espionage, blackmail or extortion.
- ATM-based fraud essentially involves either stealing the physical card or stealing the encoded credentials on the card, whether by skimming, using a hidden camera, using a card trap, or shoulder surfing.
- Card-related fraud can be defined as the use of a stolen payment card or payment card credentials (for a debit card, a credit card or a charge card) to obtain goods or services, or to obtain unauthorised funds from an account.
- False billing is the fraudulent invoicing or requesting of funds from a person for goods or services that do not exist or that were not used or provided (and never will be).
- An advanced-fee fraud usually involves a promise to transfer money into a person's bank account on receipt of confidential details or the payment of an upfront or advance fee.
- A pyramid scheme is an unsustainable business scheme that rewards people for enrolling others into the scheme.

- A Ponzi scheme is usually an investment opportunity to which investors may contribute in return for the promise of high returns.
- An affinity scam is usually an investment-related fraud that targets members or associates of a specific identifiable group.

Case study discussion questions

1. Briefly describe to Anthony Carter the ways in which personal and confidential information about him could be acquired by a fraudster.
2. Advise Anthony Carter on what actions he can take to protect himself against account-related and card-related fraud.

Self-review questions

1. Identify five simple steps a person can take to protect his or her bank account.
2. Explain the key characteristics of the following:
   - o a dead relative scam or inheritance fraud
   - o a competition win scam
   - o a work-from-home scam
   - o a fraud recovery scam
   - o a vehicle-matching scam.
3. What technologies (or countermeasures) are card issuers and retailers using to a minimise card-related fraud?
4. Define *synthetic identity theft.* Briefly explain how an identity thief can obtain personal and confidential information about her or his target victim.
5. Distinguish between a *holiday club scam* and a *timeshare fraud.*

Suggested answers to chapter activities

Activity 1

The main categories of identity theft are:

- Criminal identity theft: that is, using another person's identity when apprehended for a crime (for example, a road traffic offence such as speeding).
- Financial identity theft: that is, using another person's identity to obtain credit, goods or services.
- Identity cloning: that is, using another person's personal information to assume her or his identity in daily life.
- Medical identity theft: that is, using another person's identity to obtain medication or pharmaceuticals.
- Child identity theft: that is, using a child's identity to apply for Government benefits, to open bank accounts, to obtain credit cards or charge cards, to apply for loan finance, or to obtain utility services or rented accommodation.
- Synthetic identify theft: that is, a variation on identity theft in which an identity is completely or partially fabricated, usually using a combination of two or more real identities.

Activity 2

The ways in which a fraudster can steal either a physical card or the encoded credentials on the card include skimming, using a hidden camera, using a card trap, and shoulder surfing.

Activity 3

An advanced-fee fraud is a fraud in which the fraudster offers to transfer money into a person's bank account on receipt of confidential details or the payment of an upfront or advance fee. There are many varieties of advance-fee frauds, the most popular being the dead relative scam or inheritance fraud, the competition win scam, and the current affairs scam. Other advance-fee frauds include the psychic and clairvoyant scam, the work-from-home scam, the loan scam, the fraud recovery scam, the rental scam, the racing tipster scam, and the vehicle-matching scam.

Notes

1. For further types of fraud, see: www.actionfraud.police.uk/types_of_fraud.
2. See 'Man jailed for defrauding pensioner'. Available at: www.actionfraud.police.uk/man-jailed-for-defrauding-pensioner-nov13.
3. A card security code (CSC) is sometimes referred to as the card verification data (CVD), the card verification number (CVN), the card verification value (CVV), the card verification value code (CVVC), the card verification code (CVC), the verification code (V code), the card code verification (CCV), or the signature panel code (SPC).
4. See 'Notice to appear in court email scam'. Available at: www.actionfraud.police.uk/alert-notice-to-appear-in-court-email-scam-feb14.
5. There are many companies that can do this (but bear in mind their reputation and history, and recommendations from people you trust). See, for example: http://www.cleanitukgroup.co.uk/.
6. See: 'Facebook scam that tricks victims into hacking themselves'. Available at: www.actionfraud.police.uk/beware-new-facebook-scam-that-tricks-victims-into-hacking-themselves-jul14.
7. 'Phishing' is the fraudulent acquisition, through deception, of sensitive personal information such as passwords and credit card or finance details by masquerading as someone with a legitimate need for such information, or by using malicious and invasive software to obtain confidential and sensitive information covertly. Phishing is in essence a social engineering attack, using information technology to deceive people into revealing sensitive personal data or confidential information. Whilst historically such attacks were typically carried out through conventional telecommunication channels – for example, telephoning people to attempt to gain illicit access to personal data and confidential information – invariably such attacks are now email-based, text-based, or both.
8. 'Pharming' is the use of an email or website to trick someone into clicking on a link to a scam website in order to obtain confidential information, personal passwords, or financial information.
9. See: www.cifas.org.uk.
10. Whereas some attacks rely on technical methods, 'social engineering' attacks are non-technical methods of intrusion in which hackers rely heavily on human interaction, often in order to trick people into breaking normal security procedures.
11. 'Vishing' is the process of obtaining personal and confidential details and information by telephone – much like phishing, but over the telephone.
12. See: 'Fraudsters trick victims into revealing PIN numbers after theft'. Available at: www.actionfraud.police.uk/fraudsters-trick-victims-into-revealing-pin-numbers-after-theft-apr14.
13. This type of transaction is often referred to as nPOS-EPOS (cardholder not present at point of sale – electronic point of sale).
14. Although telephone card-not-present fraud still occurs, mail-order and online card-not-present frauds are now the major routes for fraud against retailers.
15. The card may have been compromised using a skimming device at an ATM, at a restaurant, or at a shop or retail outlet.
16. See: 'Fraudster named "Fizzy" jailed for £30 million lottery scam'. Available at: www.actionfraud.police.uk/fraudster-named-fizzy-jailed-for-30-million-lottery-scam-Jul14.
17. See: 'Fraudsters convicted for fake online adverts'. Available at: www.actionfraud.police.uk/fraudsters-convicted-for-fake-online-adverts-nov13.

18. Spoofing is a type of scam whereby an intruder attempts to gain unauthorised access to a user's system or information by pretending to *be* the user. The main purpose is to trick the user into releasing sensitive information in order to gain access to the user's bank account or computer system or to steal personal information such as passwords.
19. Hawala banking is a system for remitting money, primarily in Islamic societies, in which a financial obligation between two parties is settled by transferring the money to a third party, as when money owed by a debtor to a creditor is paid by a third person who owes the *debtor* money. Hawala transactions are usually based on trust and leave no written record. (See: www.answers.com/topic/hawala.)
20. Named after Carlo Pietro Giovanni Guglielmo Tebaldo Ponzi (1882–1949), commonly known as Charles Ponzi, who was an Italian businessman and con artist in the US and Canada, and who created the Ponzi scheme.
21. See: 'Pyramid scheme operation sees six women convicted'. Available at: www.bbc.co.uk/news/uk-29250910.
22. See: 'Police seek further victims of Ponzi scam'. Available at: www.actionfraud.police.uk/police-seek-further-victims-of-ponzi-scam-jul14.
23. Withdrawals can also be minimised by offering new plans to existing investors, such as longer-term fixed-period investments for a higher return.
24. See: www.romancescams.org.
25. See: www.independent.co.uk/news/uk/crime/conmen-killed-oil-executive-and-escort-carole-waugh-and-used-her-money-to-buy-gold-bullion-court-told-8874290.html.
26. A 'catfish' is someone who pretends to be someone he or she is not, using Facebook or other social media to create false identities, particularly to pursue deceptive online romances. See www.urbandictionary.com/define.php?term=catfish.

13

Regulation, legislation, and codes of practice

Learning outcomes

By the end of this chapter, you should be able to:

- explain the purpose of regulation
- describe the purposes and roles of the various financial market regulators
- describe relevant provisions of the *Limitation Act 1980* and of s.40 of the *Administration of Justice Act 1970*
- explain the key provisions of the Financial Conduct Authority's *FCA Handbook: Consumer Credit Sourcebook.*

13.1 Introduction

We are all part of an ever-changing world, with a global economy dominated almost exclusively by a growing complexity of financial products and services and by the erratic volatility of a huge web of interrelated financial markets, both in the UK and overseas. Whilst some economists and politicians may still believe in the absolute sanctity of the financial marketplace and its ability to control and self-regulate its own activities, history – for example, the financial crisis and banking crash of 2007/2008 – teaches us a different lesson. In today's ever more complex and ever more interconnected financial marketplace, the regulation and supervision of those providing financial products and services are an absolute imperative in ensuring, protecting and enhancing the stability of the UK financial marketplace, and in maintaining confidence in the products and services sold by financial institutions within the UK.

This chapter considers the key components of the UK legislative and regulatory framework following enactment of the *Financial Services Act 2012*, and the role of this framework in securing the continuing protection of consumers and clients and minimising financial crime.

13.2 Financial products

A 'financial product' can be defined as any facility, arrangement or contract through which an individual (or a group of individuals) can:

– make a financial investment

- manage a financial risk
- obtain credit *and/or*
- receive a means of payment.

Such financial products include bank accounts, investment products (for example, shares, bonds, and Gilts), mortgages, personal loans, credit facilities (including credit card and charge card facilities), insurance policies, and personal pension plans.

13.3 Financial services

'Financial services' are economic services that deal with the buying, selling and management of money and money-based derivatives. Such economic services are provided by a wide range of companies or organisations, including not only banks, credit card companies, building societies, consumer finance companies, direct lenders, credit unions, loan companies, and sub prime lenders (see Chapter 3), but also insurance companies, pension funds, investment funds, brokerage firms, and, of course, independent financial advisers.

13.4 Recent issues in the UK

The liberalisation of UK financial markets during the 1980s (following the *Financial Services Act 1986*, the *Building Society Act 1986*, and the *Banking Act 1987*) and the gradual incursion of new product and service providers during the 1990s (for example, the entry of large retailers such as Tesco's, Sainsbury's and Marks & Spencer into the once impenetrable banking services market) radically changed the financial services market in the UK forever. Since then, a restructuring and opening up of the financial products and services markets has seen not only a growth in competition between providers, and an increased availability of new financial products and new financial services, but also (especially in the last few years) an increase in scandals, controversies, and issues related to the fraudulent mis-selling of financial products and the deceitful provision of financial services. Examples include:

- the mis-selling of personal pension plans
- the fraudulent selling of pension liberation schemes
- the fraudulent selling of equity investments (boiler-room scams)
- the mis-selling of payment protection insurance (PPI)
- the mis-selling of endowment mortgages
- the mis-selling of equity release mortgages
- the mis-selling of tracker mortgages[1]
- the pressurised selling of credit facilities and personal loans
- the rise of payday lending.

Issues such as these have severely affected the faith, trust and confidence of customers and other businesses, not only in the particular financial product and services providers,[2] but also, and perhaps even more importantly, in the organisations that *regulate* financial services and markets. One such was the Financial Services Authority (FSA), established by the *Financial Services and Markets Act 2000*; indeed, it was the perceived regulatory failings of the FSA (especially, but not exclusively, during the financial crisis of 2007/2008) that led the UK Government to conclude that the current financial regulatory system in the UK was not fit for purpose and needed to be restructured – a process that included the abolition of the FSA.

On 19 December 2012, the *Financial Services Act 2012* received royal assent. In abolishing the FSA (with effect from 1 April 2013), the Act divided its regulatory responsibilities between the Financial Conduct Authority (FCA), the Prudential Regulation Authority (PRA), and the Bank of England.

13.5 Regulation and the UK financial marketplace

Regulation is essentially a framework of rules and laws designed to govern behaviour, and is often used to promote trust and confidence in the individuals, companies, organisations being regulated. There are, of course, many different *types* of regulation, including:
- self-regulation, in which an organisation or institution regulates its own activities
- mutual co-regulation, in which a group of related organisations or institutions regulate their own activities
- third-party imposed regulation, in which an organisation or institution is regulated by an external and independent institution or organisation.

They are also many different *forms* of regulation, for example:
- a legal restriction or requirement, imposed by a Government authority to create or limit a right or a duty
- a contractual obligation, imposed by a legally binding agreement to regulate behaviour and allocate responsibility
- a certification or accreditation framework, imposed by an industry or a profession to monitor the qualifications of its members and to enforce the use of agreed procedures and practices.

Within the UK financial marketplace, the financial regulatory system can be described as being:
- imposed (by legislation)
- hierarchical (as it has different levels of regulation) *and*
- pluralistic (as it involves a number of interrelated regulatory bodies).

Regulation generally takes the form of 'regulatory supervision': that is, a selection of rules, laws and codes of practice that govern those involved in the buying and selling of financial products and those involved in the provision and management of financial services. By enforcing minimum requirements, operational restrictions and product-related or service-related guidelines – for example, specific requirements about the disclosure of particular information – these regulations seek to promote uniformity, comparability and transparency within the UK financial marketplace.

In the buying and selling of financial products and services, a regulatory framework is important for three reasons:
- there is often an unequal distribution of knowledge and information between the buyer and the seller (usually known as 'information asymmetry')
- there may be a conflict of interests between those of the principal (the buyer) and the agent (the seller) *and*

- the cost and relative complexity of many financial products and services often means that buyers are unable to learn from experience or from repeat buying.

Following the *Financial Services Act 2012*, the main sector-based regulators and supervisory bodies within the UK are:
- the Financial Conduct Authority
- the Prudential Regulation Authority *and*
- the Competition and Markets Authority.

The Financial Conduct Authority and the Prudential Regulation Authority are in turn regulated by the Bank of England (see Figure 13.1).

In addition to the above, there are two additional bodies worthy of discussion: the Lending Standards Board and the Financial Ombudsman Service.

The Lending Standards Board is responsible for managing and administering the *Lending Code (2011)*, a voluntary code that sets standards of good practice and provides protection for customers and clients of financial institutions. The *Lending Code* applies to all current accounts, card products and services, and personal loans.

The Financial Ombudsman Service was established in 2001 following the *Financial Services and Markets Act 2000*, with the role of helping to settle disputes between consumers and UK-based businesses and institutions that provide financial services, including banks, building societies, insurance companies, investment firms, financial advisers, and finance and loan companies.

We will consider each of the above in more detail later in this chapter. In addition, we will also consider the following:
- the *Limitation Act 1980*
- s.40 of the *Administration of Justice Act 1970*
- aspects of the FCA's *Consumer Credit Sourcebook* (Financial Conduct Authority 2014).

We will also consider their implications for, and relevance and usefulness to, personal finance and personal financial management.

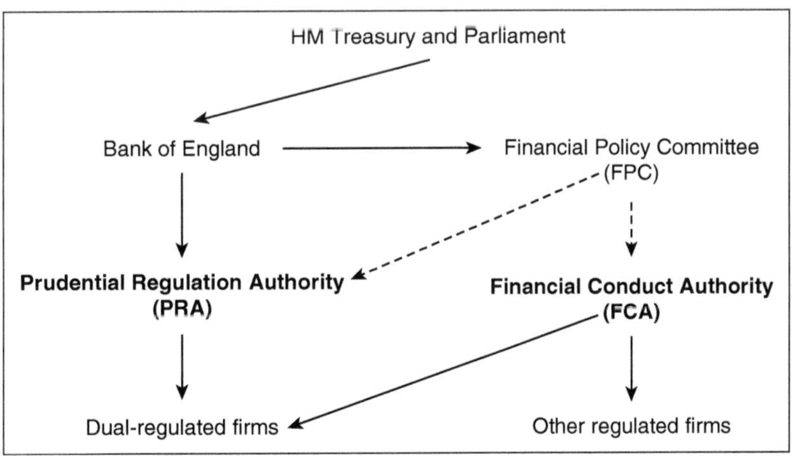

Figure 13.1 Post-2012 regulators

13.6 Independent financial advisers

A financial adviser is a professional adviser who offers clients independent information and advice on financial products and services and who makes recommendations on the suitability and availability of particular financial products and services selected from the whole of the market. Such information and advice can include, for example, investment planning advice, portfolio management, retirement planning, insurance protection, mortgage advice, advice on equity release, and also in some instances tax planning advice.

As shown in Figure 13.2, since January 2013 there have been two types of financial adviser.

Independent financial advisers (IFAs)

An *independent financial adviser* is authorised by the Financial Conduct Authority to offer advice on a range of financial products from the full range of providers in the market. This means that IFAs can make a fair and comprehensive analysis of all suitable financial products available in the market, and that they do so free from any influence that could prevent them from recommending the best financial product.

IFAs can offer advice on a range of stock market investments, life policies, personal pensions, and investment annuities.

Restricted financial advisers

A *restricted financial adviser* is only authorised to advise on a limited range of particular types of financial product, and can only recommend financial products from a limited number of providers. In essence, restricted financial advisers:

- specialise in particular types of financial product *or*
- offer a wider range of financial products, but only recommend financial products from a limited number of providers *or*
- offer a limited number of financial products from a limited number of providers.

Note: Before offering any advice, restricted financial advisers must clearly explain the nature of the restriction imposed upon them. In addition, restricted financial advisers may not describe themselves (or the advice they offer) as independent.

Advice, information only, or guidance?

Where general information about one or more financial products is provided, or where definitions or explanations of financial product terminology are provided, such information is normally referred to as 'guidance' rather than 'advice'. Financial advisers sometimes refer to it as an 'information only' or 'non-advice' service.

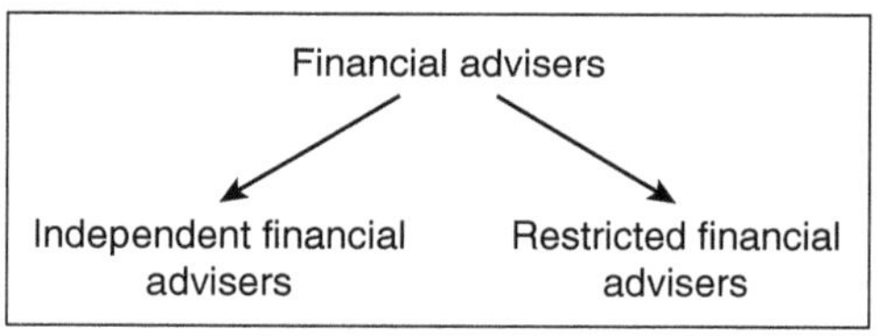

Figure 13.2 Financial advisers since January 2013

The key difference between 'guidance' and 'advice' is that when *guidance* ('information only') is provided, this is done without giving any recommendation regarding the choice of financial product; whereas when *advice* is provided, it is usually accompanied by a recommendation regarding the choice of financial product.

Which is best – independent or restricted?

All financial advisers are authorised and regulated by the Financial Conduct Authority. Whether they are independent or restricted, all financial advisers must hold a minimum qualification (see below), must subscribe to a code of ethics, and must undertake appropriate continuing professional development to maintain up-to-date knowledge of the financial markets and the range of financial products available.

Under FCA guidelines, before recommending any financial product, financial advisers must first undertake a client-based 'fact-finding' assessment to understand the client's financial circumstances, the client's attitude to risk, and the client's financial product requirements or preferences. Consequently, the quality of the advice received about specific products should be the same from both kinds of adviser; but overall, the independent financial adviser should be able to offer a more comprehensive view of the products available and their suitability for a particular client.

Fees

All financial advisers charge a fee. Their fees must be clearly stated and agreed – both the level of fee and the method of payment – in advance of any transaction.

Historically, many financial advisers received commissions from financial product providers, but since 1 January 2013 commission-based remuneration is no longer allowed for investment-related financial products, although financial advisers can still earn commission from the sale of non-investment protection products such as income protection insurance, critical illness insurance and life insurance.

Various fee-based remuneration methods are used, the most common being:

- a percentage fee: an initial percentage charge, and then a continuing annual percentage charge which can range anywhere from 0.5% to 5% *or*
- a fixed-fee per service: a fixed fee charged per visit *or*
- a time-based charge: usually per hour (as with solicitors and accountants); charges can vary, but charges up to £250 per hour are not uncommon.

Authorisation and qualifications

Any person who carries on a regulated activity (including the provision of financial advice) in the UK must be authorised, as must any firm that does so. Indeed, it is a criminal offence to give financial or investment advice without being authorised by the FCA to do so.

To offer financial advice, an individual must be an appointed representative of a firm – usually a partnership or limited liability partnership – registered with the FCA. A register of authorised financial advisers is available at www.fca.org.uk/register.

The FCA also requires that all firms ensure that the individuals who act for them have appropriate qualifications.[3] From 1 January 2013, all financial advisers are required to be qualified[4] at Level 4 or above – equivalent to completing the first year of an undergraduate degree. In addition, all financial advisers are required to obtain an annual Statement of Professional Standing – confirmation that they are suitably qualified, that they subscribe to a code of ethics, and that they actively engage in continuing professional development.

Finally – what if things go wrong?

The provision of financial services in the UK is heavily regulated: if a client purchases a financial product on the advice of an IFA, and that financial product is ultimately deemed by the client to have proved unsuitable, then the client has a right to complain; and, if the complaint is upheld, to receive compensation.

Each regulated financial services company (including IFAs) must possess its own complaint procedure. If a complaint is not dealt with satisfactorily using the company's own procedure, then the client has the option of referring the complaint to the Financial Ombudsman Service, which can conduct an independent investigation and which has the power (if necessary and warranted) to award compensation.

13.7 The Financial Conduct Authority (FCA)

On 19 December 2012, the *Financial Services Act 2012* received its royal assent, and the Financial Services Authority (FSA) as of 1 April 2013 was abolished. The FSA's responsibilities were divided between the Financial Conduct Authority (FCA), the Prudential Regulation Authority (PRA), and the Bank of England.

The FCA is a company limited by guarantee. Its strategic responsibility (following the *Financial Services Act 2012*) is to ensure that the relevant markets function well, with its main role being to monitor and regulate authorised financial services providers, both retail and wholesale, and to ensure that they comply with all the extant regulatory requirements. The FCA is responsible for regulating over 50,000 firms and organisations.[5] Detailed provisions of the FCA handbook, which apply to all FCA-regulated businesses, are available at: https://www.handbook.fca.org.uk/.

Statutory objectives and enforcement powers

The statutory objectives of the FCA (Financial Conduct Authority 2015) are:
- to secure an appropriate degree of protection for consumers
- to protect and enhance the integrity of the UK financial system *and*
- to promote effective competition in the interests of consumers.

To achieve its statutory objectives, the FCA possesses substantial rule-making and investigative powers, together with a wide range of enforcement powers – criminal, civil and regulatory – which can be used to protect consumers and to take action against firms, other organisations and individuals that do not meet FCA standards. These include:
- withdrawing authorisation to provide regulated financial services
- prohibiting or suspending firms, organisations or individuals from undertaking regulated activities
- fining firms, organisations or individuals who breach FCA rules
- fining firms, organisations or individuals who commit market abuse
- applying to the Court for injunctions and restitution orders *and*
- instigating criminal prosecutions to minimise financial crime (for example, insider-dealing or unauthorised business activities).

To ensure transparency and to maximise the deterrent effect of enforcement action, the FCA publishes information about its activities: warning notices, when it proposes to take action; decision notices, when it has decided to take action; and final notices, when it does take action. In addition, the FCA publishes lists and alerts about firms, organisations and individuals that provide financial services, including those based overseas and those in the UK operating without FCA authorisation.

On 1 April 2014, the FCA assumed responsibility for the regulation of consumer credit, which was formerly overseen by the Office of Fair Trading (OFT). All regulated companies, firms, organisations and individuals are now required to comply with the FCA's *Consumer Credit Sourcebook* (Financial Conduct Authority 2014).

Funding

The FCA is funded by the financial services firms that it regulates, through fees[6] charged to authorised firms and organisations, and is accountable to HM Treasury and to Parliament. The FCA's general powers to raise fees are set out in the *Financial Services and Markets Act 2012* (paragraph 23 of Part 3 of Schedule 1ZA).

As well as collecting its own FCA fees, the FCA also invoices on behalf of the Prudential Regulation Authority (PRA), the Financial Services Compensation Scheme (FSCS), the Financial Ombudsman Service (FOS), the Money Advice Service (MAS), and the Financial Reporting Council (FRC).

13.8 The Prudential Regulation Authority (PRA)

The Prudential Regulation Authority (PRA) is a UK-based financial services regulatory body and was created by the *Financial Services Act 2012.* A limited company, the PRA is wholly owned by the Bank of England and is one of the successors to the Financial Services Authority (FSA), abolished in 2013. The PRA is responsible for the prudential regulation and supervision of banks, building societies, credit unions, insurers and major investment firms.[7]

The PRA's primary role is to promote the safety and soundness of such companies and organisations; and, specifically for insurers, to contribute to the securing of an appropriate degree of protection for policyholders. As a secondary (albeit subservient) objective, the PRA is also responsible for pro-actively ensuring and facilitating competition within the marketplace.

The PRA works alongside the Financial Conduct Authority, and (as of late 2015), the PRA regulates approximately 1,700 financial firms (Bank of England 2015c).

The PRA Rulebook (Prudential Regulation Authority 2015) contains provisions that all PRA-regulated business must follow.

Regulation and supervision

The PRA achieves its objectives through regulation and supervision – that is, by setting standards or policies that companies, organisations and firms must adhere to, and by assessing the risks firms may pose to the PRA's primary objectives. Where necessary, it can take appropriate action to reduce or eliminate such risks.

The PRA's approach to regulation and supervision has three characteristics (Bank of England 2015a).

First, it is judgement-based: that is, the PRA uses judgement in determining whether:

- financial organisations are safe and sound
- insurers provide appropriate protection for policyholders
- organisations continue to meet the accepted threshold conditions.

Second, it is forward-looking: that is, the PRA assesses organisations not only against current risks, but also against risks that could arise in the future.

Third, it is focused: that is, the PRA focuses primarily on those issues and organisations that pose the greatest risk to the stability of the UK financial system and policyholders.

Note: The PRA Rulebook contains rules and directions made by the PRA and applies to all PRA-authorised organisations and firms. The PRA Rulebook is available at: http://www.prarulebook.co.uk/.

Funding of the Prudential Regulation Authority

To fulfil its statutory objectives, the *Financial Services and Markets Act 2000,* as amended by the *Financial Services Act 2012,* empowers the Prudential Regulation Authority (PRA) to raise fees (Bank of England 2015b).

The PRA regulates six categories or 'fee blocks' of incorporated businesses (organisations) and unincorporated businesses (firms): deposit acceptors, general insurers, life insurers, managing agents at Lloyd's, the Society of Lloyd's, and organisations or firms dealing as principal. The amount payable by members of each fee block depends on the total budgeted cost of regulating that category of organisation or firm, with the fee payable by an individual organisation or firm within each category dependent upon the size of that organisation's or firm's business.[8]

> **Activity 1**
>
> In the regulation of financial products and financial services providers, what are the main roles and responsibilities of the *Financial Conduct Authority* (FCA) and the *Prudential Regulation Authority* (PRA)?

13.9 The Competition and Markets Authority (CMA)

The Competition and Markets Authority (CMA) is a non-ministerial Government department and is responsible for strengthening business competition and minimising anti-competitive activities.

Provisionally launched in October 2013, the Competition and Markets Authority began operating fully on 1 April 2014, when it assumed many of the functions of two previous bodies, the Competition Commission and the Office of Fair Trading, both of which were abolished. In essence, the Competition and Markets Authority is responsible for making markets work well for consumers, and offers guidance on issues related to the *Competition Act 1998,* unfair practices, and consumer protection. In situations where competition could be restricted or consumer choice affected, the primary roles and responsibilities of the Competition and Markets Authority are:

- to investigate mergers and acquisitions
- to undertake market studies
- to investigate possible breaches of prohibitions against anti-competitive agreements
- to initiate criminal proceedings against individuals who commit 'cartel' offences[9]

- to enforce consumer protection legislation
- to encourage regulators to use their competition powers
- to consider regulatory references and appeals.

13.10 The Lending Standards Board and the *Lending Code*

In November 2009, the Lending Standards Board replaced the Banking Code Standards Board. The Lending Standards Board is responsible for managing and administering the *Lending Code (2011)*, a voluntary code which sets standards of good practice and which provides protection for customers and clients of financial institutions. The *Lending Code* applies to all current accounts, card products and services, and personal loans.

The Lending Standards Board has three key objectives:

- to assist firms in interpreting the *Lending Code* and in meeting its requirements
- to monitor compliance with the *Lending Code* and to take enforcement action for material breaches
- to identify any gaps and deficiencies in the *Lending Code* that could be to the detriment of consumers, and as appropriate to advocate change.

The Lending Standards Board maintains close contact with both the Financial Conduct Authority (FCA), with which it shares a Memorandum of Understanding, and the Financial Ombudsman Service, with which it shares an agreed Statement of Roles and Responsibilities.

The Board is managed by an executive board of directors, consisting of three public interest directors, an independent chairman, the executive directors of the three sponsoring trade bodies, and the chief executive of the Lending Standards Board.

The Lending Code

The *Lending Code* (Lending Standards Board 2014) provides standards of good lending practice in relation to loans, credit cards, and current account overdrafts. The *Lending Code* does not apply to non-business borrowing secured on land, nor to sales finance. In addition, the *Lending Code* offers protection only to individual consumers, to micro-enterprises,[10] and to charities with annual incomes of less than £1 million.

The *Lending Code* contains key commitments and detailed guidance on customer management throughout the whole product life cycle: that is, from services and account marketing, through customer acquisition and account opening, through account maintenance, through the provision of information on charges, terms and conditions, and interest rates, to guidance on how to deal with customers who experience financial difficulties.

A list of institutions and organisations that subscribe to the *Lending Code* is available (Lending Standards Board 2015b).

Monitoring and enforcement

As the successor body to the Banking Code Standards Board, the Lending Standards Board is an independent not-for-profit company that monitors compliance with, and enforces the provisions of, the *Lending Code*. The monitoring and enforcement activity includes pre-registration reviews, themed reviews, investigations, compliance reviews, and enforcement action.

Pre-registration reviews

The Lending Standards Board undertakes pre-registration reviews of all firms and organisations that apply to join the *Lending Code* regime. This pre-registration review will normally involve reviewing systems documentation, marketing material, internal systems and controls, and management practices; and the review will include all locations, including branches and where necessary call centres.

Themed reviews

Themed reviews involve the examination of a particular aspect of the *Lending Code* across a range of different *Code* subscribers. Such reviews can include, for example:

- credit assessments and financial difficulties
- the use of the right of 'set-off'[11]
- the handling of unauthorised credit card transactions.

Summary details of all themed reviews undertaken are published by the Lending Standards Boards (2015a).

Investigations

From time to time the Lending Standards Board receives information concerning potential breaches of the *Lending Code* by organisations or firms that subscribe to the *Code*. Such information may come from the Board's own monitoring activities, from other regulators, from consumer or debt-advice bodies, from the media, or from individual consumers. Depending on the severity of the breaches and the potential detrimental impact on past, present or future consumers, the Board can undertake specific investigations to determine the validity of the information and to identify any actions that should be taken.

Compliance reviews

Each *Lending Code* subscriber must complete an Annual Statement of Compliance (ASC), identifying and highlighting any breaches of the *Code* that have been identified by its own review. Where issues or breaches have been identified, a remedial action plan and an implementation strategy must be agreed with the Lending Standards Board.

Enforcement action

Where, because of material breaches of the *Lending Code*, enforcement action is deemed necessary, the Lending Standards Board can:

- issue directions as to the future conduct of the organisation or firm
- issue a warning or reprimand to the organisation or firm
- publish details of the material breach *and/or*
- cancel or suspend the organisation's or firm's registration.

13.11 The Financial Ombudsman Service (FOS)

The Financial Ombudsman Service (FOS) was established in 2001, as a result of the *Financial Services and Markets Act 2000*, to help settle disputes between consumers and UK-based businesses that provide financial services, including banks, building societies, insurance companies, investment firms, financial advisers, and finance companies.

The Financial Ombudsman Service provides a statutory dispute-resolution scheme, set up under the provisions of Part XVI and Schedule 17 of the *Financial Services and Markets Act 2000* (as amended), and can deal with complaints from consumers about most financial matters. These include, for example, payment protection insurance (PPI), banking, insurance, mortgages, credit cards and store cards, loans and credit, payday lending and debt collecting, pensions, savings and investments, hire purchase and pawnbroking, money transfers, financial advice, and shares, unit trusts and bonds.

Referring a dispute to the Financial Ombudsman Service

Before the Financial Ombudsman Service can intervene in a dispute and make a decision, a consumer must first give the company, organisation or individual with whom she or he is unhappy (for example, a bank, an insurance company, or a financial adviser) an opportunity to investigate the complaint. The company, organisation or individual has a *maximum* of 8 weeks to resolve the complaint. If the complaint is not resolved within 8 weeks or if the consumer is not happy with the response they have received by the end of 8 weeks, they can refer the complaint to the FOS.

The FOS will make a decision on the basis of what it judges to be fair and reasonable (given the particular circumstances of the complaint), taking into account relevant law, rules and regulations, guidance and standards, codes of practice, and (where appropriate) good industry practice.

An ombudsman's decision is the final stage of the FOS's process. If the consumer with the complaint accepts this final decision, the decision is binding on both parties and enforceable in court. If, however, the consumer chooses *not* to accept the ombudsman's decision, her or his legal rights remain unaffected and she or he can take the matter to court instead (subject to any requirements set by the courts).

Funding: levies and case fees

The FOS receives no Government funding: its service is wholly funded by levies and by case fees from the businesses covered by its work. All levies and case fees must be paid, by law.

Note: Consumers do not need to pay to bring a complaint to the FOS.

General levy

All companies, organisations and individuals covered by the Financial Ombudsman Service pay a general levy. The Financial Conduct Authority (FCA) collects the levy at the same time as it collects both its own regulatory fees and the levy for the Financial Services Compensation Scheme (FSCS). As of 2015, the general levy paid by each FCA-regulated business ranges from £100 p.a. for a small firm of financial advisers to over £300,000 p.a. for a high street bank or a major insurance company.

Case fees

Businesses covered by the FOS must also pay an individual case fee if the FOS deals with a complaint about them. All businesses are entitled to 25 *free* cases – that is, the FOS does not charge a case fee for the first 25 cases in a year, but charges £550 for the 26th and each subsequent case.[12] A fee becomes chargeable when the FOS consumer helpline passes a complaint to an adjudicator for further investigation.[13]

Note: The case fee is not payable until the complaint is resolved.

In April 2013, FOS introduced a group-account fee for the largest banking groups.

The Board of the Financial Ombudsman Service

The Board of the FOS is appointed by the Financial Conduct Authority, with the appointment of the chairman being approved by HM Treasury. The Board members are 'non-executive' members and have no involvement in individual complaints. They act as 'public interest' directors to ensure that the FOS is properly resourced and is able to carry out its work effectively and independently, and they guard the independence of the Service from undue influence by the financial services industry, trade bodies, regulators, consumer groups, or the Government.

Activity 2

Briefly explain how the Financial Ombudsman Service is funded. What types of fees may the Service impose?

13.12 The Financial Services Compensation Scheme (FSCS)

Funded by a mandatory levy on the financial services industry, the Financial Services Compensation Scheme (FSCS) is the UK's compensation fund for customers and clients of financial services companies, firms and institutions authorised and regulated by the Financial Conduct Authority (FCA) or by the Prudential Regulation Authority (PRA). In addition, European companies, firms or institutions that operate in the UK, while authorised by their home country's regulator, may also be covered. The FSCS does not, however, cover the Channel Islands or the Isle of Man.

The FSCS was created by the *Financial Services and Markets Act 2000* and became operational on 1 December 2001. It pays compensation if an authorised company, firm or institution is unable to pay claims against it because it has stopped trading or has been declared in default. (Authorised companies, firms and institutions that are *still* trading are covered by the Financial Ombudsman Service.) The FSCS protects deposits, insurance policies, insurance broking (including travel insurance, if the policy was sold alongside a holiday or other related travel), investment business, and home finance.

Because the FSCS is a fund of last resort, there are limits to the amount of compensation it can and will pay. The FSCS only pays compensation for financial loss, with the actual level of compensation dependent upon the nature and basis of the claim. The maximum levels of compensation paid by the FSCS are:

- £75,000 for deposits
- £50,000 for investments
- £50,000 for home finance (for example, mortgage advice and arranging)
- an unlimited amount for insurance.

The FSCS does not charge individual consumers for the use of its service.

For further information, see the FSCS website (Financial Services Compensation Scheme 2015).

13.13 Other relevant regulations, legislation, and codes of practice

Statute-barred debts and the provisions of the *Limitation Act 1980*

The purpose of a limitation period is to place a time limit on the period within which a creditor or a lender can commence legal proceedings or give notice of a claim. Imposed by the *Limitation Act 1980*, different limitation periods exist for different types of contractual obligations. (Limitation periods may be varied or excluded by agreement.) Once a limitation period has expired, any claim becomes statute-barred – that is, it is no longer possible for a creditor or lender to effect recovery of the outstanding debt.

The *Limitation Act 1980* provides the following:

- for a contract (for example, unsecured debt): within 6 years of the breach of contract[14] *and*
- for a contract or deed under seal (for example, a secured debt such as a mortgage): within 12 years of the breach of contract or deed.

Unsecured debt

Unsecured credit debts include those relating to credit cards, store cards, bank and building society personal loans, shopping catalogues, and finance company loans. The time limit for an action founded on simple contract is 6 years (s.5 of the *Limitation Act 1980*). Where an unsecured credit debt has been outstanding for more than 6 years, and provided that

- the creditor has not already obtained a County Court Judgment against the debtor
- the debtor has not made a payment on the debt during the last 6 years *and*
- the debtor has not written to the creditor admitting that she or he owes the debt outstanding during the last 6 years

then the debt becomes 'statute barred' and the creditor can no longer legally pursue the debt.

Where a debt is in dispute, then, under the *Data Protection Act 1998*, a debtor is entitled to have access to (that is, receive copies of) any files the creditor may possess containing the details and history of the debtor's account. *Note:* A request for such information does not constitute acceptance of the validity of the claim or an admission of liability to pay such a debt.

However, if a creditor can prove that a debtor wrote to the creditor admitting and accepting the debt, or if the debtor (or associate debtors for a debt in joint names) made a payment, then the 6 years' limitation period would run from the date on which the debtor last made a payment.

Secured debt

The time limit for an action 'upon a specialty' – for example, a deed – is 12 years. A mortgage deed made under seal is a specialty; but there are special provisions applying to mortgages in s.20 of the *Limitation Act 1980*:

- 'no action shall be brought to recover any principal sum of money secured by a mortgage or other charge on property (whether real or personal) ... after the expiration of 12 years from the date on which the right to receive the money accrued, and subject to s.20(6) and s.20(7)' (*Limitation Act 1980*, s.20(1))
- 'no action to recover arrears of interest payable in respect of any sum of money secured by a mortgage or other charge or payable in respect of proceeds of the sale of the land, or to recover damages in respect of such arrears, shall be brought after the expiration of 6 years from the date on which the interest became due' (*Limitation Act 1980*, s.20(5)).

This means that the period of limitation for recovering the principal sum advanced under a mortgage by deed is 12 years, even if the property is repossessed and sold by the mortgagee.

County Court Judgments

If the creditor has been to court and there is a County Court Judgment outstanding relating to the debt, then the *Limitation Act* cannot be used to dispute an outstanding debt. It does not matter how many years ago the creditor went to court: the County Court Judgment will still exist.

However, the creditor may not be able to enforce the Judgment without the court's permission if the Judgment is more than 6 years old. If a creditor seeks a County Court Judgment against a debtor after the debt is out of the 6-year limitation period, then the debtor can ask the court to 'set aside' or *remove* the County Court Judgment so that the debtor can use the *Limitation Act* as a defence.

It is also important to note that although the debt may be unenforceable, it is nonetheless still a legal debt, and non-payment is likely to result in details being recorded on the debtor's credit reference file.

Income Tax, VAT, and debts to the Crown

There is *no* limitation period on debts to the Crown. A debtor can always be pursued for debts related to direct taxes such as Income Tax, Capital Gains Tax and Inheritance Tax, and to indirect taxes such as VAT.

Statute-barred debts and the FCA's Consumer Credit Sourcebook

The FCA's *Consumer Credit Sourcebook* (Financial Conduct Authority 2014) provides that a firm or organisation must not attempt to recover a statute-barred debt in England, Wales or Northern Ireland if the creditor or lender (or owner of the asset) has not been in contact with the customer during the limitation period (ibid. 7.15.4).

The *Consumer Credit Sourcebook* provides that the following practices are considered unfair or improper when dealing with statute-barred debts:

- asking a debtor to pay, even after the debtor has not been contacted by the creditor during the limitation period
- advising a debtor that the creditor may take the debtor to court when the creditor is aware that the limitation period has expired
- pressurising a debtor for payment when the debtor has advised the creditor that she or he will not pay the debt because the limitation period has expired.

Harassment and the *Administration of Justice Act 1970*

'Harassment' can be defined as any course of action or behaviour directed at a specific person (for example, a debtor) that is intended to cause alarm, annoyance, or substantial emotional distress. Harassment may involve single, sporadic, or continual acts of intimidation, coercion, bullying, or verbal or physical abuse.

The harassment of people in debt by creditors or lenders, or by their representatives or agents, is a criminal offence under the *Administration of Justice Act 1970,* with s.40(1) providing that creditors and lenders, or their representatives or agents, commit an offence if, with the object of coercing another person to pay money claimed as a debt and due under a contract, they:

- 'harasses the other with demands for payment which, in respect of their frequency or the manner or occasion of making any such demand, or of any threat of publicity by

which any demand is accompanied, are calculated to subject him or members of his family or household to alarm, distress or humiliation' (*Limitation Act 1980*, s.40(1)(a))
- 'falsely represents, in relation to the money claimed, that criminal proceedings lie for failure to pay it' (*Limitation Act 1980*, s.40(1)(b))
- 'falsely represents himself to be authorised in some official capacity to claim or enforce payment' (*Limitation Act 1980*, s.40(1)(c)) *or*
- 'utters a document falsely represented by him to have some official character or purporting to have some official character which he knows it has not' (*Limitation Act 1980*, s.40(1)(d)).

Note: S.40(1)(a) above does not apply to any reasonable and legal actions taken by creditors or lenders (or by their representatives or agents) in seeking satisfaction of actual or supposed debts, or in protecting themselves from future losses.

Harassment and the FCA's *Consumer Credit Sourcebook*

The FCA's *Consumer Credit Sourcebook* (Financial Conduct Authority 2014), provides details of the kinds of activities and behaviour considered to be an unfair or improper business practice. The *Consumer Credit Sourcebook* rules and guidance provide that creditors and lenders, and their representatives or agents, should:
- treat debtors fairly
- provide clear details about what they are doing *and*
- give debtors a 'reasonable' time to repay their debts.

Unfair or improper business practices

The FCA's *Consumer Credit Sourcebook* also provides that it is unfair to communicate with consumers, by whatever means, in an unclear, inaccurate or misleading manner (Financial Conduct Authority 2014: Principle 7). The following practices are therefore unacceptable:
- sending letters that look like court claims
- failing to make clear who the company is or what its role is
- using unhelpful legal language
- failing to give balance statements about the debt when asked
- contacting debtors at unreasonable times, even when asked not to do so
- asking a debtor to contact the creditor using premium-rate phone numbers.

False representation of authority

The FCA's *Consumer Credit Sourcebook* also provides that those contacting debtors must not be deceitful – they must not misrepresent their authority or their legal position with regard to the debt or the debt recovery process (Financial Conduct Authority 2014: 7.11.1). Examples of such misrepresentation include:
- falsely claiming they work for the court or are bailiffs
- implying that action can be taken that is not legally possible (such as implying that they could take personal property, enter premises, or enforce a judgment, even though they do not in fact have the appropriate authority to do so)
- using a business name or logo that implies they represent a Government body
- implying that court action has been taken against the debtor when it has not
- implying that not paying a debt is a criminal offence
- threatening to take court action in England if the debtor lives in Scotland, or the other way round.

Physical or psychological harassment

The FCA's *Consumer Credit Sourcebook* (2014) provides that a creditor or lender must not pressurise a debtor (Financial Conduct Authority 2014: 7.3.10):

- to pay a debt in one single repayment or very few repayments
- to pay a debt in unreasonably large amounts, when to do so would have an adverse impact on the debtor's financial circumstances
- to pay a debt within an unreasonably short period of time *or*
- to raise funds to repay the debt by selling the debtor's property or borrowing money (including increasing existing borrowing).

Creditors and lenders may therefore not behave in these ways:

- contacting a debtor too frequently or at unreasonable times
- pressurising a debtor to sell property or take out more debt
- using more than one collection company, or failing to tell the debtor when the debt has been passed to another company
- pressurising a debtor to pay in full or in large instalments they cannot afford
- making threatening gestures or statements
- ignoring disputes about whether the debtor owes the money
- trying to embarrass the debtor in public
- failing to give a debtor reasonable time to seek advice or provide a payment proposal
- refusing a reasonable offer of payment from a debtor or their adviser
- continuing to pursue the debt when it is clear the debtor might have mental health problems or be unable to deal with her or his debts at that time.

Activity 3

Solicitors representing Mr Woodley have recently written to GC Services Ltd to complain about the actions of an agent working on behalf of the company.

The solicitors claim that the agent's actions amount to harassment and have cited 15 instances over a period of two weeks when the agent has contacted their client, Mr Woodley, in many instances at unreasonable times. On four separate occasions the agent has attempted to gain access to Mr Woodley's home without any appropriate authority.

Mr Woodley is 62 years old and a retired university lecturer. He lives in a small village, 10 miles north of York. His outstanding debt is £15,925. The original debt dates back to December 2011.

Do the actions of the agent working on behalf of GC Services Ltd constitute harassment?

Deceptive and unfair methods

The FCA's *Consumer Credit Sourcebook* (2014) provides that creditors and lenders, and their representatives or agents, must conduct their business with integrity – that is, dealings with debtors must not be deceitful (Financial Conduct Authority 2014: Principle 1). For example, they must not:

- send letters addressed to 'The occupier' or discuss a debt with someone without knowing whether that person is the debtor
- refuse to deal with or communicate with an adviser authorised to act on behalf of a debtor
- inappropriately pass a debtor's details to a debt management company
- refuse to accept a reasonable offer or to pass on payments made by the debtor
- try to enforce a debt when a debtor is in a debt-payment scheme (such as a Debt Relief Order or an individual voluntary arrangement)
- refuse to freeze action or fail to investigate a legitimately disputed debt *or*
- try to take larger or more frequent payments than agreed from a debtor's account (using a continuous payment authority).

Charging for debt recovery

The FCA's *Consumer Credit Sourcebook* provides that creditors, lenders and their representatives must not claim the costs of recovering a debt from a customer if they have no contractual right to claim such costs (Financial Conduct Authority 2014: 7.7.2). For example, they may not:

- claim collection costs when the original credit agreement did not allow this liability, or make the debtor think that she or he is legally liable for such costs
- seek to collect amounts added for collection costs, unless those amounts were specified in the original credit agreement *or*
- add unreasonable charges.

Debt collection visits

The FCA's *Consumer Credit Sourcebook* (2014) provides that creditors, lenders and their representatives must ensure that no person visiting a debtor's property on their behalf acts in an unclear or a threatening manner towards a debtor or the debtor's representative (see Financial Conduct Authority 2014: 7.9.14).

Examples of 'an unclear or a threatening manner' would include:

- failing to explain the reason for any visit
- failing to provide the debtor with advance notice of the time and date of the visit
- visiting a debtor when the debtor is ill or vulnerable
- entering premises without permission, or failing to leave the debtor's premises when asked by the debtor to do so
- visiting a debtor at work or in hospital.

Harassment from creditors – what can debtors do?

Unless there is also a more serious offence involved – such as violence, fraud or blackmail – it can be difficult to establish a case of harassment. Despite this, there are other actions you could take as a debtor if you believed you were being unfairly harassed. First, you should keep a detailed record of phone calls, letters, and visits received. Then you could take one of these steps, for example:

- You could write to the creditor or lender (or their representative or agent) outlining your concerns about the behaviour of the creditor, the lender, or their representative or agent.

- You could inform the creditor or lender (or their representative or agent) how you would prefer to be contacted, and ask that they confirm their agreement in writing.
- You could use a telephone call-blocking service to prevent nuisance calls.
- If the harassment relates to an unregistered or unlicensed moneylender, you could use the 'Report a loan shark hotline' (GOV.UK 2015).
- You could seek advice from the Citizens Advice Bureau consumer service or complain to your local Trading Standards office. Local Trading Standards offices have the power to take enforcement action against creditors or lenders if they contravene the provisions of the *Consumer Protection from Unfair Trading Regulations 2008*, for example by using 'aggressive commercial practices'.[15]
- You could complain (where applicable) to the creditor's or lender's trade association. Whilst a trade association's code of practice is not legally enforceable, such associations may take action against their members to prevent adverse publicity.
- You could complain to the Financial Ombudsman Service (FOS) about the behaviour of the creditor or lender (or their representative or agent). However, you would need first to have complained to the creditor or lender (or to their representative or agent) and given them an opportunity to address your concerns. If necessary, the FOS could order the creditor or lender (or their representative or agent) to correct their behaviour and could even order them to pay compensation.
- You could contact the Financial Conduct Authority (FCA) using their Consumer Helpline. Although the FCA will not address individual complaints, it will collect and collate information about complaints made, which can later be used to take action against creditors or lenders (or their representatives or agents). The FCA can, for example:
  - withdraw a company's, a firm's or an organisation's authorisation
  - prohibit an individual from working in financial services
  - suspend a company, firm or organisation for up to 12 months
  - publicise what offence a company, firm or organisation has committed *and/or*
  - impose a financial penalty.

Finally, in very serious cases of harassment or illegal behaviour, as a last resort the debtor could pursue a legal option, but this could involve considerable cost. Legal action could possibly be taken using the following laws.

Malicious Communications Act 1988

The *Malicious Communications Act 1988* deals with sending letters or articles for the purpose of causing 'distress or anxiety'. To substantiate the successful prosecution of a creditor or lender (or their representative or agent), the letter or article sent would need to contain a message that is indecent or grossly offensive, a threat, or information that is known or believed by the sender to be false. On conviction, a creditor or lender (or their representative or agent) could be fined up to £5,000 and imprisoned for up to 6 months.

Communications Act 2003

In s.127(1), the *Communications Act 2003* makes it an offence to make improper use of a public electronic communications network, with 'improper use' defined as the sending of a message or other matter that is 'grossly offensive or of an indecent, obscene or menacing character'. In s.127(2), the same Act makes it an offence to send messages 'for the purpose of causing annoyance, inconvenience, or needless anxiety to another'. This applies to messages sent by email, as well as by other forms of communication.

On conviction, a creditor or lender (or their representative or agent) can be fined up to £5,000 and imprisoned for up to 6 months.

Activity 4

In January 2015 Mr Armitage had building work carried out on his home by Redland Builders Ltd, for which he did not pay. The debt has recently been placed in the hands of Allen House Ltd, a debt collection agency, which has written to Mr Armitage. This letter is reproduced below:

> Dear Mr Armitage
>
> We have been instructed by Redland Builders Ltd to recover from you the sum of £4,567.50. You have failed to pay the above sum despite numerous requests.
>
> Unless you contact this office and arrange full and immediate payment of the amount due, we will be left with no alternative but to instruct our representatives to visit your address and seize personal assets sufficient to discharge the outstanding debt and associated costs that have been incurred by the company in the collection of this debt.
>
> We will make visits to your home and work address at times of our choosing until payment is made. This may cause embarrassment to yourself and your family.
>
> Yours sincerely
>
> Allen House Ltd.

Which of the actions threatened by Allen House Ltd constitute harassment?

Criminal Justice and Public Order Act 1994

S.4(a) of the *Criminal Justice and Public Order Act 1994* makes it a criminal offence to deliberately cause harassment, alarm or distress by using threatening, abusive or insulting words or behaviour.

Note: This behaviour can be an offence only if it happens in a public place, and the Crown Prosecution Service would have to decide whether or not to prosecute this offence.

Protection from Harassment Act 1997

The *Protection from Harassment Act 1997* makes it a criminal offence to harass an individual or to put a person in fear of violence. Such harassment would need to have occurred on at least two separate occasions. Again, the Crown Prosecution Service would have to decide whether or not to prosecute this offence.

13.14 Concluding comments

There is now a wide range of legislative pronouncements, regulatory codes of practice and established regulatory bodies and advisory agencies. However, the effectiveness (or otherwise) of the newly established regulatory system in the UK – in securing protection for consumers, enhancing the integrity of the UK financial markets, promoting effective competition, and ensuring the safety and soundness of financial products and services providers – will become evident only over the next few years.

13.15 Suggested further reading

For further reading on the following topics, see the references given.
Competition and Markets Authority:
- www.gov.uk/government/organisations/competition-and-markets-authority

Data Protection Act 1998:
- http://ico.org.uk/for_organisations/data_protection/~/media/documents/library/Data_Protection/Practical_application/the_guide_to_data_protection.pdf

Financial Conduct Authority:
- www.fca.org.uk

Financial Ombudsman:
- www.financial-ombudsman.org.uk

Lending Standards Board:
- www.lendingstandardsboard.org.uk

Prudential Regulation Authority:
- http://www.bankofengland.co.uk/pra/Pages/default.aspx

Key points

- The Financial Conduct Authority is responsible for ensuring that relevant markets function well. Its main role is to monitor and regulate authorised financial services providers.
- The Prudential Regulation Authority is responsible for the prudential regulation and supervision of banks, building societies, credit unions, insurers and major investment firms.
- The Competition and Markets Authority is responsible for strengthening business competition and for preventing anti-competitive activities.
- An independent financial adviser is authorised and competent to offer advice on a range of financial products from the full range of providers in the market.
- A restricted financial adviser may only recommend a limited range of particular types of financial product, or may only recommend financial products from a limited number of providers (or both).
- The Lending Standards Board is responsible for managing and administering the *Lending Code*.
- The *Lending Code* is a voluntary code which sets out standards of good practice, and provides protection for customers and clients of financial institutions.
- The *Lending Code* applies to all current accounts, card products and services, and also to personal loans.
- The FCA's *Consumer Credit Sourcebook* (Financial Conduct Authority 2014) is a specialist sourcebook for credit-related regulated activities.

- The Financial Ombudsman Service (FOS) helps to settle disputes between consumers and UK-based businesses that provide financial services, including banks, building societies, insurance companies, investment firms, financial advisers and finance companies.
- The *Limitation Act 1980* imposes limitation periods for different types of contractual obligations. Once a limitation period has expired any claim becomes statute-barred.
- Harassment can be defined as any course of action or behaviour directed at a specific person (for example, a debtor) that is intended to cause alarm, annoyance, or substantial emotional distress.

Self-review questions

1. According to the *Limitation Act 1980*, what are the limitation periods for an *unsecured debt* (for example, a credit card debt or personal loan), a *secured debt* (for example, a mortgage), and a *debt to the Crown* (for example, VAT or Income Tax)?
2. Distinguish between an *independent financial adviser* and a *restricted financial adviser*.
3. According to the FCA's *Consumer Credit Sourcebook* (Financial Conduct Authority 2014), what actions would be regarded as constituting physical or psychological harassment?
4. What are the statutory objectives of the Financial Conduct Authority?
5. What enforcement action can the Financial Conduct Authority take against companies, organisations or individuals that do not meet the FCA standards?

Case study discussion questions

1. Prepare a brief summary for Anthony Carter on the possible actions he could take should his bank fail to refund the money incorrectly charged to his credit card account.
2. Advise Jonathan Carter of the legitimacy of the invoice for £1,862.76 he recently received from Pandel plc, and the action (if any) the company could take to recover the outstanding debt.

Suggested answers to chapter activities

Activity 1

The responsibility of the Financial Conduct Authority (FCA) is to ensure that the relevant markets function well. Its main role is to monitor and regulate authorised financial services providers (both retail and wholesale financial services providers), and to ensure that they comply with all the extant regulatory requirements.

The role of the Prudential Regulation Authority (PRA) is to promote the safety and soundness of such companies or organisations; and, specifically for insurers, to contribute to the securing of an appropriate degree of protection for policyholders.

Activity 2

The Financial Ombudsman Service is wholly funded by levies and case fees from the business it covers. All levies and case fees have to be paid, by law. All companies, organisations and individuals covered by the Financial Ombudsman Service pay a general levy. In addition, businesses must also pay an individual case fee if the service deals with a complaint about them. All businesses are entitled to 25 free cases.

Activity 3

Yes, these actions do constitute harassment. Seeking to contact a debtor at unreasonable times and attempting to gain entry to premises without appropriate authority both contravene relevant provisions of the FCA's *Consumer Credit Sourcebook* (Financial Conduct Authority 2014).

Activity 4

Whilst requesting full payment of an outstanding debt is a legitimate business practice and does *not* constitute harassment, threatening the seizure of personal assets without appropriate legal authority and making continuous visits to a debtor's home address and work address *do* constitute harassment.

Notes

1. See: 'Thousands to complain about lifetime tracker payments'. Available at: www.bbc.co.uk/news/business-22353135.
2. Indeed, many well-known banks and financial product and services providers are now amongst the most complained about companies and organisations in the UK. See: 'Banks top complaints league table but Hargreaves Lansdown sees surge'. Available at: http://www.telegraph.co.uk/finance/personalfinance/bank-accounts/10754355/Banks-top-complaints-league-table-but-Hargreaves-Lansdown-sees-surge.html.
3. The list of appropriate qualifications is determined by the Financial Services Skills Council on behalf of the FCA.
4. For example, to have a Diploma in Financial Planning (DipFP). A more advanced qualification would be the Advanced Diploma in Financial Planning (ADipFP); and more advanced still are the Certified Financial Planner or Chartered Financial Planner (CFP) qualifications.
5. The FCA's remit includes overseeing the prudential standards of those firms and organisations that are not regulated by the Prudential Regulation Authority.
6. These fees can include: annual (periodic fees), which provide most of the funding required to carry out statutory functions; application fees, which recover some of the costs incurred in processing certain applications under FCA rules; and special project fees, to recover our exceptional supervisory costs where a firm undertakes certain restructuring transactions.
7. The PRA is not responsible for the supervision of independent financial advisers or of finance sector organisations other than banks, building societies, credit unions, insurers and major investment firms.
8. Business size is based on a specific measure for each category of organisation or firm. Organisations or firms that could cause the greatest harm to the stability of the UK financial system will be the main contributors to the PRA's funding needs.
9. Cartel offences involve collaboration between individuals or between companies, for example to reduce competition and thereby gain a financial advantage.
10. A micro-enterprise is a business that employs fewer than 10 persons and has a turnover or annual balance sheet that does not exceed €2 million. See: www.lendingstandardsboard.org.uk/thecode.html.
11. 'Setting off' means, for example, using the balance on an individual's current account or savings account to pay off outstanding loan repayments.
12. *Note:* From April 2012 to April 2014, the FOS charged a supplementary case fee of £350 for the 26th (and each subsequent) PPI mis-selling case.
13. According to the FOS (see: www.financial-ombudsman.org.uk/publications/technical_notes/QG1.pdf), fewer than one in six of the initial complaints and enquiries received becomes a chargeable case.
14. This 6-year limitation period also applies to Council Tax arrears, and to overpayments of benefits such as Income Support, Housing Benefit, and Council Tax Benefit.
15. Examples of unacceptable behaviour would include a creditor or lender (or their representative or agent) pressurising a debtor to repay a debt by contacting the debtor at unreasonable times or unreasonable locations, or a creditor or lender (or their representative or agent) threatening a debtor with action such as the use of bailiffs in order to recover money for unenforceable debts.

14

Debt, individual voluntary arrangements, and bankruptcy

Learning outcomes

By the end of this chapter, you should be able to:

- distinguish between a secured and unsecured debt
- explain what a County Court Judgment is, and how it can be enforced
- explain the function, role and power of bailiffs
- define an Individual Voluntary Arrangement and explain the process and consequences of making one
- explain the purpose, nature and consequences of bankruptcy.

14.1 Introduction

Debt can be very difficult to deal with. As suggested in Chapter 1, the stress, worry and anxiety associated with excessive personal debt can have a significant effect not only on an individual's physical and mental health, but also on his or her relationships with other people – especially with partners, but also with other family members. Surprisingly, however, many people still choose not to deal with their personal debt, instead burying their heads in the sand and hoping that the debt will somehow go away. Unfortunately, it will not: the more you ignore debt, the larger it becomes, and the worse the situation tends to get.

This chapter considers a range of topics related to personal debt, County Court enforcement actions, bailiffs, and the strategies available to deal with excessive personal debt.

14.2 Types of debt

There are essentially two types of debt: secured debt and unsecured debt.

Secured debt

'Secured debt' is debt that is tied to, or related to, an asset which is therefore considered to be collateral for the debt. In legal terms, the lender (the creditor) places a 'lien' on the asset. This gives the lender a legal right to seize the asset if the debtor fails to comply with the payment terms and conditions of the loan agreement or contract. A house mortgage and a car loan are both examples of secured debt. The house mortgage loan is secured on the property, whereas the car loan is secured on the vehicle.

Unsecured debt

'Unsecured debt' is debt that is not associated with any specific collateral. Credit card debt is the most widely-held form of unsecured debt; other popular forms include overdrafts, personal loans, student loans, payday loans, outstanding balances on utility bills, and unpaid court-ordered child support payments.

With unsecured debt, the lender has no legal right to collateral for the debt, and is not entitled to seize assets if the debtor fails to comply with the payment terms and conditions of the agreement or contract, although the lender may elect to take other forms of legal action to recover the debt. The various types of possible enforcement are discussed below.

14.3 Why things go wrong

There are many reasons why people find themselves in a situation of having excessive levels of either secured or unsecured debt, or both. This might be due to a loss of income, for example, because of sudden unemployment, redundancy or ill health; or there might be a sudden unexpected increase in personal expenditure, perhaps as a result of an addition to the family, or to the financial impact of a divorce or separation. Other possible reasons include:

- bad money management (usually involving unmonitored and excessive or unnecessary spending)
- poor budgeting skills and a lack of understanding about how much is owed
- a lack of knowledge of how to deal with accrued debt
- unwillingness to acknowledge the extent of personal debt because of the associated social stigma.

Temporary debt problems

Most people will at some time in their lives experience a temporary debt problem: a situation in which outgoings (expenses) exceed income, with the result that payments are delayed and only minimum payments are made on non-priority debts, such as overdrafts, loans, hire purchases, and the unpaid balances for credit cards, charge cards, store cards, and shopping-catalogue purchases.

Generally, the problem occurs for a short period of time, perhaps for a few months, and is then resolved – typically there is a short-term cash-flow issue, due to a sudden unexpected expense or a sudden reduction in income, and then the person adjusts to the situation and takes action to get out of debt again.

Chronic debt problems

A chronic debt problem exists where bills, invoices and statements of account are regularly ignored, and where amounts due remain unpaid – not only for non-priority debts (as above), but also for priority debts, such as property rent, mortgage repayments, and utility bills (for services such as water, gas or electricity). This can lead to reminders, final demands, and ultimately to legal action or visits from debt collection agents or court enforcement officers.

Classic symptoms of a chronic debt problem include:
- increasingly using one credit card to pay the amount owed on another credit card *and/or*
- using consolidation finance to pay off other existing loans.

14.4 Debt: some statistics

Statistics published by the Money Charity (2015) provide a startling and revealing picture about personal debt in the UK. As at October 2015:
- total personal debt was approximately £1.447 trillion (ibid.:5)
- total secured lending was approximately £1.273 trillion (ibid.:8)
- total unsecured lending was approximately £174.05 billion (ibid.:5)
- total credit card debt was approximately £62.4 billion (ibid.:5).

Every 34 minutes 20 seconds a property was repossessed (ibid.:4), and every 6 minutes 53 seconds a person was declared bankrupt. Average household debt (including mortgages) was approximately £54,178 (ibid.:5), and average personal debt (including mortgages) was approximately £28,578 (ibid.:5) – that is, nearly 112% of average earnings.

14.5 Help and advice

There is no need to pay for debt advice. Help and advice are freely and widely available from a number of reputable sources. The most popular sources of help and advice are these:
- National Debtline (see: https://www.nationaldebtline.org)
- Citizens Advice Bureaux (see: www.adviceguide.org.uk/england/debt)
- StepChange Debt Charity (see: http://www.stepchange.org)
- My Money Steps (developed by the National Debtline; see: www.mymoneysteps.org).

In addition, the Money Charity (www.themoneycharity.org.uk/), which was formerly known as Credit Action, provides a range of useful resources on personal debt and finance.

Before looking at possible strategies that can be used in tackling situations where personal debt has become excessive and unmanageable, it may be useful to explore briefly the consequences of *not* dealing with this level of debt.

14.6 County Court Judgments

Where there is a debt outstanding – that is, where a person (the debtor) has failed to make an agreed payment for goods or services used or received, or adhere to a legally binding contractual agreement – the company or individual to whom the money is owed (the creditor) may choose to 'pass on' the debt to a debt collection agency, or may elect to take legal action in order to recover the money owed.

Legal action can take place only once the creditor has warned the debtor of his or her intention. Depending on the type of debt, this warning usually takes the form of a 'default notice' or a 'letter before action'. For example, for credit agreements regulated under the *Consumer Credit Act 1974*, the debtor must be sent a default notice at least 14 days before any legal action is taken. The default notice must provide information on how the default can be remedied and must specify what legal action will be taken if the default is not remedied. A copy of the Financial Conduct Authority's default information sheet must also be provided.

Where the default is not remedied – either because of a failure to reach an agreement with the debtor, or because of the debtor's failure to reply to the notice – the creditor may then begin legal proceedings and ask for a judgment to be made against the debtor. The County Court generally handles claims for less than £50,000; claims with a monetary value over £50,000 are dealt with by the High Court. The procedures followed generally depend on the 'claims track' to which the case is allocated.

Claims tracks

Within the County Court, there are three alternative claims tracks, as shown in Figure 14.1. (Note that personal injury claims have different thresholds and are dealt with differently.)

All three tracks are formal legal proceedings. If witnesses are called by the County Court but refuse or fail to appear and give evidence, or if they fail to produce any documents required by the Court, they can be fined at the judge's discretion.

If any party to any claims proceedings in a County Court is dissatisfied with the determination of the judge (or jury), that party may, subject to certain restrictions, appeal to the Court of Appeal.

Small claims track

The small claims track is for claims with a monetary value of less than £10,000.[1] For such claims, the County Court will normally adopt an 'informal' method of proceeding; hearings usually last no more than a few hours, parties often represent themselves, as no legal fees are recoverable; and there are simplified rules regarding the use and presentation of evidence.

Court fees are on a sliding scale and depend on the sum in dispute: usually they can be recovered by the successful party as part of the sum in judgment. Depending on County Court availability, a straightforward small claims matter is typically heard between 6 and 9 months of the debt issue being brought to court.

The small claims track is generally used for claims related to:

- compensation for faulty goods or services
- disputes between landlords and tenants
- claims for wages owed or where money (wages) is to be paid in lieu of working a notice period.

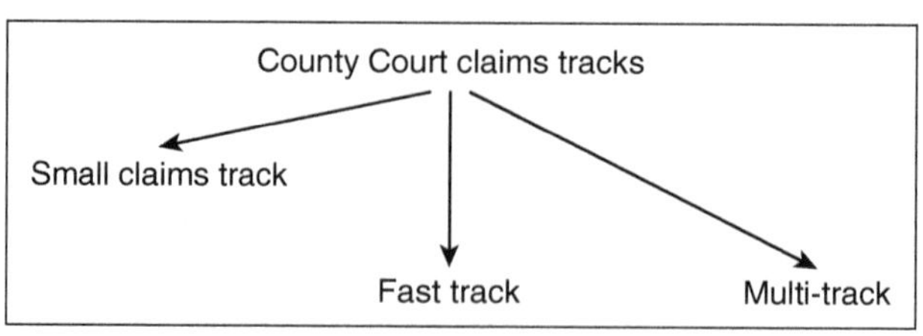

Figure 14.1 County Court claims tracks

Since April 2013, all small claims matters, as a matter of course, have been referred to small claims mediation prior to any County Court hearing.

Fast track

The fast track is the normal track for any claim with a monetary value of more than £10,000 but less than £25,000.[2]

Hearings for such claims cases normally last one day. The County Court issues directions for the management of the case, determines a timetable for the hearing, and either fixes the hearing date or sets a period (not exceeding 3 weeks) within which the hearing will occur. The costs that can be recovered in fast track hearings are strictly limited, although County Court fees are usually recoverable by the successful party as part of the sum in judgment. County Court fees are again on a sliding scale that depends on the sum in dispute, and are generally higher than those for the small claims track. Depending on County Court availability, a straightforward small claims matter is usually heard within 9 to 12 months of the debt issue being brought to court.

Multi-track

The multi-track is the normal track for all claims that do not qualify for the small claims track or the fast track; that is, for claims in excess of £25,000, but less than the County Court limit of £50,000. As with the fast track, the County Court issues directions for the management of the case; determines a timetable for the hearing; and fixes the hearing date. Final hearings usually have a time allocation of between 2 and 5 days.

County Court fees are more substantial than those for the small claims track or the fast track, but again are on a sliding scale depending on the sum in dispute, and again are usually recoverable by the successful party as part of the sum in judgment. A multi-track hearing is far more procedural.[3] Depending on County Court availability, a straightforward small claims matter is usually heard within 12 to 18 months of the debt issue being brought to court.

Obtaining a County Court Judgment

If a debt in dispute is for a fixed amount of money that is less than £100,000, an online claim can be submitted by the creditor (the claimant) using the HM Courts and Tribunals Service (HMCTS) Money Claim Online (MCOL), which is available at www.moneyclaim.gov.uk. Online claims are dealt with centrally by Northampton County Court. Claim forms are printed and distributed to the debtor (the defendant) on the next working day following receipt. Alternatively, a physical paper claim can be completed using form N1 (available from the HMCTS at www.justice.gov.uk or from any local County Court), and submitted to the County Court Money Claims Centre (in Salford), from which it is allocated to an appropriate local County Court, which advises the debtor that a claim has been made.

County Court fees are payable for the processing of both types of claim forms, but the fees are smaller for online claims than for paper-based claims.[4] Once a debtor receives notice of a County Court Claim (CCC) – which will list the amounts owed, give details of the creditor making the claim, and identify the County Court to which the hearing has been allocated – the debtor *must* take one of the following actions, usually within 14 days of receipt of the CCC:

- The debtor may admit to the CCC. In this case, the County Court will require the debtor to complete an admission form (form N9A) and to provide details of her or his income

and expenditure, so that an appropriate, realistic and affordable payment schedule can be determined. The County Court will then impose a payment order, which will stipulate the timing of payments and the amounts to be paid until the debt (together with all other agreed or imposed costs) has been paid off in full.
- Alternatively, the debtor may disagree with the CCC. In this case the County Court will require the debtor to complete a defence form (form N9B) and to provide details of his or her reasons for disagreeing with the creditor's claim. The County Court will then set a date for the case to be heard.

Once a County Court hearing has taken place, and provided that the creditor's action against the debtor has been successful, a County Court Judgment (CCJ) will be issued against the debtor. (This judgment will be recorded on the debtor's credit file for 6 years.) The debtor will be informed of the judgment (called a 'Judgment for Claimant') and will normally be offered a choice:
- the debtor may pay the amount due within 14 days (together with any additional costs awarded by the County Court) *or*
- the debtor may agree to a payment schedule imposed by the County Court.

If the debt is acknowledged, and if the amount is paid in full within the time period or the proposed payment schedule agreed to, no further County Court action will be taken. However, if a debtor fails to make the appropriate payment or agree to the proposed payment schedule, or fails to respond to the CCJ, a creditor may then ask the County Court to take further enforcement action. This request can also be made if the debtor agrees to the County Court's proposed payment schedule but then fails to make payments in accordance with that schedule.

14.7 Enforcement

The judgment of a County Court can be enforced in a number of ways, using:
- a Charging Order
- an Attachment of Earnings Order
- a Third Party Order (previously known as a 'garnishee order')
- a Warrant of Execution *or*
- the commencement of insolvency proceedings.

Each of the above has its own specific advantages and disadvantages, and which one is selected by a creditor is often determined by the creditor's assessment of the assets or income available to the debtor.

Charging Order

A Charging Order imposes a charge on the property of a debtor for the money owed, the purpose being to secure the debt. A Charging Order can only be granted when a County Court has already held that the debt to which it relates is legally owed and that payment is due (that is, there is already a CCJ). A Charging Order does not in itself provide repayment of the debt, although in certain circumstances it does allow a creditor to make a further and separate application for an 'Order of Sale' of the property.[5]

A Charging Order is generally made against a debtor's home, but it can also be made against the debtor's interest in something else, such as land (freehold or leasehold), shares, or any other investment held or asset owned by the debtor.

The application for a Charging Order has two stages: an interim order and a final order. An interim Charging Order is granted by the County Court to prevent a debtor from selling a property or asset before a final order can be considered.

If a County Court approves a final Charging Order, and if the debtor subsequently sells the property, the full amount of the charge will be paid to the creditor before any of the proceeds of the sale can be paid to the debtor. If there are a number of charges on the same property, they will be paid in order according to the dates on which the charges were registered with the Land Registry.

Attachment of Earnings Order

An Attachment of Earnings Order is an instruction by the County Court to a debtor's employer to make deductions from the debtor's earnings (which include overtime payments, fees, bonuses and commission) and to pay these to the County Court, which then forwards the payment to a creditor (or the creditor's representative).[6] Whenever an employer makes a deduction from the debtor's earnings, he or she may also deduct an amount towards administrative costs, and must provide the debtor with a written statement of the total amount deducted.

If a debtor changes his or her employment, or is made redundant or becomes unemployed, the Attachment of Earnings Order is suspended until it can be redirected to a new employer.

Before an application can be made to the County Court for an Attachment of Earnings Order, the following must apply:

- the debtor's net earnings must be above what is known as the 'protected rate' (a minimum amount determined by the Court)
- the debtor must be in arrears in respect of the County Court Judgment by least one payment *and*
- the amount owed must be £50 or more.

Third Party Order

A Third Party Order provides a different mechanism for payment. In this case, a third party (the 'garnishee') that holds money on behalf of the debtor is ordered by the County Court to pay it instead to the debtor's creditor. A Third Party Order can be issued to anyone who owes money to the debtor, and prevents the debtor from having access to that money until the County Court has made a decision about whether or not it should be paid directly to the creditor. For example, the County Court can instruct a debtor's bank (or building society) not to release any money held on behalf of the debtor, and if necessary can instruct the bank (or building society) to pay the money owed to the creditor (assuming sufficient funds are available in the bank (or building society) account).

Note: The money held by the third party (in a bank account, in a building society account, or by another individual or organisation) must be held solely for the debtor. That is, a creditor cannot apply for a Third Party Order against a joint bank account unless the judgment debt is owed by all the account holders.

An interim Third Party Order can be issued by a County Court judge without a hearing. This interim order instructs the third party not to allow the debtor to reduce the amount held by the third party to an amount less than the amount owed by the debtor to the creditor. A full hearing is required before the final order is made.

Warrant of Execution

Obtaining a County Court Judgment against a debtor does not necessarily enable the creditor to recover money owed – such debtors may (and increasingly often do) refuse to comply with judgments of the County Court. One of the most popular methods used by creditors to enforce County Court Judgments and recover monies owed is to ask County Court bailiffs to seize goods or assets belonging to the debtor.

A Warrant of Execution is an order issued by the County Court to seize goods or assets owned by the debtor. The warrant permits a bailiff to enter commercial or domestic premises and to seize goods or assets sufficient to satisfy the amount of the debt and associated costs. The process of executing the warrant is called 'levying distress'.

Once goods or assets have been seized, the debtor is usually given the opportunity to pay the debt and then to recover the goods or assets. If the debt remains unpaid, the goods or assets can be sold by the bailiffs in a public auction, with the money recovered from the sale being passed on to the creditor. The fees charged by the County Courts for using the bailiffs will be added to the amount owed by the debtor.

Note: In some cases, a debtor may be 'made of straw' – that is, the debtor may have no possessions or only possessions of very little monetary value.

If County Court bailiffs are unable to recover money sufficient to pay the debt, the County Court will normally refer the debt back to the creditor, who may then take alternative action.

Appointment of a receiver

As an alternative to the enforcement methods described above, a creditor could, in certain circumstances, commence insolvency proceedings. Provided that the amount owed to the creditor is more than £750, a 'statutory demand' could be served on the debtor. If this in turn remained unsatisfied, there could then be grounds either for issuing a 'bankruptcy petition' against the debtor (if the debtor is an individual) or for issuing a 'winding-up petition' against the debtor (if the debtor is a company).

(We will discuss this issue later in this chapter.)

Activity 1

What are each of the following known as? When would each normally be used or imposed?

- An order issued by a County Court to seize goods or assets owned by a debtor.
- An order imposing a charge on any property owned by a debtor.
- An instruction by the County Court to the debtor's employer to make deductions from the debtor's earnings and to pay these to the Court.
- An order in which a third party is ordered to pay to a creditor an amount he or she owes to the debtor.

14.8 Bailiffs

Types, roles and authority

A bailiff, sometimes referred to as an 'enforcement officer', is someone who is legally authorised to collect a debt on behalf of a creditor (a person to whom, or organisation to which, money is owed). There are four categories of bailiff:
- County Court bailiff
- High Court enforcement officer
- certificated (or certified bailiff)
- private non-certified bailiff.

County Court bailiff

County Court bailiffs are employees of Her Majesty's Courts and Tribunals Service. They are responsible for enforcing the orders of County Courts by recovering money owed under County Court Judgments. They can:
- seize and sell goods or assets to recover the amount of the debt
- serve court documents
- effect and supervise the possession of property *and*
- effect and supervise the return of goods under hire purchase agreements.

County Court bailiffs can also execute arrest warrants to secure attendance at court or committal proceedings.

For County Court bailiffs, the authority to recover money owed under a County Court Judgment is known as a 'warrant' or 'Warrant of Execution'.

High Court enforcement officer

A High Court enforcement officer (often referred to as a High Court Sheriff) is an individual who has been authorised by the Ministry of Justice to enforce High Court Judgments. High Court enforcement officers are responsible for the enforcement of the Writs of Execution issued by the High Court, the most popular being the 'Writ of Control' (formerly known as 'Writ of Fieri Facias' or 'Writ of Fi Fa'). This is a writ issued for the recovery of money owed and provides for the seizure and sale of a debtor's goods.

For further information on High Court enforcement officers, see www.hceoa.org.uk/.

Certificated bailiff

Certificated bailiffs are private companies. They are used by the Magistrates' Court to collect fines; and by local councils (once they have obtained a Liability Order from the Magistrates' Court) to collect, for example, unpaid Council Tax, fines, compensation, unpaid maintenance, and unpaid rent. For certificated bailiffs, the authority to recover money owed under a Magistrates' Court Judgment is known as a 'Distress Warrant' or a 'Liability Order'.

Note: Certificated bailiffs cannot enforce the collection of money due under a High Court Judgment or a County Court Judgment.

For further information on certificated bailiffs, see: www.civea.co.uk/.

Private non-certified bailiff

Private non-certified bailiffs are entitled to recover the money owed for a variety of debts by seizing and selling goods. Often associated with private-sector debt collection agencies, non-certified bailiffs cannot levy distress for rent, road traffic debts, Council Tax or non-domestic rates, or enforce the collection of money due under a High Court Judgment or a County Court Judgment.

Powers of entry

In general, a bailiff cannot force entry to a domestic property, except:
- to recover unpaid taxes (for HM Revenue and Customs)
- for eviction purposes (following a mortgage default) *or*
- to recover unpaid court fines (for the Magistrates' Court, the County Court, or the High Court).

A bailiff may enter a debtor's premises only if invited in. If nobody is present at the debtor's premises, a bailiff may enter if a door has been left unlocked or through a window that is already open. This is known as 'peaceful entry'. 'Peaceful entry' does *not* usually include:
- being asked in by a young child
- breaking windows, doors or locks to gain entry *or*
- pushing past people to get inside.

In certain limited circumstances, bailiffs are able to break into business premises provided that there is no living accommodation attached and that they believe there are substantial goods or assets inside the business premises. Bailiffs can also forcibly re-enter premises if they have previously been allowed in and are returning to collect goods or assets to be sold. A bailiff may also be allowed to break into a property if someone has unpaid fines following criminal conviction.

Powers of seizure

The seizure of goods is legally referred to as 'execution against goods'. Bailiffs can only seize goods that belong to the debtor – the individual (or individuals) named on a warrant (for the County Court), a Liability Order (for the Magistrates' Court), or a writ (for the High Court) – but they can seize goods that are *jointly* owned, even if the other joint owner is not party to the debt. Bailiffs can also impose 'walking possession'[7] whereby the bailiff takes legal possession (and ownership) of specific goods or assets, but does not remove them from the debtor's property.

Goods or assets that a bailiff *cannot* seize include the following:
- tools, books, vehicles and other items of equipment that are necessary to the debtor for use personally by the debtor in his or her employment or business
- clothing, bedding, furniture, household equipment or provisions that are necessary for satisfying the basic domestic needs of the debtor or his or her family
- items that are leased or rented or that are subject to hire purchase agreements (but goods on credit sale can be seized, because they are deemed to belong to the debtor)
- goods or assets that have already been seized by bailiffs acting under another warrant, order or writ *or*
- goods or assets that belong to anyone other than the person (the debtor) named on the warrant – for example, a bailiff cannot seize goods that belong to the debtor's spouse, partner or children.

Recent changes

Recent measures and reforms implementing Part 3 of the *Tribunals, Courts and Enforcement Act 2007* (effective from April 2014) provide that:

- a bailiff cannot enter premises when only children are present
- a bailiff can enter premises only between 6 am and 9 pm
- a landlord cannot use a bailiff to seize property for residential rent arrears, except with an appropriate County Court Judgment
- a bailiff cannot seize household items such as a cooker, a microwave, a refrigerator or a washing machine, because such items are deemed to be reasonably required to satisfy basic domestic needs
- a notice period of 7 days (called an 'enforcement notice') must be given to the debtor before a bailiff seeks entry to premises to take possession of the debtor's goods or assets *and*
- a bailiff cannot sell goods or assets removed from a debtor's premises until 7 days have elapsed since the date the goods were removed.

Activity 2

The County Court has recently issued a Warrant of Execution for the recovery of an outstanding debt of £4,549. What rights do bailiffs have to enter the debtor's private premises and to seize goods or assets?

14.9 Dealing with debt

There is a variety of possible debt management strategies, as shown in Figure 14.2. Each has its own specific advantages and disadvantages, and the choice of strategy will often be determined by debtors' personal circumstances. These include:

- the income and assets they possess
- the nature of the debt they have accumulated *and*
- the level of debts they have accumulated.

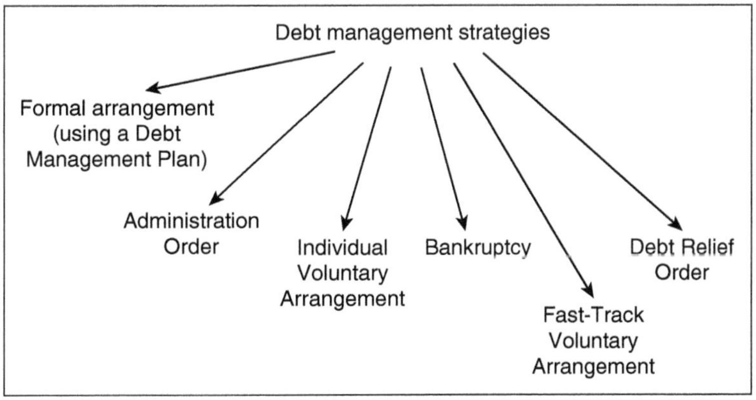

Figure 14.2 Debt management strategies

Formal arrangement

A Debt Management Plan is a formal arrangement between a debtor and his or her creditors. Such plans are usually designed, arranged and implemented by a licensed debt management company,[8] and can only be used for *unsecured* debt. The aims of a Debt Management Plan are to reduce the debtor's outstanding unsecured debts over a fixed period of time and also to help the debtor regain control of his or her finances.

Debt Management Plans are individually tailored and are based on a detailed assessment of what each debtor can realistically afford to pay on a monthly basis. A detailed income and expenditure assessment is usually made, and any surplus income (income in excess of necessary living expenses) is available to divide amongst creditors. Once the plan is in place, the debtor makes payments to a licensed debt management company. The debt management company then shares the money between the creditors *pro rata*, based on the levels of debt outstanding, having first deducted agreed fees and costs.[9] Some Debt Management Plans may also make use of facilities to consolidate any loans.

Debt management companies are licensed and regulated both by the Financial Conduct Authority (FCA) and by the Competition and Markets Authority (CMA), which provide regulatory guidance and set out minimum standards for:

- the marketing of debt management services
- the availability of pre-contract advice and information
- details of contractual terms and obligations
- the nature of services provided.

Note: Even if a formal arrangement has been agreed between the debtor and the debt management company, the creditors are not obliged to accept this arrangement. Further, even if a creditor *does* accept the proposed debt management agreement, she or he can still charge interest on any outstanding debt while the agreed payment plan is in place.

Administration Order

An Administration Order is a single County Court order, but can cover a range of debts, all of these being bound together and treated as a single debt. If approved, an Administration Order allows a debtor to make a single payment each month into the County Court. The County Court then divides the money amongst all the creditors listed in the Administration Order, on a *pro rata* basis. There is no fee payable to the County Court for an Administration Order, but the Court will normally charge a handling fee of 10%, and this fee is deducted from the payments to the County Court made by the debtor.

Note: Details of an Administration Order are recorded on a debtor's credit reference file for a period of 6 years from the date of the Administration Order.

Debtors can apply for an Administration Order if:

- they have at least two debts (that is, they owe money to at least two creditors)
- they have at least one County Court or High Court Judgment against them which they cannot pay
- their debts total less than £5,000 (including any interest and charges) *and*
- they can prove to the County Court (by providing details of their income and expenditure) that they could afford the imposed repayments.

Unlike a Debt Management Plan, an Administration Order prevents creditors from taking further action against the debtor, or at least not without prior County Court approval, and also prevents any further interest or other charges being added to the debt.

Note: Once an Administration Order is in place, it is the responsibility of the debtor to ensure that all agreed payments are made to the County Court. If this is not done, the County Court could impose an Attachment of Earnings Order, if the debtor is in employment, or simply cancel the Administration Order, which would leave the debtor open to further legal action.

Unless the County Court makes a 'Composition Order' (see below) or the debtor fails to make agreed payments, an Administration Order will continue until all the debts listed in the Order have been paid off in full.[10] When the Administration Order has been satisfied in full, the debtor can apply to the County Court for a 'Certificate of Satisfaction', for which a fee of £15 is payable.

Administration Orders can potentially last for many years, especially if the debtor has substantial debts and can only make small payments. To try to make sure this does not happen, a County Court can, at its own discretion, make a Composition Order, which means that the debtor only has to pay a proportion of his or her debts, usually an amount that he or she could reasonably manage to pay over a 3-year period. In effect, this means that only a percentage of the debt will be paid and the rest is written off.

Note: Creditors listed on the Administration Order may not take further action against the debtor once the Administration Order has ended. By that time, it is expected that the debtor will either have paid the Administration Order in full or paid the reduced amount owed under a Composition Order.[11]

Individual Voluntary Arrangement

An Individual Voluntary Arrangement (IVA) is a formal alternative for a debtor who wishes to avoid bankruptcy. Established and governed by the *Insolvency Act 1986*, an IVA constitutes a formal repayment proposal presented to a debtor's creditors by an insolvency practitioner (IP).[12] Debtors cannot propose an IVA to their creditors themselves: they must appoint an insolvency practitioner licensed to negotiate with creditors. Fees will normally be payable: an insolvency practitioner will charge both an initial fee and an ongoing fee, which will be in addition to the debt.

An IVA is essentially a contractual arrangement and involves the debtor making monthly payments based on the amount he or she can afford to pay from disposable income. It is a formal proposal to settle outstanding debt within a reasonable fixed period of time (normally 5 years), and during this time any interest and debt charges imposed by creditors are frozen. Once the final payment has been made, any outstanding debt is legally written off.

Although anybody can apply for an IVA, the suitability and success of this process depend on the debtor's personal circumstances. For example:

- personal debts must exceed £15,000
- there must be at least three different creditors
- the debtor must be able offer a reasonable monthly payment (usually a minimum of £200 per calendar month).

Usually (but not necessarily) the IVA comprises only the claims of *unsecured* creditors, leaving the rights of secured creditors largely unchanged. Any unsecured debts can be included in the IVA, including debts related to store cards, shopping catalogues, credit cards, personal loans, overdrafts, business loans (if the debtor is personally liable), and Income Tax and VAT debts. Debts related to Student Loans cannot be included, however.

The IVA process generally takes between 4 and 6 weeks. Initially the appointed insolvency practitioner will undertake a determination of the debtor's outstanding debts, followed by a detailed review of the debtor's income and expenditure. Once a formal proposal has been prepared, it will be circulated to each of the debtor's creditors. Shortly afterwards, a creditors' meeting will be held.

If the insolvency practitioner's proposal is accepted by creditors together representing 75% of the total *value* of the debt (which may not be 75% of the number of creditors), the IVA will then become legally binding on all of the creditors. The County Court is then informed, as well as all of the creditors, and normally the same insolvency practitioner is appointed to supervise the IVA.

For a debtor, an IVA has many advantages:

- The debtor only has to make a single monthly payment.
- Provided that the IVA is adhered to, the debtor could eventually be debt-free (usually within 5 years).
- All interest or late-payment charges are frozen.
- Once the IVA has been agreed and approved, it cannot be changed or varied.
- An IVA is a fixed legally binding agreement: as such, it offers the debtor protection from further legal action.
- An IVA cancels out any existing County Court Judgments.
- Because it is a private agreement, the debtor's employment and professional status remain unaffected.
- Any debts remaining at the end of an IVA are written off.

And the disadvantages?

For a debtor, the main disadvantages of an IVA are the initial qualifying conditions:

- a minimum level of debt
- a minimum level of monthly payment.

Together, these substantially limit the availability and usefulness of an IVA as a debt management strategy. In addition:

- An IVA is a legally binding agreement (for up to 5 or 6 years).
- Should a debtor fail to comply with any of the terms of the IVA, then the IVA will fail, and creditors may then petition the County Court for bankruptcy. *Note:* Any money paid into the IVA up to that time will be lost.
- While a debtor in an IVA will generally not be required to *sell* any property she or he possesses, the debtor may (as part of the IVA agreement) be expected to *re-mortgage* a property in order to release equity.
- The existence of an IVA is recorded on a debtor's credit record for a period of 6 years from the commencement of the IVA.
- During an IVA, any application for credit must first be approved by the debtor's IVA supervisor. If this is not done, the debtor would be considered in breach of the IVA, and the IVA would fail.

For further information on Individual Voluntary Arrangements, see: www.iva.co.uk.

Activity 3

Mr Arnold is a self-employed carpenter. Because of poor personal financial management and general overspending, Mr Arnold has accumulated substantial personal debts. Although his business is operating well, Mr Arnold is experiencing significant difficulties in meeting his old debts, and especially in making payments related to outstanding secured personal loans.

Mr Arnold has recently approached an approved insolvency practitioner to set up an Individual Voluntary Arrangement. Explain to Mr Arnold the requirements that need to be met for an IVA petition to be successful, and the advantages and disadvantages were an IVA to be granted.

Bankruptcy

Derived from the Italian word *bancarotta*, meaning 'broken bench', bankruptcy is a way of dealing with debts that a debtor is no longer able to pay. There are three types of bankruptcy:

- voluntary bankruptcy, also known as a 'debtor petition'
- involuntary bankruptcy, also known as a 'creditor petition' *and*
- a supervisor declaration, if a debtor was previously bound by an IVA.

The effects of bankruptcy for the debtor are the same whether it is voluntary or involuntary.

Note: A Bankruptcy Order can be made by a County Court even if the debtor refuses to acknowledge or agree to the proceedings.

Debtor petition (voluntary bankruptcy)

A debtor petition (voluntary bankruptcy) involves the debtor electing to declare herself or himself bankrupt. A debtor petition requires completion of the following:

- a bankruptcy petition *and*
- a statement of affairs.

Once completed, these must be submitted to the County Court.[13] It is the County Court that decides whether or not the bankruptcy petition is successful.

As of April 2014, the fees payable when a debtor petition is submitted to a County Court are a court fee of £180 and an administration fee of £750.

Where the debtor petition is made to the High Court, an additional fee for submission of the statement of affairs may also be payable.

Creditor petition (involuntary bankruptcy)

If a debtor owes £750 or more to a creditor and has failed to repay the debt, the creditor can petition the court to make the debtor bankrupt. However, before a creditor petition can be presented to the court, a 'statutory demand' must first be issued and then 21 days must elapse.

The statutory demand requires the debtor either to pay the demanded amount, to offer to secure the debt against any property owned (that is, to create a voluntary charge), or to offer to pay the debt in a way that is satisfactory to the creditor.

As of April 2014, the fees payable when a creditor petition is submitted to the court are a court fee of £280 and an administration fee of £750. (These fees are recoverable.)

Supervisor petition

If a debtor has an existing IVA and either fails to comply with the requirements of the agreement or acts in breach of the agreement, the IVA fails, and the IVA supervisor can petition the County Court for the debtor to be declared bankrupt.

Bankruptcy: the process

Once a petition has been received, the County Court will hold a formal hearing at which parties to the petition can attend. The County Court can rule as follows:

- if it requires further information or clarification, it can stay (or delay) the bankruptcy proceedings
- it can dismiss the petition
- if the court believes an IVA would be more appropriate than bankruptcy, it can appoint an insolvency practitioner *or*
- it can agree to the petition and make a Bankruptcy Order.

Once a Bankruptcy Order has been made by the County Court, the debtor named is officially bankrupt from the date of the Order. An Official Receiver is appointed to administer the bankruptcy, to protect and secure assets from the debtor (from the date of the Bankruptcy Order), and, where appropriate, to act as the debtor's 'Trustee in Bankruptcy' (unless the County Court appoints an insolvency practitioner to act as trustee).

The Bankruptcy Order lasts 12 months.[14] Discharge is generally automatic after a maximum of 12 months, although the time can be shorter if the Official Receiver concludes his or her enquiries sooner and files a notice in the County Court, or if the County Court annuls (cancels) the Bankruptcy Order because a change in circumstances has allowed the debtor to discharge all outstanding debts.

Once a Bankruptcy Order has been made, the debtor must:

- provide information on *all* goods or assets he or she owns (items for which he or she possesses title) to the Official Receiver
- inform the Official Receiver about any increases in assets or income during the period of bankruptcy
- not use debit cards or credit cards without informing the bank or other card provider of their status *and*
- stop making payments direct to their creditors.

Bankruptcy: implications, consequences and restrictions

There are immediate implications for a debtor of being declared bankrupt. The debtor:

- loses control of all assets
- cannot obtain credit for over £500 without informing the lender that she or he is an undischarged bankrupt
- cannot act as a company director
- cannot take any part in the management of a limited company
- cannot trade in business under any other name
- may not practise as an accountant or solicitor
- may not act as a Justice of the Peace, a Member of Parliament, or a local councillor.

Note: In terms of assets, an undischarged bankrupt can usually keep necessary employment-related items (for example, tools of trade) and essential household items (for example, clothing, bedding or furniture), although if necessary the Official Receiver or the Trustee in Bankruptcy can authorise the sale of an undischarged bankrupt's property (including his or her home) to pay off debts.

In addition to the above, there are a number of other consequences to being declared bankrupt. The most important are these:

- The bankruptcy will be reported in the press.
- The debtor's name and details will be published on a bankruptcy register (the Individual Insolvency Register).[15]
- All of the debtor's financial transactions will be investigated.
- Any business owned by the debtor may be closed and its assets seized.
- All assets acquired by the debtor during bankruptcy will be lost.
- All banks, building societies and credit institutions used by the debtor will be informed of the Bankruptcy Order.
- All bank accounts, credit accounts, loan accounts, store accounts, shopping-catalogue accounts and the like that belong to the debtor will be closed. *Note:* All bank cards, cheque books, credit cards, charge cards and store cards must be surrendered to the Official Receiver or Trustee in Bankruptcy.
- Any leased or hire purchase goods or assets in the debtor's possession will be returned.
- The debtor may suffer loss of professional status or expulsion from any professional association of which he or she was a member.

Note: Although all bank accounts will be frozen, the Official Receiver or Trustee in Bankruptcy may release any money urgently needed, for example to buy food, and may also release any funds of which the debtor is a joint account holder.

In addition, the Official Receiver or Trustee in Bankruptcy may (following an assessment of a debtor's income and expenses) make an order for an undischarged bankrupt to make monthly payments. The arrangement can last for up to 3 years and is called an Income Payments Agreement (IPA). If an undischarged bankrupt does not agree to the IPA, the Official Receiver or Trustee in Bankruptcy can ask the County Court to *order* an undischarged bankrupt to make monthly payments. This is called an Income Payments Order (IPO).

Once bankrupt, the debtor faces a number of restrictions. For the duration of the bankruptcy, a debtor cannot:

- arrange credit of more than £500 without informing the lender that he or she is bankrupt
- adopt a new business name without revealing the name under which he or she was made bankrupt
- act as a director of a company *or*
- act as an insolvency practitioner.

Bankruptcy Restrictions Order (BRO)

If the Official Receiver or appointed Trustee in Bankruptcy believes that there has been dishonest behaviour or 'unfit' conduct, a Bankruptcy Restrictions Order may be imposed by the County Court on an undischarged bankrupt. Dishonest behaviour or unfit conduct would include, for example:

- incurring additional debts when there is no reasonable chance of repaying these
- giving away goods or assets
- selling goods or assets at less than their fair market value
- deliberately prioritising payments to some creditors in preference to others
- gambling
- making rash speculations or being unreasonably extravagant
- failing to keep and produce adequate financial records to explain any losses of money or property *and/or*
- fraud or fraudulent breach of trust.

A Bankruptcy Restrictions Order can last for between 2 and 15 years, and will appear on the Individual Insolvency Register.

Activity 4

On 1 February 2014, Mr Vince, a recently qualified chartered accountant, filed a personal bankruptcy petition at his local County Court. He had never filed for bankruptcy before. At the time of his petition, his outstanding unsecured debts totalled £67,546.

What restrictions, if any, could be imposed on Mr Vince during his bankruptcy? What are the consequences for Mr Vince if the Official Receiver considers and rules that Mr Vince's conduct has been dishonest or reckless, or both?

Fast-Track Voluntary Arrangement (FTVA)

A Fast-Track Voluntary Arrangement (FTVA) is a way for a debtor who is an undischarged bankrupt to deal with debts. It is only available to someone who has already been made bankrupt. It is an agreement whereby a debtor's assets are sold to pay his or her debts. When that has been done, the bankruptcy is annulled (cancelled).

An application for a FTVA can only be made via the Official Receiver. If the Official Receiver accepts the application, she or he will refer the application to the undischarged bankrupt's creditors. The FTVA will commence if 75% of the creditors (that is, creditors representing 75% of the total value of the debts) accept the offer. It will then be binding on all of the creditors, including any who did *not* agree to the offer. Once the FTVA has been approved and accepted, the County Court Bankruptcy Order is cancelled, any assets not already sold or needed are returned to the debtor, and the FTVA is added to the Individual Insolvency Register.

For an FTVA, the Official Receiver's fees are £315 on application, and 15% of the total amount raised to pay the debtor's debts.

Debt Relief Order

Debt Relief Orders came into force in England and Wales on 6 April 2009. They were introduced in the *Tribunals, Courts and Enforcement Act 2007* and are a form of insolvency – a simplified, quicker and cheaper alternative to bankruptcy. However, they are suitable for only a small number of individuals.

Applying for a Debt Relief Order

To apply for a Debt Relief Order, a debtor should contact an authorised adviser – either an approved intermediary or a competent authority (for example, the Citizens Advice Bureau). The adviser will confirm whether the conditions for a Debt Relief Order are met, and if so can apply to the County Court Official Receiver for an Order on the debtor's behalf. If it appears that the applicant meets the requirements, the Debt Relief Order can be issued administratively by the Official Receiver without the need for a formal County Court hearing. The Debt Relief Order will cost £90, but this can be paid in instalments over six months if required.

A Debt Relief Order usually lasts for 1 year, during which time creditors will not be able to take legal action against a debtor to recover their money. At the end of the Debt Relief Order, the debtor will be free of all the debts listed in the Order.

All Debt Relief Orders are recorded in the Individual Insolvency Register, and removed 3 months after the Debt Relief Order ends.

If approved, a Debt Relief Order will remain on the debtor's credit record for 6 years. Debtors may apply for a Debt Relief Order only if:

- they have qualifying debts of £15,000 or less
- they have spare available income of £50 or less a month,[16] after paying their normal household expenses
- their assets (and any savings) are worth £300[17] or less
- they have a private pension fund worth less than £300
- they own a vehicle worth less than £1,000 (unless it has been specially adapted because the debtor has a physical disability)
- in the last 3 years they have lived, owned a property, or carried on a business in England or Wales
- they have not previously been subject to a Debt Relief Order within the last 6 years *and*
- they are not involved in another formal insolvency procedure at the time of applying for a Debt Relief Order.

In applying for a Debt Relief Order, qualifying debts are debts such as:

- credit cards debts, overdrafts, and personal loans
- rent arrears, utilities bills, telephone bills, Council Tax bills, and Income Tax bills
- benefit overpayments
- payments for hire purchase or conditional sale agreements
- 'buy now, pay later' agreements *and*
- business debts.

There are, however, certain types of debt that *cannot* be included in a Debt Relief Order. Such non-qualifying debts include:

- Magistrates' Court fines
- fines relating to criminal activity (for example, speeding fines)
- child support and maintenance
- Student Loans
- social fund loans *and*
- compensation for death and injury.

Note: Non-qualifying debts must be paid separately, and creditors for such debts can still take legal action against a debtor for recovery of the debt, even if the debtor has a Debt Relief Order.

Implications of a Debt Relief Order

During the year that a Debt Relief Order is active, the debtor will be protected from enforcement action by the creditors included in the application. At the end of the Debt Relief Order – normally 12 months from the date of the Order – the debtor will also be free from those debts included in the Order. This does not apply to any creditors whose debts cannot be scheduled in the Debt Relief Order, or to any creditors whose debts are included in the Debt Relief Order but who have successfully obtained leave from the County Court to pursue their debts.

It is, however, important to note the following:

- if the debtor is a tenant for rent arrears, a Debt Relief Order will not prevent the landlord from taking action to repossess the rented property *and*
- a Debt Relief Order will not prevent bailiffs (or enforcement officers) seizing assets or personal belongings and selling them, if they have taken control of such assets or personal belongings through a controlled goods agreement.[18]

During the Debt Relief Order period, all normal household expenses (for example, rent, Council Tax, utility bills and water charges) must continue to be paid. Payments must also be made for any debts that are *not* included in the Debt Relief Order.

In addition, the debtor is expected to provide information to, and to co-operate with, the Official Receiver, and to make arrangements to repay all of their creditors should his or her financial circumstances improve.

Note: Because a Debt Relief Order, if granted, appears on an individual's credit record for 6 years, making use of such an Order can reduce the likelihood of obtaining future credit or loans from some banks and high street lenders.

Activity 5

Which of the following debts are regarded as non-qualifying debts, and cannot be included in a Debt Relief Order?

- An overdraft.
- A Student Loan.
- A Magistrates' Court fine.
- Rent arrears.
- Non-payment of child maintenance.
- Housing Benefit overpayment.

Debt Relief Restrictions Order (DRRO)

Before applying for a Debt Relief Order and during the Debt Relief Order period, a debtor must not:

- hide or destroy any books or documents
- give away or sell goods or assets for less than they are worth

- fail to advise the Official Receiver of any change in their circumstances that would affect the Debt Relief Order.

In addition, a debtor must also adhere to certain conditions (known as restrictions). For example, a debtor must not:
- seek to obtain credit over £500 without telling the lender that she or he has a Debt Relief Order
- carry on a business in a different name *or*
- promote, manage, or set up a limited company, unless with the permission of the Court.

If the Official Receiver believes that a debtor has provided incorrect information or has acted dishonestly, she or he can apply for a Debt Relief Restrictions Order. If granted, this Order could extend the period over which the above restrictions apply, for an additional 2 to 15 years, even though the Debt Relief Order may still end after 12 months.

Activity 6

What is a Debt Relief Order? What are its key details and requirements?

14.10 Concluding comments

Debt problems are not restricted to the unemployed or poorly paid. They can happen to anyone, no matter what their education, their occupation, their income, or their social status. Indeed, history is littered with examples of the rich and famous who suffered severe personal debt problems – and even bankruptcy. Examples include Rembrandt, Oscar Wilde, Mark Twain, Abraham Lincoln, Walt Disney, and Jeffrey Archer, and there are many others.

The key to dealing with a debt problem is to *admit* that there is a debt problem. Be honest about how much money is owed, and to whom the money is owed, and then get help and advice – the sooner the better! There are many specialist agencies willing to provide guidance and assistance (free of charge) on how to deal with either a temporary or a chronic debt problem. They can provide invaluable information on simple budgeting and money management techniques and they can offer specialist advice on what alternative strategies may be available to deal with a growing debt problem. They can also provide information and advice on how to deal with aggressive and troublesome creditors, County Court Judgments, alternative County Court enforcement decisions – and, of course, bailiffs.

14.11 Suggested further reading

For further reading on the following topics, see the references given.
Bailiffs:
- www.adviceguide.org.uk/england/debt_e/debt_action_your_creditor_can_take_e/bailiffs_e.htm

Bankruptcy:
- www.adviceguide.org.uk/england/debt_e/debt_help_with_debt_e/bankruptcy.htm

Debt Relief Orders:
- www.gov.uk/options-for-paying-off-your-debts/debt-relief-orders

Individual Voluntary Arrangements:
- www.stepchange.org/Debtinformationandadvice/Debtsolutions/Individualvoluntary arrangement/IVAinformation.aspx

Key points

- There are two types of debt: secured debt and unsecured debt.
- A *temporary* debt problem is often associated with a short-term cash-flow issue.
- A *chronic* debt problem exists where both priority and non-priority debts are regularly left unpaid.
- Within the County Court, there are three alternative claims tracks: the small claims track, the fast track, and the multi-track.
- The judgment of a County Court can be enforced in a number of ways, using a Charging Order, an Attachment of Earnings Order, a Third Party Order (previously known as a garnishee order), a Warrant of Execution, or the commencement of insolvency proceedings.
- A bailiff is someone who is legally authorised to collect a debt on behalf of a creditor. A bailiff is sometimes referred to as an 'enforcement officer'.
- There are four categories of bailiff: a County Court bailiff, a High Court enforcement officer, a certificated (or certified bailiff), and a Private non-certified bailiff.
- The possible strategies available to deal with excessive or unmanageable debt include a formal arrangement (using a Debt Management Plan), an Administration Order, an Individual Voluntary Arrangement, bankruptcy, a Fast-Track Voluntary Arrangement, or a Debt Relief Order.
- There are three types of bankruptcy: voluntary bankruptcy, involuntary bankruptcy, and a supervisor declaration.

Self-review questions

1. Distinguish between *temporary debt* and *chronic debt.*
2. What service does (or can) a debt management company provide?
3. Is an IVA always the best option in all debt circumstances?
4. How far can an enforcement officer go in recovering an outstanding debt?
5. What are the main consequences of being declared bankrupt?

Case study discussion questions

1. In the last few months Jonathan and Claire Carter have become increasingly concerned about their financial situation – their overspending and their levels of personal debt. Advise Jonathan and Claire Carter on the implications and consequences of bankruptcy.
2. Provide a brief summary for Jonathan and Claire Carter of the possible alternatives to bankruptcy.

Suggested answers to chapter activities

Activity 1

An order issued by a County Court to seize goods or assets owned by a debtor is known as a *Warrant of Execution.*

An order imposing a charge on any property owned by a debtor is known as a *Charging Order*.

An instruction by the County Court to the debtor's employer to make deductions from the debtor's earnings, and pay them to the court is known as an *Attachment of Earnings Order*.

An order where a third party is ordered to pay to a creditor a debt he owes to the debtor is known as a *Third Party Order* (or a garnishee order).

Activity 2

A bailiff cannot force entry to a domestic property except to recover unpaid taxes (on behalf of HM Revenue and Customs), for eviction purposes (following a mortgage default), or to recover unpaid Court fines (on behalf of the Magistrates' Court, the County Court, or the High Court). Otherwise, a bailiff may only enter a debtor's premises if invited in. If nobody is present at the debtor's premises but a door has been left unlocked or a window is open, a bailiff may enter – this is known as 'peaceful entry'.

A bailiff may only seize goods that belong to the debtor – the individual (or individuals) named on a warrant (for the County Court), on a liability order (for the Magistrates' Court), or on a writ (for the High Court). However, a bailiff may seize goods that are jointly owned, even if the other joint owner is not named as a debtor. A bailiff may also impose 'walking possession', whereby the bailiff takes possession of goods or assets that belong to the debtor, but does not remove the goods from the debtor's property.

Activity 3

An IVA is dependent upon a debtor's personal circumstances: the debtor must have personal debts of over £15,000; must have three or more different creditors; and must also be able to offer a reasonable monthly payment as part of the IVA agreement – usually a minimum of £200 per calendar month.

For Mr Arnold, the main advantages of an IVA are that he only has to make a single monthly payment and that he could be debt-free (typically within 5 years). However, during the IVA all interest and late payment charges are frozen; and once the IVA has been agreed and approved, it cannot be changed.

Activity 4

Once declared bankrupt, Mr Vince would lose control of all his assets, and would not be able to obtain credit for over £500 without informing the lender that he was currently an undischarged bankrupt. More importantly, Mr Vince would not be able:

- to act as a company director
- to take any part in the management of a limited company
- to trade as a business under any other name
- to practise as an accountant or solicitor *or*
- to act as a Justice of the Peace, a Member of Parliament, or a Local Councillor.

If the Official Receiver deemed Mr Vince's actions to be dishonest or reckless, or both, he or she could impose a Bankruptcy Restrictions Order, which could increase the period of bankruptcy (for between 2 and 15 years).

Activity 5

The following debts are non-qualifying debts, and cannot be included in a Debt Relief Order: a Student Loan; a Magistrates' Court fine; and non-payment of child maintenance.

Activity 6

A Debt Relief Order is a form of insolvency, and usually lasts one year. During that time, those creditors included in the application are not permitted to take legal action against a debtor to recover money that is owed to them. Debtors can only apply for a Debt Relief Order if:

- they have qualifying debts of £15,000 or less
- they have spare available income of £50 or less a month[19] after paying their normal household expenses
- their assets (and any savings) are worth £300[20] or less
- they have a private pension fund worth less than £300
- they own a vehicle worth less than £1,000 (unless it has been specially adapted because of a physical disability)
- in the last 3 years they have lived, had a property, or carried on a business in England or Wales
- they have not previously been subject to a Debt Relief Order within the last 6 years *and*
- they are not involved in another formal insolvency procedure at the time of application for a Debt Relief Order.

Notes

1. Since April 2013, the County Court has had the discretion, without needing the consent of the parties involved, to deal with straightforward business-to-business disputes in excess of £10,000 by using the small claims track.
2. Since April 2013, the County Court has had discretion to use the fast track, rather than the usual small claims track, in dealing with claims of less than £10,000 in monetary value but with complex issues.
3. In general, any person, partner, company, trustee, or their legal representative may participate in multi-track proceedings, including any other persons approved by the Court to appear.
4. Details of the current court fees are available at: www.justice.gov.uk.
5. An 'Order for Sale' would force the sale of the charged property (either immediately or, if a suspended order is made, at some point in the future), and the proceeds of the sale would then be used to pay the creditor (after other secured loans of greater priority have been paid). Any equity remaining in the property would then pass to the debtor.
6. If a debtor has a number of current County Court Judgments against him or her, he or she can apply to the County Court for a 'Consolidated Attachment of Earnings Order', the result of which is that the debtor's employer only has to deduct a single monthly payment to cover all of the outstanding County Court Judgments. The County Court will then allocate the monies and make the appropriate payments to each of the named creditors (or their representatives).
7. Where a bailiff has gained peaceful entry to the premises of a debtor, a bailiff may seize any of the debtor's goods that are found on the premises (except for certain exempt categories of goods or assets). The bailiff may, however, choose not to remove the goods or assets immediately, but instead to provide the debtor with an opportunity to pay the debt (together with any additional Court costs). In such cases, a bailiff takes 'walking possession' of the goods or assets; and may require the debtor to sign a 'walking possession agreement' which lists the goods or assets that have been seized, and acknowledges that the legal title to those goods or assets no longer resides with the debtor. This means that the debtor still has the use of those goods or assets, but may not sell or otherwise dispose of them.
8. For information on how to find an authorised debt management company, see: www.fca.org.uk/consumers/protect-yourself/unauthorised-firms.
9. Some debt management companies charge both a set-up fee for the Debt Management Plan and a handling or processing fee each time a debtor makes a payment.
10. Creditors listed in the Administration Order can ask the County Court for payments to be reviewed, or apply to change the terms of the Order if they believe that the debtor's circumstances have changed.

11. For further information on Administration Orders, see: www.nationaldebtline.org/EW/factsheets/Pages/09%20EW%20Administration%20orders/Default.aspx.
12. See: www.insolvency-practitioners.org.uk/.
13. Not all courts deal with bankruptcy petitions, and a debtor must use the bankruptcy court nearest to where she or he lives or trades (whichever is for the longer period in the last 6 months). For a list of local bankruptcy courts, see: https://courttribunalfinder.service.gov.uk/.
14. Discharge is usually automatic. A Certificate of Discharge from the County Court (which costs £70) is proof of discharge.

    If the debtor is discharged early, she or he is sent a 'notice of early discharge'. This can happen if the Official Receiver (a bankruptcy court officer) finishes looking into the debtor's affairs and if the creditors do not object.
15. See: http://www.insolvencydirect.bis.gov.uk/eiir/.
16. Available spare available income includes salary or wages, welfare benefits, pension income, contributions from other household members, and any other rental income.
17. When calculating the value of assets, the following items can be excluded:
    - household equipment such as bedding, clothing and furniture
    - employment related tools of trade, books and other items of equipment
    - specially adapted vehicle which has been adapted for a physical disability and which is necessary everyday activities and
    - a motor vehicle worth less than £1,000.
18. A 'controlled goods agreement' is a formal arrangement between a debtor and a bailiff which gives the debtor time to repay what is owed. The debtor can keep his or her belongings, but they stay under the bailiff's control while the agreement is in place.
19. 'Spare available income' includes salary or wages, welfare benefits, pension income, contributions from other household members, and any other rental income.
20. When calculating the value of assets, the following items can be excluded:
    - household equipment such as bedding, clothing and furniture
    - employment-related tools of trade, books and other items of equipment
    - a specially adapted vehicle that has been modified for a physical disability and that is necessary for everyday activities *and*
    - a motor vehicle worth less than £1,000.

References

AA (2015a). 'Breakdown cover from the UK's no.1'. Available at: www.theaa.com/breakdown-cover.
AA (2015b). 'What's parts and garage cover?' Available at: www.theaa.com/breakdown-cover/breakdown-repair-cover.jsp.
Administration of Justice 1970, s.40, Available at: http://www.legislation.gov.uk/ukpga/1970/31/section/40.
Ashworth, H. (1980). *The Building Society Story*. London: Franey Publishing.
Association of British Insurers (2014). *UK Insurance Key Facts (2014)*. Available at: www.abi.org.uk/~/media/Files/Documents/Publications/Public/2014/Key%20Facts/ABI%20Key%20Facts%202014.pdf.
Bank of England (2015a). 'About the Prudential Regulation Authority'. Available at: www.bankofengland.co.uk/pra/Pages/about/default.aspx.
Bank of England (2015b). 'Funding of the Prudential Regulation Authority'. Available at: www.bankofengland.co.uk/pra/Pages/about/funded.aspx.
Bank of England (2015c). 'Prudential Regulation Authority'. Available at: www.bankofengland.co.uk/pra/Pages/default.aspx.
CIFAS (2015a). *Fraud in 2014: A summary*. Available as a link from: www.cifas.org.uk/fraudscape_latest.
CIFAS (2015b). *Identity Crime*. Available as a link from: www.cifas.org.uk/fraudscape_latest.
Citizens Advice Bureau (2014). 'Citizens Advice: evidence on bill of sale consumer lending'. London: CAB. Available at: www.citizensadvice.org.uk.
Communications Act 2003. Available at: http://www.legislation.gov.uk/ukpga/2003/21/contents.
Consumer Credit (EU Directive) Regulations 2010. Available at http://www.legislation.gov.uk/uksi/2010/1010/pdfs/uksi_20101010_en.pdf.
Consumer Credit Act 1974. Available at: http://www.legislation.gov.uk/ukpga/1974/39.
Criminal Justice Act and Public Order Act 1994. Available at: http://www.legislation.gov.uk/ukpga/1994/33/contents.
Data Protection Act 1998. Available at: http://www.legislation.gov.uk/ukpga/1998/29/contents.
Filofetch (2013). Available at: http://filofetch.com/history-of-pet-insurance/.
Financial Conduct Authority (2014). *FCA Handbook: Consumer Credit Sourcebook*. Available at: https://www.handbook.fca.org.uk/handbook/CONC/.
Financial Conduct Authority (2015) 'What we do'. Available at: http://www.fca.org.uk/about/what.
Financial Fraud Action (2014). *Fraud – the Facts 2014: The definitive overview of payment industry fraud and measures to prevent it*. London: Financial Fraud Action. Available at: www.financialfraudaction.org.uk/downloads.asp?genre=media.
Financial Services Compensation Scheme (2015). 'Financial Services Compensation Scheme'. Available at: www.fscs.org.uk.
GOV.UK (2015). 'Report a loan shark'. Available at: www.gov.uk/report-loan-shark.
Hargreaves & Lansdown (2015). 'Tax facts'. Available at: http://www.hl.co.uk/tools/tax-facts#capital-gains-tax.
HM Revenue and Customs (2014). 'Tempted by tax avoidance?' Available at: www.gov.uk/government/publications/tempted-by-tax-avoidance.
Huffington Post (2015). 'British people spend nearly £30 billion on takeaways and fast food every year'. Available at: www.huffingtonpost.co.uk/2014/03/26/takeaways-british-favourite-fast-food-spending_n_5033233.html.
Insurance Fraud Bureau (2015). 'Why report fraud?' Available at: www.insurancefraudbureau.org/insurance-fraud/why-report-fraud/.
Lending Standards Board (2014). 'The Lending Code'. Available at: www.lendingstandardsboard.org.uk/docs/lendingcode.pdf.
Lending Standards Board (2015a). 'Publications'. Available at: www.lendingstandardsboard.org.uk/pubs.php.

Lending Standards Board (2015b). 'Subscribers'. Available at: www.lendingstandardsboard.org.uk/subscriberlist.php.

Limitation Act 1980. Available at: http://www.legislation.gov.uk/ukpga/1980/58.

Link (2015) 'Statistics'. Available at: www.link.co.uk/AboutLINK/Statistics/Pages/Statistics.aspx.

Lloyds Bank (2015). 'Overdraft rates and charges'. Available at: www.lloydsbank.com/current-accounts/personal-overdrafts/charges.asp.

Money (2015). 'Compare credit cards'. Available at: www.money.co.uk/credit-cards.htm.

Money Advice Service (2013). 'The Financial Capability of the UK'. Available at: www.moneyadviceservice.org.uk.

Money Charity, The (2015). 'Debt Statistics: October 2015 edition'. Available at: http://themoneycharity.org.uk/media/Debt-Stats-Full-October-2015.pdf.

Moody, J. C. and G. C. Fite (1984). *The Credit Union Movement: Origins and Development 1850 to 1980.* Iowa: Kendall/Hunt Publishing.

Office of National Statistics (2014). 'Family Spending: 2014 edition'. Available at: www.ons.gov.uk/ons/rel/family-spending/family-spending/2014-edition/index.html.

Oxford English Dictionary (1991). Edited by E. S. Weiner and J. Simpson. Oxford: Oxford University Press.

Prudential Regulation Authority: Bank of England (2015). 'PRA Rulebook Online'. Available at: http://www.prarulebook.co.uk/.

Rand, A. (1957). *Atlas Shrugged.* London: Random House.

Santander (2015). 'Personal loans'. Santander plc. Available as a link from: http://www.santander.co.uk/uk/index.

Student Loans Company (2015a). 'Student loan repayment: How repayments are calculated: How much you will repay'. Available at: http://www.studentloanrepayment.co.uk/portal/page?_pageid=93,6678490&_dad=portal&_schema=PORTAL.

Student Loans Company (2015b). 'Student loan repayment: How repayments are calculated: How much you will repay'. Available at: http://www.studentloanrepayment.co.uk/portal/page?_pageid=93,6678784&_dad=portal&_schema=PORTAL.

List of abbreviations

ABI	Association of British Insurers
ABV	alcohol by volume
ACBUL	Association of British Credit Unions Limited
ADipFP	Advanced Diploma in Financial Planning
AEA	Action on Elder Abuse
AER	annual equivalent rate
AIA	Annual Investment Allowance
AIM	Alternative Investment Market
AMEX	American Express (charge card)
AMPS	Association of Member-directed Pension Schemes
APD	Air Passenger Duty
APR	annual percentage rate
ASC	Annual Statement of Compliance
ATM	Automated Teller Machine
AVS	Address Verification Service
BACS	Bankers' Automated Clearing Services
bn	billion (thousand million)
BRO	Bankruptcy Restrictions Order
CAB	Citizens Advice Bureau
CCC	County Court Claim
CCJ	County Court Judgment
CCTA	Consumer Credit Trade Association
CCTV	closed-circuit television
CCV	card code verification
CDF	Contractual Disclosure Facility
CFD	Contract for Difference
CFP	Certified Financial Planner; Chartered Financial Planner
CHAPS	Clearing House Automated Payments System
CIE	Continuous Insurance Enforcement
CIF	Civil Investigation of Fraud (HMRC)
CIFAS	Credit Industry Fraud Avoidance Service (*originally*)
CMA	Competition and Markets Authority
CML	Council of Mortgage Lenders
CO_2	carbon dioxide
COICOP	Classification Of Individual Consumption by Purpose
CONC	Consumer Credit Sourcebook (FCA)
CoP	Court of Protection
COP9	Code of Practice 9 (HMRC)
CPA	Continuous Payment Authority
CPI	Consumer Prices Index
CPS	Crown Prosecution Service
CRCA 2005	*Commissioners for Revenue and Customs Act 2005*
CREST	Centralised Real-Time Settlement System
CSC	card security code
CSOP	Company Share Option Plan
CVC	card verification code

CVD	card verification data
CVN	card verification number
CVV	card verification value
CVVC	card verification value code
DD	direct debit
DipFP	Diploma in Financial Planning
DLA	Disability Living Allowance
DMO	Debt Management Office
DRRO	Debt Relief Restrictions Order
DVLA	Driver and Vehicle Licensing Agency
DWP	Department for Work and Pensions
ECA	Enhanced Capital Allowance
ECC	Economic Crime Command
ECJ	European Court of Justice
EEA	European Economic Area
EFRBS	employer-financed retirement benefits schemes
EHIC	European Health Insurance Card
EIB	European Investment Bank
EIS	Enterprise Investment Scheme
EMI	Enterprise Management Incentive
EPA	Enduring Power of Attorney
ERNIE	Electronic Random Number Indicator Equipment
ESA	Employment and Support Allowance
ETF	exchange-traded fund
ETL	Energy Technology List
EU	European Union
EURIBOR	Euro Interbank Offered Rate
FCA	Financial Conduct Authority
FIFO	'first in, first out'
FLA	Finance and Leasing Association
FOREX	Foreign Exchange
FOS	Financial Ombudsman Service
FPC	Financial Policy Committee
FPS	Faster Payments Systems
FRC	Financial Reporting Council
FSA	Financial Services Authority
FSCS	Financial Services Compensation Scheme
FTSE 100	Financial Times Stock Exchange Share Index; top 100 shares (by share value)
FTSE 250	Financial Times Stock Exchange Share Index: top 250 shares (by share value)
FTSE AIM	Financial Times Stock Exchange Share Index: Alternative Investment Market
FTVA	Fast-Track Voluntary Arrangement
FYA	First Year Allowance
GAIN	Gone Away Information Network
GBP	Great Britain pound
GEMM	Gilt-Edged Market Maker
GSIPP	group self-invested personal pension
HCJ	High Court Judgment
HMCTS	HM Courts and Tribunals Service
HMO	House in Multiple Occupation
HMRC	HM Revenue and Customs
HNC	Higher National Certificate
HND	Higher National Diploma
HSCTC	high-cost short-term credit
IAL	Insurance Advisory Letter

ICVC	investment company with variable capital
IFA	independent financial adviser
IFB	Insurance Fraud Bureau
IHT	Inheritance Tax
IP	insolvency practitioner
IPA	Income Payments Agreement
IPO	Income Payments Order
ISA	Individual Savings Account
ISIN	International Securities Identification Number
ISP	Internet Service Provider
IT	Information Technology
IVA	Individual Voluntary Arrangement
JSA	Jobseeker's Allowance
LIBOR	London Interbank Offered Rate
LLP	limited liability partnership
LPA	Lasting Power of Attorney
LSE	London Stock Exchange
m	million
MAS	Money Advice Service
MCOL	Money Claim Online
MIB	Motor Insurers' Bureau
MTIC	missing trader intra-community fraud
NASDAQ	National Association of Securities Dealers Automated Quotations (*originally*)
NBFC	non-banking financial company
NCA	National Crime Agency
NEST	National Employment Savings Trust
NHS	National Health Service
NICs	National Insurance contributions
NINJA	'No Income, No Job or Assets'
nPOS-EPOS	cardholder not present at point of sale – electronic point of sale
NS&I	National Savings and Investments
NSIN	National Securities Identifying Number
OEIC	open-ended investment company
OFT	Office of Fair Trading
OPG	Office of the Public Guardian
ORB	Order book for Retail Bonds
p.a.	per annum
P2P	peer-to-peer
PAYE	Pay As You Earn
Paym	mobile payment
PC	personal computer
PEP	Personal Equity Plan
PET	Potentially Exempt Transfer
PGCE	Postgraduate Certificate of Education
PIBS	Permanent Interest Bearing Shares
PIN	Personal Identification Number
PIP	Personal Independence Payments
PLC	Public Limited Company
POAT	Pre-Owned Asset Tax
PPI	payment protection insurance
PPP	personal pension plans
PRA	Prudential Regulation Authority
PRR	Private Residence Relief
QUP	quarter-up price

RAC	retirement annuities contract
REIT	real estate investment trust
RPI	Retail Prices Index
s.	section
S2P	State Second Pension
SAV	Share and Assets Valuation (HMRC)
SAYE	Save As You Earn
SCI	Special Civil Investigations (HMRC)
SDRT	Stamp Duty Reserve Tax
SEIS	Seed Enterprise Investment Scheme
SEPA	Single Euro Payments Area
SERPS	State Earnings-Related Pension Scheme
SHP	stakeholder pension
SIM	Subscriber Identity Module
SIP	Share Incentive Plan
SIPP	self-invested personal pension
SMS	Short Message Service
SO	standing order
SORN	Statutory Off Road Notification
SPC	signature panel code
SSAS	small self-administered schemes
SSP	Statutory Sick Pay
Strip	Separate Trading of Registered Interest and Principal Securities
SVR	standard variable-rate mortgage
SWIFT	Society for Worldwide Interbank Financial Telecommunication
TESSA	Tax Exempt Special Savings Account
TGCA 1992	*Taxation on Chargeable Capital Gains Act 1992*
TMA 1970	*Taxes Management Act 1970*
UC	Universal Credit
UCIS	unregulated collective investment schemes
URL	Uniform Resource Locator
V code	verification code
VAT	Value Added Tax
VCT	Venture Capital Trust
VED	Vehicle Excise Duty
WDA	Writing Down Allowance
WTL	Water Technology List

Index

References to figures and tables are in **bold** type.

www.ingramcontent.com/pod-product-compliance
Ingram Content Group UK Ltd.
Pitfield, Milton Keynes, MK11 3LW, UK
UKHW051417150926
475561UK00005B/206

9 781137 471871